D1261019

Narcissism and the Novel

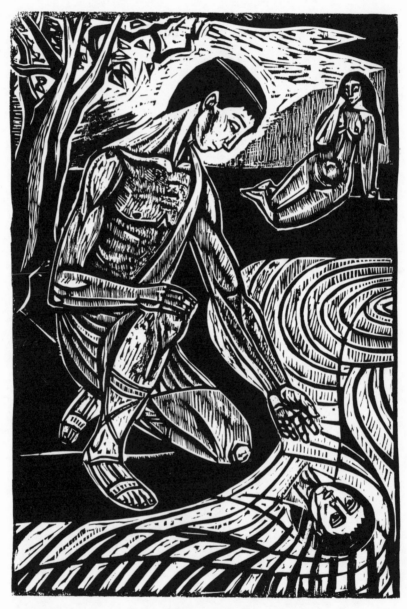

Narcissus by Irving Amen. By permission of the artist

Narcissism and the Novel

Jeffrey Berman

New York University Press
NEW YORK & LONDON

Library of Congress Cataloging-in-Publication Data
Berman, Jeffrey, 1945–
Narcissism and the novel / Jeffrey Berman.
p. cm.
Includes bibliographical references.
ISBN 0-8147-1132-4 (alk. paper)
1. English fiction—History and criticism. 2. Narcissism in
literature. 3. Psychoanalysis and literature. I. Title.
PR830.N355B47 1990   89-13047
823.009'353—dc20   CIP

New York University Press books are printed on acid-free paper,
and their binding materials are chosen for strength and durability.

Book design by Ken Venezio

To my parents, Roslyn and Isadore Berman

Contents

Acknowledgments

Many people have helped me to research and write this book, and I am deeply grateful to them. Professor Marshall W. Alcorn, Jr., of Northern Illinois University alerted me to important theoretical issues; his forthcoming book on narcissism has aided my own work. Three of my colleagues at the State University of New York at Albany—Professors Randall Craig (English), Warren Ginsberg (English), and Jerome Eckstein (Judaic Studies)—have been close readers as well as dear friends. Jerry, in particular, read my manuscript so carefully that his commentary could be published as a separate book. The author of two books on Plato, he would have completed his forthcoming *Metaphysical Drift* much sooner had he not drifted so generously with me.

Nor can I adequately thank Sophie Freud, professor of social work at Simmons College and author of the remarkable *My Three Mothers and Other Passions* (New York University Press, 1988), for her insights and friendship. She has been my mentor in the vast field of human development, and she has rightly insisted that psychoanalytic theory is useful only to the extent that it is supported by rigorous empirical studies. Where I have not followed her suggestions, I have probably gone astray. In her independent thinking, keen intellect, and boldness, she is (to paraphrase Ernest Jones's remarks on Anna Freud) a true granddaughter of an immortal sire.

Special thanks also go to Professor Daniel Ross of Allentown College and to James Twiggs, a university press editor and author of *Transferences*, a wickedly funny novel about the dark side of psychotherapy.

I wish to thank Professors William Dumbleton and Eugene K. Garber, chair and former chair, respectively, of the SUNY-Albany English Department for their help in allowing me to teach a course called "Narcissism in Literature," where I was able to teach the novels on which I was simultaneously writing. As always, my students have helped me to clarify many of the issues under discussion. In teaching a graduate seminar on psychoanalytic criticism, I was fortunate to meet two students, Peggy Johnstone and Janet Tarella, whose doctoral dissertations I later supervised. Peggy and Janet were, in turn, kind enough to read and criticize my own manuscript. Gladly would they learn and gladly would they teach.

The State University of New York awarded me a Summer Faculty Research Grant to complete the manuscript. A SUNY-Albany Center for the Arts and Humanities Fellowship also provided timely assistance. Sally Stevenson and Wendy Deiber of the SUNY-Albany Interlibrary Loan were once again indispensable.

The chapter on *Jude the Obscure* appears, in slightly different form, in *Compromise Formations*, edited by Vera J. Camden (Kent State University Press, 1989).

I am most grateful to the staff of New York University Press for their efficiency and expertise. Kitty Moore, senior editor, and Despina P. Gimbel, managing editor, have been invaluable, as they were for *The Talking Cure*, in guiding the manuscript through the various stages of production.

The stunning woodcut of Narcissus that appears on the book jacket was specially designed by Irving Amen, whose friendship I value as much as his art.

Finally, I wish to thank my family for their love and support: my wife, Barbara; my daughters, Arielle and Jillian; and my parents, Roslyn and Isadore Berman, to whom I dedicate this book.

ONE

Introduction: Narcissus Revisited:
From Myth to Case Study

Ovid's Myth of Echo and Narcissus

I burn with love of my own self; I both kindle the flames and suffer them. What shall I do? Shall I be wooed or woo? Why woo at all? What I desire, I have; the very abundance of my riches beggars me. — Ovid, *Metamorphoses*[1]

Few ancient legends are as haunting or timeless as the myth of Echo and Narcissus. The story of the beautiful youth who languished after seeing his own reflection in a body of water has seized the imagination of readers everywhere. From its origins in the *Metamorphoses*,[2] a lively collection of Greco-Roman stories completed in the year 8 A.D., when Ovid was banished from Rome by the Emperor Augustus for irreverence against the state, the Narcissus legend has undergone countless retellings. The richness of the myth is inexhaustible. Narcissus dramatizes not only the cold, self-centered love that proves fatally imprisoning, but fundamental oppositions of human existence: reality/illusion, presence/absence, subject/object, unity/disunity, involvement/detachment. These dualisms continue to preoccupy literary theorists, psychologists, and philosophers.

Literary historians have impressively documented the Narcissus theme in poetry, drama, and fiction. Douglas Bush's *Mythology and the Renaissance Tradition in English Poetry* (1932)[3] records the major English versions of the Narcissus legend through 1680; and Louise Vinge's *The Narcissus Theme in Western European Literature Up to the Early Nineteenth Century* (1967)[4] explores in abundant detail the hundreds of literary transformations of the myth. More recently, literary theorists have adopted the term *narcissistic narrative* to describe the contemporary self-reflexive novels that force the reader to become a cocreator of the fictional process. In *Narcissistic Narrative* (1980), Linda Hutcheon uses the Ovidian adjective to describe textual self-awareness in fiction that comments on itself or its own linguistic identity.[5]

Although the myth of Narcissus is two thousand years old, psychologists did not begin to explore its implications until the end of the nineteenth century. Havelock Ellis was the first to invoke the figure of Narcissus to describe a normal state of psychology with morbid exaggerations. In 1898, he published a paper called "Auto-Erotism: A Psychological Study," in which he mentions a "Narcissus-like tendency" for the sexual emotions to be absorbed and often entirely lost in self-admiration. Ellis viewed the tendency as an extreme form of autoerotism, a term devised "to cover all the spontaneous manifestations of the sexual impulse in the absence of a definite outer object to evoke them, erotic dreams in sleep being the type of auto-erotic activity."[6] Paul Näcke, a German psychiatrist, read Ellis' paper and coined the term *Narcismus* as a translation of the phrase "Narcissus-like tendency."

Freud's ground-breaking 1914 essay, "On Narcissism: An Introduction," postulated narcissism as a normal transitional state between autoerotism and object love. He identified the concept with nothing less than the entire development of the self. As we shall see, Freud linked narcissism to the libido theory and distinguished primary narcissism from secondary narcissism. After Freud, many analysts placed the concept of narcissism at the very center of the psychological universe—an irony Ovid would have appreciated. The enormous theoretical and clinical interest in narcissism has stimulated research in other fields. In *Eros and Civilization* (1955), Herbert Marcuse associates Narcissus with Orpheus, both "symbols of a non-repressive erotic attitude toward reality."[7] This is an untypically affirmative interpretation of Narcissus, for narcissism has become widely associated with self-absorption, vanity, and illusory love. Indeed, the word now signifies a cultural phenomenon, embedding itself as firmly in the popular imagination as T.S. Eliot's *The Waste Land* did half a century ago.[8] Christopher Lasch's influential *The Culture of Narcissism* (1979) generalizes Ovid's myth into a social and cultural phenomenon, "a way of life that is dying—the culture of competitive individualism, which in its decadence has carried the logic of individualism to the extreme of a war of all against all, the pursuit of happiness to the dead end of a narcissistic preoccupation with the self."[9]

The astonishing popularity of the term has led, inevitably, to a loss of precision. Narcissus began as a literary figure, emerged into a psychological concept, and now has attracted the attention of political scientists and sociologists. Lasch complains that as the word *narcissism* becomes part of our everyday vocabulary, its clinical meaning becomes lost. The warning can be carried one step further: the mythic origins of Narcissus and Echo have been forgotten. Before proceeding further, then, let us turn to Ovid's delightful story.

Ovid begins by telling us that Cephisus raped a water-lady, named Liriope, in a winding brook and nearly drowned her. In due time she gives birth to a boy. Even as a baby, Narcissus inspires girls with thoughts of love. Anxious about her son's life, Liriope asks the prophet Tiresias whether Narcissus will live to old age. "If he ne'er know himself" (149), the seer enigmatically answers, contradicting the Delphic oracle's injunction to "know thyself." Reaching his sixteenth birthday, Narcissus retains his boy-like qualities and proves irresistible to both sexes. But he remains proud and aloof, indifferent to the feelings of his admirers. One day he meets Echo, a maiden condemned to repeat the sounds of others. She has been deprived of normal speech because of punishment inflicted upon her by the goddess Juno for having deceived her about Jove's infidelities. Infatuated with Narcissus, Echo cannot express her feelings toward him. She pursues the elusive youth until he calls out, "Is anyone here?" "Here!" she cries (151), but when they finally meet, Narcissus coldly rejects her attempted embrace. "Hands off! embrace me not! May I die before I give you power o'er me!" Echo repeats his last six words and then vanishes into the woods, metamorphosing into a disembodied voice. Narcissus continues to spurn a host of lovers until one lovesick boy cries out in despair: "So may he himself love, and not gain the thing he loves!" Nemesis hears the brokenhearted boy's curse and executes a fitting revenge. When Narcissus bends down to drink from a bright pool of water, he is suddenly enraptured by his image. The curse comes true; Narcissus cannot take his eyes off himself. "Unwittingly he desires himself; he praises, and is himself what he praises; and while he seeks, is sought; equally he kindles love and burns with love" (155).

There is both comedy and pathos in Narcissus' attempts to kiss the watery image. Immobilized by his reflection and oblivious to hunger or sleep, he is tormented by the quest for impossible unity. "O fondly foolish boy," Ovid exclaims, "why vainly seek to clasp a fleeting image? What you seek is nowhere; but turn yourself away, and the object of your love will be no more" (155). Cursed by his love for a shadow, Narcissus begins to pine away, as Echo did earlier. Tiresias' prophecy comes true: once Narcissus comes to see (know) himself, his life ends. Narcissus realizes he is in love with himself; he knows that "I am he." Nevertheless, intellectual knowledge brings no relief. Awareness of his paradoxical situation—is he the lover or the be-loved?—only heightens his confusion. Since he is what he longs for, his riches make him poor.

Echo sees Narcissus mortifying his body and takes pity on him, empathically repeating his cries. But no one can help him. Gazing down into the water, he utters his last fateful words before bidding farewell: "Alas, dear boy, vainly beloved!" Contrary to the popular idea that Narcissus inadvertently drowns in pursuit of his watery reflection, Ovid's story concludes with the youth placing his head deep in the cool grass as death shuts fast his eyes. He crosses the narrows of darkest hell and sees the floating image of his lost shade within the Stygian waters. Ovid's story ends on a note of grief as Narcissus' beloved followers search in vain for his vanished body. The only trace of his existence is a gold flower with white-rimmed petals.

Of all the tales in Ovid's *Metamorphoses*, the myth of Echo and Narcissus has undergone the most retellings and reinterpretations.[10] In another version of the myth, by the second-century Greek writer Pausanias, the image confronting Narcissus is that of his deceased twin sister, who exactly resembles him in appearance. "It is utter stupidity to imagine that a man old enough to fall in love was incapa-ble of distinguishing a man from his own reflection," Pausanias writes,[11] evidently unable to accept the idea of self-love. Curiously, Freud ignored the incestuous implications of Pausanias' version. In a still earlier version of Narcissus and Echo by the Greek mythographer Conon (36 B.C.–A.D. 17), the rejected lovesick youth who is avenged by the gods is named Ameinias, to whom Narcissus has cruelly sent a sword with which to commit suicide.[12] Imitating Ameinias, Narcissus later commits suicide in an act of atonement. Unlike Ovid, both Pausanias and Conon replace Narcissus' specular reflection with a real lover. The effect, Tobin Siebers observes in *The Mirror of Medusa* (1983), is to negate the theme of narcissism, the fatal attraction of self-love.[13] Siebers adds that the impulse to eradicate narcissistic love may be seen in all later versions of the myth, at least until the Romantics, who viewed Narcissus as the personification of the sensitive, alienated artist. Twentieth-century avatars of Narcissus are often associated with sacred martyrdom: an early draft of *The Waste Land,* for example, contains a section entitled "The Death of Saint Narcissus," linking self-love to autoerotism, self-punishment, and prophetic knowledge.

A love story fraught with disturbing ironies and paradoxes, Ovid's myth of Echo and Narcissus contains the psychological complexity of a Freudian case study. The two major parts of Ovid's tale, the Echo episode and the reflection episode, embody numerous interrelated motifs, as Vinge shows: motifs of error or illusion, beauty, rejected or frustrated passion, hunger and thirst, discovery or recognition, death, and obliteration. Despite its unambiguous warning of the folly of vanity and self-deception, Ovid's myth raises more questions than it answers. Tiresias, that shrewd clinician, prophetically cautions Narcissus to avoid self-knowledge. The youth never succeeds in translating intellectual self-awareness into deeper emotional understanding. The blind Tiresias sees what the clear-sighted Narcissus remains oblivious to: the unreliability of surface perception. Narcissus' dilemma, Robert Langbaum points out in *The Mysteries of Identity* (1977), anticipates a basic problem in the theory of knowing and perceiving. "The epistemological counterpart to narcissism is solipsism," the belief that the self is the only object of real knowledge.[14] The reasons for Narcissus' fall lie deeper than the mirror reflection that greets his eye.

How would Ovid's myth of Echo and Narcissus be interpreted psychoanalytically? Though little is revealed about Narcissus' childhood—Ovid is a mythographer, not an analyst—the story reflects fascination with one's origins and identity. The striking fact about

Narcissus' past is that his birth originates from a sexual crime. His fatal attraction to water seems to be a repetition of his mother's near drowning. Entranced by his reflection in the body of water, Narcissus may be gazing at the maternal body, as Hyman Spotnitz and Philip Resnikoff suggest. "Narcissus by identification with Cephisus was predestined also to seek the love object in water. Hence, part of the fascination exerted on Narcissus by the image he saw reflected in the pool stemmed from his incestuous strivings, i.e. his yearning for his mother." [15] The incest taboo awakens fears of stern punishment. Echo already bears witness to the frightful punishment meted out by the gods—her tongue has been cut out. And the ever-wakeful Nemesis stands ready to enforce swift retribution.

Contemporary analysts emphasize the pre-Oedipal implications of Narcissus' story, particularly the search to recover lost maternal love. Narcissus suffers from a tenuous identity, compelling him to search for maternal mirroring and confirmation from external objects. Perhaps this is why Liriope seeks Tiresias' counsel; given the details of Narcissus' conception, it would be understandable for his mother to feel ambivalent toward him. Narcissus' mirror is analogous to maternal mirroring, essential to identity development, object relatedness, and self-esteem. In Ovid's story, however, the mirror reflects little genuine empathy or pleasure, suggesting that beneath Narcissus' self-love lies self-hate. His self-neglect hastens his death.

Ovid's story darkly hints at a repetition compulsion principle, traumatic events reenacted but not mastered. Narcissus seems intent upon humiliating men and women alike for crimes committed in the past. By converting past traumatic injuries into present triumphs, Narcissus gains the controlling hand. Yet he is finally condemned to experience the injuries he has inflicted upon others, including Echo and the lovesick youth. Narcissus thus begins as a victim, becomes a victimizer, and ends as both self-victim and self-victimizer. The dialectical interplay between self and other in Ovid's myth recalls Freud's discussion of the "fort/da" game in *Beyond the Pleasure Principle* (1920), in which the child magically enacts a game of disappearance and return, not unlike looking at one's shadow. The child utters the word *fort* (gone) as he throws a wooden reel with a piece of rope attached to it, then utters the word *da* (there) as he retrieves it. [16] Freud interprets the act as the child's need to revenge himself on his mother for going away from him. By making the reel alternately disappear and return, the child symbolically kills his mother and then brings her to life again. Narcissus, too, is engaged in a compulsive ritual in which he makes an object—himself—disappear and return. There is no pleasure in the game, however, and in the end he loses his shadow and himself.

If Narcissus were in therapy, the analyst would seek to uncover the lost connections between past and present. The analyst would attempt to decipher the hidden script in which Narcissus acts out childhood conflicts. Analytic sessions would shift the story to the youth's relationship with his parents and his enactment of maternal and paternal roles. For example, when Narcissus warns Echo not to touch him, lest he die, he seems to be repeating his mother's terrifying experience of sexual union. Ovid tells us that Cephisus "embraced" and "ravished" Liriope in a winding stream; later, when Echo feverishly pursues Narcissus, the hysterical youth flees, crying "Hands off! embrace me not!" Narcissus prefers death to Echo's entangling arms. He seems to be projecting onto Echo an image of an assaultive, smothering mother whose touch threatens to absorb or devour his own identity. This is indeed what happens when he gazes into the pool. Narcissus' fear of intimacy reflects, on one level, his identification with his mother, the victim of a violent sexual crime. On a second level, the son's fear of intimacy reveals the threat of being engulfed by the mother, who is now seen as a potential victimizer. And on a third level, Narcissus' fear of intimacy represents a defense against absent love. Narcissus' pride is "so cold," Ovid remarks, that "no youth, no maiden touched his heart," suggesting that he has never truly been loved. Narcissus' sadistic behavior toward others recalls his father's treatment of Liriope: both men seem incapable of love.

What emerges, then, is a portrait of a youth who is both overloved and underloved, and who in turn becomes overloving and underloving. Overloving and underloving, Sophie Freud notes, are typical narcissistic problems, often arising from parents who are alternately overinvolved and underinvolved with their children.[17] Overloving and underloving are close on the emotional continuum, and one may easily turn into the other. Overloving parents tend to be possessive, anxiously overprotective, and infantilizing; consequently, they prevent their children from achieving autonomy and independence. Thus,

Narcissus sees all relationships as threatening, engulfing, which is symptomatic of the child's ambivalence toward the symbiotic mother. Fatherless, Narcissus cannot distance himself from an overanxious mother. Though psychoanalysis has tended to ignore the father's role in the infant's development, Peter Blos argues that the "dyadic" or pre-Oedipal father is especially crucial for the son's ability to separate himself from the mother.[18]

The myth of Echo and Narcissus contains ideas that are as old as the ancient Greeks and as modern as the latest clinical research. The story dramatizes the consequences of thwarted desire, the problem of identity, the role of sexuality and aggression in mental illness, the double and mirror image, the interplay between self and other. These subjects form the themes of countless novels, poems, and plays. For artists and psychoanalysts alike, the myth of Echo and Narcissus remains a treasure trove.

Lionel Trilling has observed that when Freud was greeted as the "discoverer of the unconscious," he disclaimed the honor and instead paid tribute to the poets and philosophers who had long ago discovered the unconscious self.[19] Freud may have been thinking not only of Sophocles, Shakespeare, and Dostoevsky, from whom he tirelessly and effortlessly quoted, but of literary figures such as Ovid, whose myth of Narcissus ranks second only to *Oedipus Rex* in shaping psychoanalytic theory. Unlike Oedipus, who did not, after all, have an Oedipus complex, Narcissus was undeniably narcissistic—a perfect subject, paradoxically, for psychoanalytic theorizing.

Despite the centrality of the Oedipus complex in psychoanalytic theory, narcissistic issues—that is, pre-Oedipal issues—take precedence in child development. Ovid's myth illustrates the main reason for people now entering psychotherapy: problems of self-esteem and self-fragmentation. The myth of Narcissus and Echo reveals a pathological union of two individuals who succeed in tormenting each other. The absence of boundaries in their relationship, the failure to distinguish between self and other, indicates two selves that have never come into independent existence. To use Margaret Mahler's terminology in *The Psychological Birth of the Human Infant* (1975), Narcissus and Echo have failed to work through the separation-individuation phase and are, consequently, unable to achieve separate identities.[20] The more desperately Echo pursues Narcissus, the more cruelly he rejects her. His actions silence her as effectively as if he had cut out her tongue. Echo suffers two painful narcissistic injuries. Silenced by Juno and spurned by Narcissus, she retreats into the woods and feeds her love on melancholy until her body withers away. Echo's crippling dependency on Narcissus betrays a self that cannot exist on its own. "To be unable to start a conversation," Martin Bergmann observes, "is a symbolic way of saying that Echo lacks an independent self."[21] Without a man, she feels worthless, empty, incomplete. Echo's unrequited love for Narcissus has the effect of further depleting her self-esteem, while her adulation succeeds only in reinforcing his grandiosity. Victoria Hamilton's insight in *Narcissus and Oedipus* (1982) vividly captures the sadomasochistic relationship between Narcissus and Echo. "Like all echoes, she drives Narcissus deeper into the whirlpool of his pride and his delusions of self-reference. Every time she speaks, she validates his belief in his irresistible attraction for, and justifiable disparagement of, women. What else could he feel but revulsion towards someone who is so blindly and idiotically attracted?"[22]

Echo's situation reflects empathy without insight, the opposite of Narcissus' dilemma, (in)sight without compassion. Each character is associated with a form of repetition or duplication that leads to thwarted desire.[23] The lack of meaningful communication between Echo and Narcissus dramatizes the empty nature of narcissistic discourse.[24] Both Echo and Narcissus suffer from insatiable hunger, despite the abundance surrounding them. Both are depleted by shadows. In one sense, Narcissus' shadow may be viewed simply as absence; in another sense, the shadow represents the presence of an actively depleting self, an internalized persecutory object.[25]

The first critic to point out the persecutory symbolism of the double in literature was Otto Rank, who concluded in his pioneering psychoanalytic study, *"Der Doppelgänger,"* that "the double, who personifies narcissistic self-love, becomes an unequivocal rival in sexual love; or else, originally created as a wish-defense against a dreaded eternal destruction, he reappears in superstition as the messenger of death."[26] Rank's essay, first published in 1914 in the journal *Imago* and expanded into a book in 1925, contains the first extended discussion of the theme of narcissism in mythology and literature. The last chapter of *The Double* is called "Narcissism and the Double" and is filled with original insights, including the observation that the self-love implicit in Ovid's myth conceals the idea of death. For death remains, quite simply, the ultimate narcissistic blow to self-esteem. Rank notes that the defense against narcissism manifests itself in two forms: "in fear and revulsion before one's own image," or, as in most cases, in the "loss of the shadow-image or mirror image," a loss resulting in the double's pursuit and persecution of the self (73). For Rank, the creation of the double represents the effort to defy death; the slaying of the double in literature frequently turns out to be a suicidal act, as in Oscar Wilde's *The Picture of Dorian Gray*. The first nonmedical analyst and the first psychoanalytic literary critic, Rank laid the groundwork for future investigations of narcissism in literature. Coincidentally, his essay on the double appeared in the same year Freud published his major work on narcissism. It is to Freud's work that I now turn.

Freudian Theory of Narcissism

In the last resort we must begin to love in order not to fall ill, and we are bound to fall ill if, in consequence of frustration, we are unable to love. — Sigmund Freud, "On Narcissism: An Introduction" [27]

Freud did not refer to the subject of narcissism in his early writings, but he gradually realized its importance to psychoanalytic theory. References to narcissism abound in the middle and late years of his career. The first reference appears in a 1910 footnote to the *Three Essays on the Theory of Sexuality* (1905), where he links narcissism to homosexuality. [28] Freud's major statement appears in the 1914 essay "On Narcissism: An Introduction." In this highly theoretical and condensed paper, Freud breaks new ground by erecting an elaborate metaphysical structure of the relationship between the self and object world. He distinguishes primary narcissism from secondary narcissism and greatly expands the libido (sexual energy) theory. After the 1914 essay, Freud returned often to the theoretical implications of narcissism, especially in Lecture 26 of the *Introductory Lectures on Psycho-Analysis* (1916–1917), "Mourning and Melancholia" (1917), *The Ego and the Id* (1923), and *Group Psychology and the Analysis of the Ego* (1921). The last reference to narcissism appears in the post-humously published *An Outline on Psycho-Analysis* (1940), written a few months before Freud's death in London in 1939. In total, there are just under four hundred references to narcissism in the *Standard Edition*, considerably below the number of references to hysteria and obsessional neurosis but on a par with the phobias, paranoia, and melancholia.

"On Narcissism" remains, after three-quarters of a century, indispensable for anyone interested in the subject. The essay is problematic, however, and Ernest Jones reports that it was "disturbing" even to Freud's early adherents.[29] Freud himself confessed dissatisfaction with the essay, and Jones quotes a letter Freud wrote to Karl Abraham in 1914, in which Freud admits that "the narcissism [paper] was a difficult labor and bears all the marks of a corresponding deformation" (2:304). Before examining "On Narcissism," I shall briefly note the biographical events surrounding its origin.

We know, as a consequence of Freud's theory of transference and countertransference, that the observer is always part of the observed. All personality theories reflect elements of the personality theorists, and the subject of narcissism is particularly treacherous to speculate upon, if only because the speculator's own narcissism is at stake. While writing "On Narcissism," Freud was also proceeding with *On the History of the Psycho-Analytic Movement* (1914), "fuming with rage," as he wrote to Sandor Ferenczi, over the defections of Adler and Jung (Jones, 2:304). Nothing less than the survival of psychoanalysis was at issue here, along with Freud's own place in history. Two years later, in the *Introductory Lectures on Psycho-Analysis*, Freud referred to the three major blows dealt by science to human self-love: the Copernican discovery that the earth revolved around the sun, the Darwinian discovery of the ineradicable animal nature in humankind, and the psychoanalytic discovery of the unconscious. Of these three revolutions, Freud asserts, psychoanalysis constitutes the "most wounding blow" to "human megalomania," since the ego "is not even master in its own house, but must content itself with scanty information of what is going on unconsciously in its mind."[30] It is ironic, then, that Freud began conceiving of narcissism at a time when he was riddled with narcissistic fears over the future of psychoanalysis. Freud's identity was merged with the subject matter of psychoanalysis, and he experienced criticisms of his theory as a narcissistic attack, deserving immediate counterattack. Jones has stated that Freud dealt "objectively" with narcissism, but Reuben Fine is closer to the truth when he argues that "some of the obscurity and inconsistency of his 1914 paper derives from his frustration with his departed disciples."[31]

Freud begins the 1914 essay by observing that narcissism, as a sexual perversion, represents the attitude of a person who treats his body as a sexual object: "who looks at it, that is to say, strokes it and fondles it till he obtains complete satisfaction through these activities" (*Standard Edition*, 14:73). Freud then suggests that narcissism may not be restricted to psychological disorders, but may claim a place in normal human sexual development. Although Freud distinguished narcissistic neuroses from transference neuroses, judging the former untreatable, he later changed his mind and adopted a continuum theory, implying quantitative, not qualitative differences between health and illness. As early as 1909, Freud observed in *Analysis of a Phobia in a Five-Year-Old Boy*—the case of Little Hans—that no sharp line can be drawn between "neurotic" and "normal" people. The concept of "disease," he realized, is a purely practical one.[32]

Freud defines *primary narcissism* as inherent in all infants, unlike *secondary narcissism*, which occurs when libido is later withdrawn from the external world and reinvested into the self, as in schizophrenia. Freud theorizes that at birth there is an original libidinal cathexis of the self; ego cathexis is gradually given off to objects. Central to Freud's theory is the assumption that the infant is at one with the mother and not yet able to distinguish objects or relate to the world. The two forms of cathexis are related, Freud suggests, "much as the body of an amoeba is related to the pseudopodia which it puts out" (*Standard Edition*, 14:75). The zoological metaphor evidently pleased Freud, and he used it often to describe the energic relationship between ego cathexis and object cathexis. The fullest account of the flow of libido appears in the *Introductory Lectures on Psycho-Analysis*:

Think of those simplest of living organisms which consist of a little-differentiated globule of protoplasmic substance. They put out protrusions, known as pseudopodia, into which they cause the substance of their body to flow over. They are able, however, to withdraw the protrusions once more and form themselves again into a globule. We compare the putting-out of these protrusions, then, to the emission of libido on to objects while the main mass of libido can remain in the ego; and we suppose that in normal circumstances ego-libido can be transformed unhindered into object-libido and that this can once more be taken back into the ego. (*Standard Edition*, 16:416)

Freud cites as evidence for the existence of primary narcissism the child's overestimation of his wishes and mental acts: the "omnipotence of thought." Freud's observations led him to the conclusion that children resemble certain types of patients, such as megalomaniacs, who exaggerate their power and importance. Unlike these patients, who remain fixated on their narcissistic ego, children have the ability to convert self cathexis into object cathexis. In normal child development, self cathexis is slowly converted to object cathexis, resulting in the child's awareness of the external world, the distinction between self and other, and the ability to form interpersonal relationships.

Libido, then, operates as a flow of energy on a two-way avenue, able to reverse direction during health or illness and to invest in or attach itself to other objects. Freud is unclear whether libido is a physical or mental force. He usually defines it as the latter, the force in which the sexual instinct is represented in the mind. The normal course of development, Freud believed, is from narcissism to object love, from self to others. The highest phase of development of which object love is capable may be seen in the state of being in love, when the individual renounces ego cathexis in favor of object cathexis. But not all libido passes from ego to object: a certain quantity remains in the ego, even during the state of being in love. Freud observes elsewhere that the "ego is a great reservoir from which the libido that is destined for objects flows out and into which it flows back from those objects." [33] Complete psychological health, Freud insists, requires full mobility of libido.

"On Narcissism" contains valuable statements about the psychology of love. Freud affirms, for example, the inestimable therapeutic value of love in the prevention of illness. He defines psychological health as the ability to love and work, both of which strengthen the individual's ties to the external world. Freud recognizes, however, the ambiguities of being in love. Love is necessary for psychological well-being, yet unrequited love, the depletion of self cathexis in favor of object cathexis, may lead to a narcissistic injury. Freud returns to this subject in *Group Psychology and the Analysis of the Ego*, where he suggests how the object, so to speak, consumes the ego. "Traits of humility, of the limitation of narcissism, and of self-injury occur in every case of being in love."[34] Unhappy love becomes a form of bondage in which the lover finds him- or herself held hostage by the love object. Freud does not emphasize, as contemporary analysts do, the grave narcissistic injuries caused by a parent's rejection of a child. Freud always stresses Oedipal over pre-Oedipal issues. Nevertheless, he shrewdly observes in *Beyond the Pleasure Principle* that loss of love leaves behind a permanent injury to one's self-esteem in the form of a "narcissistic scar," which contributes more than anything to the "sense of inferiority" so common in neurotics (*Standard Edition*, 18:20–21).

Freud also distinguishes between two types of object choices: the *anaclitic* or *attachment* type, which usually begins with the child's dependent relationship to the mother, the earliest sexual object; and the *narcissistic* type, in which the child chooses not the mother but him- or herself as the primary love object. Both kinds of object choice are open, though the individual may show a preference for one or the other. "We say that a human being has originally two sexual objects —himself and the woman who nurses him—and in doing so we are postulating a primary narcissism in everyone, which may in some cases manifest itself in a dominating fashion in his object-choice" ("On Narcissism, *Standard Edition*, 14:88).

There are several problems with "On Narcissism," apart from its theoretical abstractness and stylistic unwieldiness. Modern infant research has vigorously rejected the parallel between adult pathology and infantile behavior. Emanuel Peterfreund refers to two fundamental conceptual fallacies that have dominated psychoanalytic thought: "the adultomorphization of infancy, and the tendency to characterize early states of normal development in terms of hypotheses about later states of psychopathology."[35] In addition, Freud's theory of primary narcissism has been challenged by recent observational studies indicating that infants begin to experience a sense of emergent self from birth. One of the most important new books on the infant's subjective life is Daniel Stern's *The Interpersonal World of the Infant* (1985). Synthesizing the findings of developmental psychologists, Stern concludes that infants "never experience a period of total self/other undifferentiation. There is no confusion between self and other in the beginning or at any point during infancy."[36] Disagreeing with Mahler's concept of infantile autism, Stern points out that infants never live in total isolation; they are born with a readiness for relating. Consequently, infants are much more responsive to their environment than Freud's generation realized, and the child's symbiotic (re)fusion with the mother appears to be a secondary phenomenon. The facts arising from contemporary research suggest that the infant possesses a rudimentary sense of self far earlier than Freud believed, earlier, perhaps, than the acquisition of language.

Freud, master theory-builder that he was, would have had no difficulty in revising his own view of human development in light of the latest scientific data. He was fond of quoting Charcot's dictum: "La théorie c'est bon; mais ça n'empêche pas d'exister" (Theory is good, but it doesn't prevent things from existing.)[37] Elsewhere Freud stressed the empirical nature of psychoanalysis, arguing that "it keeps close to the facts in its field of study, seeks to solve the immediate problems of observation, gropes its way forward by the help of experience, is always incomplete and always ready to correct or modify its theories."[38] Freud's speculative side was often at odds with his empirical side, it is true, and in our own highly theoretical age, psychoanalytic literary critics have become enamored with his boldest, most imaginative ideas, such as the so-called death instinct. Yet few analysts—Lacan is a notable exception—now take seriously Freud's death instinct, and the enduring achievements of psychoanalysis will be determined through observational research.

Nowhere is Freud's theory of narcissism more suspect than in its dismaying generalizations about women. Freud claims that anaclitic object choice is characteristic of most men, while narcissistic object choice is characteristic of perverts, homosexuals, and women. Additionally, Freud insists that unlike men, who are capable of complete object love, women take themselves as the love object, which results in their complacency. "Women, especially if they grow up with good looks, develop a certain self-contentment which compensates them for the social restrictions that are imposed upon them in their choice of object. Strictly speaking, it is only themselves that such women love with an intensity comparable to that of the man's love for them" ("On Narcissism," *Standard Edition*, 14:88–89). Freud compares women to children and certain animals, such as cats and large beasts of prey, whose charm lies in their inaccessibility. This charm has a darker side, he asserts, in that the lover's identification with a narcissistic woman arises over her enigmatic nature and self-centeredness. Freud ends his brief discussion by assuring his readers that his description of female psychology "is not due to any tendentious desire on my part to depreciate women"—an assurance that is not likely to persuade us.

Freud's unconscious bias, part of his Victorian legacy, is responsible for the psychoanalytic devaluation of women. In the name of disinterested science, Freud inflicts a narcissistic injury on women that explains, in large part, feminist criticism of psychoanalytic theory.[39] Indeed, the twentieth-century interest in narcissism as a psychological concept has been associated from the beginning with subtle misogyny. The first published paper on narcissism, Havelock Ellis' 1898 "Auto-Erotism, A Psychological Study," asserts that the "Narcissus-like tendency" is found more frequently in women than in men —and when found in men, mainly in those who are "feminine-minded."[40] Ellis cheerfully reports that a narcissistic woman inspired him to write the 1898 paper. "She has never known—though it might please and would certainly amuse her to know—the stimulus she has provided to psychological conceptions." That the unknown woman might have been angered at the antifeminism implicit in the early psychoanalytic theorists—all of whom were male and who identified women as the narcissistic sex—has remained uncommented upon in psychoanalytic literature. It is ironic, then, that while Ovid's Narcissus is a male, psychoanalysis has identified the phenomenon of narcissism with the female. It is true that some female analysts, such as Sabina Spielrein and Helene Deutsch, have also accepted narcissism as a peculiarly feminine characteristic, but the assertion still lacks scientific credibility. Psychoanalysis thus has invested the myth of Narcissus with another myth, a distressing subtext couched in clinical language, proclaiming female inferiority. Interestingly, one prominent analyst, James Masterson, has reported that narcissistic disorders are more common in boys than in girls.[41]

Freud's discussion of the role of narcissism in the parent-child relationship is also problematic. He argues that parents narcissistically invest themselves in their children, seeing their offspring only in terms of themselves. "If we look at the attitude of affectionate parents towards their children, we have to recognize that it is a revival and reproduction of their own narcissism, which they have long since abandoned." Parents idealize the child, to whom they refer as "His Majesty the Baby." In addition, parents live vicariously through their children and achieve immortality through them. "Parental love, which is so moving and at bottom so childish, is nothing but the parents' narcissism born again, which, transformed into object-love, unmistakably reveals its former nature" ("On Narcissism," *Standard Edition,* 14:90–91).

Freud's writings here are vulnerable to charges of cynicism and reductivism. Is parental love nothing more than childish, selfish love? Can all parenting be reduced to the wish for vicarious pleasure? Cannot parents see their children without overidealizing them? We do not have to accept Freud's cynical belief that all selfless acts inevitably spring from or are transformations of selfish feelings. Moreover, not all parents narcissistically invest themselves in their children to the same degree. Freud misses the opportunity to distinguish between healthy and unhealthy forms of parenting, between unconditional and conditional love. He also remains silent on the social, political, cultural, and economic factors that contribute to narcissism. We know, for example, that each gender has its own developmental problems with respect to narcissistic conflicts. Sophie Freud points out that men have more outlets for their narcissistic strivings than women do. Men are also more prone to alcoholism, antisocial behavior, and suicide, while women are more vulnerable to depression.[42]

There are other criticisms of Freud's theory of narcissism, beginning with the obvious fact that no one has ever observed narcissistic libido. Psychoanalysts may agree on the observable symptoms of a narcissistic patient but sharply disagree on a theoretical or metaphysical framework. The energic concept of narcissism is closer to nineteenth-century science, with its mechanistic implications, than to twentieth-century psychotherapy, with its emphasis upon the contextual and transactional dynamics of the self. Robert Holt has pointed out that the concept of narcissistic libido is tautological in that "the only data by means of which it can be assessed are the very ones it is invoked to explain."[43] Freud's theory of the relationship between narcissism and object love corresponds, by way of analogy, to the image of the fluid levels in a U-shaped tube. The rise of fluid in one level results in a proportionate fall of fluid in the other level. But, as

Heinz Kohut remarks, "the sense of heightened self-esteem, for example, that accompanies object love demonstrates a relationship between the two forms of libidinal cathexis that does not correspond to
that of the oscillations in a U-tube system."[44]

Freud believed narcissism was inseparable from the libido theory,
based on the flow of energy between self and object, but he soon
began to expand his thinking into other areas. For instance, how do
narcissistic injuries lead to depression? "Mourning and Melancholia,"
published three years after "On Narcissism," represents a pivotal
work. There Freud shifts from the biological framework of id psychology to a model based upon defense and explores the concept of
identification. His investigation of the dynamics of aggression, including masochism and sadism, still remains one of his most original
contributions to psychological theory. Freud begins with the symptoms of depression: profound dejection, cessation of interest in the
external world, inability to love, general inhibition of all activity, and
a lowering of self-esteem, culminating in an expectation of punishment. In reconstructing the origins of depression, Freud suggests that
the loss of a love object may cause an individual to withdraw libido
into the self in such a way as to preclude future displacements toward
other love objects. The individual now identifies with the abandoned
object. Freud reasons that depression is caused by the internalization
of an object originally loved but now hated because of its association
with rejection or disappointment. The cause of narcissistic injury,
then, is the incorporation of a poisonous object. "The self-tormenting
in melancholia, which is without doubt enjoyable, signifies, just like
the corresponding phenomenon in obsessional neurosis, a satisfaction
of trends of sadism and hate which relate to an object, and which have
been turned round upon the subject's own self."[45] In both depression
and obsessional neurosis, individuals punish themselves in order to
take revenge on people who have failed them.

Freud's insights into narcissism result in startling paradoxes. Behind narcissists' self-love lies self-hate; beneath their grandiosity lies
insecurity. The shallowness and emptiness characteristic of narcissism
are defenses against virulent inner forces assaulting a person's self-
esteem. These psychic forces represent, to use Freud's theoretical
framework in "Mourning and Melancholia," the ego's unconscious

identification with the lost love object. The narcissistic person thus craves love that has never been forthcoming. Freud concluded that the narcissistic patient has no capacity for transference, since impaired object relations prevent the individual from forming even a minimal relationship to the analyst. None of Freud's five major case studies directly involves a discussion of narcissism, although there are, of course, narcissistic injuries in the lives of Dora, Little Hans, Schreber, the Rat Man, and the Wolf Man. Freud remains pessimistic about the treatment of narcissistic disorders. Using a metaphor in the *Introductory Lectures on Psycho-Analysis* he seldom uses elsewhere, he remarks: "In the narcissistic neuroses the resistance is unconquerable; at the most, we are able to cast an inquisitive glance over the top of the wall and spy out what is going on on the other side of it" (*Standard Edition*, 16:423). It is rare for the Promethean Freud, disturber of the world's sleep, to acknowledge an unconquerable psychological problem. The subject of narcissism posed one of his greatest intellectual challenges.

Since Freud first peered over the wall, many psychoanalytic researchers have extended his vision of narcissism. Predictably, there are almost as many different interpretations of narcissism as there are interpreters. Psychoanalysis is hardly the monolithic point of view its detractors have claimed—or that some of its supporters have also claimed, thus dismissing any "deviation" from orthodoxy. Narcissism has proven to be particularly troublesome to define, explain, and treat. Where on the nosological spectrum does it lie in relation to neurosis and psychosis? Is narcissism a normal or abnormal developmental process? Is the patient best served by the analyst's cool understanding or warm empathy? Debates over narcissism have produced the most fruitful—and rancorous—discussions in psychoanalytic circles. Of the conflicting theories emerging in the last twenty years, two have seized hold of the psychoanalytic community. The more classical view of narcissism has been set forth by Otto Kernberg, influenced by Melanie Klein and the British school of object relations. The more revolutionary view comes from Heinz Kohut, who, until his death in 1981, was the founder and leader of a new school of psychoanalysis called self psychology. It is to these major post-Freudian theorists that I now turn.

Post-Freudian Theories of Narcissism:
Otto Kernberg and Heinz Kohut

In the voluminous literature on narcissism, there are probably only two facts on which everyone agrees: first that the concept of narcissism is one of the most important contributions of psychoanalysis; second that it is one of the most confusing.—Sydney Pulver, "Narcissism: The Term and the Concept"[46]

Narcissism has been a major topic of interest in psychoanalysis since Freud's 1914 paper, but the concept has been as elusive as Narcissus' shadow. Analysts use the term in several different ways: to refer to a special type of object choice; to an early, nondifferentiated stage of development; to a mode of relating to others; and to a personality disorder. Only in the last few years, however, has narcissism been officially recognized as a psychiatric illness. The American Psychiatric Association's introduction of the term *narcissistic personality disorder* in the third edition of the *Diagnostic and Statistical Manual of Mental Disorders* in 1980 formally legitimized the illness for the first time. (By contrast, there is no mention of narcissism in the second edition, published in 1968.) *DSM-III*, as it is popularly called, defines Narcissistic Personality Disorder in the following way:

a grandiose sense of self-importance or uniqueness; preoccupation with fantasies of unlimited success; exhibitionistic need for constant attention and admiration; characteristic responses to threats of self-esteem; and characteristic disturbances in interpersonal relationships, such as feelings of entitlement, interpersonal exploitativeness, relationships that alternate between the extremes of overidealization and devaluation, and lack of empathy.[47]

Richard Chessick has pointed out that although *DSM-III* presents an accurate description of narcissism, the language is judgmental, reflecting the belief that the narcissist "would clearly be somebody that no one could like, an individual who is obviously maladapted and headed for serious trouble in life."[48] This view of narcissism, Chessick continues, reveals the philosophy of *DSM-III*, which describes psychiatric disorders as diseases that require medical attention rather than problems in living. Reuben Fine also criticizes *DSM-III* for rejecting the concept of a continuum between normal behavior and abnormal disorders. "All people are narcissistic; the difference is only one of degree" (*Narcissism, the Self, and Society,* 67). These criticisms will be especially important for my discussions of how narcissistic conflicts in literary characters demonstrate a continuum between normal and abnormal behavior.

DSM-III succeeds, however, in capturing the paradoxical features of narcissism, in which a sense of self-importance alternates with feelings of unworthiness. Fantasies of achieving unlimited power, wealth, beauty, or ideal love are pursued with a driven, pleasureless quality. The narcissist seeks admiration but is more concerned with appearance than reality. The narcissist's fragile self-esteem results in a sense of entitlement, the expectation of receiving special favors without assuming reciprocal responsibilities. In addition, the narcissist alternates between idealization and devaluation, as when a man repeatedly becomes involved with women whom he worships yet disdains. Depression is extremely common, along with painful self-consciousness, hypochondria, and chronic envy of others.

DSM III lists five diagnostic criteria for the narcissistic personality disorder: (1) grandiose sense of self-importance; (2) preoccupation with unrealistic fantasies; (3) exhibitionism; (4) cool indifference or feelings of rage, inferiority, shame, humiliation, or emptiness in response to criticism; (5) at least two of the following interpersonal disturbances: entitlement, exploitativeness, alternation between over-idealization and devaluation, lack of empathy. *DSM-III* points out that while the narcissistic personality disorder appears to be more prevalent now than in the past, this may be due merely to greater professional interest in the subject.

Since the middle 1960s, Otto Kernberg, professor of psychiatry at Cornell, has been considered one of the two leading authorities on narcissism. Kernberg has presented the "most systematic and wide-sweeping clinical and theoretical statements of the last decade, perhaps even since Freud."[49] He has synthesized the work of earlier psychoanalysts, reconciled Freudian instinct theory and object relations theory, and worked out a coherent psychiatric classificatory system. Kernberg's work represents a systematic analysis of borderline patients—that is, patients whose presenting symptoms do not easily fall into the traditional categories of neurosis and psychosis.

Kernberg's major book, *Borderline Conditions and Pathological Narcissism* (1975), has become a classic in its field.[50] Nearly every

book or article published on narcissism in the last decade cites this
work in its bibliography. Its readability, uncommon in psychiatry,
contributes to its wide influence. Kernberg classifies the narcissistic
personality as a subgroup of borderline disorders, variously called
over the years the *schizoid personality structure* or the *as if personality*.
Admitting that *narcissism* as a descriptive term has been both abused
and overused, Kernberg reserves the term *pathological narcissism* for
those patients with severe disturbances in their self-esteem and object
relations, a term signifying the depth of an individual's internal relations with other people. On the surface, narcissistic people often do
not seem ill, and they have better self-control than other patients.
Narcissists' adaptive behavior contributes to their success. Highly
intelligent people with a narcissistic personality structure may be
found in many fields, Kernberg observes, including business, indus-
try, and art, not to mention medicine and psychotherapy. If these
people appear symptom-free and well-functioning, how does one
detect a narcissistic personality? Kernberg's description captures the
bewildering contradictions of narcissism:

These patients present an unusual degree of self-reference in their interactions
with other people, a great need to be loved and admired by others, and a
curious apparent contradiction between a very inflated concept of themselves
and an inordinate need for tribute from others. Their emotional life is shallow.
They experience little empathy for the feelings of others, they obtain very
little enjoyment from life other than from the tributes they receive from others
or from their own grandiose fantasies, and they feel restless and bored when
external glitter wears off and no new sources feed their self-regard. They envy
others, tend to idealize some people from whom they expect narcissistic
supplies and to depreciate and treat with contempt those from whom they do
not expect anything (often their former idols). In general, their relationships
with other people are clearly exploitative and sometimes parasitic. It is as if
they feel they have the right to control and possess others and to exploit them
without guilt feelings—and, behind a surface which very often is charming
and engaging, one senses coldness and ruthlessness. Very often such patients
are considered to be dependent because they need so much tribute and adoration from others, but on a deeper level they are completely unable really to
depend on anybody because of their deep distrust and depreciation of others.
(227–28)

We have all experienced some of these problems at one time or
another, and probably no one has escaped narcissistic injuries. How,
then, does Kernberg recognize a pathological narcissist from another

person who has experienced normal narcissistic injuries? Without rejecting the continuum approach to mental health and illness, Kernberg argues that narcissists may be recognized, clinically speaking, by the degree and duration of their injuries. A telltale sign of pathological narcissism for Kernberg is the relationship between narcissistic idealization and grandiosity. Unlike healthy idealization, narcissistic (or defensive) idealization reveals a cold, envious, angry quality that reflects the patient's projection of his or her grandiosity onto the analyst. Narcissistic idealization implies, for Kernberg, the patient's denial of the analyst as an independent person. The narcissist usually turns against formerly idealized individuals because of their failure to supply him or her with sufficient admiration or attention. The tension between overvaluation and devaluation evokes the pattern of elevating certain individuals onto a pedestal only to cast them off later.

Kernberg maintains that the haughtiness and grandiosity are a defense against paranoid traits related to the projection of inner rage, which is central to the narcissist's pathology. The narcissist uses primitive defense mechanisms, such as splitting, denial, omnipotence, and projective identification—the process in which a person projects aggressive impulses onto another, with whom he or she then actively identifies. A major problem of the narcissist, all psychoanalysts agree, is the inability to tolerate aggression. A healthy person is able to integrate love and hate; a narcissist, by contrast, perceives others as shadowy persecutors endowed with sinister powers. The narcissist's aggression arises from traumatic injuries suffered in early childhood. Following Melanie Klein, Kernberg interprets narcissistic (or oral) rage and envy as the result of the child's primitive fantasy that the mother is aggressively withholding gratification. This rage must be confronted in therapy, Kernberg insists, if the narcissistic patient is to make progress.

Unlike Freud, who believed that narcissists' lack of object relations prevents them from establishing transference relationships with analysts, Kernberg argues that beneath the surface narcissists exhibit intense, primitive object relations of a frightening kind and an inability to depend on good objects. During analysis, the narcissist's hidden paranoia, hatred, and envy erupt, making the transference relationship treacherous. Kernberg and other analysts believe that narcissism can be treated successfully through psychoanalysis, but the prognosis often remains guarded. The narcissist is often the most intractable patient to treat because of the need to devalue the analyst and deny the analyst's existence as an independent person.

Following the work of other psychoanalytic theorists, most notably Edith Jacobson,[51] Kernberg hypothesizes that in the early stages of normal child development, separation between self and object images leads to the formation of identity. Agreeing with Heinz Hartmann's definition of narcissism as the "libidinal investment of the self,"[52] Kernberg views healthy narcissism as synonymous with a general sense of well-being, and he equates it with the capacity for object love. But Kernberg has less to say about healthy narcissism than about pathological narcissism, and he tends to associate narcissism with its unhealthy manifestations.

Pathological narcissism arises in early childhood, Kernberg suggests, as a result of chronically cold, unempathic parents who fail to provide the infant with the love and attention necessary for psychological health. Disruptions in the mother-child bond may bring about a refusion of self and object images, resulting in identity diffusion and an inflated or grandiose (narcissistic) self. Kernberg's composite picture of the narcissist's family environment includes a parental figure, usually a mother or mother surrogate, who functions well on the surface but with a degree of callousness, indifference, and spiteful aggression. The mother often overinvests herself in the child's life, using the child as an extension of herself, a way to fulfill her own narcissistic needs. Children of such mothers later sense that they are loved not for their own sake but for the gratification they supply to others. Yet even if they reject conditional love, they demand it from others, thus perpetuating the intergenerational conflict.

In time, narcissists become entrapped in delusions of grandiosity. Rejected, they take vengeance by rejecting others. The impossibility of maintaining the grandiose self may result in a psychotic breakdown, with its attendant blurring of ego boundaries, loss of ability for reality-testing, and regression to more infantile modes of behavior. However, narcissists appear to be less vulnerable to breakdowns than other types of patients. Indeed, because narcissists often function well in society, a vicious circle arises in which success only heightens grandiosity. Feelings of self-hatred, deriving from a punitive and accusatory superego (conscience), may occasionally drive narcissists to suicide, but this is unusual. More typically, a terrible narcissistic hunger develops that can never be fulfilled.

The strength of Kernberg's theory lies in its internal coherency and plausibility, its integration of the major schools of psychoanalytic thought, its detailed descriptions of character pathology, and its logical developmental model of narcissism. Reading Kernberg's work, one is struck by his remarkable grasp of both clinical and theoretical material, his broad historical overview of the psychoanalytic movement, and his organizational brilliance. He covers more territory than perhaps any other figure, and his self-assurance never falters.

This self-assurance, paradoxically, is both a strength and weakness of Kernberg's work. He rarely admits to the doubts and uncertainties other analysts frequently acknowledge about the field of psychiatry, notorious for its subjectivity and imprecision. The exactness of Kernberg's diagnostic categories seems more appropriate to neurology than psychiatry. He writes like a man who has discovered the clear truth and is now prepared to impart his insights to a confused and demoralized profession.[53] He is professorial in style, confident about method of treatment, and authoritative in his judgments. His approach to narcissism is based on cool detachment, not warm empathy. His clinical style is reflected in his prose style: objective, impersonal, controlled, prescriptive. By talking about extreme narcissism as a form of pathology, Kernberg leaves no doubt about the value judgment he assigns to it. He equates narcissism with cancer, and he refers to severe cases of character pathology as "terminal" and "malignant." By focusing relentlessly on the hidden aggression, envy, and controlling impulses of narcissistic patients, Kernberg runs the risk of being seen as unempathic, if not openly sadistic. Ironically, his approach may represent another narcissistic blow to his patients' wounded self-esteem. Kernberg remains essentially an orthodox psychoanalyst— and quick to detect deviations from Freudian theory. The recent empirical research on children, emphasizing the high degree of differentiation in the infant-mother relationship, has not caused Kernberg to alter significantly his developmental model, including his belief that the infant splits objects into good and bad. "How can one postulate a 'good self' and a 'bad self' before there is a 'self'?" Daniel Stern asks, concluding that the present research on infants permits no such assumption (*The Interpersonal World of the Infant*, 251–52).

In contrast to the orthodox Kernberg, Heinz Kohut has long had a problematic relationship to the psychoanalytic community. The Viennese-born neurologist came to the United States after World War II and then began his training in psychiatry and psychoanalysis. An inspiring teacher, he was professor of psychiatry at the University of Chicago and a training analyst at the Chicago Institute for Psychoanalysis. He has developed an almost mystical following among his disciples; to this extent, he resembles Jacques Lacan, whose current authority among psychoanalytic literary critics is no less remarkable.

Kohut's approach to narcissism differs sharply from Kernberg's.[54] The disagreement ranges from their metapsychological theories of narcissism to methods of clinical treatment. Kernberg views pathological narcissism as a pathological self-structure clearly distinct from normal or primary narcissism; by contrast, Kohut perceives pathological narcissism as a fixation or developmental arrest of an archaic though normal primitive self. Kohut sees nothing malignant or evil about narcissistic personality disorders, and he urges an empathic, nonjudgmental attitude toward narcissistic patients. Indeed, Kohut argues that the pejorative connotations of narcissism are due to the inappropriate intrusion of the altruistic value system of Western civilization.

The radical implications of Kohut's psychology are clear. He urges not only a new theoretical and clinical approach to narcissism, but a fundamental shift in our attitude toward self-love. Kohut would agree with Erich Fromm's conclusion that the problem of our culture is not that there is too much selfishness but too little genuine self-love.[55] One of Kohut's most far-reaching beliefs is that the phenomenon of narcissism, both in its normal and abnormal functions, affects all people. Consequently, he concludes that a new psychoanalytic paradigm must be devised to treat individuals suffering from problems of the self.

In *The Analysis of the Self* (1971), Kohut postulates two separate and largely independent developmental lines: "one which leads from autoerotism via narcissism to object love; another which leads from autoerotism via narcissism to higher forms and transformations of narcissism."[56] The belief that narcissism follows an independent and potentially healthy line of development is a striking departure from earlier psychoanalytic thinking. Kohut dispenses with the traditional term *narcissistic self* and replaces it with *grandiose self*. He argues that when a child's primary narcissism is disturbed by inevitable deficiencies of parental care, the child responds in two ways: first, by creating a grandiose self, with characteristics ranging from solipsism to delusional thinking; and second, by giving over the previous perfection to an admired, omnipotent "selfobject," the "idealized parent imago." Kohut coins the term *selfobject* (which he sometimes writes as two words or hyphenates) to describe an object (usually another person) that is psychologically experienced as part of the self. The selfobject is crucial for the preservation of a stable and healthy sense of self. Kohut uses the metaphor of oxygen to describe how an individual lives in a matrix of selfobjects from birth to death. "He needs selfobjects for his psychological survival, just as he needs oxygen in his environment throughout his life for physiological survival."[57]

Under optimal developmental conditions, the grandiosity and exhibitionism of the self are tamed, with self-love leading to object love. But if the child suffers extreme narcissistic injuries—and here Kohut and Kernberg agree on the grave consequences of parental empathic failures—the child retains the unrealistic idealized parent imago in the structure of the self. The result, according to Kohut, is a fixation or developmental arrest of the archaic selfobject and an intense form of object hunger that cannot be fulfilled. The narcissistic hunger may manifest itself in pervasive feelings of emptiness, depression, or dehumanization. The self is depleted because of the unrealistic demands imposed by an archaic grandiose self, hungering for perfection and omnipotence. The major anxiety experienced in narcissistic personality disturbances is the self's fear of fragmentation or loss of the idealized object.

Kohut identifies two types of transference relationships mobilized by the narcissistic patient in therapy: the idealizing transference and the mirror transference. Both transference relationships represent the self's efforts to preserve in its psychic structure the image of parental omnipotence withdrawn or destroyed in external reality. The idealizing transference relationship is the therapeutic revival of the omnipotent object lost in early childhood. Persons who have suffered severe narcissistic injuries are forever attempting to achieve a union with the idealized object. The mirror transference represents the therapeutic revival of the child's efforts to preserve its original narcissism by concentrating perfection and power upon the self and by rejecting the disappointments of the external world.

There are interesting similarities between Kohut's mirror transference and Jacques Lacan's discussion of the *stade du miroir* in *The Language of the Self* (1978).[58] Any discussion of narcissism must make at least passing reference to the increasingly influential French psychoanalyst. Independent of each other's influence, Lacan and Kohut center their developmental systems on the image of the mirror. Lacan's looking-glass theory rests upon the assumption that infants go through a mirror phase in which they define their identity to fit the image reflected in the mirror. Lacan sees the *stade du mirror* as a developmental phase involving a dialectical process between subject and object. Infants mistakenly assume the mirror image, which they see as unified, to be an accurate representation of themselves. It remains unclear whether Lacan views the *stade du miroir* as an actual event or as a structural concept. In either case, Lacan privileges the mirror phase, which he views as the source of all future identifications. The *moi*, or alienated self, escapes its own self-fragmentation only by entering the symbolic world of language. Lacan's system of the imaginary, symbolic, and real seeks to explain the tension between desire and fulfillment. "It is in the nature of desire to be radically torn," Lacan writes in book 2 of *The Seminar* (1988). "The very image of man brings in here a mediation which is always imaginary, always problematic, and which is therefore never completely fulfilled."[59]

Lacan's metapsychological system is vastly different from Kohut's and Kernberg's. Along with Foucault and Derrida, Lacan postulates a radical decentering of the self, and he shares the poststructuralist tendency to value linguistic over biological approaches to human development. Lacan calls into question the existence and autonomy of the self, and he views the ego as a destructive illusion, a symptom of mental illness. He also rejects the idea of an autonomous, conflict-free ego. By contrast, Kohut and Kernberg agree with the traditional ego psychology emphasis upon strengthening the individual's adaptive and integrative abilities.

Lacan's ideas have been clarified by Ellie Ragland-Sullivan and others,[60] yet it remains to be seen how valuable his theories are in describing and accounting for human development, in general, and narcissism, in particular. Lacan's theory of narcissism is more encompassing than either Kernberg's or Kohut's, and it assumes an inherent lack of being in infancy. Lacan sees narcissism as the irreducible and atemporal condition of human reality. Rather than attributing narcissistic wounds to faulty mirroring or empathic failures, Lacan locates narcissistic difficulties in the child's unfulfilled desire for the mother. Yet Lacan offers remarkably little clinical material to support his psychoanalytic epistemology, and he rarely speaks about the child's real mother. He thus ignores crucial differences in the types of mothering to which children are exposed. Lacan also ignores the attunement and mutual reinforcement between the infant and mother that researchers like Daniel Stern have recently discovered.

Indeed, Lacan dismisses any attempt empirically to validate psychoanalytic theory or integrate it with a general psychology. "No empiricism is possible without an advanced conceptualisation, as Freud's work clearly shows," Lacan states (*The Seminar*, 93.) But surely Lacan has it backwards here: theories come into existence to explain facts. For all their differences with each other, Kohut and Kernberg both incorporate clinical findings to buttress their systems, and, as with all researchers who claim scientific credibility, their chief importance years from now will depend upon the extent to which their theories are useful to treatment endeavors.

The experience of reading Lacan is strikingly different from reading Kernberg or Kohut. Lacan is a master ironist whose devious paradoxes, like Derrida's, always destabilize meaning. One is never sure whether to read Lacan literally or metaphorically. Is he primarily a scientist, whose authority is based upon observational research; a philosopher, whose influence rests upon his problematic redefinitions; or a poet, whose power resides in his vivid language? "As long as his verbal performances dazzle and stimulate us to new possibilities of encountering texts, or to unconventional lines of inquiry, we are enriched," Daniel Dervin remarks. "But if we press his metonymies and metaphors too closely we can expect disappointment."[61]

Kohut, too, has a tendency toward obfuscation, but there is one subject on which he has been clear: the importance of empathy. Unlike Kernberg, who argues that the psychoanalyst must remain clinically detached, neutral, and objective, intervening only to analyze and interpret, Kohut maintains passionately that the analyst's empathy completes a developmental process arrested in early childhood. Kohut's greatest originality may lie in the simple but eloquent affirmation of empathy. He disagrees with Freud, who advises his colleagues in "Recommendations to Physicians Practising Psycho-Analysis" (1912) to model themselves on the surgeon, "who puts aside all his feelings, even his human sympathy." Using a mechanistic metaphor, Freud urges the analyst to "turn his own unconscious like a receptive organ towards the transmitting unconscious of the patient. He must adjust himself to the patient as a telephone receiver is adjusted to the transmitting microphone."[62] Though Freud did not follow his own injunction to remain a "blank screen" to the patient, he felt that only through the preservation of strict objectivity and detachment could the analyst maintain control of his own countertransference—the tendency to project unresolved fears, fantasies, and conflicts onto the patient. Freud also believed that if psychoanalysis was to become scientifically respectable, the analyst must retain the impartiality characteristic of other scientists.

The role of empathy was surprisingly neglected during the early years of the psychoanalytic movement. Ernest Wolf reports, for example, that Freud never elaborated on the concept of empathy and only rarely alluded to its theoretical significance. In the twenty-four volume English *Standard Edition* of Freud's writings, there are only fifteen references to empathy, suggesting its unimportance to psychoanalytic theory.[63] Empathy is the English translation of the German word *Einfühlung*, coined by Theodore Lipps in 1903, which means to feel oneself into something or somebody. Empathy is thus a modern concept, less than a century old. Though it is often equated with sympathy, empathy signifies a more active projection of one's personality into another person's point of view.

Without explicitly condemning Freud's statements on analytic detachment, Kohut declares that the elimination of empathy in the area of psychological observation leads to a mechanistic and lifeless conception of psychological reality. Since the publication of "Introspection, Empathy, and Psychoanalysis" in 1959, Kohut has defined his theoretical framework in terms of the "empathic-introspective stance."[64] If dreams are for Freud the royal road to the unconscious, empathy is for Kohut the unerring passageway into the self. Empathy serves three functions for him. First, it is an indispensable tool of observation, the mode by which one person understands the feelings and thoughts of another person. Second, it constitutes a powerful bond between people, counteracting human destructiveness. Finally, it is an invaluable psychological nutriment that sustains life. Boldly revising Freudian theory, Kohut asserts that the major observational tool of psychoanalysis is not free association but the empathic-introspective stance.

There are ambiguities, however, in Kohut's definition of empathy. Joseph Lichtenberg, one of Kohut's supporters, suggests that empathy comprises intuition,[65] though Kohut categorically states that "empathy is not intuition and must not be confused with it."[66] Nor is the difference between empathy and sympathy entirely clear. Part of the uncertainty over Kohut's concept of empathy lies in whether psychoanalysis is mainly a science or art. Kohut attempts to objectify empathy by asserting that it is in essence neutral, value-free, nonsubjective, and employed only for data-gathering. Like most analysts, Kohut still views psychoanalysis as a science rather than an art. In his technical definition, Kohut sees empathy as vicarious introspection, analogous in the physical sciences to vicarious extroversion. Yet, more broadly, Kohut affirms empathy as an instrument of cognition and a humanizing force. To this extent, the analyst becomes an artist, studying human emotions no less than a poet or sculptor. In *The Search for the Self* (1978), Kohut asserts that empathy is the "power that counteracts man's tendency toward seeing meaninglessness and feeling despair" (2: 713). Kohut's affirmation of empathy recalls Buber's dialogical "I-Thou" philosophy.[67] Kohut suggests, however, that the widespread existential malaise of our times derives not from a philosophical but from a psychological problem: faulty empathic responses encountered in infancy, when the self was being formed. Yet, at the same time, Kohut must have felt ambivalent about elevating empathy into a transcendent value; in the posthumously published *How Does Analysis Cure?* (1984), he warns that "we must beware of mythologizing empathy, this irreplaceable but by no means infallible depth-psychological tool."[68]

Kohut also recommends a new paradigm for therapeutic cure. Since narcissistic disorders are caused by empathic failure, they can be cured only by unwavering empathic support. Empathy enables the individual to proceed from primitive narcissism to more mature forms of narcissism. Kohut greatly expands the role of the analyst-as-mirror;

whereas the mirror in Ovid's myth of Echo and Narcissus is emotionally unresponsive, in Kohut's writings mirroring assumes an affirmative, joyful quality. He affirms the "glint in the mother's eye" in mirroring the child's buoyant strivings. Empathic mirroring remains for Kohut a Kantian imperative, and he celebrates, with almost religious fervor, the child's search for empathically responsive selfobjects. Empathic failures, he stresses, may lead to disastrous consequences. For example, the analyst's failure to express empathic support represents a repetition of earlier empathic failures that initially gave rise to the patient's narcissistic personality disorder. In *How Does Analysis Cure?*, Kohut makes the heretical claim that as long as the analyst remains empathic, excellent therapeutic results can be obtained, even if the analyst's interpretation of the patient's psychopathology may be in error (91).

Kohut's emerging psychology of the self, as it is now called, has been moving steadily away from classical Freudian theory, yet Kohut has been anxious not to break completely with traditional psychoanalysis. He candidly acknowledges in *The Search for the Self* that his hesitation in proclaiming an independent system was grounded in his fear of creating a new schism in psychoanalysis (2: 935). Rather than abandoning classical Freudian theory, with its emphasis upon sexual and aggressive drives, Kohut urges the principle of complementarity: the existence of a conflict psychology that explains classical problems, such as hysteria and obsession-compulsion, and a self psychology that works better in the treatment of narcissistic personality disorders. In a larger sense, self psychology represents a shift away from the Freudian model of psychopathology to a theoretical framework emphasizing the struggle for creative growth. Sounding like R. D. Laing, Kohut proposes that "psychological disturbance should not be looked upon as a disease—or at any rate not exclusively so—but as a way station on the road for man's search for a new psychological equilibrium" (*The Search for the Self*, 2: 539).

Indeed, Kohut's most endearing characteristics are the extraordinary therapeutic hope and warmth conveyed in his writings, along with an openly inspirational tone. He puts into practice in his writings the empathic stance that he advocates in psychoanalysis. His recognition that the narcissistically disturbed individual yearns for praise, approval, and merger with a selfobject is reflected in a prose style that is itself empathic, soothing, and generous. There is a disarming quality about Kohut that allows the reader to forgive his occasional lapses into psychoanalytic jargon. In his own terminology, these stylistic lapses are temporary, nontraumatic failures. Like Freud, Kohut is aware of his tendency toward theoreticism and tries to resist being seduced by it. "It is my impression that theory has achieved a position of somewhat exaggerated significance in modern psychoanalysis. I love theory, and I am unable to conceive of our science without the serious-minded pursuit of framing relevant general statements. But theory must not become our master; it must be our servant" (*The Search for the Self*, 2: 928). At times Kohut sounds like a cheerleader, as when he proclaims the principle of complementarity: "Three cheers for drives! Three cheers for conflicts! They are the stuff of life, part and parcel of the experiential quintessence of the healthy self. The same can be said of anxiety and guilt."[69] Above all, Kohut is willing, as few analysts are, to acknowledge his mistakes and trust his patients' perceptions. "If there is one lesson that I have learned during my life as an analyst," he writes in *How Does Analysis Cure?*, "it is the lesson that what my patients tell me is likely to be true—that many times when I believed that I was right and my patients were wrong, it turned out, though often only after a prolonged search, that *my* rightness was superficial whereas *their* rightness was profound" (93–94).

Predictably, Kohut has come under sharp criticism, and he remains unquestionably the most controversial figure in American psychoanalysis. His last-minute abandonment of drive theory has incurred the disapproval of many analysts who would otherwise be sympathetic to his teachings. He has been criticized for the illogicality of the principle of complementarity—the belief in a sharp dichotomy between the structural conflicts, amenable to classical psychoanalysis, and the developmental (narcissistic) defects, conducive to self psychology. Kohut's theory-building, with its elaborate reifications and at times obscurantist prose, is particularly vulnerable to criticism. One of the most trenchant critiques of Kohut's work comes from Morris Eagle, who observes that what Kohut calls "healthy narcissism" would be called by others "minimal narcissism."[70] In addition, critics charge that Kohut's elevation of empathy to a mystical ideal only gratifies the narcissist's—and analyst's—grandiosity.

Kohut has also come under attack from literary critics. Steven Marcus questions his distinction between "Guilty Man," suffering from what classical Freudian psychoanalysis identifies as structural conflicts, and "Tragic Man," suffering from what self psychology identifies as narcissistic disorders. Kohut singles out Kafka's writings as an exemplary illustration of tragic man. But, as Marcus rightly points out, "To sever or separate guilt from tragedy is the equivalent of performing *Hamlet* without the prince. Guilt is in fact the central emotion dealt with in tragedy, and it is impossible to imagine the history of the genre without that emotion."[71]

Whether self psychology is a natural and organic outgrowth of classical psychoanalysis remains to be seen. Only time will tell whether Kohut's treatment of narcissistic personality disorders yields good therapeutic results. One of his most controversial ideas is that human aggression is not the manifestation of a primary drive, as Freud resolutely asserted, but a "disintegration product" of the fragmented self. Kohut traces aggression to empathic failures—a less pessimistic view of human nature than Freud's, but also less tough-minded. Critics charge that were it not for his death, Kohut would have repudiated Freudian theory altogether, as many of his disciples have done. Indeed, Kohut feared the bitter divisions that have beset the psychoanalytic movement from its inception. In *The Search for the Self*, he wryly asks himself whether he is the "Pied Piper who leads the young away from the solid ground of the object-libidinal aspects of the Oedipus complex" (2: 622).

Indeed, there is an intriguing passage near the end of *The Analysis of the Self* reflective of Kohut's ambivalence over originality in psychoanalytic research. In some potentially creative analysts, he remarks, aspects of a narcissistic transference toward the training analyst may become shifted onto Freud, the founding father of psychoanalysis. A researcher's departure from Freudian theory may mobilize deep fears of the loss of the father. "Fears aroused by the loss of the narcissistic transference may, for example, block the carrying to completion of truly original steps that would significantly transgress the scope of Freud's own discoveries" (319–20). Kohut's insight recalls Harold Bloom's theory of literary creativity in *The Anxiety of Influence*.[72] Bloom's Oedipal-based interpretation argues that the strong (original) poet unconsciously fears he has come too late onto the scene and must, therefore, silently deidealize or defeat the parent-creator. In *The Search for the Self,* Kohut hints at the anxiety of influence, observing that the death of the idealized parent can have two results: deidealization can bring about rebellious destruction of the father's values and goals, or it can bring about a surge of independent initiative (2: 667). Kohut is himself an original thinker who, transgressing the scope of Freudian theory, experiences the anxiety of the rebellious son usurping the father's authority.

Whatever the disagreements of Kernberg and Kohut, both analysts expand our understanding of the elusive nature of narcissism. It is not necessary to choose either one theory or the other: both models offer valuable insights. Kernberg's most important contribution to the study of narcissism may be the detailed descriptions of the intense rage lying under surface calm. No analyst has written more persuasively about the paradoxical relationship between the narcissist's self-love and self-hate. Kohut's most important contribution may be the importance of empathy both as an observational tool and as a psychological antidote for poisoned self-esteem. Kernberg writes like an omniscient parent, Kohut like an all-forgiving one. No one can accurately predict the future of self psychology and its relationship to classical theory, but both writers have revitalized and enriched contemporary psychoanalytic discourse. And nowhere is the issue of narcissism more central than in literature, where Ovid's spectral hero continues to haunt writers and critics.

Narcissism and the Study of Character

"Spare me that word 'narcissism,' will you? You use it on me like a club."

"The word is purely descriptive and carries no valuation," said the doctor.

"Oh, is that so? Well, you be on the receiving end and see how little 'valuation' it carries!"—Philip Roth, *My Life as a Man*[73]

Since Freud's earliest forays into drama and fiction, there has been a continuing debate over the application of psychoanalysis to literature. No less than the partisans of Kernberg and Kohut, psychoanalytic literary critics are engaged in impassioned arguments over fundamental theoretical issues. These include the extent to which psychoanalysis ought to be privileged in literary discussions, the uses and abuses of psychoanalytic criticism, the vexing problem of representation, and the postmodern challenge to Freudianism. Before these issues can be confronted, however, it is important to understand historically the troubled relationship between the artist and psychoanalyst. These tensions originate in Freud's ambivalence toward the artist.

Freud's best known statement on the artist appears in the *Introductory Lectures on Psycho-Analysis,* where he observes that the artist is "in rudiments an introvert, not far removed from neurosis" (*Standard Edition,* 16: 376). Oppressed by powerful instinctual needs, the artist "desires to win honour, power, wealth, fame and the love of women; but he lacks the means for achieving these satisfactions." Consequently, the artist turns away from reality and retreats into the world of art, where he makes his dreams come true. Art, then, represents for Freud a substitute gratification enabling the artist to escape illness. "It is well known, indeed," Freud writes in the same passage, "how often artists in particular suffer from a partial inhibition of their efficiency owing to neurosis. Their constitution probably includes a strong capacity for sublimation and a certain degree of laxity in the repressions which are decisive for a conflict."

Freud's portrait of the artist as a neurotic is, of course, hopelessly condescending, but there is a disquieting irony we must acknowledge. There is some scientific evidence supporting the link between suffering and art. The relationship between genius and insanity has been hinted at for centuries; and numerous investigators, ranging from Cesare Lombroso to Havelock Ellis, have speculated that genius and mental illness are somehow allied. None of these studies was scientifically rigorous, though, and the evidence remained largely anecdotal. One study, however, undertaken in the mid-1970s, supports Freud's contention that the artist is more vulnerable than others to neurotic conflicts. Nancy Andreasen, a trained literary critic and psychiatrist, conducted a study of writers at the University of Iowa Writers' Workshop for the purpose of examining the prevalence of psychiatric symptoms in a group of poets and novelists. She discovered that the interviewed writers had a significantly higher incidence of illness and psychiatric treatment than did a matched control group. Nine out of the fifteen writers had previously seen a psychiatrist, eight had been in treatment, and four had been hospitalized. Most of the writers described symptoms of mood disorder, which appears to be the illness most associated with creativity. Interestingly, relatives of the writers also experienced a higher incidence of psychiatric symptoms and creativity than did the control group, suggesting that mood disturbance may be genetically determined. Andreasen theorizes that mood disorders increase a writer's insight into human experience. Unlike more serious forms of mental illness, such as schizophrenia, mood disorder is not incapacitating, and there are prolonged normal periods conducive to creativity.[74]

Andreasen's findings have been confirmed by a 1986 study of forty-seven major British artists and writers. Kay Jamison, a UCLA psychiatrist, reported that 38 percent of the sample had been treated for an affective illness, three-quarters of whom were either hospitalized or given antidepressants or lithium. The percentage is strikingly high, Jamison notes, when compared to the normal incidence of manic depression (about 1 percent) and other major depressive disorders (about 5 percent). Jamison's explanation for the high rate of affective illness among artists is that periods of intense creativity seem to overlap with periods of hypomania (a relatively mild form of mania in which a person is still able to function).[75]

Had Freud not singled out the "neurotic artist" for attention, but widened his generalization to include a possible link between other creative individuals and suffering, his theory would have been less offensive to literary writers. By insinuating that artists were both inhibited and inefficient, Freud linked creativity to psychopathology —a theory of creativity that has rightly engendered widespread suspicion and hostility among writers. It goes without saying that not all artists are neurotics, nor are all neurotics artists—despite Freud's tendency to collapse the distinctions between them.

Indeed, Freud knew better than anyone that creativity and suffering are mysteriously allied, and his letters affirm the connection in his own life. The discovery of the Oedipus complex arose from his anguished feelings toward his father, whose death was the central impetus behind the writing of *The Interpretation of Dreams*.[76] Biographers have documented Freud's depressions and migraine attacks, his cardiac symptoms and stomach complaints, his fainting spells (in the presence of Jung and others) and fatal nicotine addiction. Nor did these neurotic symptoms disappear after his self-analysis, as Ernest Jones misleadingly implies. These neurotic symptoms do not invalidate Freud's discoveries, any more than a writer's breakdown invalidates (or, conversely, authenticates) his or her literary achievement. Rather, the link between creativity and suffering is not limited only to writers. Had Freud remembered this, the relationship between the artist and analyst would have been a less troubled one.

George Pickering has coined the term *creative malady* to describe the role of illness in otherwise dissimilar figures as Charles Darwin, Florence Nightingale, Marcel Proust, Elizabeth Barrett Browning, and Freud. "The illness was an essential part of the act of creation rather than a device to enable that act to take place."[77] As I shall seek to show in discussions of representative nineteenth- and twentieth-century British novelists, writers may be more vulnerable than other types of people, not because writers are repressed or inefficient, as Freud implies, but because their bursts of creativity seem to be related to the intensity of their moods. Andreasen reports that most of the interviewed writers described a nagging sense of self-doubt and loneliness and believed that they were literally engaged in a life-or-death battle during the act of creation. They also experienced a corresponding delight when they successfully transmuted their conflicts into art. Writing serves an adaptive and counterphobic function that becomes, for many artists, a form of personal therapy.[78] Freud was one of these "neurotic artists," and his monumental discoveries were closely allied to the personal conflicts he sought to understand and master.

Rather than including himself among the artists, however, Freud insisted that psychoanalysts were scientists, temperamentally inclined toward heroic self-restraint. The artist was, by contrast, narcissistic— like woman—and thus self-centered. Freud's psychobiography, *Leonardo da Vinci and a Memory of His Childhood* (1910), unambiguously links the artist to the narcissist. Freud also suggests that both the artist and woman embody mysterious, seductive secrets they cannot fathom. "Kindly nature has given the artist the ability to express his most secret mental impulses, which are hidden even from himself, by means of the works that he creates; and these works have a powerful effect on others who are strangers to the artist, and who are themselves unaware of the source of their emotion."[79] Both artists and women, then, represented the mysterious other to Freud; they were to be praised from a distance, lest his own power and independence be called into question.

Though Freud admired artists and looked to them for confirmation of his theories, he subtly denigrated their achievements, which seemed less valuable to him than scientists'. "People who are receptive to the influence of art cannot set too high a value on it as a source of pleasure and consolation in life," he writes in *Civilization and Its Discontents* (1930). "Nevertheless the mild narcosis induced in us by art can do no more than bring about a transient withdrawal from the pressure of vital needs, and it is not strong enough to make us forget real misery."[80] In the *New Introductory Lectures on Psycho-Analysis* (1933), Freud goes even further in devaluing the artist's effect upon reality. Of the three powers that may dispute the basic position of science—religion, art, and philosophy—only religion is to be taken seriously as an enemy. "Art is almost always harmless and beneficent; it does not seek to be anything but an illusion. Except for a few people who are spoken of as being 'possessed' by art, it makes no attempt at invading the realm of reality."[81] As Jack Spector notes, Freud never regarded the artist's intuitive insights as comparable to the psychoanalyst's rational understanding.[82]

Freud's confidence in the analyst's rational understanding led him to believe that psychoanalysis would eventually dominate and subdue other fields of human inquiry. To many critics, his incursions into literary criticism represent intellectual imperialism. As usual, Freud was partly to blame for this literary adventurism. While acknowledging in "Dostoevsky and Parricide" (1928) that "before the problem of the creative artist analysis must, alas, lay down its arms,"[83] Freud never ceased his own militant efforts to understand the artist's motivation and to establish a unifying connection between the creator and creation. Freud was fond of quoting a derisive comment by Heinrich Heine about the philosopher who searches for coherency: "With his nightcaps and the tatters of his dressing-gown he patches up the gaps in the structure of the universe."[84] Yet Freud was precisely one of these philosophers, and his faith in psychoanalysis to patch up the gaps in human knowledge never wavered. The "fertilizing effects" of psychoanalytic thought on other disciplines, he wrote in 1919, "would certainly contribute greatly towards forging a closer link, in the sense of a *universitas literarum*, between medical science and the branches

of learning which lie within the sphere of philosophy and the arts."[85]
And in 1924 he wrote that the "aesthetic appreciation of works of art
and the elucidation of the artistic gift are, it is true, not among the
tasks set to psycho-analysis. But it seems that psycho-analysis is in a
position to speak the decisive word in all questions that touch upon
the imaginative life of man."[86]

In our own time, literary scholars and philosophers have made us
dizzyingly aware of the gaps and discontinuities in language and
thought, the impossibility of speaking the decisive word on any subject. The *universitas literarum* Freud envisioned is startlingly different
from the present university scene, where a crisis of interpretation
reigns. Conquistador that he was, Freud continues to dominate our
imagination, but in ways that he could not have anticipated. "No
20th-century writer—not even Proust or Joyce or Kafka—rivals
Freud's position as the central imagination of our age," Harold Bloom
remarks. "Freud has contaminated every 20th-century intellectual discipline, and this in a time when each discipline fights desperately for
its own ground."[87]

In emphasizing Freud's "contamination" of culture, Bloom uses a
disease metaphor that is at once appropriate yet suspect: appropriate
in that American psychoanalysis has rested upon a medical model of
disease; and suspect in that the metaphor identifies psychoanalysis
with the contagions it seeks to eliminate. One is reminded of Karl
Kraus's sardonic characterization of psychoanalysis as the disease of
which it purports to be the cure. It is well known that Freud's
influence has exerted a far greater impact on American university
departments of English than on psychology departments; it is less well
known that prominent literary critics have embraced Freudian analytic
tools while denying or largely ignoring psychoanalysis' ability to
discover truths, however provisional, about human nature. Thus Peter
Brooks opens his essay "The Idea of a Psychoanalytic Literary Criticism" (1987) by disapproving of the entire tradition of Freudian criticism. "Psychoanalytic literary criticism has always been something of
an embarrassment. One resists labeling as a 'psychoanalytic critic'
because the kind of criticism evoked by the term mostly deserves the
bad name it largely has made for itself."[88]

Brooks's attack on psychoanalytic criticism is formidable, especially since he repeats the concerns of other eminent literary scholars identified with Freudian criticism, including Lionel Trilling and Frederick Crews. Brooks criticizes the subjects with which depth psychology has traditionally been concerned: the author, fictional characters, and, more recently, the reader. The first subject, study of the author, constitutes the classical locus of psychoanalysis, but is now the most discredited, Brooks insists, though acknowledging that biographical criticism is the most difficult to extirpate. The second subject, study of fictional characters and their "putative unconscious," has also fallen into disrepute. Brooks extends his criticism here to feminist studies of literature. In analyzing how the female psyche "refuses and problematizes" the views imposed upon it by patriarchal society, feminist criticism, according to Brooks, has yielded to a regressive interest in studying fictional character. The final subject of psychoanalytic inquiry, reader response criticism, similarly displaces the object of analysis from the text to a person or to another psychoanalytic structure, a displacement Brooks hopes to avoid. All these approaches are methodologically disquieting to him. Implicit in his argument is that, however valid interdisciplinary approaches to literature may be, the only proper psychoanalytic criticism should concern itself with uncovering the structure and rhetoric of literary texts. Brooks finally urges a neoformalist approach to psychoanalytic criticism, one that involves Lacan, Roland Barthes, and the erotics of form.

Brooks and others associated with the Yale school of criticism implicitly privilege linguistic and philosophical forms of psychoanalytic criticism over psychological models based upon empirical and observational data. In *Reading for the Plot* (1984), for example, Brooks invokes Freud the semiotician, "intent to read all the signs produced by humans, as individuals and as a culture, and attentive to all behavior as semiotic, as coded text that can be deciphered, as ultimately charged with meaning."[89] By contrast, Brooks is not concerned with the scientific credibility of Freudian theory, with discovering which psychoanalytic concepts have or have not been substantiated.[90] By reducing Freudianism to a series of metaphors, these critics deny the possibility that either literature or psychoanalysis can tell us anything about "reality," which is now seen as inherently ineffable or unknowable. The result is a psychoanalytic criticism that has become even

more theoretically minded than Freud would have desired and a turning away from the empiricism and verifiability that any social science
must demonstrate if it is to be taken seriously.

For all their differences with each other, Lacan and Derrida share a
common mistrust of the American empirical tradition, and in literary
studies their commentaries on Freud are now accorded an honored
status that is denied to clinicians, scientists, and developmental psychologists, who continue to explore a reality that has not been banished through endless problematizings. Thus Geoffrey Hartman invokes Derrida and the hermeneutics of indeterminacy, while Shoshana
Felman applies Lacan's synthesis of psychoanalysis, philosophy, and
linguistics to literature. Brooks, Hartman, and Felman are part of the
postmodern sensibility that has radically steered psychoanalysis away
from its traditional objects of inquiry to new and highly theoretical
issues. In forcing us to accept a more complicated relationship between literature and psychoanalysis, one based on mutuality, these
critics have performed a valuable service. They have also turned the
tables on Freud, or, I should say, repositioned the analyst on his own
couch, where he lies exposed in all his contradictions and rhetorical
deviousness. There is poetic justice in this, given Freud's inveterate
need to expose the artist's neurotic conflicts. At the same time, however, the new theoreticism has repudiated the effort to determine the
nature of the Freudian legacy and its application to literature.[91]

In observing this, I am not denying Derrida's brilliant insights so
much as questioning whether he has indeed expelled reality from
literary studies and, in the process, banished psychoanalysis to a
labyrinthine crypt to which deconstruction alone holds the key. No
one who has read Derrida's cunning deconstruction of Beyond the
Pleasure Principle can avoid the conclusion that Freud was ensnared
in the very processes he sought to unravel. Derrida shows how Beyond the Pleasure Principle reenacts in its structure the child's fort/da
game, with Freud, like his grandchild, casting away the pleasure
principle only to summon it back magically. Interpreting Freud's
repetition compulsion principle in terms of an elaborate "auto-bio-
thanato-hetero-graphic writing scene," Derrida reads Beyond the
Pleasure Principle as a story about Freud's ambivalence toward the
legacy he bequeaths to his family and the world.[92] Derrida ingeniously

demonstrates that the observer is always caught up in the observed: there is no context-neutral observation.

It is possible to accept Derrida's observation but reject his nihilistic conclusion that *Beyond the Pleasure Principle* is a text with no thesis, with nothing beyond the *mise en abîme* of language. The subjective bias of the personality theorist does not automatically refute the validity of the personality theory. We can intuit conflicts in ourselves that are also present in others and through the truth of the imagination apprehend what it means to be human. Freud's idea about the need to recreate a traumatic experience for the purpose of self-mastery has received confirmation from a variety of disciplines, and there is little doubt that psychic identity is maintained through repetition. Freudian reconstruction and Derridean deconstruction are part of an ongoing dialectical tension between unity and disunity, presence and absence. Freud and Derrida may be viewed as doubles, each representing a permanent thrust of the human imagination, one trying to uncover the essential unity in the structure of the universe, the other relentlessly exposing the patches and gaps.

Freud always tried to steer a course between the Scylla of subjectivity and the Charybdis of objectivity. He discovered, on the one hand, the projective mechanisms of interpersonal relationships, including transference and countertransference, that make perfect human objectivity impossible, while he clung no less tenaciously, on the other hand, to the hope of analytic neutrality. That he always failed to maintain a perfect balance between the two does not discourage us from the attempt. To this extent, psychoanalysis and deconstruction are strikingly similar in their recognition that the interpreter can never locate a sufficiently expansive or stable position to render any interpretation definitive. Texts, whether they be human, historical, or literary, resist monolithic interpretations and contain within themselves contradictions and discontinuities. Reading always leads back to an irresolvable paradox or *aporia* that forever disrupts unity or certainty. Freud's theory of overdetermination, Heisenberg's principle of uncertainty, and Derrida's hermeneutics of deconstruction all suggest that there is no way to trace one's origins, human or textual, to a single originary event. Everything is thus caught up in an endless flow of signifiers. "What has become indeterminate," Elizabeth Freund

remarks in *The Return of the Reader* (1987), "is precisely the relationship between a hypostatized original experience (the author's, let us
say, presumably placed *in* the text) and the reader's extrapolation of
that experience (presumably triggered by the text). Giving free reign
to the poetic sign puts at risk the very possibility of communication."[93]

At issue, then, is whether reality can ever be known and, if so,
accurately communicated. Freud rarely lost confidence in meaning,
but this faith has been shattered by the postmodern recognition that
there is no immaculate perception. Freud saw no incommensurability,
as we do now, between language and reality, the signifier and signi-
fied. Like Heine's tireless philosopher, Freud strove to fill up the gaps
in the universe. What psychoanalysis aims at and achieves, he wrote
in the *Introductory Lectures*, "is nothing other than the uncovering of
what is unconscious in mental life" (*Standard Edition*, 16: 389). He
expressed this wish in a variety of formulations: making conscious the
unconscious, lifting repressions, filling gaps in the memory. Today
these aspirations may seem to be, in the light of postmodernism, naïve
positivism. The best that we can do, it appears, is to re-present, to
acknowledge the complexity of discovering and conveying elusive
reality. "The central problem for the critic," Murray Schwartz observes, "can be seen as one of making representation 'presentable,'
that is, of communicating in a language that can be 'heard' by the
audience he seeks."[94]

Like Shakespeare, to whom he has often been compared, Freud
reflects and transcends his own cultural age. The Freud to whom we
return in the age of postmodernism is surely different from the Freud
of only a quarter of a century ago. The relationship between psychoanalysis and literature is no longer the master-slave bond of the past.
Because Freud initiated an unequal relationship between the analyst
and artist, writers and literary critics understandably have sought to
end the tyranny, but we may have created a new inequality, in which
the body of Freud's work is endlessly autopsied. After such knowledge, what forgiveness?

And yet the analyst and artist can mutually appreciate each other's
work. Freud realized this from the beginning. In "Jensen's *Gradiva*"
(1907), he anticipates the objections of critics who argue that the study
of character or author demonstrates misplaced critical attention. "Per-

haps, too, in most people's eyes we are doing our author a poor service in declaring his work to be a psychiatric study. An author, we hear them say, should keep out of the way of any contact with psychiatry and should leave the description of pathological mental states to the doctors." The truth is, Freud declares, that from time immemorial the creative writer has been the precursor of the scientist: the domain of both is the human mind. Freud's conclusion is that the "creative writer cannot evade the psychiatrist nor the psychiatrist the creative writer, and the poetic treatment of a psychiatric theme can turn out to be correct without any sacrifice of its beauty."[95]

The relationship between the creative writer and psychiatrist is potentially a valuable one, but if it is to succeed better than it has in the past, it must focus again on the study of human character. For Lacan, Derrida, and the postmodern critics, character does not exist, at least not in its recognizably humanistic form. By arguing that the human being is a decentered subject, they imply that characters, fictional and human, are merely passive elements of an impersonal linguistic system they can neither understand nor control. As Lacan writes about Poe's "The Purloined Letter," "One can say that, when the characters get a hold of this letter, something gets a hold of them and carries them along and this something clearly has dominion over their individual idiosyncracies" (*The Seminar of Jacques Lacan*, Book II, 196). Gone is the notion of free will and causality we associate with character; characters do not act but are acted upon, and they never know what they are saying because they are ensnared in language.

Fortunately, the once-honorable study of character in literature has been making a revival in recent years, by psychoanalytic and nonpsychoanalytic critics alike. While acknowledging that character analysis has suffered a bad reputation, Meredith Skura points out in *The Literary Use of the Psychoanalytic Process* (1981) that it is not only traditional Freudians who remain interested in the subject but also, surprisingly, revisionary critics, like Geoffrey Hartman and John Irwin.[96] Some of the most influential proponents of deconstruction, including J. Hillis Miller, repeatedly return to character analysis, which they do exceedingly well. Baruch Hochman's recent book, *Character in Literature* (1985), demonstrates how subtle and theoretically sophisticated this approach to literature can be. "Characters in

literature have more in common with people in life than contemporary
critical discourse suggests," Hochman argues. "What they have in
common is the model, which we carry in our heads, of what a person
is. Both characters and people are apprehended in someone's consciousness, and they are apprehended in approximately the same
terms."[97] Real and fictional characters are not always identical, but
they have an ontological parity. When we talk about fictional people
we must always approach them as one element in the larger literary
text as a whole. For years the study of character has resulted in
excellent literary criticism, and, however old-fashioned it may strike
some readers, character study will continue to preoccupy readers as
long as there are characters who read literature. Bernard Paris' observation in *A Psychological Approach to Fiction* is as true now as it was
in 1974: "We are coming to see, among other things, that character is
central in many realistic novels and that much of the characterization
in such fiction escapes dramatic and thematic analysis and can be
understood only in terms of its mimetic function."[98]

The revival of character study is related to the larger resurgence of
humanism, which has been under siege since the 1960s. Barbara Johnson's distinction between deconstruction and humanism is an extreme
example of how the liberal humanistic tradition has been dismissed by
critics who view all literature as allegories of reading. "Deconstruction
is a reading strategy that carefully follows both the meanings and the
suspensions and displacements of meaning in a text, while humanism
is a strategy to stop reading when the text stops saying what it ought
to have said."[99] Yet humanism cannot be reduced to a strategy of
reading or, worse still, a strategy to stop reading. No less than deconstruction, humanism allows us to discover the paradoxes, ironies, and
contradictions inherent in literature and life. In addition, humanism is
inseparable from a system of beliefs and values without which we
cannot live. Humanism implies that we can approach an understanding of the external world without, of course, fully realizing the quest.
Deconstruction is not the terroristic belief in meaninglessness that its
opponents have claimed, but it is also not sufficient to explain the
pleasure and richness of reading about fictional characters and their
relationship to our life experience. Without denying the insights of
deconstruction and postmodern criticism, with their emphasis upon
textuality and rhetoricity, we can agree with Daniel Schwarz in *The*

Humanistic Heritage (1986) that fiction imitates a world that precedes the text. Like Paris and Hochman, Schwarz argues that human behavior is central to most novels and should therefore be the major concern of analysis. "Although modes of characterization differ, the psychology and morality of characters must be understood as if they were real people; for understanding others like ourselves helps us to understand ourselves."[100] A corollary to the belief in character is that, however discontinuous real and fictional people appear to be, they possess a core, stable self.

This is, admittedly, an essentialist position, and thus antagonistic to the existentialist and poststructuralist positions that have dominated recent thought. But here the literary critic can turn to psychoanalysts, who have accumulated overwhelming clinical evidence to confirm an essential "identity theme" that remains remarkably constant in all people. The term comes from Heinz Lichtenstein, who argues that Freud's repetition compulsion principle is a manifestation of the necessity for maintaining human identity. "Identity, in man, requires a 'repetitive doing' in order to safeguard the 'sameness within change' which I believe to be a fundamental aspect of identity in man."[101] This identity theme is irreversible but capable of variations. Lichtenstein compares human identity to thematic development in music: both are developed while undergoing variations. The variations finally revert back to a primary theme, originating, in the case of human development, in early infancy. Lichtenstein's model influenced Norman Holland's transactive criticism, in which a reader transforms a literary text according to his or her own identity theme. Both Lichtenstein's analytic model and Holland's literary model assume an essential unity of personality, whether it be the author, fictional character, or reader. "That is, if we imagine a human life as a dialectic between sameness and difference," Holland writes in *The I* (1985), "we can think of the sameness, the continuity of personal style, as a theme; we can think of the changes as variations on that theme."[102]

In arguing this position, analysts and literary scholars affirm a self that is not, as the poststructuralists insist, constituted solely by language. The linguistic analogy, Richard Freadman points out in *Eliot, James and the Fictional Self* (1986), privileges systems over selves when it is applied to characters. While acknowledging that the theory of a core, essentialist, preverbal self is difficult to prove, Freadman invokes a number of arguments, including the traditional belief in referential reality. Admitting that he is "writing against the current," Freadman nevertheless maintains that fictional characters are not merely parts of sign systems, but selves who possess, like real characters, an interiority that can be apprehended through intuition, introspection, and inferences from our experience of the world.[103]

Fictional characters, no less than real ones, reveal narcissistic elements, and it is here that we can confront, at last, the question of narcissism and character. Beginning with his birth in Ovid's *Metamorphoses* two thousand years ago, Narcissus occupies a permanent position in our lives, not only as an immortal myth, but as a psychic force. He dwells, in all his healthy and unhealthy manifestations, in fictional and real characters alike. Narcissus embodies a meaning that endures throughout the ages but changes from generation to generation, even from reader to reader. Camus' Sisyphus, condemned eternally to push a stone up a mountain only to watch helplessly as it rolls down again, represents the plight of the early twentieth-century individual, confronting existentialist problems. Ovid's Narcissus, condemned to fall in love with a treacherous double, represents the plight of the late twentieth-century individual, confronting problems of wounded self-esteem, blurred self-object boundaries, and grandiosity.

We cannot say for certain whether we are indeed living in a new age, the culture of narcissism, or simply becoming more aware of a situation that has always been with us. Researchers from a variety of disciplines have wrestled with this vexing question. As early as 1950, Erik Erikson suggested that modern patients suffer from different problems than those seen in patients fifty years earlier. "The patient of today suffers most under the problem of what he should believe in and who he should—or, indeed, might—be or become; while the patient of early psychoanalysis suffered most under inhibitions which prevented him from being what and who he thought he knew he was."[104] Culture defines psychopathology, and as the forms of society change, so do the forms of mental illness. And yet it seems probable that the feelings of emptiness, meaninglessness, and wounded self-esteem characteristic of narcissism have always been part of the human character.

Narcissistic issues appear conspicuously in the body of literature I will be looking at: selected nineteenth- and early twentieth-century

British novels. *Frankenstein, Wuthering Heights, Great Expectations, The Picture of Dorian Gray, Jude the Obscure, Sons and Lovers,* and *Mrs. Dalloway* all contain characters who exhibit the elements of narcissism defined by *DSM-III*: grandiosity; exhibitionism and the need for constant attention and admiration; emotional shallowness, hostility, or indifference to the feelings of others; and severe disturbance in their interpersonal relationships. These novels' characters are not, I should hasten to add, unduly self-preoccupied. With the exception of *The Picture of Dorian Gray,* their characters are probably no more or less narcissistic than those of other representative novels. I chose these novels, not because they illustrate a particular theory of narcissism, but because they powerfully dramatize the dynamics of the endangered self. And while each of these novels has amassed a formidable body of psychological commentary, surprisingly little has been written from the standpoint of narcissism.

There is obviously limited value in labeling characters *narcissistic,* even if they exhibit all the symptoms of *DSM-III*. Accordingly, I will use the word as sparingly as possible. A cataloguing of narcissistic qualities similarly has limited significance, as does any classificatory system. To attach a clinical label to characters is to distance ourselves from them. In addition, the concept of narcissism is so inherently problematic, the word so judgmental, that one is tempted to dispense with it altogether and find a less ambiguous substitute. Contrary to what Dr. Spielvogel tells Peter Tarnopol in Philip Roth's *My Life as a Man,* the word "narcissism" is not purely descriptive or value-free. If one cannot dispense with the word, one can try not to use it as a club. [105]

Narcissistic issues exist on four separate but interrelated levels: fictional character, text, author, and reader. I will seek to show how the heroes and heroines in each of the following novels suffer severe narcissistic injuries, almost always as a result of a childhood event, and then spend the rest of their lives struggling to come to terms with this experience. Indeed, it is virtually impossible to offer any psychological commentary on Victor Frankenstein, Heathcliff, Pip, Dorian Gray, Jude Fawley, Paul Morel, or Clarissa Dalloway without exploring fundamental narcissistic issues, such as grandiosity, idealization, identity diffusion, and empathic failure. The problems experienced by characters in their adult lives may be traced, with few exceptions, to early parent-child conflicts, particularly to an overloving or underloving (or, in some cases, an absent) mother and a father who fails to provide steady love and attention. I cannot prove that narcissistic injuries always arise in early childhood—correlation is not causation—but I can show the patterns of repetition that govern each novel.

In attempting to reconstruct a fictional character's life, I have encountered the difficulties an analyst experiences in reconstructing a real character's life. In one sense, the literary critic's task is harder, since the critic knows less—sometimes nothing—about a fictional character's past history. Insofar as representing is re-presenting and remembering is misremembering, the task is seemingly impossible.[106] Yet the situation is not entirely hopeless.

Confronting the problem of historical reconstruction, Daniel Stern coins the term *narrative point of origin* to describe how an analyst attempts to recreate a patient's remembered history. The narrative point of origin, Stern remarks in *The Interpersonal Life of the Infant*, is the "potent life-experience that provides the key therapeutic metaphor for understanding and changing the patient's life" (257). The narrative point of origin is the moment when the patient recollects the beginning of pathology, regardless of when it occurred in actual point of origin. Therapy rarely if ever proceeds back to the preverbal stages when the actual point of origin may have occurred. Instead, it is sufficient, both theoretically and therapeutically, to discover the narrative point of origin. Stern's important concept has wide application to literary criticism, and in my discussions I shall explore the key metaphors surrounding the characters' remembered beginning of conflict.

In the following chapters the findings of noteworthy contemporary theorists and clinicians, including Otto Kernberg, Heinz Kohut, Erik Erikson, Margaret Mahler, John Bowlby, Robert Stoller, Sophie Freud, and others, will be integrated into the discussions in an attempt to show how real and fictional characters have more in common than recent literary criticism would indicate. In both life and literature, for example, when narcissistically injured children grow up and become parents, they tend to injure their children in ways that strikingly repeat their own past. When subjected to improper mirroring in childhood, real and fictional characters tend in later life to be joyless

or distorting mirrors to their children. Narcissism is thus an intergenerational issue.

In arguing that real and fictional characters undergo similar responses to narcissistic injuries, and that, by implication, past and
present are continuous, I do not wish to sacrifice complexity and
ambiguity for narrow coherency and stability. As Steven Marcus
argues in "Freud and Dora," psychoanalysis creates a coherent narrative of life, but this narrative inevitably breaks down upon close
scrutiny. And so, while acknowledging that Freud's case study of
Dora is a creative narrative of the highest order, Marcus also points
out its narrative insufficiency, incoherence, and incompleteness. He
also reminds us that "reality" should always be surrounded by quo-
tation marks.[107]

Narcissistic issues show up variously in a text: in the blurred
boundaries between two characters or in the reliance upon primitive
defense mechanisms, such as splitting, projective identification, or
idealization. Victorian repression was particularly conducive to the
development of the *Doppelgänger,* illustrating the essential oneness of
two characters. Although the theme of the divided self has been fully
documented in nineteenth-century literature,[108] its relationship to narcissism has not been well understood. Nor has the subject of ambition
been treated primarily as a narcissistic issue. Subtitled a "Modern
Prometheus," *Frankenstein* is no less about a "Modern Narcissus."
Like other narcissists, Victor never recognizes the extent to which he
is implicated in monstrous crimes. Predating Kohut by a century and
a half, Mary Shelley's novel could not be more modern in its understanding of the dynamics of narcissism.

However we define it, narcissism involves empathic failure, and
narcissistic texts, no less than narcissistic people, manipulate us into
withdrawing sympathy from deserving characters. The "vast importance of the novel," D. H. Lawrence affirms in *Lady Chatterley's
Lover,* is to "inform and lead into new places the flow of our sympathetic consciousness, and . . . lead our sympathy away in recoil from
things gone dead."[109] The ebb and flow of a novel's sympathy is a
reliable indicator of its internal equilibrium. If a novel reveals a pattern
of consistent empathic failure or solipsistic thinking, or if one character can maintain self-esteem only by undercutting another character's
self-esteem, then we suspect that the novelist is implicated in the text's

narcissistic conflicts. In such cases, problems of narrative distance occur.

Textual issues invariably involve biographical ones, and we should not be surprised that a story's narcissistic conflicts ultimately relate back to the novelist's life and, in a larger sense, to society and culture. These narcissistic conflicts may range from normal to abnormal on the continuum and arise from early childhood loss. We know from the work of John Bowlby and other attachment theorists that the loss of a parent in early infancy has a profound effect upon a child's subsequent development. Consequently, I will explore the link between narcissism and maternal loss. Mary Shelley lost her mother during childbirth, and Emily Brontë was three when her mother died. Virginia Woolf was older, thirteen, when she lost her mother, but her biographers agree that this was the central traumatic event of her life. A child may also experience narcissistic injuries from deficient parenting. Dickens and Hardy perceived their mothers to be underprotective, while Wilde and Lawrence perceived their mothers to be overprotective.

Fathers are also implicated in narcissistic disturbances. Thus, *Frankenstein* dramatizes a cold, disapproving father reflective of William Godwin, Mary Shelley's father; *Great Expectations* portrays a father surrogate who, in failing to come to the aid of his abused son, recalls the failure of Dickens' own father; and *Sons and Lovers* reveals a father whose expulsion from the family results in the son's wounded image of masculinity—a problem that D. H. Lawrence wrote about from experience.

It was common in the nineteenth- and early-twentieth centuries to lose a parent or child at an early age, and I will observe the different responses to early loss. Victor Frankenstein enacts a birth fantasy in which he dispenses with his mother altogether during the act of creation. The motherless Cathy Linton refuses even to think about her mother or the consequences of parental loss in *Wuthering Heights*. Pip has lost his biological mother but cannot escape from the sadistic treatment of his two mother surrogates, Mrs. Joe and Miss Havisham. Dorian Gray is another motherless youth whose idealization of women conceals deep mistrust. Jude Fawley attempts to drown himself immediately after learning that his mother committed suicide years ago. Paul Morel's love-hate relationship toward his mother culminates in an act that partakes of both euthanasia and matricide in *Sons and Lovers*. And Clarissa Dalloway's suicidal double, Septimus Warren Smith, cannot come to terms with the tragic loss of his beloved Evans.

Mourning occupies a central role in all these novels, and a writer's imaginative interest in the subject inevitably arises from personal experiences with loss. "There is no greater threat in life than that we will be deserted, left all alone," Bruno Bettelheim writes in *The Uses of Enchantment*. "Psychoanalysis has named this—man's greatest fear —separation anxiety; and the younger we are, the more excruciating is our anxiety when we feel deserted, for the young child actually perishes when not adequately protected and taken care of. Therefore, the ultimate consolation is that we shall never be deserted."[110] Perhaps the ultimate consolation for novelists is that through fiction they memorialize loss, thus achieving for their characters and themselves a measure of immortality.

Narcissism also plays a role in the act of reading. As Marshall Alcorn and Mark Bracher observe in a provocative 1985 *PMLA* article, literature provides the opportunity for the "re-formation" of the reader's self. The reader forms a "narcissistic alliance" with a fictional character who, like the psychoanalyst, "becomes interposed between the reader and the perceived threat to the reader's self."[111] The act of reading involves both stasis and change in the reader, repetition and variation in the reader's identity. Like psychoanalysis, though to a lesser extent, literature can alter the reader's self by changing his or her perceptions of the world, pursuit of ideals, recognition of human limits, and empathic responses. Reading is a narcissistic activity, Alcorn and Bracher suggest, but not necessarily a solipsistic activity; the act of reading enables the self to pursue grandiose aspirations while, at the same time, discovering human limits.

In one important sense, however, the act of reading may not be narcissistic. Our hunger for reading confirms the powerful need for object relatedness, and if we remain attuned and attentive to the text, respecting its unique otherness, then we overcome the tendency toward narcissistic reading. The dynamics of reading require, no less than the dynamics of all interpersonal activities, a negotiation between the need for merging, on the one hand, and the impulse toward separation, on the other.

In his two remarkable books, *With Respect to Readers* and *The*

Look of Distance, Walter Slatoff has analyzed the tensions between separateness and oneness, distance and closeness, loneliness and connectedness.[112] Slatoff does not relate these issues to narcissism, but it is easy to see how the growth of empathy and the preservation of a delicate balance between self and other are antidotes to narcissism. The text is the (m)other we yearn for yet finally must separate ourselves from if we are to maintain our own identity as well as the text's. To confuse or collapse these separate identities, the reader's and the text's, is to risk the fate of Narcissus.

Since we are human, we cannot achieve a perfect balance between sympathy and criticism or a perfect understanding of the text. Insofar as narcissistic defenses in a text tend to provoke the reader's narcissistic defenses, it is particularly difficult to maintain an empathic stance toward a novel like *The Picture of Dorian Gray.* Even the almost limitless empathy of a Kohut would be challenged by the novel's cynical observations about human nature. The novel's aesthetic brilliance is at odds with its moral hollowness, and we cannot appreciate the former without being distressed by the latter. Nor does Dorian's death at the end convincingly repudiate Wilde's infatuation with the aesthetics of narcissism, especially since the novelist makes no effort to distance himself from or repudiate Dorian's hedonistic mentor and tempter, Lord Henry Wotton. The best we can do is to try to remain as empathic as possible, recognizing that we are bound to be offended or threatened when an author's value judgments are so different from our own. Only the nonexistent ideal reader can maintain perfect empathy—the human reader cannot.[113]

We cannot be perfect readers, but we can become, to modify D. W. Winnicott's concept, good enough readers. The good enough mother, Winnicott writes, "is one who makes active adaptation to the infant's needs, an active adaptation that gradually lessens, according to the infant's growing ability to account for failure of adaptation and to tolerate the results of frustration."[114] The good enough mother is not perfect but sufficiently reliable, predictable, empathic, and available to aid the child's development. Like mothers and analysts, readers can be good or not good enough. We are good enough readers if we are attentive to the text; appreciative of its literary, psychological, philosophical, biographical, and historical complexity; and tolerant of its ability to frustrate our desire to understand and control it. And we are good enough readers if we remember that no theory of literature or aesthetics can substitute for human experience, in the same way that no guide can teach someone to become a good parent. Apologizing, then, in advance for my inevitable empathic lapses and textual inattentiveness, let me turn to *Frankenstein*, where we see the disastrous consequences of not good enough parenting.

TWO

Frankenstein;
or, The Modern Narcissus

Ask readers to describe the physical appearance of the monster in Mary Shelley's *Frankenstein* and most will immediately conjure up the image of a gigantic eight-foot high creature with yellow skin, shriveled complexion, straight black lips, and dull, watery eyes, a "hideous phantasm of a man"[1] whose bones and limbs are collected from charnel houses and assembled in Victor Frankenstein's "workshop of filthy creation" (55). The same readers will easily recall the monster's crimes: the unprovoked murder of Victor's young brother, William; the killing of Victor's best friend, Henry Clerval; and the strangulation of Victor's wife, Elizabeth, on the night of their honeymoon. It is a tribute to the enduring power of the novel that we remember so vividly the haunting imagery of the Frankenstein Creature and his terrible acts. But can we confidently identify the real monster in the story and the nature of his misdeeds? Robert Walton, the young explorer who hears Victor's and the Creature's narrations, has no difficulty in locating the embodiment of evil. For Victor and Walton, the monster is born in the scientist's laboratory. Many readers, especially those who confuse Frankenstein with the Creature, would doubtlessly agree with this interpretation. And yet as we shall see, the real monster in *Frankenstein* is the scientist whose monstrous empathic failure comes back to haunt him.

Published in 1818 to immediate popular and literary acclaim, *Frankenstein* has been slow to receive the close psychoanalytic scrutiny it richly deserves. The neglect is more surprising in light of the numerous reprintings of the novel, its translation into many languages, and the legendary status of the Frankenstein movies.[2] Freud was unaware of the novel's existence, and the early psychoanalytic literary critics ignored it in favor of other stories. Otto Rank did not mention *Frankenstein* at all in *The Double,* despite the fact that Shelley's novel powerfully illustrates his thesis.[3] Nor did the extraordinary popularity of the Boris Karloff film adaptation in 1931, only one of more than a hundred cinematic versions, stimulate much psychological interest in the work. It was not until the mid-1970s that a spate of books and essays employing depth criticism appeared on *Frankenstein.* In *The Unspoken Motive* (1973), Morton Kaplan and Robert Kloss were among the first critics to explore Shelley's intriguing use of the *Doppelgänger* technique;[4] subsequently, nearly every critic has alluded, if only in passing, to the way in which the Creature embodies Victor Frankenstein's monstrous sexual and aggressive passions. Kaplan and Kloss offer an Oedipal interpretation of the novel, viewing Victor's obsession with the origin of babies as an ambivalent wish to present his mother with another child. Immediately after Victor succeeds in animating the Creature, the scientist dreams he is embracing Elizabeth; seconds later the dream changes, and Victor imagines he is holding the corpse of his dead mother in his arms.[5]

Ellen Moers' brilliant essay "Female Gothic," first published in the *New York Review of Books* in 1974, represents a milestone in Mary Shelley scholarship. Moers interprets the novel as a "phantasmagoria of the nursery," an elaborate fantasy of birth trauma evoking a woman's deepest fears of conception and childbirth.[6] One of the earliest critics to probe a text's gender identity, Moers reads *Frankenstein* as "distinctly a *woman's* mythmaking on the subject of birth precisely because its emphasis is not upon what precedes birth, not upon birth itself, but upon what follows birth: the trauma of the afterbirth" (81). Moers does not mention Otto Rank, but it is clear that she offers a female revision of *The Trauma of Birth.* Moers also brings in compelling biographical information on Mary Shelley's personal tragedies. Her mother, Mary Wollstonecraft, died as a consequence of giving birth to her, and Mary Shelley almost died herself in childbirth. With one exception, all of her children died either in infancy or in early childhood. "Death and birth," Moers writes, "were thus as hideously intermixed in the life of Mary Shelley as in Frankenstein's 'workshop of filthy creation' " (84).

Other articles and books followed, with critics exploring in abundant detail the psychological complexity of *Frankenstein*. J. M. Hill argues in *"Frankenstein* and the Physiognomy of Desire" (1975) that Victor's "dominant incestuous root for Promethean sin seems to take hold in uncompromising psychic wishes for exclusive love, and in possession of the mother—the source of first love."[7] In articles appearing in the 1975 issue of *Hartford Studies in Literature*, Gerhard Joseph suggests that Victor's terror of incest is the veiled cause of his disintegration,[8] while Gordon D. Hirsch concludes that the "monster is psychologically a lady, or perhaps one should say, a little girl."[9] Mark A. Rubenstein (1976) discusses the primal scene imagery in *Frankenstein*, ingeniously showing how it "penetrates into the very structure of the novel and becomes part of a more deeply hidden search for the mother."[10] Martin Trop's *Mary Shelley's Monster* (1976) and David Ketterer's *Frankenstein's Creation: The Book, the Monster, and Human Reality* (1979) offer additional psychological interpretations.[11] *The Endurance of Frankenstein* (1979) contains several excellent essays, including U. C. Knoepflmacher's "Thoughts on the Aggression of Daughters," which demonstrates that *Frankenstein* is a novel of emotionally distant fathers and absent mothers.[12] A psychiatrist argues in a 1982 essay that Mary Shelley conceived of herself as an "exception to the rules," an individual who sensed that she had suffered unjustly because of her mother's death.[13] More recently, Mary Poovey fuses feminist and psychoanalytic criticism in *The Proper Lady and the Woman Writer* (1984),[14] while William Veeder suggests in *Mary Shelley & Frankenstein* (1986) that the novel reflects the author's lifelong concern with the psychological ideal of androgyny and its opposite, bifurcation.[15] The brief history of psychoanalytic criticism on *Frankenstein* thus reveals a movement from Oedipal to pre-Oedipal approaches.

Surprisingly, the narcissistic implications of the story have not yet been directly confronted.[16] Mary Shelley subtitled *Frankenstein* the "Modern Prometheus," but she could have also referred to it as the "Modern Narcissus." Victor exhibits, in fact, all the characteristics of the narcissistic personality disorder as defined in *DSM-III:* a grandiose sense of self-importance; preoccupation with fantasies of unlimited success; exhibitionism; cool indifference or feelings of rage in response to criticism; and interpersonal disturbances, including exploitativeness, alternation between overidealization and devaluation, and lack of empathy. Moreover, Victor demonstrates the paradoxical nature of narcissism, where self-love exists with self-hate, and fragile self-esteem results in a sense of entitlement, the expectation of receiving special favors from others without assuming reciprocal responsibilities. In addition, Victor pursues fantasies of unlimited power and glory with a pleasureless, monomaniacal intensity. He experiences the profound depression often accompanying a narcissistic disorder: dejection, loss of interest in the external world, inability to love, and a lowering of self-esteem, culminating in an expectation of punishment. It is as if he has internalized a poisonous object, the Creature, who is now consuming his heart.

The supreme horror story of nineteenth-century English fiction, *Frankenstein* is, like Ovid's myth of Echo and Narcissus, a tragic love story leading to madness and despair. The parallels between the ancient myth and the Gothic novel are striking. No novel illustrates more graphically the destructive consequences of withheld love. "Treat a person ill and he will become wicked," Percy Bysshe Shelley observes in his Introduction to *Frankenstein*. "Requite affection with scorn; let one being be selected for whatever cause as the refuse of his kind—divide him, a social being, from society, and you impose upon him the irresistible obligations—malevolence and selfishness." [17] Like Narcissus, Victor coldly spurns an individual who asks for love; like Echo, the Creature remains hopelessly devoted to a man who callously rejects him. Both Echo and the Creature make futile efforts to validate themselves through another's approval. Distance becomes problematic: the Creature can neither live with Victor nor live without him. Ovid's myth and Shelley's novel both reveal a pathological union of two individuals who sadomasochistically torment each other. Unrequited love culminates in shattered self-esteem, crippling dependency, and uncontrollable rage.

Frankenstein warns, furthermore, of the dangers of surface perception and solipsism. Both Narcissus and Victor are blinded by superficial impressions that are reflections of their own inner conflicts. Haunting and hunting each other, Victor and the Creature reveal not only an absence of self-object boundaries, but an identity that has never come into independent existence. Functioning as a selfobject, the Creature embodies Victor's narcissistic rage. Victor narcissistically invests himself in his offspring, the helpless Creature; but contrary to Freud's belief that parents idealize their children, Victor imposes a monstrous identity on the "demoniacal corpse." With fitting poetic justice, Victor finds himself punished by his shadowy double.

Victor Frankenstein is the first of several narcissistic characters who will occupy our attention, characters who rationalize their empathic failures and seek to escape the consequences of their actions. To understand Victor's narcissism, we must confront the most vexing issue in *Frankenstein:* his failure to understand and empathize with an innately benevolent individual. Victor's failure points to a major irony in *Frankenstein:* it is easier to discover the secret of bestowing animation upon lifeless matter than to unlock the mystery of human development. Before exploring Victor's wish to destroy life, however, I must consider the complex motives behind his wish to create life.

"The world was to me a secret which I desired to divine. Curiosity, earnest research to learn the hidden laws of nature, gladness akin to rapture, as they were unfolded to me, are among the earliest sensations I can remember" (36). The highly charged erotic language suggests more than a simple infatuation with science. Victor is "deeply smitten with the thirst for knowledge," and he describes himself as "always having been embued with a fervent longing to penetrate the secrets of nature" (39). The language suggests a link between sexual and intellectual discovery. Viewed from the Freudian theory of sublimation, Victor's interest in the science of anatomy reflects his fascination with the structure of the human body, a wish to participate in the mysteries of sexuality and usurp the mother's role in the act of procreation. "In *Frankenstein*," George Levine observes, "we are confronted immediately by the displacement of God and woman from the acts of conception and birth." [18]

Victor's decision to create new life also seems related to his efforts to master fears of death. Is it merely accidental that his philosophical interest in regeneration immediately follows his mother's death? Despite his acceptance of maternal loss and rejection of the mourning process, Victor attempts to reverse the forces of time by resurrecting the dead. He thus enacts a rescue fantasy, not unlike the service Robert Walton performs for him. "You rescued me from a strange and perilous situation; you have benevolently restored me to life" (26). Both Ellen Moers and U. C. Knoepflmacher speak eloquently about the fantasy of restitution in *Frankenstein* that would reconcile the apparently antagonistic aims of resurrecting a lost mother and regaining a father's undivided love.

These two important motives for scientific research, birth fantasy and restitution fantasy, help us to understand Victor's need to create new life, but they do not explain the narcissistic implications of his scientific work. Why, for example, does he create a larger-than-life figure who will invariably attract attention and inspire awe? Victor claims that "as the minuteness of the parts formed a great hindrance to my speed, I resolved, contrary to my first intention, to make the being of a gigantic stature; that is to say, about eight feet in height, and proportionably large" (53–54). It is difficult to take this explanation seriously, however, and he remains fixated on the magnitude of his creation. Similarly, he demands egotistically that his offspring glorify him as the creator and pay him tribute. "A new species would bless me as its creator and source; many happy and excellent natures would owe their being to me. No father could claim the gratitude of his child so completely as I should deserve theirs" (54). Victor wishes to give birth to gigantic and numerous offspring whom he can omnipotently control. Although he claims, earlier, that his quest for the elixir of life is prompted by the noble wish to "banish disease from the human frame, and render man invulnerable to any but a violent death" (40), narcissism, not humanitarianism, dictates the gigantic shape of his progeny.

For if Victor truly were motivated by humanitarianism or Prometheanism, as he claims, his rejection of the Creature would be inconceivable. We could not then reconcile Victor's view of himself as an intellectually curious scientist, free from superstition and fear, with the picture of a terrified and morally revolted individual who flees during the moment of his greatest success. Victor asserts that "during every hour of my infant life I received a lesson of patience, of charity, and of self-control" (34). Why, then, does he lose patience, charity, and self-control when he accomplishes what he has set out to do? He states that as a youth he never trembled at a tale of superstition, feared the apparition of a spirit, or avoided the dark. Yet why does he repeatedly address the Creature as "daemon," assume that he is inherently malevolent, and consign him to eternal darkness? And why does Victor deliberately choose the Creature's ill-formed anatomical parts only to reject his handiwork on the grounds of physical deformity?

Victor offers several explanations for the rejection of the Creature, but they turn out to be rationalizations. He cites the changeable feelings of human nature to explain why, after nearly two years of labor to infuse new life into dead matter, the beauty of the dream suddenly vanishes. Victor would rather justify his own fickleness as an aspect of human nature than as a uniquely individual failure. His description of the awakening Creature evokes the image of a sadistic beast ready to devour its prey: "His jaws opened, and he muttered some inarticulate sounds, while a grin wrinkled his cheeks. He might have spoken, but I did not hear; one hand was stretched out, seemingly to detain me, but I escaped, and rushed down stairs" (58). The Creature's narrative portrays the opposite image, that of a helpless and dependent baby, desperately seeking human contact. Victor agrees at first to the Creature's request for a female companion, but then, months later, inexplicably destroys the nearly completed figure, citing the fear that the two monsters might propagate a race of devils upon the earth. Surely a simple change of design in the female creature's anatomical parts would lay to rest Victor's reproductive nightmare.

If, as we sense, grandiosity is the secret motive behind Victor's creativity, then his horrified retreat from the Creature may lie in the psychic mechanism of projective identification, the projection of virulent aggression onto another figure, who is then perceived as a deadly persecutory double. Victor's paralyzed overidentification with the Creature and subsequent revulsion and dread suggest not only projective identification, but the other primitive defense mechanisms characteristic of pathological narcissism: splitting, denial, defensive idealization, omnipotence, and devaluation. As such, Victor's personality bears an uncanny resemblance to the case study material found in Otto Kernberg's psychiatric text, *Borderline Conditions and Pathological Narcissism*. Consider this description, for example:

I describe patients with narcissistic personalities as presenting excessive self-absorption usually coinciding with a superficially smooth and effective social adaptation, but with serious distortions in their internal relationships with other people. They present various combinations of intense ambitiousness, grandiose fantasies, feelings of inferiority, and overdependence on external admiration and acclaim. Along with feelings of boredom and emptiness, and continuous search for gratification of strivings for brilliance, wealth, power and beauty, there are serious deficiencies in their capacity to love and to be concerned about others.[19]

There are, admittedly, several potential dangers in applying a psychiatric diagnosis to a literary character. To begin with, we must be careful not to reduce art to illness or subordinate literature to psychiatry. There are key differences between a fictional and real character. A fictional character, Lillian Feder reminds us in *Madness in Literature,* is "rooted in a mythical or literary tradition in which distortion is a generally accepted mode of expression; furthermore, the inherent aesthetic order by which his existence is limited also gives his madness intrinsic value and meaning."[20] Clinicians acknowledge that descriptive diagnosis is innately ambiguous, with no clear line existing, as Freud admitted, between normal and neurotic behavior. In addition, it is often more difficult to locate pathology in a fictional character than in a real person. The fictional character does not consent, after all, to lie on the therapist's couch and offer the free associations that are indispensable to analysis. Moreover, we will never know more about a fictional character than the text gives us.

Nevertheless, psychoanalytic theory can illuminate a literary character's conflicts and interpersonal relationships. In particular, a comparison of Victor Frankenstein to a narcissistic personality yields new and valuable insights into his disturbed inner world. From an object relations point of view, Victor's inner world—the internalized objects that shape his pattern of interpersonal relationships—is highly unstable. Good object relations involve "the capacity both to love well, and to hate well, and particularly to tolerate varying combinations of loving and hateful feelings" (Kernberg, 308). Victor's reliance upon splitting, the division of the world into "all good" and "all bad" objects, betrays the inability to acknowledge ambivalence, or to integrate the good and bad self into a single totality. Two of the most common defenses of narcissism, omnipotence and devaluation, reflect Victor's overinvolvement and subsequent underinvolvement with the creation of new life. These two defenses, Kernberg writes, represent the patient's "identification with an 'all good' object, idealized and powerful as a protection against bad 'persecutory' objects" (33). De-valuation of external objects inevitably accompanies omnipotence. "If an external object can provide no further gratification or protection, it is dropped and dismissed because there was no real capacity for love of this object in the first place" (33). Victor experiences the Creature either as a remote, distant object or as a persecutory self. He never sees his offspring as a related other who remains, paradoxically, both inside and outside the self.

Victor also demonstrates the all-or-nothing behavior common to narcissism. He repudiates violently the ideas and ideals that no longer interest him. His brief infatuation with science is a good example. His delight in a volume of Cornelius Agrippa prompts his father to look carelessly at the book's title page and exclaim: "Ah! Cornelius Agrippa! My dear Victor, do not waste your time upon this; it is sad trash" (39). Victor rebels against his father's harsh judgment but internalizes his dismissive attitude. The same dismissiveness is echoed later in Victor's professor of natural philosophy, M. Krempe, who derides the ancient masters: " 'Have you,' he said, 'really spent your time in studying such nonsense?' " (45). Not only does Victor dethrone the "lords of his imagination"—Agrippa, Albertus Magnus, Paracelsus—but he later regards their work as contemptible. "By one of those caprices of the mind, which we are perhaps most subject to in early youth, I at once gave up my former occupations; set down natural history and all its progeny as a deformed and abortive creation; and entertained the greatest disdain for a would-be science, which could never even step within the threshold of real knowledge" (41). Victor similarly sees the Creature as "sad trash," a "deformed and abortive creation."

Victor's reliance upon defensive idealization represents one of the most conspicuous narcissistic features of his narration. He repeatedly makes statements affirming the happiness and tranquility of his earlier life, as when he says: "No human being could have passed a happier childhood than myself!" (37). Indeed, a major problem in reconciling Victor's idyllic childhood and tragic adulthood is the radical disconti-nuity between past and present. How could a loving son enjoy an unconflicted relationship with his parents and then become a mon-strous father? "What went wrong?" Christopher Small asks in *Ariel Like a Harpy* (1972) and then proceeds to accept at face value Victor's assertions of an untroubled past. "Frankenstein has suffered no deprivation, on the contrary he has been doted on, and his upbringing by parents equally loving and judicious, in an atmosphere uniformly high-minded, approaches the Rousseau-Godwin ideal. He certainly cannot say that he is wicked because he has been ill-treated: nor does he."[21] Small is deceived, however, by Victor's repeated denials. Quite simply, Victor protests too much. His celebration of childhood suggests not merely the repression of normal anxieties and conflicts but a massive falsification of reality.

Otto Kernberg has written extensively on defensive idealization and describes how, in the early stages of analysis, the narcissistic patient develops fantasies that his analyst is perfect, God-like, devoted exclusively to fulfilling the patient's every need. The patient's idealization of the analyst soon shifts to intense devaluation, symptomatic of the grandiose self's rejection of imperfection. The devaluation is neither healthy nor realistic, since it does not allow the patient to see the analyst as a fellow human being, with both strengths and weaknesses. The devaluation represents a symbolic destruction of both the analyst and the potentially therapeutic possibilities of analysis. Devaluation confirms the patient's deepest fear that others cannot be trusted or loved. Defensive idealization, Kernberg argues, "reveals defensive functions against the emergence of direct oral rage and envy, against paranoid fears related to projection of sadistic trends on the analyst (representing a primitive, hated, and sadistically perceived mother image), and against basic feelings of terrifying loneliness, hunger for love, and guilt over the aggression directed against the frustrating parental images" (280–281).

Victor sentimentalizes his childhood in order to deny past disappointments. The story he conceals is more significant than the one he reveals. His rejection of his intellectual mentors—the "lords of my imagination"—precedes his repudiation of the Creature and repeats, transferentially, the dislocation of his privileged position in the family. The first-born child, Victor claims that he was his parents' "plaything and their idol, and something better—their child, the innocent and helpless creature bestowed on them by Heaven" (33). The Creature also appears, at first, innocent and helpless—and the "first-born child" of his creator. Both characters mythologize an idyllic past, deriving what Victor calls "exquisite pleasure in dwelling on the recollections of childhood, before misfortune had tainted my mind" (38). Victor would have us believe that he experiences no sibling rivalry when his mother unexpectedly brings home Elizabeth Lavenza, an Italian foundling. A similar situation arises in *Wuthering Heights* when Mr. Earnshaw returns from London with a curious, dark-skinned waif. Hindley and Catherine immediately welcome Heathcliff with hisses and imprecations—Catherine even spits at him. Victor, by contrast, promises dutifully to accept Elizabeth and to "protect, love, and cherish" her (36). She quickly becomes the center of attention in the family, displacing Victor.

When Victor is seventeen, Elizabeth falls ill with scarlet fever, and Mme. Frankenstein nurses her back to health, sacrificing her own life in the process. During Elizabeth's illness, "many arguments had been urged to persuade my mother to refrain from attending upon her. She had, at first, yielded to our entreaties; but when she heard that the life of her favourite was menaced, she could no longer control her anxiety" (42). Nor can Victor control his own anxiety—his sarcastic anger over the recognition that his mother favored Elizabeth above everyone else. Victor does not tell us about the specific arguments his family used to dissuade Mme. Frankenstein from attending to Elizabeth, but presumably they involved the mother's obligations to the rest of the family. We may assume from what Victor says that he was prepared to accept the necessity of Elizabeth's death to save the mother's life. Mme. Frankenstein's "watchful attentions triumphed over the malignity of the distemper," Victor tells us. "Elizabeth was saved, but the consequences of this imprudence were fatal to her preserver" (42). We can thus detect Victor's anger over his mother's "imprudence," which forever destroyed the family's intactness. His anger spills over to Elizabeth, the adopted child who is indirectly responsible for his mother's death. Victor cannot express this anger directly, however, especially since Mme. Frankenstein's last wish was for him and Elizabeth to marry one day. Such a last wish reveals an overcontrolling mother, narcissistically invested in her children's lives.

The birth of William, the youngest brother, further displaces Victor's position in the family. There is no description of overt sibling rivalry, but M. Frankenstein's letter, announcing the news of William's murder, is filled with thinly veiled criticism of his distant son. "And how, Victor, can I relate our misfortune? Absence cannot have rendered you callous to our joys and griefs; and how shall I inflict pain on my long absent son?" (71). M. Frankenstein scolds Victor for his untimely absence, hints ominously that his son has become insensitive, and confers sainthood on the murdered William. "William is dead!—that sweet child, whose smiles delighted and warmed my heart, who was so gentle, yet so gay!" (71). The father thus plays off William, the good son, against Victor, the bad son. "How shall I inflict pain on my long absent son?" conceals a disguised threat that is probably not lost on the former "idol" of his parents. The father even signs the letter with his full name, heightening the cold formality of the communication. Family and friends eulogize the martyred William with imagery befitting an angel. "Poor William!" laments Ernest, the middle brother, "he was our darling and our pride" (78); "Poor William!" exclaims Henry Clerval, "dear lovely child, he now sleeps with his angel mother" (73); "William, dear angel!" intones Victor, "this is thy funeral, this thy dirge!" (76).

When we actually see William, however, he hardly justifies the lavish praise bestowed upon him. The child seems thoroughly spoiled and obnoxious, almost deserving his fate. The epithets he hurls at the Creature—"monster," "ugly wretch," "ogre," "hideous monster"— are forms of discrimination, like racial prejudice, that a child generally learns from his or her family. Significantly, these are the same hateful words that Victor uses to describe the Creature. Thus, for the second time, we see a family that repudiates otherness, that either overloves (as in the case of the mother's willingness to die for Elizabeth) or underloves (strangers).

Consequently, William's sadistic treatment of the Creature calls into question the family's sentimentalized descriptions of the slain boy, underscoring the problem of narrative reliability. Apart from the Creature, who alone knows the truth of William's capacity for monstrous judgments, the other characters in *Frankenstein* collude in a defensive idealization of him. Had William been as innocent as the others claim, he would have either remained paralyzed with fright at the fearful-looking stranger or attempted to run home. Of course, if William were truly gentle, he would have befriended the helpless Creature. Instead, William makes a fatal error, invoking in the Creature's presence the power of a stern, wrathful father. "Hideous monster! let me go. My papa is a Syndic—he is M. Frankenstein—he will punish you" (142). Discovering William's relationship to the hated creator, the Creature executes his first act of revenge.

William's death, consequently, unmasks Victor's murderous feelings, his revenge on a family that metes out swift punishment to "hideous monsters," be they deformed creatures or long-absent sons. William is not the real object of the Creature's (hence, Victor's) rage, but only a symbol of deeper disappointments. These disappointments lead inevitably to Victor's troubled childhood, particularly to a mother whose premature death is perceived as an act of abandonment and to a father whose emotional coldness is reproduced, with a vengeance, in his unempathic son. These disappointments, moreover, lead to Mary Shelley's own troubled childhood, particularly her anger toward the two "Williams" in her life, her father and her half-brother.[22]

Indeed, Victor seems to have inherited from his father an inability to express deep feeling or acknowledge loss. Victor's stony heart later prevents him from empathizing with the Creature's feelings. Victor's reaction to his mother's unexpected death illustrates his failure to mourn. Telling us that his mother "died calmly" (which may represent wishful thinking), Victor resolves stoically not to succumb to excessive emotion.[23] "The time at length arrives, when grief is rather an indulgence than a necessity; and the smile that plays upon the lips, although it may be deemed a sacrilege, is not banished" (43). Victor's sacrilegious smile, we suspect, reveals his secret hatred of his mother for dying—and for playing favorites. Victor is simply too angry to mourn his mother's death, just as he is later too angry to mourn the Creature's deformed birth. In denying himself the opportunity to mourn, Victor cannot work through the normal emotions associated with maternal loss: confusion, anger, and despair. To this extent, Victor's "rationalism" echoes his father's mistrust of emotion. We do not learn about M. Frankenstein's reaction to his wife's death, but we hear him reproach Victor for feeling depressed over William's death. " 'Do you think, Victor,' said he, 'that I do not suffer also? No one could love a child more than I loved your brother'; (tears came into his eyes as he spoke;) but is it not a duty to the survivors, that we should refrain from augmenting their unhappiness by an appearance of immoderate grief?' " (90–91). M. Frankenstein's language is revealing: he removes himself and Victor from the class of survivors, implying that neither man should grieve over William's death. Although his tears make him seem more human, M. Frankenstein is better at reproaching than consoling Victor. Both father and son avoid talking about the dead subject. Significantly, Victor rejects immoderate grief but not immoderate rage.

Unable to work through his grief and guilt, Victor falls ill to a mysterious "nervous fever" and is confined for several months. The illness, which immediately follows the Creature's birth, is a kind of postpartum—and postartem—depression. "The form of the monster on whom I had bestowed existence was for ever before my eyes, and I raved incessantly concerning him" (62). Like other forms of psychological illness, Victor's nervous breakdown has secondary advantages, allowing him to avoid confronting the consequences of a disabling subject—a Creature who is, like himself, helpless, dependent, and demanding. The illness represents Victor's conscious repudiation of the Creature, on the one hand, and unconscious identification with him, on the other. The breakdown enables Victor to regress and become a child again, wholly dependent on the ministrations of his devoted friend, Henry Clerval. "But I was in reality very ill; and surely nothing but the unbounded and unremitting attentions of my friend could have restored me to life" (62). Clerval functions as both nurse and mother, supplying Victor with the love and empathy Victor himself cannot offer to the Creature. Clerval becomes a fantasy mother, nonjudgmental and infinitely empathic, and his devoted care temporarily restores Victor to life.

Unlike Victor, the Creature has no devoted friend to care for him. Nor does he have a loving family, however distant, to maintain the illusion of support. (The De Laceys function as a family, but they quickly turn against him in horror.) The Creature's narcissistic injuries are apparent in his shattered self-esteem, massive rage, and blurred self-object boundaries. Victor's relationship to the Creature dramatizes the theme of defective parenting, as critics have realized. "The story of the monster's beginnings is the story of a child," M. K. Joseph observes.[24] Moreover, throughout Mary Shelley's fiction there are, Elizabeth Nitchie points out, "many orphans and half-orphans among her heroes and heroines."[25] The Creature's story reveals the futile search for loving parent surrogates to replace the "real" parents who have failed him. The Creature experiences the worst narcissistic injury imaginable: the recognition that his sole parent tried to abort him and, failing that, cruelly abandoned him. Victor's rejection defines the Creature's identity, and as the Creature reads Victor's journal, he is appalled by his "accursed origin." " 'Hateful day when I received life!' I exclaimed in agony. 'Accursed creator! Why did you form a monster so hideous that even *you* turned from me in disgust?' " (130).

Mary Shelley's depiction of aggression in *Frankenstein* is a textbook example of narcissistic rage, and Kohut's description applies to both Victor and the Creature:

Narcissistic rage occurs in many forms; they all share, however, a specific psychological flavor which gives them a distinct position within the wide realm of human aggressions. The need for revenge, for righting a wrong, for undoing a hurt by whatever means, and a deeply anchored, unrelenting compulsion in the pursuit of all these aims which gives no rest to those who have suffered a narcissistic injury—these are features which are characteristic for the phenomenon of narcissistic rage in all its forms and which set it apart from other kinds of aggression.[26]

Underlying narcissistic rage, both Kohut and Kernberg agree, is the struggle to maintain the perfection of the grandiose self, which has come into existence as a defense against rejection. The grandiose self demands absolute control and perfection, devaluing those individuals unable to fulfill its demands. Unlike healthy or reactive aggression, which can be successfully discharged, narcissistic rage feeds off itself, with revenge becoming an end in itself. "Narcissistic rage enslaves the ego," Kohut writes, "and allows it to function only as its tool and rationalizer" (387). The Creature's twin sides—the gentle, benevolent figure and the violent, malevolent monster—embody the radical split between the good and bad self.

The actual moment of the Creature's self-alienation occurs when he gazes down at a transparent pool of water and, like Narcissus, is paralyzed by his reflection. "At first I started back, unable to believe that it was indeed I who was reflected in the mirror; and when I became fully convinced that I was in reality the monster that I am, I was filled with the bitterest sensations of despondence and mortification" (114). Mirrors are dangerous to narcissists, reminding them of their tenuous identity and imperfection. In a twist on Lacanian theory, the Creature experiences no jubilation during the *stade du miroir* scene, no merging with an idealized image. The mirror affects Narcissus and the Creature differently, awakening the former's self-love and the latter's self-hate. Unlike Narcissus' death, which is poetic justice for a life of self-preoccupation, the Creature's fate is undeserved. Innately benevolent, the Creature is born with a finely developed sensibility. He is struck by the gentle manners of the De Laceys, moved by their poverty. He is also attentive to their moods. "When they were unhappy, I felt depressed; when they rejoiced, I sympathised in their joys" (112).

Although the Creature's exquisite empathy is improbable, psychologically speaking, the novel's optimistic developmental theory reflects Mary Shelley's acceptance of the prevailing Romantic belief in innate human goodness propounded by Rousseau and Godwin. Erik Erikson's "basic trust," with which the Creature is generously endowed, develops not in a vacuum but as a result of loving, empathic parents, attentive to the child's needs. Denied from "birth" the maternal mirroring necessary for healthy development, the Creature exhibits an empathic responsiveness that remains one of the mysteries of his character.

The story of the De Laceys reenacts the Creature's personal childhood myth of *Paradise Lost*. His idealized portrait of the De Laceys is pure fantasy, like Victor's distorted memory of his own family life. The two recreations are, in effect, the same story, products of a narcissistically injured child's defensive idealization. In both stories there is an absent mother, a father unable to keep the family together, and a son who falls in love with an orphaned female. (Felix's relationship to Safie repeats Victor's relationship to Elizabeth.) Parent-child hostility and sibling rivalry may be glimpsed, but only beneath the narrative's surface calm.

Throughout *Frankenstein* hovers the idealized father, whose function is to preserve the illusion of a perfect, omnipotent creator. De Lacey remains a phantom father, a mirage existing beyond the Creature's anguished reach. Unable to win the good father's love, Victor and the Creature keep alive the bad father by "nurturing" narcissistic rage. Revenge fills the void created by parental absence. Victor realizes that revenge is the "devouring and only passion of my soul" (200); "revenge alone endowed me with strength and composure" (201). Although narcissistic rage seems preferable to emotional deficit, it ultimately becomes self-depleting.

Victor and the Creature are essentially indistinguishable in their psychology, but we respond to them differently. Victor is the more narcissistic of the two, and the more solipsistic. He is self-justifying, always seeking to thwart our identification with the Creature. The Creature, by contrast, readily confesses to his repugnant crimes. By refusing to minimize these acts, he accepts full responsibility for them. We condemn the Creature's acts but not the Creature himself. Unlike Victor, who would obliterate the Creature's point of view, the Creature does not seek to destroy his other self. Victor urges us to dispose heartlessly of all monsters, to abort the ill formed; the Creature compels us, by contrast, to empathize with those who, through no fault of their own, are bereft of protectors and friends. The possibility exists, of course, that the Creature is playing upon our sympathy, seducing us by his eloquence. This is what Victor warns Robert Walton at the end. "He is eloquent and persuasive; and once his words had even power over my heart; but trust him not. His soul is as hellish as his form, full of treachery and fiendlike malice" (209). Nevertheless, we can empathize with the Creature without condoning his crimes, and he expands our understanding of all creatures great and small.

Victor's failure as a narrator parallels his failure as a scientist. In both activities, he authors defective texts. He precedes his narration by admonishing Robert Walton to "deduce an apt moral from my tale" (30). Victor frequently interrupts his narration, however, to prevent Walton from deducing anything other than a prescribed meaning. "Learn from me, if not by my precepts, at least by my example, how dangerous is the acquirement of knowledge, and how much happier that man is who believes his native town to be the world, than he who aspires to become greater than his nature will allow" (53). The phrasing of the sentence is revealing. Even as Victor attempts to repudiate his ambitions, he idealizes those who, like himself, aspire to become greater than their nature will allow, and devalues those who narrow-mindedly believe their native town to be the world. When he does acknowledge guilt, he refuses to locate the true meaning of his crime. Thus, Victor sees himself as a failed Promethean rather than as a pathological narcissist. By interpreting his defeat in terms of the acquisition of forbidden knowledge, instead of empathic failure, Victor heroicizes his story. His last words to Walton indicate the belief that his ambition has been noble and blameless. "Farewell, Walton! Seek happiness in tranquility and avoid ambition, even if it be only the apparently innocent one of distinguishing yourself in science and discoveries" (217–18). Like T. S. Eliot's Gerontion, Victor has the experience but misses the meaning.

Indeed, Victor's narcissism is more pronounced at the end of the story, when he is presumably penitent, than in the beginning. Viewing Robert Walton as a younger version of himself, the dying Victor exhorts the captain and his crew to undertake a "glorious expedition" to slay the hated Creature (214). Like his mother, but only to a greater extent, Victor attempts to influence the living even after death. He is as careless with Walton's life as he has been with the Creature's. In a speech charged with emotion, Victor exclaims: "You were hereafter to be hailed as the benefactors of your species; your names adored, as belonging to brave men who encountered death for honour, and the benefit of mankind" (214). Ironically, Victor calls Walton and his crew the "benefactors of your species." Earlier Victor has invoked the same argument to justify his experimentation with lifeless matter. "A new species would bless me as its creator and source; many happy and excellent natures would owe their being to me" (54). The Creature was made to show Victor's parents how an offspring ought to be conceived and framed, how, ideally, offspring should be treated; but Victor's motivation is inherently grandiose, causing him to abandon the Creature at birth. Victor's allegiance has been, from the beginning, not to the creation but the destruction of life. Notwithstanding his admonition to Walton to avoid ambition, Victor megalomaniacally believes that he alone can save humankind from monstrous evil.

Victor finds the right audience in Robert Walton, his younger counterpart. Like Victor, Walton has a strained relationship with his father: "my father's dying injunction had forbidden my uncle to allow me to embark in a seafaring life" (17). He is also prone to depression, which, as in Victor's case, spurs him to Promethean activities. (Their Prometheanism seems to be the manic phrase of depression.) Like Victor, Walton hungers for a friend who will fill the terrible void in his life. Walton's objectivity is impaired by his idealization of Victor, whom he sees as "noble," "gentle," and "wise" (27). Walton's relationship to Victor anticipates Marlow's pursuit of Kurtz in *Heart of Darkness,* both captains irresistibly drawn to brilliant alter egos whom they see as dying stars.

Unlike Marlow, who becomes ambivalent toward the "nightmare of my choice," Walton reaches no comparable insights. Marlow realizes Kurtz's "exalted and incredible degradation," while Walton remains blind to Victor's similarly oxymoronic identity. Walton's purpose in voyaging to the North Pole, we gradually realize, has been to find a man to whom he can devote his life and receive, in turn, the love and validation necessary for his self-esteem. Walton's driving force seems to originate from the same hunger that underlies Victor's scientific ambitions. William Walling has commented on the paradoxical split within Walton that radiates from his ambition: he wants to benefit humanity and, at the same time, achieve an eminence that will separate him from the human community.[27] Fortunately, Walton's egotism is not as dangerous as Victor's, and he reluctantly heeds the crew's demands to return home. Ironically, Walton finds himself in the Creature's situation, bereft of the support of the one person who can validate his life.

Walton and the Creature confront each other in the last scene in *Frankenstein,* each regarding himself as the true offspring of Victor, who now lies dead. The rivalry between them is intense, with Walton the good son, the Creature the bad son. Torn between Victor's dying request to slay the fearful Creature, on the one hand, and the promptings of his own curiosity and compassion, on the other, Walton allows his rival to speak, though not without branding him a "hypocritical fiend!" (220). Walton's language faithfully echoes Victor's undying enmity, which cannot equal the Creature's self-hate. Committing himself wholly to Victor's version of reality, Walton continues the creator's deformation of his work. The Creature's eloquence renders Walton speechless, however, and the last five pages of the novel contain the Creature's almost uninterrupted narration. As *Frankenstein* closes, the Creature refers to the funeral pyre that will consume the ashes of his "miserable frame." Even in his dying moments he cannot rid himself of a deformed self-image. The closing of the novel —the Creature's wrenching farewell and Walton's awed description of the figure being "borne away by the waves, and lost in darkness and distance" (223)—constitutes one of the most moving endings in fiction.

There is only one character in *Frankenstein* who might not be appalled at the Creature's appearance—and who would not, therefore, echo Victor's monstrous rejection of him. A minor character, admittedly, M. Waldman has been ignored by commentators. A benevolent chemistry professor, he stimulates Victor's imagination and stirs his soul. Whereas Victor's other professor, M. Krempe, dismisses the achievements of the old philosophers, Waldman wisely evaluates them in the proper context. "The labours of men of genius, however erroneously directed, scarcely ever fail in ultimately turning to the solid advantage of mankind" (49). Waldman offers a valuable perspective on the nature of creativity. He views intellectual progress as arising, not from one generation of scientists repudiating the findings of the preceding generation, but from the painstaking accumulation of knowledge. He thus offers a theory of creativity based not on the anxiety of influence, but on a careful synthesis of knowledge: he is committed to the ego, not the id or superego. He also urges a broad course of studies, including every branch of natural philosophy. Waldman alone is the truly Promethean figure in *Frankenstein,* a scientist and humanist who remains devoted to ideals.

Equally important, unlike the vain and mean-spirited Krempe, Waldman has transcended egotism. He is an idealized figure, to be sure, but he represents the healthy idealism necessary for all genuine creativity. He affirms not only scientific progress but, more importantly, evolutionary development. He invites Victor to identify with him, to be his "disciple"—but without imposing any demands on the student other than a commitment to the pursuit of truth. Waldman's temperament is conciliatory, good natured, reasonable. It is Victor's misfortune that he never confides in this Kohutian figure. Waldman alone would accept, we sense, what Victor and the others condemn as monstrous deformity. Observe again Waldman's statement: "The labours of men of genius, however erroneously directed, scarcely ever fail in ultimately turning to the solid advantage of mankind." Do we not hear in these words an affirmation of the strivings of humankind, a tolerance for inevitable error and imperfection, a recognition that all labor—scientific, artistic, procreative—is potentially valuable? Waldman is an inspiring scientist and a wise analyst, and his statement uncannily anticipates Kohut's affirmation of humanistic growth, particularly the realization that "Freud's writings are not a kind of Bible but great works belonging to a particular moment in the history of science—great not because of their unchanging relevance but, on the contrary, because they contain the seeds of endless possibilities for further growth." [28] In remaining committed to an ideal larger than the self, Waldman escapes the paralyzing narcissism and solipsism to which Victor succumbs.

So, too, does Mary Shelley avoid Victor Frankenstein's deadly self-preoccupation. It is appropriate to recall here the origins of *Frankenstein* and the novelist's feelings toward her creation. In the 1831 introduction to *Frankenstein,* she vividly recalls how the story first seized hold of her imagination. One night, following lively philosophical conversations with her husband and Byron, she found herself unable to sleep. A series of images suddenly arose in her mind. "I saw —with shut eyes, but acute mental vision,—I saw the pale student of unhallowed arts kneeling beside the thing he had put together" (9). In a paragraph filled with extraordinary imagery, she identifies with Victor's hope that, left to itself, "the slight spark of life which he had communicated would fade; that this thing, which had received such imperfect animation, would subside into dead matter" (9). Like Victor, she is appalled by the "hideous corpse" terrifying both scientist and artist. She seems to assume, along with Victor, that the Creature's physical appearance reflects moral deformity. She certainly gives the impression that she endorses Victor's efforts to abort the creature.

And yet, unlike the fictional scientist, the novelist does not attempt to destroy or disown the product of her imaginative labors. Quite the opposite: she is entirely devoted to the Creature, despite its "imperfect animation." She goes on to describe the excitement when she realized that her "hideous phantom" would make a wonderful ghost story. Her remarks indicate that the "spectre"—both the Frankenstein Creature and the novel *Frankenstein*—is no longer an enemy but an ally capable of delighting as well as terrifying readers. As the introduction closes, she bids her "hideous progeny go forth and prosper." "I have an affection for it, for it was the offspring of happy days, when death and grief were but words, which found no true echo in my heart" (10). Artistic creativity, she implies, is a magical defense against the fear of death. The hideous progeny has won its Creator's blessing and, like any labor of love, filled her heart with joy that can withstand the severest ordeal.

Mary Shelley and Victor Frankenstein both may be viewed as Promethean, but they are not equally narcissistic. Shelley's hideous progeny is not only the Creature, but the novel, to which she lovingly gives birth. There is an analogy, David Ketterer notes, between the birth of the novel and Frankenstein's creation. "The process of literary creation is presented in the Introduction as exactly parallel to the initial phases of the monster's apprehension of his existence."[29] Whatever her feelings about the "effect of any human endeavour to mock the stupendous mechanism of the Creator of the world" (9), she conceives and nurtures a literary work that has, in its own way, engendered countless offspring. In a Winnicottian sense, the affection she lavishes on her fictional characters affirms her good enough mothering and authoring. Despite its minor aesthetic "deformities"—improbable plotting, superficial development of minor characters, and a tendency toward melodrama—*Frankenstein* remains an admirable novel, fulfilling Victor's dream of "pour[ing] a torrent of light into our dark world" (54).

THREE

Attachment and Loss in
Wuthering Heights

"Come in! come in!" Heathcliff sobs at the beginning of *Wuthering Heights*,[1] imploring his beloved Catherine, dead for twenty years, to reenter his empty life. Moments earlier, Lockwood, falling asleep in Catherine's old coffin-like bed after reading several pages of her journal, dreams he hears a voice and a child's face crying: "Let me in—let me in!" (67). To his intense horror, Lockwood discovers an icy cold hand seizing his arm, which he had thrust through the window. Terror makes Lockwood cruel, and, instead of letting the waif in, he grinds her wrist onto the broken glass. When that fails, he hurriedly piles up several books in a pyramid against the window, hoping to block the child's forced entry.

For decades now critics have been trying, like Catherine's departed spirit, to enter the mysterious world of *Wuthering Heights* (1847), only to find, along with Heathcliff, that entry has been barred. Unlike Lockwood, who shrinks nervously from confronting Catherine Earnshaw's secrets, critics have not been daunted. Indeed, innumerable scholarly books and articles have accumulated, pyramiding in a way that Lockwood—and Emily Brontë—never could have dreamed.

From the beginning, critics have encountered obstacles. Of all English novels, *Wuthering Heights* is, as Dorothy Van Ghent observes, "the most treacherous for the analytical understanding to approach."[2] The novel is especially treacherous for psychoanalytic critics, who have discovered that it invites yet defies interpretation. Since the early 1950s, critics have been peering through the novel's windows, trying to decipher its characters' enigmatic dreams, fantasies, and conflicts. The richness and complexity of *Wuthering Heights* make it a Freudian's delight. The novel's psychosexual conflicts, sibling rivalries, incestuous motifs, castration imagery, primal scenes, and transference dynamics constitute the drama and poetry of psychoanalysis. And yet the sheer number of contradictory conclusions reached by critics indicates the failure to reach a consensus over the meaning of Brontë's novel.

Much of the psychological criticism on *Wuthering Heights* published in the 1950s and 1960s focused, not surprisingly, on its Oedipal and incestuous motifs. Several critics commented on the metaphorical incest between Heathcliff and Catherine, one critic even suggesting that Heathcliff might possibly be Mr. Earnshaw's illegitimate offspring, thus making their love relationship literally incestuous.[3] Viewing Heathcliff as the embodiment of the Freudian id, Thomas Moser argues that *Wuthering Heights* dramatizes, through its imagery of locks, windows, and doors, the lover's violent entry into Catherine's life.[4] Other critics interpreted in great detail the many dreams in the novel, concluding that they all point to incest and the crime against one's kin.[5]

In the early 1970s, critics began noting Catherine's narcissistic relationship to Heathcliff. In *The Female Imagination* (1975), Patricia Meyer Spacks describes the lovers as "transcendent narcissists," two adolescents who have never grown up.[6] Relying upon the classical Freudian view of narcissism, Helene Moglen analyzes *Wuthering Heights* in terms of the development of female identity in a masculine universe. Like Spacks, she refers to the "childish, narcissistic nature of Catherine and Heathcliff's relationship."[7] In *A Future for Astyanax* (1976), Leo Bersani reads *Wuthering Heights* as an ontological psychodrama. Combining psychoanalysis and deconstruction, he concludes that Brontë is "less interested in the psychological continuities which make personality possible than in those radical discontinuities and transformations which explode the myth of personality."[8]

The most significant criticism of *Wuthering Heights* published in the last decade appears in Sandra Gilbert and Susan Gubar's *The Madwoman in the Attic* (1979), a feminist reading of nineteenth-century literature. Noting that, like Mary Shelley, Emily Brontë lost her mother in early childhood—she was three when her mother died from stomach cancer—Gilbert and Gubar point out the intriguing similarities between *Wuthering Heights* and *Frankenstein,* with their emphasis upon orphans and beggars. The "problems of literary orphanhood seem to lead in *Wuthering Heights,* as in *Frankenstein,* not only to a concern with surviving evidence but also to a fascination with the questions of origins."[9] For a writer who suffers early childhood loss, these origins inevitably lead to the "absent mother"—the title of Philip Wion's recent psychoanalytic study of Brontë's strategies to deal with this loss.[10]

What has not yet been explored, however, is the larger subject of attachment and loss in *Wuthering Heights*—how attachments are formed, dissolved, and reformed. The intense possessiveness, anxiety, and anger arising in Heathcliff following Catherine's death reveal characteristics of pathological mourning. Clinical research on attachment and loss indicates that adults who demonstrate abnormal mourning have generally experienced loss of a parent in childhood or adolescence. Nor is Heathcliff alone in losing parents and loved ones: nearly all the characters in the novel experience early loss. In addition, *Wuthering Heights* demonstrates the vicious circle frequently surrounding maternal loss, where separation from the attachment figure provokes hostility within the child, leading in turn to further rejection by loved ones. Behind the visible grieving of the fictional characters lies the hidden grieving of Emily Brontë, who experienced multiple losses in her brief life. Not only did she lose her mother at the age of three, but she lost her two older sisters before she turned seven. Her brother, Branwell, died three months prior to her own death in 1848, at the age of thirty. In many ways Brontë's death seemed, like Heathcliff's and Branwell's, self-induced. Before turning to *Wuthering Heights,* however, I shall examine the subject of attachment and loss.

Child psychiatrists have amassed overwhelming clinical evidence to indicate the crucial importance of the mother-child bond. Hundreds of large-scale studies conducted by investigators from widely differing theoretical backgrounds conclude that the child's happiness and well-being depend upon the existence of a warm, intimate, and continuous relationship with the mother or mother surrogate, especially during the first three years of life. Curiously, Freud had little to say about the importance of early childhood, and it was only in the last ten years of his life that he began to appreciate the child's early tie to the mother. Freud always emphasized Oedipal over pre-Oedipal issues. In "Female Sexuality" (1931), he suggests that a girl's intense attachment to her father is preceded by a phase of exclusive and equally passionate attachment to her mother. Freud seemed to despair that this very early stage in human development could ever be resurrected in analysis. "Everything in the sphere of this first attachment to the mother seemed to me so difficult to grasp in analysis—so grey with age and shadowy and almost impossible to revivify—that it was as if it had succumbed to an especially inexorable repression."[11]

None of the early psychoanalysts explored the precise way in which infants and young children attach themselves to their mothers, nor what happens when the maternal bond is suddenly shattered. How does a young child react, for example, to prolonged separation from the mother? What are the factors that determine whether the reattachment will become problematic or not? Does the early loss of a parent predispose the child to what we now call narcissistic disturbances—problems of self-esteem, empathy, self-object boundaries, interpersonal relationships? It gradually became clear that the subject of attachment and loss has the most profound importance in human development.

Attachment and Loss is also the appropriate title of the major study on the subject by the distinguished English psychoanalyst, John Bowlby. His comprehensive three-volume work—*Attachment* (1969), *Separation* (1973), and *Loss* (1980)[12]—uses as its principal data detailed records of how young children respond to the experience of being separated from and later reunited with their mothers. In contrast to the tendency among many psychoanalysts to construct elaborate, often unverifiable theory, Bowlby is rigorously empirical; and he has sought the help of ethnologists and cognitive psychologists to explain what has come to be called *attachment behavior*. Expressed simply, attachment behavior implies that infants possess an instinctive propensity to cling to other human beings, a desire for a human object that is as primary as the need for food. The "child's tie to his mother," Bowlby writes, "is a product of the activity of a number of behavioural systems that have proximity to mother as a predictable outcome" (*Attachment*, 179). Attachment behavior is activated within most children usually in the first year of life, and it tends to become less easily activated after their third birthday, when proximity to the mother becomes less imperative. Bowlby refers to attachment behavior in terms of certain behavioral systems that are activated or deactivated. These behavioral systems are the result of the child's interaction with the environment, particularly with the mother. The child's characteristic actions during the first years of life—sucking, clinging, following, crying, and smiling—have the effect of maintaining closeness to the mother. The young child's hunger for mother's love and presence is as intense as the hunger for food. When this hunger cannot be fulfilled, the child reacts with a powerful sense of loss and anger.

Bowlby makes a distinction between "dependency" and "attachment." In the early weeks of life, an infant is dependent upon the mother but not yet attached to her. Conversely, an older child is less dependent upon but more attached to her. Dependency is maximum at birth and steadily diminishes until maturity is reached, while attachment is absent at birth and steadily increases. Although Bowlby avoids using the word *dependency* because of its pejorative value connotations of weakness and immaturity, we may continue to use it as long as we affirm the adaptive and self-preservative implications of the child's bond to the mother. Acts that might ordinarily be interpreted as weakness, such as weeping, clinging, and appealing to others for help, reflect the effort to obtain strength and support for the self. These gestures have survival value, confirming Darwin's conclusions on the evolutionary significance of grief. Bowlby does not cite Heinz Kohut's work, but many of the implications of attachment behavior find support in self psychology, especially the positive value of attachment bonds and the developmental importance of empathy.

One of the most important and repeatedly validated conclusions reached by Bowlby and his associates is that children from fifteen to thirty months old who have had a secure family relationship will commonly demonstrate a predictable sequence of behavior when they are separated from their mothers. This sequence of behavior can be classified into three phases: protest, despair, and detachment. The initial phase, protest, reflects the child's acute distress upon realizing the mother's absence. The child will cry loudly, shake his or her cot, and search eagerly for any sight or sound that might prove to be the missing mother. Bowlby claims that the child is likely to reject substitute figures, although other researchers have challenged this finding.

In the middle phase, despair, the child remains preoccupied with the absent mother but experiences increasing hopelessness. The child becomes withdrawn, inactive, quiet, as if in a state of deep mourning. Sooner or later the child enters the final phase, detachment, in which he or she begins to show renewed interest in the surroundings and no longer rejects offers of food and toys. The detachment phase may seem to reflect the child's recovery, but this is misleading, Bowlby suggests, because when the mother returns, the child remains remote and apathetic, if not openly hostile. Each of the three phases of the child's response to separation, Bowlby argues, corresponds to a central area of psychoanalytic theory. Thus, protest involves separation anxiety, despair implies grief and mourning, and detachment represents a defense mechanism.

After reunion with the mother, the child is likely to remain either emotionally detached or excessively clinging. The period of detachment depends mainly on the length of separation. The longer the child remains separated from the mother, the longer the detachment. Should the child come to believe that another separation is likely, he or she will become acutely anxious. If the child loses not only the mother but mother surrogates, he or she will gradually withdraw from all human contact and become unable to form new attachments. This often occurs during prolonged hospitalization, when the child turns inward, becoming increasingly self-preoccupied and self-centered. Children who have suffered prolonged separation or loss are particularly vulnerable to threats of further abandonment. These threats are expressed in several ways. The child may be told that he or she will be sent away for bad behavior or told that the parent will leave home if he or she persists in being disobedient. A more subtle anxiety-provoking threat occurs when the child learns that if he or she is not good, the mother or father will become ill and die (*Separation*, 226). These threats may achieve the intended goal of controlling the child, but they frequently produce unintended or unwelcome side effects. Maternal behavior can unconsciously affect the intensity of the child's attachment behavior. For example, when a mother rebuffs a child for wishing to be near her, the child may become more clinging than ever.

The most prevalent types of disturbances of attachment behavior in the Western world are either too little mothering or a succession of different mother surrogates. Disturbances arising from excessive mothering are less common. These disturbances arise, not because the child has an insatiable need for love and attention, but because the mother insists on being too close to the child. Like many analysts, Bowlby interprets a parent's overprotective or overindulgent behavior as symptomatic of either unconscious hostility toward the child or a desire to cling to him or her. A mother's undercloseness or overcloseness to the child affects the way in which he or she will later relate to others, including future children. Attachment behavior thus reflects intergenerational as well as cultural patterns. While viewing parents as playing a major role in their child's attachment disturbances, Bowlby reminds us that we should not be morally condemning, since parents were themselves children at one time, shaped by early childhood experiences.

In the final volume of his trilogy, Bowlby draws attention to four pathological variants of adult mourning and to the fact that most individuals who demonstrate these responses have lost a parent during childhood or adolescence. The four variants include: unconscious yearning for the lost person; unconscious reproach against the lost person, combined with conscious and often unremitting self-reproach; compulsive caring for other persons; and persistent disbelief that the loss is permanent (*Loss*, 15–16). Bowlby emphasizes that pathological variants of adult mourning are only exaggerations or distortions of normal processes. For example, in both normal and abnormal mourning, anger and hatred play a role. "Loss of a loved person gives rise not only to an intense desire for reunion but to anger at his departure and, later, usually to some degree of detachment; it gives rise not only to a cry for help, but sometimes also to a rejection of those who respond" (*Loss*, 31).

All investigators of childhood bereavement note that children who have lost one parent are terrified they will lose the other parent, either by separation or death. The fear that the surviving parent will die is intensified by other deaths in the family. These fears are inevitable, but they can be aggravated by the surviving parent's refusal to explain to the child the cause of the other parent's death. They can also be aggravated by remarks that implicate the child either in the absent parent's death or in the surviving parent's health. The child's fear of further loss may be heightened when the surviving parent implies that life is no longer worth living or that suicide would be the best course.

Those who have suffered childhood bereavement are often at risk of suicide, Bowlby cautions. The motives for attempting suicide can be understood as responses to the loss of the attachment figure. These motives include a wish for reunion with the lost object, a desire for revenge, a need to punish oneself for harboring murderous feelings toward the dead person, and a feeling that life is not worth living without the future prospect of loving another person (*Loss*, 304). We know that suicide and homicide are closely related and that the anger aroused in children and adults may be internalized or externalized.

It may seem at first improbable that contemporary clinical research on attachment and loss can illuminate *Wuthering Heights*, which appears to stand outside time and space. The early twentieth-century critics certainly believed that Brontë's fictional universe was remote from ordinary human concerns. Closer examination reveals, however, that *Wuthering Heights* dramatizes the dynamics of maternal loss and bereavement. Many of the central conflicts among Brontë's characters may be attributed to parental loss or discontinuities in the parent-child relationship. *Wuthering Heights* does not confirm faithfully all the conclusions of attachment behavior. There is no reason why it should: we are reading a novel, after all, not a psychiatric textbook. The story reveals two surprising contradictions: first, Brontë's attachment figures are fathers, not mothers, and second, attachments tend to be formed not at birth but usually several years later. Both observations contradict Bowlby's findings, which suggest that in most infants attachments are formed with the mother during the first year of life. Brontë offers in *Wuthering Heights* a "revisionist" interpretation of attachment and loss, in which the death of the most important mother in the novel—Catherine Earnshaw Linton—remains conspicuously unmourned by her daughter.

Wuthering Heights also raises important narrative issues with respect to attachment and loss. In a novel that returns obsessively to the subject of maternal separation and loss, it is curious that the children neither grieve over nor even mention their mothers' deaths. It is as if maternal loss is a forbidden subject. It may not be surprising that Catherine Earnshaw refuses to remark on her mother's death; but it certainly is surprising that Catherine's daughter, Cathy Linton, never once inquires into the circumstances of her mother's life and death.

Indeed, Cathy goes out of her way to avoid acknowledging any attachment to her mother, who has died while giving birth to her. Nor does Ellen Dean, an ambivalent mother surrogate who reflects the novel's disparagement of mothering, allude, in Cathy's presence, to her mother's death. We sense, not simply narrative silence over the absent mother, but a pattern of narrative evasiveness and concealment. Cathy's refusal to grieve over her mother's death differs strikingly from Heathcliff's obsession with Catherine's memory. Yet even as Cathy seeks, with Ellen Dean's tacit approval, to deny her maternal roots and thus, by implication, to deny a connection to the past, she demonstrates, in her actions toward her father, the fear of further separation and loss—a fear shared by the other major characters in the novel.

It is never precisely clear why Mr. Earnshaw unexpectedly brings home a young orphan to Wuthering Heights. The father never tells anyone that he is going to Liverpool for this purpose. His wife is ready to fling the waif out the door upon his arrival. Earnshaw tries halfheartedly to explain that the orphan was starving and homeless, claiming that it was somehow easier to take the poor boy back with him to Wuthering Heights than to remain in Liverpool and find a home for him. The explanation pleases no one. We have one clue, however, to the father's behavior. The orphan is christened Heathcliff, the name of a son who died in childhood. The dead son is never mentioned again, and nothing in the novel leads us to believe that this detail may be significant. Yet it is not fanciful to believe that the father has adopted the youth in an effort to undo a past loss. In a double sense, Heathcliff symbolizes a lost child to Earnshaw, and the way in which he suddenly opens his great coat and pulls out the child bundled up in his arms may suggest a birth fantasy, with the father, not the mother, linked to procreation.

In bringing Heathcliff home to Wuthering Heights, Earnshaw incurs the monstrous wrath of his family. They immediately treat the outsider as a Frankenstein Creature, reducing him into an "it." He even sounds like a monster. "When it was set on its feet, it only stared round, and repeated over and over again some gibberish that nobody could understand" (77). Catherine grins and spits at the creature, Hindley instantly hates him, and the usually temperate Ellen puts the orphan on the landing of the stairs, hoping he might disappear in the morning. Even after the family's initial shock subsides, they treat the child contemptuously. Only Earnshaw takes an interest in him. Ironically, the father's closeness to Heathcliff results in their estrangement from the family. No one can understand Earnshaw's attachment to the sullen boy, who rarely shows any sign of affection or gratitude. Heathcliff is not insolent to his benefactor, merely insensible. Treating Heathcliff as the favored child, the father ignores his natural children, thus provoking more ill will in the family.

If Earnshaw's attachment to Heathcliff represents an attempt to create a new son to replace a lost one, the effort fails. For the father succeeds only in alienating his natural son and quarreling with his daughter. Hindley sees Heathcliff as the usurper of his father's affections and broods endlessly over the loss of paternal love. Mrs. Earnshaw's death, two years after Heathcliff's arrival, has no visible impact upon the family. Catherine's growing closeness to Heathcliff does nothing to improve the strained father-daughter relationship. "Nay, Cathy," Earnshaw tells her, "I cannot love thee; thou'rt worse than thy brother. Go, say thy prayers, child, and ask God's pardon. I doubt thy mother and I must rue that we ever reared thee!" (84). Earnshaw's stern reprimand makes Catherine cry at first, but subsequent rebukes harden her, and she dismisses Ellen's request to apologize to her father. The last exchange between father and daughter is revealing. "Why canst thou not always be a good lass, Cathy?" To which she laughingly replies, "Why cannot you always be a good man, father?" (84). With that he dies.

Unlike Catherine and Heathcliff, who express grief over Earnshaw's death, Hindley remains permanently estranged from his father. He astonishes everyone by returning to the funeral with a new wife, but there is something odd about both the timing of the marriage and the particular woman he marries. Ellen describes Frances as filled with "hysterical emotion" and morbidly afraid of death (86). She is ill from the moment she arrives at Wuthering Heights and dies not long after giving birth to a son, Hareton. It is as if Hindley has unconsciously chosen a dying woman to marry, whose death repeats earlier losses in his life. Upon Frances' death, he immediately falls apart, his life ruined. As Ellen prophetically observes, "he had room in his heart only for two idols—his wife and himself—he doted on both, and adored one, and I couldn't conceive how he would bear the loss" (105).

In fact, Hindley cannot bear loss. Married to Frances only about a year before she dies, he spends the rest of his brief life bewailing the loss. He succeeds finally in drinking himself to death at the age of twenty-seven. It is hard to say whether Hindley's self-destructive behavior is motivated more by his inconsolable anguish over Frances' death or by his implacable rage toward Heathcliff. Both gratify his despair. His "sorrow was of that kind," Ellen observes, "that will not lament, he neither wept nor prayed—he cursed and defied—exe-crated God and man—and gave himself up to reckless dissipation" (106). For all of his raging defiance of God and man, Hindley remains a needy child, dependent upon an absent figure. His inability to tolerate his wife's loss has its counterpart in the child's inability to tolerate parental loss. Like the children Bowlby describes who have lost their mothers, Hindley goes through the phases of protest and despair, corresponding to separation anxiety and mourning, respec-tively. These phases define the central issues behind Hindley's tor-mented life. He apparently does not reach the final stage, detachment, in which the child superficially shows renewed interest in his or her surroundings. On a deeper level, however, Hindley remains funda-mentally detached from life, unable to form new attachments or re-sume old ones.

Significantly, none of the other characters in the story interprets Hindley's behavior as a cry for help. They see him as willful, perverse, raging, suicidal—but not as dependent. They make little effort, con-sequently, to come to his assistance or assuage his loss. To be sure, Hindley would spurn their aid, since he does not regard himself as weak or clinging. He forms his identity around the twin themes of loss and victimization. He would rather rage against his wife's death than commit himself to his son's robust life. He is unable to see himself as a victimizer, a father who has abandoned his child. Nor can he see the conflicting signals he gives to others; his self-destructive behavior, for example, is an effort to elicit support from the very people he pushes away. "He was always greedy," Catherine says, "though what he grasps with one hand, he flings away with the other" (138).

Hindley's pathological mourning reflects two characteristics of those who have lost a parent during childhood or adolescence: unconscious yearning for the lost love object and severe reproaches against the dead parent for having abandoned the child. In Hindley's case, anger and hatred predominate. Triggered by his wife's death, his self-destructive behavior may be understood as a response to the loss of an attachment figure. His actions are motivated by, to repeat Bowlby's findings, a wish for reunion with the lost object, a desire for revenge, a need to punish himself for harboring murderous feelings, and a feeling that life no longer holds meaning.

If Frances is an attachment figure, a problem immediately arises. She seems too inconsequential to explain the magnitude of Hindley's despair. The problem is aesthetic and psychological: aesthetic, in that we are merely told about rather than shown their love; and psychological, in that we cannot imagine Hindley loving Frances or anyone else. He is too self-hating to love anyone. Consequently, Hindley's pathological response to his wife's loss must symbolize deeper conflicts in his life. These conflicts point to the father's embittered disconfirmation of his son: "Hindley was naught, and would never thrive as where he wandered" (82). Hindley seems intent upon fulfilling this prophecy. A rejected son, Hindley becomes a rejecting father to Heathcliff and Hareton. Hindley's hatred of Heathcliff, we suspect, is a displacement of his feelings toward his father. "It is some devil that urges me to thwart my own schemes by killing him" (177). The devil is, transferentially speaking, Hindley's unconscious image of himself as the bad son, projected onto Heathcliff and Hareton.

Transference is, as Freud notes, the "playground" in which past conflicts are repeated in the present and either acted out or worked through.[13] The literary implications of transference are intriguing. "Story telling is a regular function of intra- and extra-analytic transference," Stanley Olinick and Laura Tracy point out in a recent issue of *The Psychoanalytic Review*, "an active effort to influence and manipulate the imagined reader or listener consonant with transference needs, conflicts, and defenses."[14] The content of Hindley's story suggests his inconsolable anguish over his wife's death, while the form of his story reveals his inability to sustain relationships. His love-hate relationship to the terrified Hareton reflects intense ambivalence toward maternal union. "Hareton was impressed with a wholesome terror of

encountering either his wild-beast's fondness, or his madman's rage—
for in one he ran a chance of being squeezed and kissed to death, and
in the other of being flung into the fire, or dashed against the wall"
(114). Alternately overloving and underloving, Hindley is never able
to strike a balance in his affections or achieve healthy distance from
others.

Hindley degrades Hareton and, before him, Heathcliff, because he
wishes to degrade himself. There are several reasons for this: to express rage toward those who abandoned him, to atone for his complicity in their deaths, to confirm his father's judgment that he is worthless, and to be reunited, finally, with the lost attachment figures. No
one ever laments Mrs. Earnshaw's passing, but Hindley's violent
response to his wife's death inevitably raises the specter of maternal
loss. Abandoned children often grow up to become abandoning parents, and Hindley's impulse toward infanticide—he threatens to break
Hareton's neck and actually drops him over the banister of the stairs
—reflects the active hostility of adults toward their children in the
novel. As Wade Thompson remarks, *Wuthering Heights* reveals a
"world of sadism, violence, and wanton cruelty, wherein the children
—without the protection of their mothers—have to fight for very life
against adults who show almost no tenderness, love, or mercy."[15]
These infanticidal impulses seem to originate from the child's perception of parental abandonment and neglect. Thus, Hindley remains an
example of a child who has never worked through feelings of parental
loss. To this extent, he resembles his sister, Catherine, who also wills
herself out of existence.

Like Hindley (and Heathcliff), Catherine attaches herself to others
with either a wild-beast's fondness or a madwoman's rage. Asked by
her father what she desires from Liverpool, she requests a whip.
Earnshaw brings back Heathcliff, whom she uses, not as a whipping
boy, but as a creature whose passion she whips into a fury. The two
become inseparable, until Catherine decides to marry Edgar Linton.
The belief that she can maintain control and possession of both men is
illusory. Contrary to Ellen's remark that she has a "wondrous capacity to old attachments" (106), Catherine is committed to the destruction of attachments. Realizing that she cannot possess both Heathcliff
and Edgar, she vows to punish them, even if it means punishing
herself. "Well, if I cannot keep Heathcliff for my friend—if Edgar

will be mean and jealous, I'll try to break their hearts by breaking my own" (155). To accomplish this purpose she starves herself, believing, as Ellen says, that "at every meal, Edgar was ready to choke for her absence" (158.) Catherine knows precisely what she is doing. Long before Freud began theorizing about the dynamics of aggression, she authoritatively refers to the link between suicide and homicide. "If I were only sure it would kill him . . . I'd kill myself directly!" (159).

Staring at her reflection in a mirror, Catherine is startled by the image. She is not enamored of her reflection, as Narcissus is, but horrified by it. The mirror confirms her narcissistic personality: her self-preoccupation, need for constant attention and admiration, and rejection of the feelings of others. The mirror also reveals that she is wasting away, consumed by inner rage. Mirrors are instruments of ontological insecurity, and when Catherine gazes at herself, she is haunted by, in Leo Bersani's words, "alien versions of the self" (208). She breaks down in tears, prompting Ellen to remark: "our fiery Catherine was no better than a wailing child!" (162). Catherine indeed becomes a wailing child again during this scene, and the regression to childhood indicates the wish to return to her old bed at Wuthering Heights.

Catherine dreams that she is enclosed in the oak-paneled bed at home, her heart aching with intense grief. She realizes that the grief originates in past events. Perplexed by the meaning of the dream, she probes deeper and deeper into her unconsciousness. Suddenly the last seven years of her life dissolve, and she is transported back into a twelve-year-old girl. "I was a child," she tells Ellen; "my father was just buried, and my misery arose from the separation that Hindley had ordered between me, and Heathcliff" (163). The dream offers Catherine a glimpse into the abyss, overwhelming her with despair. She imagines for the first time how Heathcliff must have felt when he was driven into exile. Returning to present time, Catherine tells Ellen she is burning with fever and longing to go outdoors. "I wish I were a girl again, half savage and hardy, and free . . . and laughing at injuries, not maddening under them!" (163). Springing up from bed, the delirious woman throws open the window and bends out into the misty dark night, "careless of the frosty air that cut about her shoulders as keen as a knife" (164).

Catherine's dream reveals, significantly, the association between her father's death and Heathcliff's separation. In her unconscious mind, the two men are thus one. Prior to her loss of them, Catherine imagined that the attachment would continue unbroken. Even when she marries Edgar, she is convinced that she will always remain connected to Heathcliff. "Who is to separate us, pray?" she defiantly asks Ellen. "They'll meet the fate of Milo!" (121). She reaffirms this in her central speech in the novel. "My love for Heathcliff resembles the eternal rocks beneath—a source of little visible delight, but necessary. Nelly, I *am* Heathcliff—he's always, always in my mind—not as a pleasure, any more than I am always a pleasure to myself—but as my own being—so, don't talk of our separation again" (122).

Improbable as it may seem, Catherine regards Heathcliff as a parent surrogate, and the loss awakens in her feelings of anger, grief, reproach, and abandonment. Heathcliff's loss of Catherine awakens, as we shall see, similar feelings in him. Each views the other as part of the same unchanging, unbroken identity. Each remains incomplete without the other, unable to survive alone. Neither character recognizes the concept of otherness or object love. Mirror images, Catherine and Heathcliff enact the roles of Narcissus and Echo, alternately embracing and rejecting the other's advances. In addition, Catherine's relationship to Heathcliff reenacts her stormy relationship to her father. She passionately loves both men—but vexes them to death.

Like Hindley, Catherine acts out early narcissistic disturbances. Her father had told her when she was twelve that he could not love her, since she was worse than her brother. The daughter responded first by crying, then by hardening her heart to further criticisms. Seven years later the nineteen-year-old dying woman angrily accuses Heathcliff of breaking her heart:

> "I wish I could hold you," she continued, bitterly, "till we were both dead! I shouldn't care what you suffered. I care nothing for your sufferings. Why shouldn't you suffer? I do! Will you forget me—will you be happy when I am in the earth? Will you say twenty years hence, 'That's the grave of Catherine Earnshaw. I loved her long ago, and was wretched to lose her; but it is past. I've loved many others since—my children are dearer to me than she was, and, at death, I shall not rejoice that I am going to her, I shall be sorry that I must leave them!' Will you say so, Heathcliff?"(195)

We cannot understand this extraordinary passage without remembering that Catherine is pregnant at this point in the novel. Her fear of giving birth awakens earlier fears of separation and loss. She does not allude to her pregnancy, but she refers ominously to her fear of being displaced in Heathcliff's life by his future children. These children are, symbolically, the offspring of her fantasied union with Heathcliff. Interpreted Oedipally, Catherine's desire for Heathcliff symbolizes the daughter's wish to possess the father's love. For Catherine, love is exclusive: as a child, she demands exclusive attention from her father; as an adult, she demands exclusive attention from her husband and lover. Interpreted pre-Oedipally, Catherine's desire for Heathcliff symbolizes the child's wish for union with the lost mother. Since dreams and symbols are overdetermined, it is not surprising that both wishes inhere in Catherine's speech. Additionally, Catherine's fear of abandonment conceals her wish for Heathcliff to abandon his children in order to be reunited with her. Catherine is, in fact, the abandoned child and the abandoning mother.

Catherine's motives for self-destruction closely resemble Hindley's, including the wish to punish those who have abandoned her, which is followed by the wish for reunion with them in death. Her self-punishment takes the form of anorexia. It appears likely that Catherine's self-starvation, like the eating disorders found in many teenage females, is symptomatic of unresolved mother-daughter conflicts, particularly sexual fears, deformed body image, and regressive behavior. Catherine never mentions her mother, but during her delirium she sees Ellen as an "aged woman," a "withered hag" (161). Although Ellen is Hindley's age—thus, only eight years older than Catherine—she has functioned as Catherine's nurse and mother surrogate since childhood. Ellen makes little effort to conceal her displeasure with Catherine, whom she considers selfish and willful. The two women are locked in an ambivalent relationship, in which power frequently shifts back and forth. Catherine sees Ellen as the bad mother, and when she hears Ellen tell Edgar about Heathcliff's presence at Thrushcross Grange, she furiously refers to the older woman as a "traitor," "hidden enemy," and "witch" (166.). For her part, Ellen sees herself as Catherine's faithful servant and rejects all statements to the contrary. The truth is that the two women infuriate each other. Ellen ignores Catherine's efforts to starve herself, thus heightening her rage. Ellen's tendency to dismiss Catherine as "mad" and to be alternately neglectful and overcontrolling has caused one critic to label her as the "villain" in *Wuthering Heights*.[16] Ellen is not sadistic, but she is not consistently empathic, and there is little doubt that she is implicated in Catherine's death.

Catherine's death, moreover, has a remarkable effect on Ellen. She prides herself on being a "steady, reasonable kind of body" (103), and though she is often preachy, she is rarely sentimental. Consequently, her rhapsodic description of Catherine's appearance in death surprises us. "No angel in heaven could be more beautiful than she appeared; and I partook of the infinite calm in which she lay. My mind was never in a holier frame, than while I gazed on that untroubled image of Divine rest" (201). Ellen's perception of Catherine's "infinite calm" recalls Victor Frankenstein's smiling face as he contemplates his dead mother. In both cases, it seems easier to love a person after she is dead. Catherine's death elicits Ellen's most intriguing observation in the novel: "I don't know if it be a peculiarity in me, but I am seldom otherwise than happy while watching in the chamber of death, should no frenzied or despairing mourner share the duty with me. I see a repose that neither earth nor hell can break; and I feel an assurance of the endless and shadowless hereafter—the Eternity they have entered —where life is boundless in its duration, and love in its sympathy, and joy in its fulness" (201–2).

In idealizing death, Ellen validates Catherine's mystical longings, her wish to escape from the "shattered prison" of life into the "glorious" other world. Catherine desires to be in that other world, "not seeing it dimly through tears, and yearning for it through the walls of an aching heart; but really with it, and in it" (196–97). Catherine's otherworldliness is mystical, of course, and cannot be explained rationally. Yet, without implying that the mystical impulse can be reduced to a psychological wish, I can suggest that Catherine's movement away from life toward death is motivated by the need to triumph over separation and discontinuity, to reattach herself to the circumambient universe. Ellen is not by temperament mystical, as Catherine and Heathcliff are, but her beatific description of Catherine—she uses words like "perfect peace," "infinite calm," and "blessed release"— evokes a similar image of ecstatic unity. Ellen's devout Christian faith enables her to believe that earthly death is the beginning of eternal life.

No easy acceptance of death awaits Heathcliff. His raging protest and despair over Catherine's loss elevate him into one of the great Byronic characters in literature. Heathcliff dwarfs his male rivals, particularly Hindley, and at first glance their response to loss seems quite different. Both are devastated and inconsolable; but whereas Hindley is shown to be dependent without being attached, Heathcliff is attached without being dependent. Hindley never mentions Frances after her death, while Heathcliff remains obsessed with Catherine's memory. Hindley is pathetic, Heathcliff is tragic. Heathcliff despises his former tormentor, judging him weak, dissipated, and ineffectual, while he himself demonstrates preternatural strength, inflexible will, and ruthless success. He is mythologized into a larger-than-life figure, an "unreclaimed creature," in Catherine's vivid words, "without refinement, without cultivation; an arid wilderness of furze and whinstone" (141). He's not a "rough diamond," she continues, but a "fierce, pitiless, wolfish man." Hindley's violence is mainly self-inflicted, while Heathcliff's shockingly graphic violence is directed toward others. He hangs his wife Isabella's dog; wrenches Hindley's pistol from his grip, slitting mercilessly his attacker's wrist with the attached knife; and later flings a dinner knife at Isabella. When Catherine's daughter, Cathy, becomes enraged enough to bite her persecutor, Heathcliff viciously administers a shower of slaps to her head.

Yet despite these outward differences, Heathcliff and Hindley reveal remarkably similar responses to separation and loss, reflective of the child's reaction to maternal loss. Heathcliff and Hindley show heightened anxiety following loss and are unable to attach themselves to other people. They remain fixated on the first two phases of loss: protest and despair. Heathcliff's despair is surely unexceeded in literature. After Catherine's death, he withdraws from life, remaining listless, depressed. Like Hindley, Heathcliff experiences intense rage over loss, and his appetite for revenge is insatiable. Hindley execrates God and man for Frances' death; Heathcliff hurls his reproaches directly at Catherine. "You loved me—then what *right* had you to leave me?" (197). Both *Frankenstein* and *Wuthering Heights* dramatize the paradoxical nature of narcissistic rage, which temporarily maintains life while eroding the will to live. Heathcliff's and Hindley's violent mourning resembles the pattern of bereavement of individuals who have lost a parent during childhood or adolescence: unconscious yearning for the lost person, bitter reproaches and self-reproaches, and denial of the permanency of loss.

Significantly, another character in *Wuthering Heights* illustrates the phases of protest, despair, and detachment through which children pass in response to maternal loss. Linton, Heathcliff's son, elicits no sympathy from readers, and he seems to have none of his father's qualities. The product of the disastrous union between Heathcliff and Isabella, Linton appears from birth as an "ailing, peevish creature" (218). Isabella dies when Linton is not yet twelve, but his response to maternal loss is that of a much younger child. Taken to Thrushcross Grange, he spends the first day or two sitting in a corner of the library, too depressed to read or play. Ellen's description of him is brutally forthright. "A pale, delicate, effeminate boy, who might have been taken for my master's younger brother, so strong was the resemblance; but there was a sickly peevishness in his aspect, that Edgar Linton never had" (235). Nor does Ellen expect the "weakling" (236) to live very long. Linton's health deteriorates further when he is taken to live with his father at Wuthering Heights, and he gradually wastes away. Ellen's description of his gradual alteration strikingly resembles Bowlby's clinical descriptions of despairing children who have lost their mothers. "The pettishness that might be caressed into fondness, had yielded to a listless apathy; there was less of the peevish temper of a child which frets and teases on purpose to be soothed, and more of the self-absorbed moroseness of a confirmed invalid, repelling consolation, and ready to regard the good-humoured mirth of others, as an insult" (293). When Linton does indeed die, shortly after coercing young Cathy to marry him, no one mourns his death.

It is easy to see why the others dislike Linton. He is weak, complaining, hypochondriacal, selfish, and cowardly—like Hindley. Linton shamelessly manipulates Cathy into marrying him, coolly indifferent to her suffering. Unlike his counterpart, Hareton Earnshaw, who is depicted as good nature put to bad use, Linton appears to be innately defective. He makes no attempt to conceal his bad nature from Cathy. "I hate everybody! I *am* worthless, and bad in temper, and bad in spirit, almost always—and if you choose, you may say good-bye—you'll get rid of an annoyance" (285). Linton is a textbook example of a narcissistic personality disorder. He suffers from

low self-esteem, requires constant attention and admiration, and remains highly self-preoccupied. He demonstrates characteristic disturbances in interpersonal relationships, most notably, feelings of entitlement and exploitativeness. He is utterly devoid of empathy. Behind
his self-pity lie feelings of rage, inferiority, and shame. Linton's "sickly
peevishness" may be another term for the depression that is extremely
common among narcissistic people. Accompanying the depression are
painful self-consciousness, hypochondria, and chronic envy of others.

For all the differences between Heathcliff and Linton, father and
son display similar narcissistic injuries. Stripped of their Byronic energy and romantic overtones, Heathcliff's speeches reveal the same
anxiety over separation and loss that can be seen in his son. Stripped
of their meanness, Linton's speeches reveal the same need for intense
attachment that can be seen in his father. Compare the following two
speeches, for example. In the first, Linton acknowledges that he has
betrayed Cathy but begs her to remain with him, even die with him.
" 'Oh!' he sobbed, 'I cannot bear it! Catherine, Catherine, I'm a
traitor, too, and I dare not tell you! But leave me and I shall be killed!
Dear Catherine, my life is in your hands; and you have said you loved
me—and if you did, it wouldn't harm you. You'll not go, then? kind,
sweet, good Catherine! And perhaps you *will* consent—and he'll let
me die with you!' " (299). In the second speech, Heathcliff weeps
upon learning of Catherine's death and implores her to return to life.
"Catherine Earnshaw, may you not rest, as long as I am living! You
said I killed you—haunt me then! The murdered *do* haunt their
murderers. I believe—I know that ghosts *have* wandered on earth.
Be with me always—take any form—drive me mad! only *do* not
leave me in this abyss, where I cannot find you! Oh God! It is
unutterable! I *cannot* live without my life! I *cannot* live without my
soul!" (204).

Given their hidden similarities, why do we identify with Heathcliff's story and counteridentify with Linton's? The question cannot
be explained entirely by the contrast between the heroism of the
former and the pathos of the latter. These judgments obscure the fact
that neither character can cope with separation and loss. Nor can they
form new attachments following loss. To this extent, they resemble
Hindley and Catherine, who reveal the same disturbances in their
attachment behavior. Of the four characters, however, only Linton is

explicitly associated with being a "mama's boy"—and in this association lies a clue to the novel's enigmatic attitude toward loss. Ellen
Dean, the chief mother surrogate in *Wuthering Heights*, unsympath-
etically describes Linton as "effeminate" the first time she sees him.
She never alters her opinion that he has been corrupted by maternal
overattachment. Linton asks Cathy to sit on the settle and allow him
to lean on his knee—"That's as mamma used to do, whole afternoons
together" (274). Cathy obligingly treats him like a baby; she resolves
to make a "pet" of him, stroking his curls, kissing his cheek, and
offering him tea in her saucer, "like a baby" (236). Later she tells
Ellen: "He's a pretty little darling when he's good. I'd make such a
pet of him, if he were mine" (275). Ellen makes little effort to conceal
her contempt for Linton, referring to his behavior as the "mere per-
verseness of an indulged plague of a child" (273). Heathcliff actively
despises Linton, wondering how he could have produced such a son.
"Thou art thy mother's child, entirely! Where is *my* share in thee,
puling chicken?" (242). The possibility remains, then, that the novel
blocks our empathy toward Linton precisely because he is identified
with maternal attachment.

Beginning with Lockwood's pompous reference to his "dear mother"
(47), *Wuthering Heights* reveals a consistent pattern of disparaging
remarks on motherhood. As a lover, Lockwood remains Heathcliff's
ironic foil. In rejecting the advances of a woman at a vacation resort,
Lockwood refers to her as persuading her "mamma" to decamp (48).
Catherine never would have referred to her own mother in this way.
The young Edgar Linton appears to be overindulged by his mother,
and his cry of "Oh, mamma, mamma!" (90) when Catherine and
Heathcliff first visit Thrushcross Grange finds sharp contrast in the
toughness of the Earnshaw children, who never rely upon their own
mother. When Heathcliff expresses the wish to have Edgar's light hair
and fair skin, Ellen replies sneeringly, "And cried for mamma, at
every turn" (97). Provoking Heathcliff into violence at Wuthering
Heights, Edgar sobs: "I promised mamma that I wouldn't say one
word to him, and I didn't" (99). The one time Catherine uses the
word *mother* occurs when she praises herself for her compliancy
during arguments. "I yield like a foolish mother," she complacently
tells Ellen (137)—though one can hardly imagine Catherine more
intransigent. These references associate mothers and mothering with

softness, indulgence, and sentimentality. "There's harm in being too soft," remarks Ellen (152), who earlier dismisses Edgar as the "soft thing" (112).

There is no danger that Ellen is too soft, since she has limited patience and empathy for the characters she nurses. Brontë's portrait of Ellen Dean is a masterpiece of psychological complexity. As a nurse and foster mother, Ellen honestly admits that she resents her numerous responsibilities. Forced to nurse the Earnshaw children after their mother dies and they fall ill with the measles, Ellen confides that she took little pleasure in doing so, though she does feel proud when the doctor commends her care of them. She becomes, in effect, Heathcliff's mother, cheering him up when he unfavorably compares himself to the refined Edgar. Yet, even as she tries to inculcate Christian virtues among the children, she is not averse to using pugilistic metaphors to express her disapproval of softness. She insinuates, for example, that Edgar is a weakling and tells Heathcliff that he could "knock him down in a twinkling" (97). Although she informs Heathcliff that it is "for God to punish wicked people; we should learn to forgive" (101), she herself has difficulty in forgiving Catherine, Heathcliff, Linton, and the others. She neatly summarizes her attitude toward human nature by pragmatically observing: "Well, we *must* be for ourselves in the long run; the mild and generous are only more justly selfish than the domineering" (132).

Like the other characters in *Wuthering Heights*, Ellen Dean holds to the hypothesis prevalent in the nineteenth century that an excess of parental affection spoils children by making them excessively demanding and intolerant of frustration. Overloving parents who narcissistically invest themselves in their children's lives can indeed cause serious developmental problems, but these problems differ from those associated with what Bowlby calls "anxious attachment." There is no evidence to support the theory that anxious attachment is the result of an excess of parental affection and attention. In fact, all the evidence points to the opposite conclusion—namely, that the child's heightened anxiety over separation and loss of love is a reaction to fears of parental abandonment. Bowlby quotes an observation by Dorothy Burlingham and Anna Freud in *Infants Without Families* (1944): "The child is all the more clinging the more it has an inner conviction that separation will repeat itself" (*Separation,* 237). The child who is spoiled or overindulged usually has not received genuine parental love, and, as a consequence, the child fears that the parents will remain inaccessible and unresponsive. The child will then adopt a strategy of remaining close to the attachment figures in order to insure sufficient love and attention from them.

Linton's anxious attachment arises as a result, not of overindulgence, but of early childhood loss. He clings to others from the conviction that they will abandon him. And, indeed, they do repeatedly abandon him. Growing up without a father, Linton is entirely dependent upon his mother, and once Isabella dies, he is thrust into the frightening world of Wuthering Heights. When he first meets his father, whose grim, sneering face would dishearten the most stalwart adult, Linton clings in terror to Ellen. "Don't leave me! I'll not stay here! I'll not stay here!" he cries (244), to no avail. How many children would not be terrified to live with Heathcliff? The next time we hear about Linton is three years later, when Heathcliff tells Cathy, "As true as I live, he's dying for you—breaking his heart at your fickleness, not figuratively, but actually" (266). Insofar as Heathcliff is incapable of being an attachment figure, Linton remains, in effect, utterly abandoned and detached from life. When Cathy finally meets him, he bitterly reproaches her: "Why didn't you come before?" (270). Ellen and Heathcliff ridicule Linton's frightened dependency, but their behavior only exacerbates his insecurity, which is merely a distortion or exaggeration of a normal process of mourning. As Bowlby points out, children respond poorly to loss if they are made to feel that there is something wrong with them for expressing sorrow. "Especially adverse effects are attributed to disparaging and sarcastic remarks by parents and parent-surrogates made whenever a child is distressed and seeks comfort. The injunctions 'Don't cry,' 'Don't be a cry-baby,' 'I won't love you if you cry' can . . . do untold harm, especially when uttered in contemptuous tones" (*Loss*, 228).

And so, contrary to Ellen's emphasis upon Linton's defective nature, a more persuasive interpretation of his anxiety lies in his failure to overcome traumatic loss. "All children love their parents" (239), Ellen platitudinizes, but then continues to narrate a story in which children helplessly struggle to protect themselves from parents bent upon infanticide. Thus, Hindley tortures Heathcliff, who in turn neglects or mistreats Hareton and Linton, while the dying Catherine predicts bitterly that Heathcliff will betray her memory by loving his own children more than he loves her. Catherine need not worry. Heathcliff does everything he can to deform the three children under his influence: Hareton, Linton, and Cathy. In short, not only do we fail to see children being spoiled or overindulged by their parents, but we see the opposite situation, in which children and adults become anxious, dependent, and clinging because of their inner conviction that they are not genuinely loved.

Indeed, mothers remain conspicuously absent from *Wuthering Heights*. Mrs. Earnshaw tries to throw the waif Heathcliff out the door when her husband brings him home. She dies shortly thereafter, her absence unnoticed. That is all we learn about her, in contrast to her husband, who evokes strong feelings from his children. Hindley's wife, Frances, dies shortly after giving birth to Hareton. Heathcliff's wife, Isabella, dies before Linton turns twelve; we see her interact briefly with her husband but not with her son. And, in what constitutes the central parent-child relationship in the novel, Catherine Earnshaw Linton dies while giving birth to her daughter, Cathy. If we exclude the two first-generation women, Mrs. Earnshaw and Mrs. Linton, all the women who marry die prematurely, two of them (Catherine and Frances) either during or immediately following childbirth. Moreover, Edgar's mother dies as a consequence of nursing the dangerously ill Catherine back to health early in the novel. "The poor dame had reason to repent of her kindness," Ellen observes; "she, and her husband, both took the fever, and died within a few days of each other" (128). Mrs. Linton may thus be viewed as another mother who perishes as a result of birthing or nursing children. Fathers, by contrast, seem to be omnipresent, ranging from Earnshaw's old servant, Joseph,[17] to Edgar Linton, the only loving parent in the novel. Fathers may not live longer than mothers in *Wuthering Heights*, but they are not at risk solely because of procreation. The same pattern holds true, as we have seen, in *Frankenstein*.

Like Heathcliff, who is named after an Earnshaw child who died in childhood, young Cathy is named after her dead mother, suggesting the wish for intergenerational continuity. We learn a good deal about the similarities and differences between mother and daughter. Cathy embodies the qualities of both parents, the Earnshaws and Lintons. She has the Earnshaws' handsome dark eyes and the Lintons' fair skin and small features. She is high spirited, like her mother, but more sensitive and affectionate. Cathy's "capacity for intense attachments reminded me of her mother," Ellen observes; "still she did not resemble her; for she could be soft and mild as a dove, and she had a gentle voice, and pensive expression: her anger was never furious, her love never fierce; it was deep and tender" (224). Ellen acknowledges in the same breath Cathy's faults: "a perverse will that indulged children invariably acquire, whether they be good tempered or cross" (224). Few modern readers would call Cathy an "indulged" child; her father loves her but does not overlove her. Cathy not only combines the best features of the two ancient families, but she has a complexity of form and substance that can be captured only through oxymorons. Thus, when she reaches her full height, her figure is "both plump and slender, elastic as steel" (250).

Whereas Linton Heathcliff is described as a "mama's boy," Cathy is a "daddy's girl." Ellen speculates that Cathy's father never uttered a harsh word to her; if he reproved her, even by a look, she would be crushed. Cathy adores Edgar, and her ability to empathize with others, including Linton and Hareton, arises from her loving relationship with her father. Secure in her attachment to him, Cathy is capable of intense attachments to others. Father and daughter mirror each other's love and devotion without blurring the distinction between self and other. Edgar's love for Cathy reflects the "glint in the mother's eye" that Kohut argues is so important for the child's development. Cathy's capacity for object love is itself an objective reflection of her father's feelings for her. Ellen gratefully acknowledges Cathy's admirable devotion to her during a period of illness: "she was the fondest nurse that ever watched: she must have had a warm heart, when she loved her father so, to give so much to me!" (276). When Edgar's health begins to fail, Cathy despairs, telling Ellen: "I love him better than myself" (264)—an echo of her mother's earlier characterization of Heathcliff as "more myself than I am" (121). Unlike her mother, Cathy does not reject Edgar. Beseeching Cathy to marry him, Linton repeats Heathcliff's assertion that she may grow to love him more than she loves her father. Cathy gravely rebukes Linton. "No! I should never love anybody better than papa" (271). She consents to marry Linton only so that she may visit her dying father. "If papa thought I had left him, on purpose, and if he died before I returned, could I bear to live?" (307). Cathy is saddened but not devastated by her father's death, and despite the painful loss, she is able to form a new attachment to Hareton.

Given Cathy's intense family loyalty, it is astonishing that she seems totally uninterested in discovering anything about her deceased mother. And it is no less astonishing that critics have failed to notice this point, even critics who have written sensitively on issues of maternal loss, female identity, and orphanhood in *Wuthering Heights*. The fact remains that Cathy Linton—imaginative, inquisitive, and adventurous—not once, neither as a child nor as a young woman, inquires about her mother. In *Frankenstein* Victor usurps the mother's role in the act of creation; in *Wuthering Heights*, another motherless novel, Cathy denies that her mother has ever existed. It is as if Cathy emerges full blown from her father's great coat, like Heathcliff's "birth" into Wuthering Heights. Cathy knows that her mother has died, of course, but she knows none of the details of Catherine's life or death. The daughter never mentions her mother's name, even when the opportunity arises.

This becomes strikingly evident when Cathy and Linton find two balls among a heap of old toys in a cupboard at Wuthering Heights, Catherine Earnshaw's ancestral home. Cathy's narration is revealing, not for what she says, but for what she doesn't say. "One [ball] was marked C., and the other H.; I wished to have the C., because that stood for Catherine, and the H. might be for Heathcliff, his name; but the bran came out of H., and Linton didn't like it" (280). A child far less curious than Cathy would immediately realize that the ball had once belonged to her mother and would wonder about her mother's past. But Cathy seems unwilling to imagine her mother's life or to identify with her in any way. We have only circumstantial evidence that Cathy knows her mother died in childbirth. Ellen tells us, for example, that when Cathy turns sixteen, no one celebrates her birthday—or any of her birthdays, for that matter. "On the anniversary of her birth we never manifested any signs of rejoicing, because it was, also, the anniversary of my late mistress's death. Her father invariably spent that day alone in the library" (246).

Indeed, there is a conspiracy of silence surrounding Catherine's death, beginning with Ellen. When Cathy expresses alarm over her father's health, Ellen scolds her. " 'Oh, fie, silly child!' I exclaimed.

'If you had any real griefs, you'd be ashamed to waste a tear on this little contrariety. You never had one shadow of substantial sorrow, Miss Catherine' " (257). Evidently, the loss of one's mother does not qualify as a shadow of substantial sorrow for Ellen. She seems to believe that a child can lose her mother at birth without suffering ill consequences. Nor does Ellen bring up the mother's tragic death, even when it would explain the daughter's acute anxiety over losing her father. At one point Cathy bursts into sobs when she contemplates life without Edgar and Ellen. Her anxiety over loss is heightened by the fact that her father's sister, Isabella, died young. (She might also have mentioned the early deaths of Hindley and Frances Earnshaw.) Ellen responds by saying that she herself is still strong and hardly forty-five, while her own mother lived to the age of eighty. Cathy is not biologically related to Ellen Dean, however, but to a woman who died at the age of nineteen—which is only a few years older than Cathy's present age. No wonder she fears loss.

Cathy's refusal to explore her maternal roots remains the most conspicuous omission in *Wuthering Heights*. We can speculate on the reasons behind her reluctance to resurrect the shadow of substantial loss, beginning with the understandable fear of her own complicity in her mother's death. The fear is particularly intense, Bowlby reminds us, among children who have lost their mothers in childbirth. Heathcliff alludes darkly to this when he tells Cathy that her father cursed the day on which she was born. "Catherine, his happiest days were over when your days began. He cursed you, I dare say, for coming into the world (I did, at least). And it would just do if he cursed you as *he* went out of it" (306). Heathcliff insidiously plays upon Cathy's unconscious guilt over her mother's death and father's despair. Cathy does not respond to Heathcliff's provocation, but she cannot be unaware of his meaning. Nor can she be unaware of her father's anger at Heathcliff's role in Catherine's death. Warning Cathy to stay away from Heathcliff and Wuthering Heights, Edgar cannot conceal his hatred toward the diabolical enemy. " 'She might have been living yet, if it had not been for him!' was his constant bitter reflection; and, in his eyes, Heathcliff seemed a murderer" (256). Immediately following Catherine's death, Ellen reports that Edgar's "distraction at his bereavement is a subject too painful to be dwelt on; its after effects showed how deep the sorrow sunk" (201). These after effects include, Ellen adds, treating Cathy as an "unwelcome infant." They "redeemed the neglect afterwards" (201), but the gloomy facts of her birth compel her to repress any thought of mother. *Wuthering Heights* reveals, to recall Ellen Moers' description of *Frankenstein*, the trauma of the afterbirth, resulting in the daughter's denial that she ever had a mother.

But if, as I suggested earlier, Cathy adores her father, is it reasonable to conclude that she does not feel some resentment toward those who "neglected" the "unwelcome infant"? How do we know that her idealization of Edgar is not really defensive, intended to conceal anger? The question is difficult to answer because we don't know when Edgar's neglect of Cathy ended. The evidence that I used earlier to argue for Cathy's healthy idealization of her father can also be used to suggest her defensive idealization of him. Thus, the belief that she loves her father better than herself may strike us as suspect, along with her assertion that she will never love anybody better than she loves her father. Does she protest too much?

The possibility cannot be lightly dismissed. She becomes very distressed by the thought that she is responsible for Edgar's failing health, which itself may reflect denial. Ellen warns her, for example, that if she is reckless enough to marry Linton against her father's wishes, she might actually be responsible for Edgar's death. The fear terrifies Cathy, and she confides a secret wish to Ellen. "I pray every night that I may live after him; because I would rather be miserable than that he should be—that proves I love him better than myself" (264). But the question is, not whether Cathy loves her father, but whether the love is tinged with ambivalence; her confession to Ellen may "prove" guilt as well as love. Cathy's love for Edgar may well contain elements of guilt over her mother's death and anger over her father's early neglect of her.

Cathy's need to affirm her love for her father does not carry over to inquiries about her mother. It is as if Cathy intuitively knows what her mother was like—and prefers to remain motherless. Catherine Earnshaw Linton would hardly have been an empathic, nurturing mother. Recall Catherine's bitter accusation to Heathcliff shortly before her death: "Will you say twenty years hence . . . 'I've loved many others since—my children are dearer to me than she was' "

(195). Had Cathy come across these remarks in a journal, she would have been horrified. In short, if she knew her mother, Cathy would not wish to become a "second edition" of her.

Consequently, Cathy refuses to mourn her mother's death or seek information about her life. Several times she goes out of her way to remain disconnected from her. When she asks Heathcliff why he and her father quarreled years ago, she is told: "He thought me too poor to wed his sister . . . and was grieved that I got her" (251). Cathy refuses to pursue the subject. "Linton and I have no share in your quarrel," she responds, foreclosing her parents' history. She reacts more emotionally to Linton's mischievous narration of Heathcliff's relationship to her parents. Angered by Linton's assertion that Catherine hated Edgar and loved Heathcliff instead, Cathy gives Linton's chair a violent push, causing him to fall and experience a coughing seizure. Curiously, she makes no effort to confirm or deny his version of the truth.

Once, significantly, Cathy refers obliquely to her mother. Imprisoned by Heathcliff at Wuthering Heights and forced to marry Linton, Cathy offers to give her new husband a gold locket from her neck if he will help her to return to Thrushcross Grange to be with her dying father. The locket contains two small pictures of her mother and father when they were young. It comes as a surprise to learn that Cathy has actually worn a picture of her mother around her neck. Nothing in the story prepares us for this symbolic attachment. When Linton greedily decides to seize the pictures, claiming that all her possessions are now his by reason of marriage, Cathy resists. Hearing Heathcliff approach, she breaks the hinges of the locket and divides the case into two. She gives Linton her mother's picture but attempts to hide her father's picture. The Oedipal symbolism is evident: Cathy wishes to dispose of her mother and husband in order to preserve the attachment to her father. Heathcliff seizes Catherine's picture from Linton and jealously preserves it, while he wrenches Edgar's picture from Cathy and crushes it with his foot. After Heathcliff leaves, Cathy gathers up the shattered pieces of her father's picture and grieves over its destruction. The torn picture foreshadows Edgar's demise—he dies two pages later. It is entirely appropriate that Cathy should mourn the loss of Edgar's picture. She remains daddy's girl to the end.

Edgar has many failings, as critics have pointed out. Arguing that his rule over Thrushcross Grange is based upon physical and spiritual violence, Gilbert and Gubar link him to repressive patriarchy.[18] As a child Edgar is obnoxious, as a husband, ineffectual. Contrasting Edgar to Heathcliff, Catherine sees her husband as faint-hearted and unheroic, with veins full of ice water, unlike her own, which are constantly boiling. It is certainly true that husband and wife are mismatched. Catherine is infuriated when Edgar retreats into his library among his books. He is capable of anger and cruelty, as when he disowns Isabella for marrying Heathcliff. "We are eternally divided," Edgar coldly proclaims (183), sounding like Heathcliff.

And yet Edgar is one of the few characters in *Wuthering Heights* who grows in stature. The weak and timid child who Ellen predicts is "doomed" by his "soft" nature develops into an admirable figure, serving as Cathy's mother and father. His growing attachment to his daughter enables him to accept his wife's loss and return to the world of the living. Remarkably, Edgar never confuses the two Catherines or seeks to create his daughter into a second edition of his wife. He calls his daughter Cathy, not Catherine, so that the child, in Ellen's words, "formed to him a distinction from the mother, and yet, a connection with her; and his attachment sprang from its [Cathy's] relation to her, far more than from its being his own" (219).

Edgar remains attached, in other words, to the living and the dead. Unlike his contemporaries—Hindley, Heathcliff, and Catherine—he respects the otherness of relationships. He adores his daughter but does not seek to possess or control her. Nor does he treat her as Catherine's echo. Catherine's bitter premonition that Heathcliff's devotion to his future children will eventually obliterate his love for her is true neither for him nor Edgar; the latter remains devoted to both his wife's memory and his daughter. Shortly before Cathy turns seventeen, Edgar confides to Ellen that often he lies on the mound of his wife's grave, yearning for the time when he will be beneath it. One can only wonder how Cathy would feel if she overheard her father's remarks. Her attachment to her father is so intense that it would be difficult for her to share him with any other woman— especially with her mother. Edgar intuits this, which may account for his reluctance to evoke Catherine's memory until the final moments of his life, when his last words to Cathy invoke her mother's spirit.

"I am going to her, and you, darling child, shall come to us" (315). With that, he dies, a rapt, radiant expression on his face. Cathy makes no response, other than to sit near the death bed, brooding over her loss. She cannot fail to notice, however, that Edgar fully expects her to join them when the time comes.

Cathy's abiding love for her father makes possible her growing attachment to Hareton Earnshaw, another motherless child. Hareton is neglected by all the caretakers in his life. Neither his biological father, Hindley, nor father surrogate, Heathcliff, values Hareton for his own sake. Hindley sees Hareton as a younger version of himself and despises him; Heathcliff sees him as a younger version of Hindley and degrades him. Ellen cares for the child for the first five years of life, teaching him the alphabet, but after she leaves Wuthering Heights to accompany the newly married Catherine Earnshaw Linton to Thrushcross Grange, Hareton's education ends. When Ellen returns to Wuthering Heights sixteen months later, he hurls stones at her and curses her. His baby features, she remarks in horror, are distorted into a "shocking expression of malignity" (148). His new master, he tells her, is "Devil daddy"—Heathcliff. Ellen does not realize it, but Hareton's rage is a reaction to her abandonment of him. His angry rejection of her, in fact, is only an exaggeration of the typical responses of a child who is reunited with the mother after prolonged separation.

Hareton miraculously survives parental neglect and mistreatment; his good nature is stunted but not permanently deformed by his upbringing. Comparing Hareton to Linton, Heathcliff concludes, "one is gold put to the use of paving-stones; and the other is tin polished to ape a service of silver" (253). Brontë does not allow us to invoke either nature or nurture alone, heredity or environment, to account entirely for Hareton's development.[19] Unlike Linton, Hareton is able to form intense attachments, but not to a mother figure. Indeed, no character demonstrates consistent loyalty to a mother or mother surrogate in *Wuthering Heights*. Despite Ellen's statement that she and Hareton were "all the world" to each other (129), there is little warm recognition between them. Thus, it is not surprising that Hareton's attachment figure is Heathcliff. The parallel is inexact, but Hareton's attachment to Heathcliff recalls Heathcliff's earlier attachment to Mr. Earnshaw. Heathcliff cannot entirely despise Hareton, whom he recognizes as a younger counterpart. Ironically, Heathcliff's revenge plan is thwarted by Hareton's uncanny resemblance to Catherine, his maternal aunt. "When I look for his father in his face, I find *her* every day more!" Heathcliff exclaims. "How the devil is he so like? I can hardly bear to see him" (334).

At the end of *Wuthering Heights*, Heathcliff sees in both Hareton and Cathy features of his beloved Catherine. In pursuit of his unearthly vision, Heathcliff wills himself out of existence. "The dead are not annihilated!" (362), he tells Ellen shortly before he expires. Ignoring Ellen's advice to repent for his selfish, unchristian life, he defiantly proclaims that he has done no injustice and thus has nothing to repent. Death allows Heathcliff and, before him, Edgar, to be reunited with Catherine, the lost love object.

Loyalty is the supreme value in *Wuthering Heights*, and Hareton's attachment to Heathcliff matches Cathy's allegiance to Edgar. Both youths remain intensely attached to their father figures. When Cathy tries to tell Hareton about Heathcliff's reprehensible conduct toward Hindley, the young man stops her, asking how she would feel if her father were disparaged. Cathy instantly understands Hareton's feelings and desists, recognizing, in Ellen's words, that he is attached to Heathcliff "by ties stronger than reason could break—chains, forged by habit, which it would be cruel to attempt to loosen" (351). Only recently have investigators like John Bowlby realized the strength of these attachment chains, confirming once again, if further confirmation is needed, Freud's recognition that the poets and philosophers— and, we might add, the novelists—discovered the unconscious side of life long before the psychoanalysts did.

Some critics have been distressed by the fact that Cathy and Hareton are conceived on a less intense scale than Catherine and Heathcliff. "How Lord David [Cecil] and most other Brontë critics can take seriously the affair between Cathy and Hareton remains a mystery," Thomas Moser complains, noting that the characters in the second half of *Wuthering Heights* suffer "feminization."[20] Leo Bersani refers to the "rather boring second half of the novel," presumably because it contradicts his thesis that *Wuthering Heights* is concerned with the radical discontinuities that subvert the unity of personality.[21] Notwithstanding these criticisms, the relationship between Cathy and Hareton reveals the triumph of (re)attachment over loss, thus making possible, in Arnold Kettle's words, the "continuity of life."[22] Cathy and Hareton demonstrate the capacity for love and forgiveness; to this extent, they escape their predecessors' narcissistic entrapment. Hareton's absence of lingering rage toward Heathcliff may be unrealistic, but we are not troubled by this. The ability to forgive is finally not explainable.[23] It is ironic that Hareton, the most wronged character in the novel, is the only one who mourns Heathcliff's death. Hareton's filial love for Heathcliff remains beyond question, and out of this love arise loyalty, empathy, and strength of character.

Indeed, "Filial Love" is the title of a brief essay written in French by Emily Brontë while studying at a Brussels boarding school in 1842. One of her few surviving prose works, "Filial Love" is only four paragraphs long but eloquently affirms the commandment "Honor thy father and thy mother—if thou wilt live."[24] That such a commandment is necessary, Brontë sadly declares, reveals the baseness of human nature. It is unfortunate that human beings must be threatened to perform the "tenderest and holiest of all duties." It is a law of human nature, she insists, that parents love their children: "the hind does not fear the hounds when her young is in danger, the bird dies on its nest." Children experience a similar bond to their parents. The "virtuous soul" shuns the "monsters" who neglect their filial responsibilities. "Memory of their youth has never recalled the hopes and affection of the father whom they disobey; the long hours of patient suffering, the cares, the tears, the tireless devotion of the mother they are killing by the cruellest of deaths, turning into poison the boundless love that should have been the comfort of her unhappy old age."

Losing her own mother at the age of three, Emily Brontë was never able to demonstrate filial love toward her. Did she feel that her mother had sacrificed her life so that her children might live? Was Brontë's own death hastened by the refusal to mourn maternal loss? We have an intimate portrait of Catherine Earnshaw Linton in *Wuthering Heights* and can speculate, therefore, on the reasons for Cathy's refusal to inquire into her mother's life and death. But we do not have an intimate biography of Emily Brontë, and we know nothing about her all too brief relationship with her mother. However much Brontë may have identified with Cathy Linton, we cannot automatically equate the novelist with her character, nor conclude that their feelings about maternal loss were identical.

There is no question, though, about the unique relationship Emily Brontë enjoyed with her father or the extent to which this relationship influenced Cathy's intense attachment to Edgar in *Wuthering Heights*. Of all his talented children, Patrick Brontë was closest to Emily, and the two had many interests in common. There was a close and easy relationship between them, according to Patrick Brontë's biographers. "His golden-haired son [Branwell] in his childhood days had been his hope; in old age necessity would make Charlotte his only support; but nature had made Emily Jane his most beloved, his favourite."[25]

With the early deaths of her mother, two older sisters, and brother, Emily Brontë's attachment to life soon perilously weakened, and she became increasingly preoccupied with death, as her poetry indicates. Withdrawing from life, she never left her house again after Branwell's funeral. Within three months she was dead, of a severe cold that progressed into inflammation of the lungs. Until the very last moments, she rejected all efforts to seek medical attention. The final months deepened the enigma surrounding the "Sphinx of Literature." If she did not will herself to die, as Hindley, Catherine, and Heathcliff do, she nevertheless did nothing to fight for life. We cannot know whether she did indeed wish to die, Winifred Gérin concludes in her biography; but "if, as appears all too probable from the signs of her sorrow, her visions had deserted her, her pursuit of them beyond death could explain her rejection of life."[26] Brontë's most recent biographer suggests that a factor in her death may have been guilt arising from the belief that she did not do more to avert the deaths of her two sisters and brother.[27]

In her brief life, Emily Brontë had many experiences with attachment and loss, a subject which stands at the center of her only novel. Since the life span in her native Haworth was so short in the mid-nineteenth century—only about thirty years—she may never have expected to live beyond that age. Given, then, her family history and background, the multiple losses she experienced could not help but indelibly shape her imagination. Even as *Wuthering Heights* remains, on one level, almost impervious to interpretation, it becomes, on another level, highly accessible through attachment theory. To say this is not, finally, to explain the novel's greatness, but to find an entry into a world that is, for all its apparent remoteness, powerfully similar to our own. Like Catherine and Heathcliff, Brontë viewed death as a form of liberation, a final reunion with the lost love object. "Death's touch is to the hero what the striking off his chains is to the slave," she wrote at the end of "Portrait," her French essay on King Harold on the eve of the Battle of Hastings.[28] So different in life, Edgar and Heathcliff have a similar expression of exultation in death. The lifeless Catherine appears to Ellen as partaking of the infinite calm of the other world. Ellen herself is never happier than when she watches in the chamber of death, assured of the endless, shadowless hereafter. Born from the novelist's repeated experience with the chamber of death, *Wuthering Heights* remains a novel of resurrection and renewal,[29] a miraculous bridge between the living and the dead.

The Autobiography of Fiction: The Crime Against the Child in *Great Expectations*

Of all the stories Charles Dickens wrote, none is more haunting than the Autobiographical Fragment. John Forster, Dickens' closest friend and biographer, records how he once asked the novelist a question about an acquaintance who claimed to have seen him working as a boy in a warehouse. Forster concluded, from Dickens' prolonged silence, that he had unintentionally touched upon a painful memory. Weeks later, Dickens acknowledged that he could never forget the childhood experience, which continued to distress him to the present day. Shortly afterwards, in 1845 or 1846, Dickens wrote the Autobiographical Fragment, in which he poured forth the details of the infamous experience working in Warren's Blacking Warehouse. Forster published the Autobiographical Fragment soon after Dickens' death in 1870. Only then did Dickens' wife and children learn about the event.

The details of the story are by now legendary. John Dickens was a kindhearted but irresponsible individual who always seemed to be precipitating a financial crisis. Priding himself on his middle-class respectability, he raised his oldest son to be a "gentleman," but the dream was cruelly shattered when the family moved to London in 1823, forcing Charles to discontinue his schooling. Two days after his twelfth birthday, he was sent to work pasting labels on blacking pots in a warehouse owned by a distant relative. A few days later John Dickens was arrested and sent to the Marshalsea Debtors' Prison, where his large family, except for Charles, was allowed to move in with him. The boy continued to work in the warehouse ten hours a day, from Monday morning to Saturday night. He lived apart from his family, in a dangerous and depressing lodging house. He felt utterly abandoned by them, receiving neither financial nor emotional assistance. "No advice, no counsel, no encouragement, no consolation, no support, from any one that I can call to mind, so help me God."[1] The six shillings he earned a week were barely enough to pay for his food, and sometimes he roamed the streets with other hungry children. He continued to toil in the warehouse even after his father was released from prison, though by this time the family's financial situation had improved. Only when the father argued with the owner of Warren's Blacking was the boy taken from work and allowed to return to school. Though Dickens could not remember how long he worked in the blacking warehouse, Edgar Johnson estimates that it was no more than five months, at most. "But that had nothing to do with what it seemed to the child, or with the lasting impression it made upon the man. The boy had no way of knowing when his bondage there would ever end, or *if* it would ever end, and he was in a state of absolute despair."[2]

The theme of the Autobiographical Fragment is the child's expulsion from Eden, a fall from grace into poverty, neglect, shame, and despair. Written more than twenty years after the event, the Autobiographical Fragment poignantly captures the feelings of confusion, disbelief, and helplessness Dickens experienced as a youth. The narration is clearly from a child's point of view. Time did not soften the impact of the experience. "It is wonderful to me how I could have been so easily cast away at such an age," Dickens writes. "It is wonderful to me, that, even after my descent into the poor little drudge I had been since we came to London, no one had compassion enough on me—a child of singular abilities, quick, eager, delicate, and soon hurt, bodily or mentally" (Forster, 25). Dickens blamed his parents for taking him out of school and forcing him to endure degrading factory work. In his view, they seemed to be perfectly satisfied with him working night and day in the warehouse, even if that meant the end of his hope to educate himself and rise in the world. "My father and mother were quite satisfied. They could hardly have been more so, if I had been twenty years of age, distinguished at a grammar-school, and going to Cambridge" (Forster, 25).

Indeed, the Autobiographical Fragment dramatizes the boy's shattered pride and self-esteem, his horrified disbelief that his parents could so easily sacrifice him to shore up their own failing resources. The anguish in Dickens' voice over the impossibility of attending university anticipates the situation of another figure I will be discussing, Jude Fawley, who is denied entrance into his beloved Christminster (Oxford). But Jude is older and more self-reliant when he realizes that he is locked out of the university system. For all his despair, Jude never experiences the brutal working conditions of the Industrial Revolution. Dickens, on the other hand, suffered unspeakable humiliation by the contrast between his past happiness and present gloom:

> No words can express the secret agony of my soul as I sunk into this companionship; compared these every day associates with those of my happier childhood; and felt my early hopes of growing up to be a learned and distinguished man, crushed in my breast. The deep remembrance of the sense I had of being utterly neglected and hopeless; of the shame I felt in my position; of the misery it was to my young heart to believe that, day by day, what I had learned, and thought, and delighted in, and raised my fancy and my emulation up by, was passing away from me, never to be brought back any more; cannot be written. My whole nature was so penetrated with the grief and humiliation of such considerations, that even now, famous and caressed and happy, I often forget in my dreams that I have a dear wife and children; even that I am a man; and wander desolately back to that time of my life. (Forster 26–27)

Was Dickens exaggerating the severity of the blacking warehouse experience, blaming his parents for an economic system that oppressed countless other children and adults? He had no particular reason to distort the experience, since he did not expect the Autobiographical Fragment to see the light of day. Nevertheless, we know that all narratives, including those that claim to be objective or autobiographical, contain elements of unreliability. Childhood memories, furthermore, are subject to particular distortion in later life. The recent controversy over Freud's seduction theory, for example, has highlighted the vexing problem of separating fact from fiction, historical from psychological reality.

Two recent critical studies suggest that, whatever the historical reality might have been, Dickens indeed held his parents, particularly his mother, responsible for his humiliating childhood experience. In *Dickens and Women* (1983), Michael Slater points out the inconsis-

tency between Dickens' bitterness toward his mother in the Autobiographical Fragment and the lack of corroborating evidence found
either in his letters or in reminiscences of him by others. Based on a
reading of the Autobiographical Fragment, Slater concludes that an
"enduring sense of horrified dismay and ultimate betrayal—such feelings as these must, at the deepest level, have been those of Dickens
towards his mother for the rest of his life."[3] These feelings, Slater
continues, surface in the long line of bad mothers who appear in
Dickens' stories. Gwen Watkins' psychoanalytic study, *Dickens in
Search of Himself* (1987), similarly argues that, although there is no
way to discover from actual biographical evidence whether Dickens
was the child of a neglectful mother, this is precisely the theme that
emerges from his fictional writings.[4] Both critics agree that Dickens
believed he was raised by a mother unable to give him the love and
support he needed.

Historical evidence suggests that if Dickens' parents were actually
indifferent to his welfare, they were not typical of their class. Although it was not unusual for working-class children to toil day and
night in gloomy factories, it was less common for middle-class children to do so. In addition, even the working-class parents who sent
their children into the factories were generally concerned for their
welfare and distressed by the working conditions. Linda Pollock has
shown in *Forgotten Children* (1983), a study of parent-child relations
from 1500 to 1900, that nineteenth-century parents were reasonably
aware of the importance of childhood and tried to protect their children as much as possible. An examination of the records of the
Children's Employment Commissions set up in England in the early
nineteenth century indicates that interviewed parents were appalled
by the long hours their children were forced to work. Not long after
Dickens' experience at Warren's Blacking, Parliament began propos-
ing legislation to limit the working hours of children to ten hours a
day and to forbid the employment of children under twelve.[5] Unfortunately, the legislation came too late to help Dickens.

As a number of historians argue, although middle-class reformers
were horrified at the long work hours for children, this may not have
been true for working-class families, to whom children's income was
essential. For these families, a child's earnings often made the difference between poverty and comfort. And yet, as F. M. L. Thompson

notes in *The Rise of Respectable Society* (1988), even working-class parents generally realized the value of a child's formal education and did their best to make this possible. "An education was a passport to respectability and a necessary ticket for entry to many trades; many fathers would pay an extra penny or so a week so that a son could be taught some additional subject like drawing, and thus get a flying start in following a father's footsteps as a skilled carpenter, shipwright, or engineer."[6] That Dickens' parents failed to provide him with such a passport remained a source of bitterness for the rest of his life.

The history of Dickens scholarship reveals an increasing awareness of his preoccupation with the child's plight. No less than *Frankenstein* or *Wuthering Heights*, Dickens' novels are haunted by the crime against the child. As early as 1953, Dorothy Van Ghent pointed out in *The English Novel* that the "child-parent situation is the dynamic core of the Dickens world."[7] Dickens was the first English novelist, Frank Donovan asserts in *Dickens and Youth* (1968), "in whose stories children and young people played central parts" and "virtually the first to introduce children into English literature."[8] Angus Wilson observes in "Dickens on Children and Childhood" (1970) that "Dickens's novel are more full than any others of parents who fail their children."[9] The only substitute parent whose influence succeeds in saving his child, Wilson remarks, is Joe Gargery in *Great Expectations* —though Joe proves to be an ineffectual father figure to Pip, as we shall see.

The most significant study of Dickens' lifelong interest in the child is Arthur A. Adrian's *Dickens and the Parent-Child Relationship* (1984). Adrian examines in detail four recurring patterns. These involve: "(1) orphans who are left to the mercy of surrogate parents, (2) unwanted or ignored children who are hurt by unfeeling or indifferent parents, (3) children who have been misguided or corrupted by their parents, and (4) children who have been exploited by unprincipled or ineffectual parents to assume family responsibilities."[10] These patterns suggest that Dickens viewed his own parents, in particular, and biological parents, in general, as unable to provide the child with a secure and loving environment, with what Erik Erikson calls the "basic trust" arising from nurturing caretakers.[11] Dickens looked to adoptive or surrogate parents—a generous benefactor, almost always male—to repair the damage caused by biological parents to their children.

On the basis of observations regarding the traumatized child in Dickens' fiction, critics have concluded that the novelist was traumatized in his own youth and remained obsessed with the subject. In his highly influential essay "Dickens: The Two Scrooges," published in in *The Wound and the Bow* (1941), Edmund Wilson argues that for the "man of spirit whose childhood has been crushed by the cruelty of organized society, one of two attitudes is natural: that of the criminal or that of the rebel. Charles Dickens, in imagination, was to play the roles of both, and to continue up to his death to put into them all that was most passionate in his feeling." [12] Wilson might have quoted two sentences from the Autobiographical Fragment that particularly convey Dickens' indignation: "I know that I have lounged about the streets, insufficiently and unsatisfactorily fed. I know that, but for the mercy of God, I might easily have been, for any care that was taken of me, a little robber or a little vagabond" (Forster, 29–30). That Dickens strongly identified in his fiction with robbers and vagabonds is beyond doubt. Other critics have agreed with Wilson, arguing, as Edgar Johnson does, that Marshalsea and Warren's Blacking had a formative influence on Dickens' life.

Nevertheless, one of Dickens' most persuasive psychoanalytic critics, Albert D. Hutter, has questioned whether the warehouse experience could have the status of a "formative trauma." In "Reconstructive Autobiography: The Experience at Warren's Blacking" (1977), Hutter suggests that Edmund Wilson, Johnson, and other critics overvalue external events and underplay the extent to which they mobilize much earlier fantasies and conflicts within the child. When psychoanalysts speak of formative influences, Hutter reminds us, they usually emphasize events in the first few months and years of a child's life. Dickens' personality was probably well formed by the time he started work at Warren's. Gwen Watkins (who does not cite Hutter's article) makes a similar point, arguing that most children would survive such an experience without permanent damage if they believed, as Dickens apparently did not, that they were loved by their parents.

And yet we know from recent history that formative traumas may occur later in life. The prevalence of post-traumatic stress disorder confirms this. The traumatic event can be reexperienced in a number of ways, and, according to *DSM-III*, the disorder can occur at any age. A formative trauma, then, is not limited to childhood. Just as

Vietnam veterans are at greater risk in developing post-traumatic stress disorder if they or their families are unable to talk about the severity of the war experience, so might Dickens have been more vulnerable by his inability to discuss his experience at Warren's Blacking with his family and friends.

In emphasizing the traumatic nature of the warehouse experience, we must remember that Dickens was not merely a passive victim. He was also an active, resourceful person, coping with what Erikson would call a "normative crisis" of adolescence. Hutter writes: "we need to see Warren's both as something that happened to Dickens and as something he did to himself, something that he used positively in his own self-development."[13] Viewed from this perspective, a developmental crisis can provide the opportunity to convert trauma into triumph.

Consequently, we need to view Dickens' experience as a traumatic and triumphant event: traumatic in that it forever shattered the boy's conception of the world, triumphant in that it demonstrated his own inner resources. The ambiguity of the event was bound to confuse him, and he could not decide whether he was a passive victim or an active hero. Given his fierce desire to rise in the world, we can understand his wish to play down his competitive strivings while he was employed at Warren's. To admit being an ambitious young gentleman, grandiosely self-important and entitled to the rights and privileges he had been unfairly denied in his childhood, might threaten the reader's identification with him.

We also need to recognize the fictionality of autobiography and the autobiography of fiction. Even in his most autobiographical disclosures, Dickens was reluctant to reveal the figure behind the veil. Unlike Forster, who confidently concluded that he could separate fact from fiction, we must remain more skeptical in reconstructing the novelist's life. Dickens himself was at once candid and evasive in his autobiographical disclosures. "It does not seem a tithe of what I might have written, or of what I meant to write," he tantalizingly observes at the end of the Autobiographical Fragment (Forster, 39). It is idle to speculate on what the rest of the story was or why he decided to break off writing the Autobiographical Fragment. No doubt his novelistic instinct saw the possibility of fictional development in *David Copperfield,* one of his two novels written in the first person. But before turning to *Great Expectations,* the other first-person novel which dramatizes a boy's struggle to overcome his traumatic childhood in order to become a gentleman, we must understand what Dickens prepared to reveal—and conceal—about his early developmental crisis.

The victimized child Dickens portrays in the Autobiographical Fragment resembles another early nineteenth-century character who suffers injury and rejection. In both stories we sympathize with unformed youths who are suddenly wrenched from their homes, inexplicably abandoned by their parents, forsaken for more favored siblings, and rendered into social outcasts. They are children of singular abilities, quick, eager, delicate, easily hurt. Their exquisite sensibility naturally sets them apart from their contemporaries. In an evil hour they are cast away and deprived of the pleasure and protection enjoyed by other children of their age. No one has compassion on them. Thwarted in their efforts to improve themselves through education and culture, they remain inconsolable in their grief and humiliation, unable to confide their disgrace to anyone. Repeated protestations to their fathers prove futile. Forced to search for food and shelter and to contend with innumerable indignities, they slowly degenerate into almost animal-like behavior. Feelings of loneliness, resentment, and self-contempt crush their spirit. Both come to regard themselves as Cains, banished forever from the human community.

It may seem an exaggeration to compare Dickens' self-portrait in the Autobiographical Fragment with the Frankenstein Creature. But parallels exist, both in Shelley's plot and Dickens' narrative and in their emphasis upon the victimization of an innocent child. In both stories we see a child abandoned by his parents, deprived of love and protection at a crucial developmental stage, and consumed by unspeakable shame. The protagonists return obsessively to the scene of the crime in order to understand what happened. They cannot redress past crimes, however. Victimized by his own rage, the Frankenstein Creature finally acts out the hateful identity his creator has defined for him. No Frankenstein Creature, Dickens nevertheless seemed surprised that he did not become a robber or vagabond. He might also have become a monstrous narcissist, driven by rage and wounded pride.

Dickens generally succeeds in controlling his indignation in the

Autobiographical Fragment, but anger occasionally breaks through. Reluctant to censure his father, Dickens first praises him, then sadly observes that "he appeared to have utterly lost at this time the idea of educating me at all, and to have utterly put from him the notion that I had any claim upon him, in that regard, whatever." The next sentence is more damning. "So I degenerated into cleaning his boots of a morning, and my own; and making myself useful in the work of the little house; and looking after my younger brothers and sisters (we were now six in all); and going on such poor errands as arose out of our poor way of living" (Forster, 16). Even as Dickens strives to temper his criticisms, he uses the word *degenerated*, evoking the seething indignation of the Frankenstein Creature, oppressed by Victor, or of Hareton, tyrannized by Hindley or Heathcliff. The word seems strangely inconsistent with the rest of the sentence, which catalogues the usual household activities a youth may be required to perform in a large family. Dickens' anger reflects, not the physical indignities the Frankenstein Creature or Hindley is forced to endure, but the psychological indignities arising from shattered self-esteem and feelings of entitlement. In another passage Dickens recalls working at Warren's and seeing his father, now out of prison, enter the warehouse. "I saw my father coming in at the door one day when we were very busy, and I wondered how he could bear it" (Forster 37).

Dickens' anger toward his mother is even sharper. After beginning with an obligatory denial of anger, he makes no attempt to praise his mother before criticizing her readiness to return him to the blacking warehouse. "I do not write resentfully or angrily: for I know how all these things have worked together to make me what I am: but I never afterwards forgot, I never shall forget, I never can forget, that my mother was warm for my being sent back" (Forster, 38). The intensity of the rhetoric, the insistence upon never forgetting his mother's actions, captures Dickens' outrage. The word *warm* carries ironic connotations; far from being a warm, nurturing mother, Mrs. Dickens stands condemned for abandonment, even betrayal. In a letter to Washington Irving, Dickens described himself as a "very small and not-over-particularly-taken-care-of boy" (Forster, 7), and this is the way he portrays himself throughout the Autobiographical Fragment.

Dickens was unable to forgive those who were responsible for his employment at Warren's Blacking Warehouse, and he recasts the entire episode in imagery of crime and punishment. The specter of debtors' prison loomed throughout Dickens' childhood, symbolizing not only the danger of financial catastrophe, but a deficit of parental empathy and support. John Dickens' last words to his son before being carried off to prison were to the effect that "the sun was set upon him for ever"; the novelist recalls that his own heart was also broken (Forster, 20). It must have been especially hard for a child to express anger toward a father who now was sitting disgraced in prison. Wasn't the father punished enough without having to face the additional humiliation of his son's angry words? But where, then, did Dickens' anger and desire for revenge go?

Not into the Autobiographical Fragment, at least not directly. In writing about his past, the adult Dickens could not help portraying himself as an innocent boy, crushed by adversity, unable to pursue the aspirations rightfully destined to him by reason of birth, class, and natural talent. At one point he parenthetically compares himself to a "small Cain . . . except that I had never done harm to any one" (Forster, 28). It would be unreasonable to assume, of course, that the child had never harmed anyone or never expressed, in thought or deed, anger or jealousy. To cite one example, Dickens told Forster that when his older sister Fanny was sent to the royal academy of music, he experienced the event as a "stab to his heart," since he felt denied the opportunity of returning to school. When Fanny won a prize, Dickens burst into tears. "I could not bear to think of myself —beyond the reach of all such honourable emulation and success. The tears ran down my face. I felt as if my heart were rent." He then quickly adds, and Forster concurs, "There was no envy in this" (Forster, 36–37). Yet, as Hutter observes, Dickens protests too much. In *Frankenstein* we recall the Creature's murderous rage upon confronting the favored William, who smugly invokes the protection of the powerful father against the claims of the despised son. Dickens does not cast Fanny into a William Frankenstein, but he does cast himself into an innocent, abandoned creature, a martyr. And he never stopped believing that his family had betrayed him.

Dickens claimed to have enjoyed his parents' protection, only to lose it; but we can now question whether he ever had his mother's love during the crucial formative years of his life. It is not the absent mother who appears in Dickens' novels, as she does in *Frankenstein* and *Wuthering Heights*, but a sadistic mother, who narcissistically injures her son. We cannot determine conclusively whether Dickens' feelings of inferiority arose for the first time from his experiences at Warren's Blacking or at a much earlier date; but we can say that he portrays children who have been repeatedly denied maternal love, paternal support, and healthy mirroring.

Dickens recognized a split in his personality that seemed to arise over wounded self-esteem, and he was determined to maintain his distance from the other workers at Warren's Blacking, lest he be viewed as one of them. "Though perfectly familiar with them, my conduct and manners were different enough from theirs to place a space between us. They, and the men, always spoke of me as 'the young gentleman' " (Forster, 30). The young gentleman kept his own counsel and did his own work, knowing that if he could not work as hard as the other laborers, he would incur their contempt.[14] He wanted the workers to know that he was different from them. When a woman rebelled against his title of the "young gentleman," another worker rushed to his defense and upheld his privileged position. It must have seemed an empty victory, however, for he still could not imagine rescue from such an existence.

Years later, long after rescue had finally come, Dickens returned imaginatively to the scene of Warren's, replaying in fiction what he could convey only fragmentarily in autobiography. Like other novelists, he found autobiography too limiting. In fiction he was able to reveal the details he had largely concealed in autobiography, including the traumatic and triumphant implications of his experiences in the blacking warehouse.

Dickens' humiliation, which his characters share with the same intensity, strikingly resembles Kohut's definition of narcissistic rage:

Narcissistic rage occurs in many forms; they all share, however, a specific psychological flavor which gives them a distinct position within the wide realm of human aggressions. The need for revenge, for righting a wrong, for undoing a hurt by whatever means, and a deeply anchored, unrelenting compulsion in the pursuit of all these aims which gives no rest to those who have suffered a narcissistic injury—these are features which are characteristic for the phenomenon of narcissistic rage in all its forms and which set it apart from other kinds of aggression.[15]

Dickens was hardly a narcissistic person, if by the term we mean a grandiose individual lacking in empathy. Quite the opposite: he was among the most compassionate of writers. No novelist was more sympathetic to the strivings of ordinary men and women, and no writer worked harder, publicly and privately, to diminish suffering and eradicate injustice. At the same time, however, there was in Dickens a darker side, exhibiting some of the characteristics we now associate with narcissistic injuries, including rage, the "secret agony" of his soul he never permitted himself to forget.

Psychoanalysts have postulated several driving forces behind rage, including (1) converting a passive experience into an active one, (2) identifying with the aggressor, and (3) seeking revenge for past humiliations. Freud noticed that, contrary to what might be predicted by the pleasure principle, shell-shocked soldiers often relived their traumatic injuries. This led him to advance, in *Beyond the Pleasure Principle* (1920), the repetition compulsion principle, in which an individual converts a passive experience into an active one for the purpose of mastery.[16] Anna Freud used the phrase *identification with the aggressor* to describe how children learn to imitate the sadistic actions of their parents. "By impersonating the aggressor, assuming his attributes or imitating his aggression, the child transforms himself from the person threatened into the person who makes the threat."[17] More recently, Robert Stoller has stated that the motive of humiliation exists in all acts of perversion. "By *humiliation*, I mean the mechanism, within the script that makes up the excitement, of revenge—humiliating another as payment for others' having humiliated one."[18]

Dickens is understandably loath to humiliate his humiliators in the Autobiographical Fragment, and he must have been fearful of unleashing the rage engendered by Warren's Blacking. The most beloved novelist of his time did not want to appear vindictive or ungenerous to his loyal readers. He realized, moreover, that he was not the only one who suffered during the period described in the Autobiographical Fragment. His father was, after all, sitting disgraced in prison, while his mother was overworked by the demands of a large family. In addition, Dickens knew that the complicated story of untamed ambition, wounded pride, and yearning for success—a story we would today subsume under the category of narcissism—is exceedingly risky to disclose.

For Victorian novelists, the story of narcissism was no less problematic than that of sex. As Kohut notes, narcissism calls into question our deeply ingrained value system, which extols altruism and disparages egotism and self-concern. "I think that the overcoming of a hypocritical attitude toward narcissism is as much required today as was the overcoming of sexual hypocrisy a hundred years ago" ("Thoughts on Narcissism and Narcissistic Rage," 365). But it is not clear whether it is possible to overcome this "hypocritical" attitude, since the line between healthy and unhealthy narcissistic strivings is so unclear. Dickens must have realized the difficulties of such an undertaking, which required firm narrative distance and fictional disguise. For an author driven by prodigious hunger for fame, enormous talent, and a consuming need to rise from the world of Warren's Blacking to become a young gentleman, the proper story about the pursuit of great expectations was not in an autobiographical fragment but in a novel.

Few novels have received closer psychoanalytic scrutiny than *Great Expectations* (1860), Dickens' masterpiece. Noting the varying degrees of depth and profundity of this criticism, Leonard Manheim, the founder of two major journals in the field, *Literature and Psychology* (1951) and *Hartford Studies in Literature* (1967), lamented that, with few exceptions, the state of Dickens psychoanalytic criticism "seems to be approaching the point of no return which characterized the gradual demise of the New Criticism." [19] Manheim was particularly concerned about the tendency of psychoanalytic literary scholars to avoid Freudian and immediate post-Freudian theory in favor of dissident schools. Oddly enough, no psychoanalytic critic, either from a classical or contemporary point of view, has explored the subject of narcissism in *Great Expectations*.

Dickens offers in *Great Expectations* a parable of the narcissistic condition. As the novel opens, Pip gazes upon the tombstones of his mother, father, and five brothers; the gloomy churchyard cemetery mirrors his bereavement. Pip has been adopted by his older sister, a physically violent and verbally abusive termagant who employs an instrument of torture called the "Tickler" with which she brings him up "by hand." Pip is one of the earliest abused children in literature, and his story demonstrates the dynamics of child abuse. His loving but ineffectual father figure, Joe Gargery, remains unable to prevent severe injury to the child. Pip's world is literally turned upside down when a convict enters his life and forces him to break the law. Introduced into the artificial world of Miss Havisham, an embittered woman who raises her adopted daughter, Estella, to "break men's hearts," Pip suffers unspeakable humiliation. The three women treat him as an object of ridicule and scorn, an identity he comes to accept. Aided by a mysterious benefactor, Pip pursues his great expectations in London, only to become subtly corrupted by false ideals. The arrival of the convict Magwitch shatters Pip's illusions and marks the beginning of his renunciation of ambition. At novel's close he is sadder but wiser.

A summary of *Great Expectations* cannot capture, however, the unresolved narcissistic tensions in Pip's life. His ambition is gradually tamed and transformed into more realistic strivings, but he can make peace with his tormentors only after unleashing frightful violence. Torn between gratitude toward his supporters, on the one hand, and rage toward his enemies, on the other, Pip alternately engages in idealization and devaluation. The characters whom he most admires at the end, such as Joe and Biddy, are precisely those who seem the least convincing to us, aesthetically and psychologically. Pip's idealization of Estella remains problematic, reflecting either pathological narcissism (Kernberg) or a developmental arrest (Kohut). Pip retains our sympathy even during his fall from grace, but there is a darker, unredeemed side, embodied in the sinister Orlick, Pip's disavowed self. The two characters haunt and hunt each other, highlighting grandiosity and rage. Their struggle to the death recalls, as we have seen, another story of monstrous revenge.

Like the Frankenstein Creature, Pip has no mother, but he must endure the humiliation of a stepmother whose cruelty exceeds that of any Gothic figure. The opening description of Mrs. Joe seems a parody of the phallic castrating woman. "She was tall and bony, and almost always wore a coarse apron, fastened over her figure behind with two loops, and having a square impregnable bib in front, that was stuck full of pins and needles. She made it a powerful merit in herself, and a strong reproach against Joe, that she wore this apron so much."[20] With her ever-present "Tickler," a cane worn smooth by its collisions with Pip's frail body, Mrs. Joe is a figure out of a nightmare. Obsessed with order, cleanliness, and control, she has, in Pip's words, "an exquisite art of making her cleanliness more uncomfortable and unacceptable than dirt itself" (54). With her sexual sadism, rigid need for omnipotent control, phallic hardness, and contempt for masculine softness, Mrs. Joe is the forerunner of a long tradition of castrating women, culminating in Ken Kesey's "Big Nurse" in *One Flew Over the Cuckoo's Nest*. Mrs. Joe's method of cutting bread and butter reveals her oral aggression and wish to injure her family. "First, with her left hand she jammed the loaf hard and fast against her bib— where it sometimes got a pin into it, and sometimes a needle, which we afterwards got into our mouths" (42). As Ian Watt notes, the hundreds of references to food and drink make *Great Expectations* one of the most oral of novels, and a character's attitude toward eating has moral and psychological significance.[21]

Treating Pip as if he were, in the words of Mr. Hubble, "Naterally wicious" (57), Mrs. Joe is the evil stepmother of mythology and folklore and the narcissistic mother of psychiatric literature. She is totally self-preoccupied: she repeatedly bemoans her fate, deprecates her husband and stepchild, and flies into a rage at the least provocation. Mrs. Joe never thinks about her deceased parents and brothers, never attempts to conceal from Pip her wish that he, too, were dead. Pip experiences her rejection as another indication that he never should have been born. Her lack of mirroring and confirming responses, withholding of love and approval, and association of Pip's natural curiosity with criminality, all contribute to the boy's narcissistic injury. The subject of mothering is so painful to Pip that he never allows himself to imagine what his biological mother was like or whether all mothers conform to the image of Mrs. Joe. His refusal to call her either "mother" or by her first name (which is, ironically, their mother's name) suggests the cold impersonality of their relationship.

Only when Pip travels to Satis House and is humiliated by Miss Havisham and Estella does he give vent to years of pent-up bitterness and rage. Crying, kicking the brewery wall, twisting his hair, he offers one of the most moving commentaries found anywhere on the outrage of child abuse:

My sister's bringing up had made me sensitive. In the little world in which children have their existence whosoever brings them up, there is nothing so finely perceived and so finely felt, as injustice. It may be only small injustice that the child can be exposed to; but the child is small, and its world is small, and its rocking-horse stands as many hands high, according to scale, as a big-boned Irish hunter. Within myself, I had sustained, from my babyhood, a perpetual conflict with injustice. I had known, from the time when I could speak, that my sister, in her capricious and violent coercion, was unjust to me. I had cherished a profound conviction that her bringing me up by hand, gave her no right to bring me up by jerks. Through all my punishments, disgraces, fasts and vigils, and other penitential performances, I had nursed this assurance; and to my communing so much with it, in a solitary and unprotected way, I in great part refer the fact that I was morally timid and very sensitive.(92)

Given Mrs. Joe's deficient mothering, it is remarkable that Pip is able to retain, much less develop, his natural sensitivity, trust, loyalty, hopefulness, and capacity for love. To this extent, Pip's innate deli-cacy of feeling recalls that of the Frankenstein Creature and Hareton. To judge from *Great Expectations* (and the Autobiographical Frag-ment), Pip's (and Dickens') exquisite sensitivity does not appear to arise from his maternal legacy. That Pip is so unlike his sister, with whom he counteridentifies in almost every way, remains one of the surprises of the story. For often—too often—children internalize precisely those qualities in their parents that are most disliked, such as a violent temper, overcontrolling behavior, or empathic lapses. Mrs. Joe is indeed a violent, overcontrolling, unempathic person, and Pip needs to guard against the internalized bad mother.

Why doesn't Joe Gargery, the tender-hearted blacksmith, rush to Pip's defense? Joe is one of the most paradoxical characters in *Great Expectations*. He demonstrates Dickens' intuitive awareness that an abusive parent cannot terrorize a child without a spouse's complicity. Joe is a "mild, good-natured, sweet-tempered, easy-going, foolish, dear fellow—a sort of Hercules in strength, and also in weakness" (40). Pip loves Joe and values his tender simplicity, but he cannot understand why the powerful blacksmith does not make more of an effort to protect him. Not that Joe fails to try: he catches Pip when Mrs. Joe hurls him like a connubial missile, and he is quite willing to bear as much physical abuse from his wife as possible in the hope that the boy will be spared. Why, then, cannot Joe defuse his wife's terrible violence?

Dickens offers some clues into Joe's personality. The early section

of *Great Expectations* reads as much like a psychiatric case history as
a grim fairy tale. Joe's father, a blacksmith, was an alcoholic, unmercifully battering his wife and son. Several times the two victims ran
away, only to be caught and dragged home, where the vicious cycle
would repeat itself. Joe was taken out of school and forced to work in
the forge to support the family, and when his father died from an
apoplectic fit, he continued to support his mother. After his mother's
death, Joe fell in love with Pip's sister, generously inviting her to
bring the boy along to the forge. Joe's loyalty to his family reflects,
as he himself observes, a conscious decision not to repeat his father's
violent behavior. "I see so much in my poor mother, of a woman
drudging and slaving and breaking her honest hart and never getting
no peace in her mortal days, that I'm dead afeered of going wrong in
the way of not doing what's right by a woman, and I'd fur rather of
the two go wrong the t'other way, and be a little ill-conwenienced
myself" (p. 80). Since Pip is more than a little inconvenienced by
Joe's passivity, we need to ask why he remains strangely powerless.

Joe's own explanation remains contradictory. He says, to begin
with, that he fears his own potential violence, but he has no trouble
using his vast strength defensively against Orlick, when the journey-
man threatens Mrs. Joe. Why does Joe defend his wife but not his
stepson? Surely Pip is more vulnerable than Mrs. Joe. If Joe can
defeat Orlick, why cannot he prevent Mrs. Joe from abusing Pip?
How can Joe claim that Mrs. Joe is a "fine figure of a woman" (78)
when everyone else knows that she is a shrew? If, as he maintains, he
sees his wife as a version of his beloved mother, then either Mrs. Joe
is less monstrous than Pip firmly believes, or Joe's mother is less
noble than her son pretends. In either case, we cannot reconcile the
blacksmith's idealized portrait of Mrs. Joe with the woman who is
always on the rampage. Nor can we understand his gigantic helplessness.

On the basis of his admissions and family dynamics, Joe is implicated in his wife's sadistic treatment of Pip. An abused child, he seems
to have chosen a spouse who resembles his abusive father. Unable to
defend himself from a battering father, Joe prefers not to defend Pip
from a battering stepmother. From the viewpoint of ego psychology,
Joe identifies with the aggressor, suggesting his unconscious collusion
with his wife's violence. Joe chooses to be helpless against his wife's

onslaught, chooses to allow Pip to be abused. Bartleby's maddening refrain, "I would prefer not to," seems relevant to Joe's passive-aggressive behavior. Ironically, his passivity infuriates his wife, further endangering Pip.

Admittedly, the interpretation of Joe as a passive aggressive sharply disagrees with the prevailing critical view. Most critics would agree with Curt Hartog's observation that Joe provides a "model of masculine gentleness that goes far toward shaping Pip's character." Hartog also notes that Joe teaches Pip "how to bear suffering by the example of his own patience before his shrewish and dominating wife."[22] Lawrence Jay Dessner similarly argues that Joe is the most self-sacrificing of men, "incapable of anger."[23] This is certainly the view to which Pip subscribes, at least on a conscious level, and he declares repeatedly his love for Joe, the best and noblest of men. Nor can it be denied that Joe is empathic and understanding. He is always eager to comfort Pip, nurse him when he falls ill, and pay his debts at the end of the novel. No matter how ungrateful Pip grows toward Joe, no matter how the young gentleman recoils from the blacksmith's lack of education and genteelness, Pip expects and receives Joe's blessing. And Joe is always ready to forgive Pip, just as Joe always forgave his abusive father. The inscription Joe wishes to place on his father's tombstone embodies the principle of love and compassion. "Whatsume'er the failings on his part, Remember reader he were that good in his hart" (77). How, then, can we suggest that Joe colludes with his wife's aggression, when Dickens strives to affirm the gentle blacksmith's Christ-like virtues?

The problem may well lie in Dickens' ambivalent feelings toward his father, whom he loved but felt had abandoned him.[24] It is risky to explain a fictional character's inconsistency in terms of the writer's unconscious conflicts,[25] but in this case biography intrudes into art, and we cannot help recalling Dickens' anguished conviction that his father had failed him. Through Joe, Dickens indicts yet finally exonerates his ineffective father. Pip is incredulous that Joe views his wife as a "master-mind" (79), a judgment that invests her with additional power and rationalizes his own passivity. Joe's abandonment of Pip is less conspicuous than De Lacey's desertion of the Frankenstein Creature, but both failures are severe enough to produce confused and angry sons. Pip's traumatic disappointment with his father surrogate produces a wounded image of masculinity, resulting in the fear of maternal omnipotence implicit in the misogynistic portrait of Mrs. Joe.[26] It is painful for Pip to acknowledge ambivalence toward Joe, and when he does so, he offers superficial reasons. Pip simply cannot bring himself to admit that he is angry over Joe's failure to protect him from a rampaging mother.

Significantly, Pip's yearning for an idealized, omnipotent father compels him to mythologize Joe into a Herculean figure. Pip needs to idealize his father in order to restore his own wounded image of malehood. Additionally, Pip's idealization of Joe repeats the black-smith's Christ-like forgiveness of his father. As if wryly to acknowledge Joe's autobiographical meaning, Dickens cannot resist introducing a private joke into the novel, Joe's otherwise inexplicable reference to visiting a "Blacking Ware'us" on his way to seeing Pip in London (244). Pip has known all along about Joe's ineffectuality and has tried hard not to express bitterness or disillusionment. From the beginning of the novel, there has been a role reversal between the two men, with Pip treating Joe "as a larger species of child, and as no more than my equal" (40). By regarding Joe as a child, Pip removes him as a competitor, and the two men, fellow-sufferers at the hands of Mrs. Joe, form a lasting bond.

Understandably, Pip has more difficulty forgiving Mrs. Joe. He cannot forgive her, in fact, until he participates vicariously in Orlick's brutal attack upon her. Since the reader's identification with Pip would be seriously impaired if his matricidal feelings became overt, Dickens shrewdly introduces Orlick, the hero's dark double, who is permitted to act out Pip's secret wishes. In chapter 1 the convict foreshadows Orlick's later arrival when he refers ominously to a terrible young man who will tear out Pip's heart and liver. "A boy may lock his door, may be warm in bed, may tuck himself up, may draw the clothes over his head, may think himself comfortable and safe, but that young man will softly creep and creep his way to him and tear him open" (38). Orlick's entry into the novel coincides with the beginning of Pip's dissatisfaction with his old way of life. Meeting at Joe's forge, Pip and Orlick instantly dislike each other, Pip explaining that "when I became Joe's 'prentice, Orlick was perhaps confirmed in some suspicion that I should displace him" (140). Pip is right in more than one way. He not only succeeds in displacing Orlick as Joe's apprentice, but also displaces his pent-up rage onto his shadowy nemesis.

Q. D. Leavis, in an article entitled "How We Must Read *Great Expectations*" (1970), dogmatically dismisses the "antics of critics searching for Freudian explanations" of Orlick's role.[27] Presumably she refers to Julian Moynahan's essay "The Hero's Guilt" (1960), which convincingly describes Orlick not only as Pip's "would-be murderer, but also as a distorted and darkened mirror-image."[28] Orlick represents a parody of Pip's upward progress throughout the novel. Orlick's psychological role in the novel may be viewed in several related ways. In Rankian terms, he is Pip's narcissistic double, personifying pathological self-love; in Kleinian terms, he represents Pip's tendency toward projective identification, the projection of rage upon another object, with whom the self then actively identifies and fears; in Kohutian terms, he represents Pip's grandiose self, which comes into existence as a defense against intolerable reality. However we view Orlick, he remains a mirror image of Pip's repressed self.

In addition, Orlick uncannily embodies the dynamics of narcissistic rage, including the need for revenge, for righting a wrong, and for undoing a hurt by whatever means. Orlick sees himself as the injured party in life, the besieged outsider, and he vows to punish his enemies. Orlick is a thoroughly abhorrent character, but his criticisms of Pip are accurate, since Pip does everything he can to thwart his rival's demand for love and acceptance. Pip cannot see that Orlick's feelings of entitlement reflect his own feelings as well. Pip is threatened by Orlick's interest in Biddy, and he later advises Jaggers to secure Orlick's dismissal as Miss Havisham's gatekeeper. Orlick incarnates the fearful rage Pip must continually ward off if he is to remain in control of his life. The imagery identifies Orlick with insatiable orality, with the wish to tear open a person's insides and devour his heart and liver. Feeding off his own rage, Orlick is one of the most malignant characters in Dickens' world. Orlick's boundless wish to avenge injury represents not only his own driving passion, but that of Miss Havisham, Estella, and Magwitch as well.

Enacting Pip's secret thoughts and wishes, Orlick alone has the audacity to call Mrs. Joe a "foul shrew" to her face (142). He calls her "Mother Gargery," a recognition of her symbolic role in the novel. Orlick alone is willing to challenge her matriarchal power, vowing to choke her into submission. His threat of violence intimidates Mrs. Joe, instantly transforming her from an omnipotent matriarch into a weak, hysterical woman. Orlick thus succeeds in magically dispelling her mythic power. Dickens does not allow us to overhear Pip's thoughts, but we cannot escape the conclusion that had Mrs. Joe's violence been challenged years earlier, she would not have continued to terrorize the helpless child.

Once Mrs. Joe's mythic power is broken, her control over Pip comes to an end. Dickens does not dramatize Orlick's savage beating of her—the account would be too violent for readers, awakening sympathy for a woman the novelist is not yet ready to forgive. Instead, we are merely told about the tremendous blow she receives on the back of her head, dealt by an unknown hand. Never again, Pip tells us, will she be on the rampage. Pip immediately feels guilty for the act, and indeed he is, through the omnipotence of thought: Orlick enacts Pip's fantasy of the taming of the shrew. Pip is implicated in the crime since the weapon, a convict's leg-iron, had been removed by Magwitch as a result of the file Pip surreptitiously brought him. Apprehended at the end of the novel, Orlick cunningly disclaims responsibility for the attack. "But it warn't Old Orlick as did it; it was you. You was favoured, and he was bullied and beat. Old Orlick bullied and beat, eh? Now you pays for it. You done it; now you pays for it" (437). Orlick echoes Pip's rage over having been bullied and denied the rights to which he was entitled. Pip is both victim and victimizer, the abused child, demanding revenge, and the ambitious young gentleman, willing to displace others in the pursuit of great expectations.

Mrs. Joe's change of heart raises a number of questions. Biddy reports how, with her assistance, Mrs. Joe placed her limp arms around Joe's neck and laid her head contentedly on his shoulder. Mrs. Joe's dying words indicate a plea for forgiveness. "And so she presently said 'Joe' again, and once 'Pardon,' and once 'Pip' " (302). Insofar as she has always regarded herself as a victim, Mrs. Joe's sudden willingness to see herself as a victimizer strains credibility. Ironically, she is now truly a victim, yet she uncharacteristically foregoes the opportunity to complain and vent her aggression. It is certainly poetic justice that the boy who has been raised "by hand" should have a hand in his victimizer's death. Dickens' cartoon depiction of Mrs. Joe prevents us, however, from taking her death entirely seriously. Dickens has it both ways by implicating Pip in Mrs. Joe's death yet softening his hero's crime, which makes possible his sister's miraculous change of heart. Significantly, Mrs. Joe's death does not release Pip from destructive mother figures, as he discovers from Miss Havisham.

Few minor characters in literature are as memorable as Miss Havisham. Secluded in a dismal house of horrors appropriately named "Satis House," which evokes its sadistic environment, Miss Havisham has tried to stop time. The clocks in her house are stopped at twenty minutes to nine, signifying the bridegroom's abandonment of her on their wedding day. The withered wedding gown she still wears every day reflects her faded, decayed life. On her dressing table lies a looking-glass, mirroring her only real interest in life. A jilted bride, she remains married to suffering. Miss Havisham has much in common with Mrs. Joe, including a cold heart, blinding self-preoccupation, and a need for omnipotent control. They represent similar images of a narcissistic mother, brooding, hypochondriacal, inattentive to the child's needs. Both women are furious with men, whom they regard as weak, ineffective, and, in Miss Havisham's case, treacherous. The two women fail Pip in important ways, provoking his murderous rage. Before dying, they seek forgiveness for their crimes against the child. Their legacy of bitterness, however, outlives them.

No character, not even Victor Frankenstein, is more narcissistic. Both are consumed by monstrous rage, which temporarily sustains but ultimately depletes their lives. But Miss Havisham nourishes her injury, believing that it is the only way to keep alive her identity. "It is Miss Havisham herself who chooses to make her betrayal the central event and meaning of her life," J. Hillis Miller observes. "And in so choosing she makes herself responsible for it."[29] Rage is the energy from which she draws her strength and the fire which eventually consumes her. The rage defends against the deeper fear of depression and emptiness. Like Victor Frankenstein, Miss Havisham projects her rage onto a creature who finally turns against the creator.

But whereas we sympathize with Victor, at least until we recognize his unreliable narration and abrogation of parental responsibilities, we only pity Miss Havisham. She has created, deliberately and systematically, a monster in Estella, who will redress her creator's grievous

injury. "You can break his heart" (89), she tells Estella, then derives
malignant enjoyment as she watches her weapon in action. Miss Havisham fully believes that she is entitled to revenge, and she cannot
imagine any script in life other than revenger's tragedy. The wish to
break men's hearts reveals the motives behind narcissistic rage: to
right a wrong, undo a hurt by whatever means, humiliate the humiliator.

The most striking quality of Miss Havisham's love for Estella is its
sadomasochistic nature. She tells Pip: "If she favours you, love her. If
she wounds you, love her. If she tears your heart to pieces—and as it
gets older and stronger, it will tear deeper—love her, love her, love
her!"(261). Real love, she breathlessly continues, is "blind devotion,
unquestioning self-humiliation, utter submission, trust and belief against
yourself and against the whole world, giving up your whole heart and
soul to the smiter—as I did!" (261). The ravenous intensity with
which she kisses Pip's hand before lecturing him on the meaning of
love intimates the insatiable orality of her desire, as if she wishes
literally to devour the distance between self and other. Miss Havisham's wish to merge with a hated love object calls into question her
brief relationship with her mother, who died young, as well as the
type of mother she becomes to Estella.

"Motherhood," Nancy Chodorow writes in *The Reproduction of
Mothering* (1978), "may be a (fantasied) attempt to make reparation to
a mother's own mother for the injuries she did (also in fantasy) to her
mother's children (her siblings). Alternatively, it may be a way to get
back at her mother for (fantasied) injuries done by her mother to
her."[30] Both of these motives, reparation and revenge, characterize
Estella's relationship to her adoptive mother, Miss Havisham. Estella
is truly her mother's daughter. Dickens captures the intensity of the
bondedness characteristic of so many mother-daughter relationships.
Chodorow and other gender theorists, such as Dorothy Dinnerstein
and Carol Gilligan,[31] argue that for complicated biological, psychological, and cultural reasons, girls have more difficulty than boys in
separating from their mothers. The consequence, Chodorow observes, is that the "mother does not recognize or denies the existence
of the daughter as a separate person, and the daughter herself then
comes not to recognize, or to have difficulty recognizing, herself as a
separate person" (103). Although these findings have been challenged

by other researchers, it appears that girls tend to experience themselves as the self of the mother's fantasy, while boys learn to become
the other.

For all her apparent independence, Estella remains hopelessly tied
to her mother. Taught at an early age to break men's hearts, she
succeeds in breaking her mother's heart. In the process, she breaks
her own. Estella is a sadistic Narcissus, coldly spurning her lovers,
and a masochistic Echo, helplessly repeating other voices. Pip sees her
as a brilliant star, but she also resembles a spectral moon, reflecting
her creator's nonexistence. She is Pip's Medusa, turning his heart into
stone. And she is, of course, the quintessential Frankenstein Creature,
as Miss Havisham discovers too late. Estella's story is not a psychiatric
case history but a how-to book illustrating the creation of a monster.
She marries Bentley Drummle, not because she loves him or expects
happiness or independence, but because she wishes to revenge herself
on her mother. Given Miss Havisham's overcloseness with Estella, it
is surprising that the young woman has anything to do with men.
Estella is always bonded to her mother; her rebellion at the end, when
she seems to turn against Miss Havisham, is in reality a confirmation
of their essential oneness.

Unlike Pip, who struggles to free himself from the destructive
influence of his two mother surrogates, Estella is remarkably accepting of the grievous narcissistic injury done to her. She makes no effort
either to understand its psychological consequences or to soften its
impact. Nor does she try to empathize with her mother's situation. In
one crucial sense she differs from other children, including Pip. Estella
has no father or father surrogate to help distance her from the symbiotic mother. In *Great Expectations* Dickens portrays a male-domi-
nated society in which, as is typical of most patriarchal cultures, the
father is conspicuously absent in matters of parenting and child care.
(The exception is the maternal Joe Gargery, but he is symbolically
absent to Pip.) The absence of a father in Estella's life prevents her
from counteridentifying with her mother or even recognizing the
unnaturalness of their relationship. Mother and daughter remain locked
in a fused relationship, and neither can imagine being other than she
is or separating from the other. Estella remains a psychological fatal-
ist. The best she can do to control her appetite for revenge is warn Pip
to stay away from her, a warning he perilously disregards.

Why, then, does Pip continue to idealize a woman whom everyone else advises him to forget? This constitutes one of the most intriguing questions in the novel. No single explanation can entirely account for Pip's obsession with her. "The unqualified truth is, that when I loved Estella with the love of a man, I loved her simply because I found her irresistible"(253). Estella's irresistibility is heightened by her unobtainability; Pip is in love with elusive, ethereal beauty, and the icy remoteness of the glittering star-like Estella makes her burn more brightly in his imagination. Indeed, inaccessibility may inhere in all infatuations.[32]

Pip's idealization of Estella may be interpreted in different ways. Classical psychoanalytic theory suggests that his infatuation with Estella is a repetition of earlier relationships with rejecting women. Estella's scornful, belittling personality, her haughty and capricious manners, remind us of Pip's stepmother. Mrs. Joe is a "foul shrew," in Orlick's words, while Estella is a "Tartar" (200), in Herbert's words. Pip's early description of Estella accurately characterizes Mrs. Joe. "Sometimes, she would coldly tolerate me; sometimes, she would condescend to me; sometimes, she would be quite familiar with me; sometimes, she would tell me energetically that she hated me" (123). The two women may be viewed, Oedipally, as phallic castrating women and, pre-Oedipally, as highly narcissistic.

A Kernbergian approach would suggest that Pip engages in a defensive idealization of Estella. Pip cannot admit that he sees Estella as cold and spiteful because this would force him to confront his mother again, also cold and spiteful. Estella's self-characterization—"I have no softness there, no—sympathy—sentiment—nonsense" (259)— applies equally well to Mrs. Joe. Both women physically and verbally abuse Pip and treat him as a "little coarse monster"(111), in Estella's disdainful words. To this extent, they transform him into a Frankenstein Creature, awakening his indignation and anger. But whereas Pip acknowledges his keen disappointment with Mrs. Joe, he cannot bring himself to renounce his pursuit of Estella, since he is masochistically attached to her. She thus confirms the "monster" identity he has unconsciously internalized from Mrs. Joe. Pip cannot entirely free himself, then, from years of pathological love for his mother. In addition, Pip's love for Estella, "against reason, against promise, against peace, against hope, against happiness, against all discouragement that could be" (253–54), parallels his stepfather's equally hopeless love for Mrs. Joe. In loving a cold, rejecting woman, Pip recreates his stepfather's situation. Joe claims that he is in love with his wife, but it is an unlikely, undramatized love.

A Kohutian approach would emphasize, by contrast, the search for idealized, omnipotent selfobjects—objects experienced as part of the self. Kohut speaks about narcissistic love, not as a pathological development, but as a developmental arrest of a normal process. If a child suffers a traumatic disappointment, he or she will experience an intense need to restore the lost unity and bliss of childhood. The child creates a grandiose self and invests unlimited power and perfection in an idealized parent, a fantasy parent, so to speak. The child searches for other idealized selfobjects in an effort to merge with their power. These idealizations must be welcomed, Kohut argues, to tame the grandiose self's unrealistic ambitions and goals. Kohut postulates two separate developmental lines, one leading from autoerotism via narcissism to object love, the other leading from autoerotism via narcissism to higher forms and transformations of narcissism.[33] Pip's infatuation with Estella reflects, then, the wish to create and preserve the image of perfect beauty and bliss lost in childhood. His belief in Estella is not inevitably self-destructive but essential for the growth of his self-esteem. "Estella, to the last hour of my life, you cannot choose but remain part of my character, part of the little good in me, part of the evil" (378). Pip remains faithful to Estella, for she remains part of his existence. She personifies his grandiose and exhibitionistic strivings, his ambitions and goals. Through Estella, Pip wishes to recover, not merely the gleam in his mother's eye, but the dazzling light of her star. Pip's overestimation of Estella represents the grandiosity that must be acknowledged and gradually tamed.

Great Expectations abounds in mirror images,[34] and nowhere is Dickens' reliance upon doubling more apparent than in his portraits of Pip and Estella, each of whom is victimized from birth by a murderous mother and an ineffective or absent father. Indeed, Pip and Estella may be viewed as reflections of the same character. "Pip cannot relinquish his desire for Estella without abandoning the idea of himself," Lawrence Frank notes.[35] Both are orphans adopted by the same woman who vows to break men's hearts. Duplicity and deception surround their childhoods; Estella is not, in fact, an orphan, and Pip is not adopted by the person he believes. Miss Havisham is Estella's adoptive mother and Pip's sham mother, and she projects false values upon both children. They also share, symbolically, the same father. Abel Magwitch, Estella's biological father, describes himself to Pip as "your second father" (337). Like Miss Havisham, Magwitch is obsessed with a single idea, to make Pip into a gentleman, and he is prepared to sacrifice his life to this end. The parental wish to provide Estella and Pip with great expectations seems motivated less by genuine love than by the need to live vicariously through the children and achieve revenge upon society. To be sure, Magwitch also wishes to repay Pip's act of kindness in the churchyard. Like Miss Havisham, Magwitch magnifies his self-disgrace, unable to forget the past. Both parents treat their adoptive children as selfobjects, thus denying their otherness.

Like Cathy in *Wuthering Heights*, Estella never attempts to discover her biological mother—and for good reason. A violent and fearful-looking woman, Molly remains an enigmatic character, and little has been written about her. Seeing her for the first time, Pip describes her face "as if it were all disturbed by fiery air, like the faces I had seen rise out of the Witches' caldron" in *Macbeth* (235). Pip learns about her from three characters, Wemmick, Herbert Pocket, and Jaggers, each of whom provides him with additional information about her shadowy past. Wemmick calls her a "wild beast tamed" (404) and relates how, twenty years ago, she was tried at the Old Bailey for the murder of a woman. "It was a case of jealousy" (405), Wemmick cryptically says, relating how she was also suspected of frantically destroying her three-year-old child to revenge herself on her common-law husband. We never learn the details of Molly's jealousy or why she believes infanticide is a fitting punishment. Through Jaggers' efforts, she was acquitted and "tamed" into service. Herbert, who hears Magwitch's side of the story, fills in some of the details to Pip. According to Magwitch, on the night when the woman was murdered, Molly told him that she would destroy their young child, of whom he was exceedingly fond. Molly then vanished, along with the child, and Magwitch assumed she kept her terrible oath. Fearing he would have to testify in court about his murdered child and thus be the cause of his wife's execution, Magwitch disappeared. After her acquittal, she also disappeared, and Magwitch never saw her again.

Jaggers supplies additional details, frequently interrupting his narration to deny any personal role in the story. Without clarifying whether the mother was prepared to commit infanticide, Jaggers explains how he persuaded her to give up the child for adoption, sparing it from the sordid fate awaiting most children of its class. Referring to himself in the third person, Jaggers declares:

Put the case that he lived in an atmosphere of evil, and that all he saw of children, was, their being generated in great numbers for certain destruction. Put the case that he often saw children solemnly tried at a criminal bar, where they were held up to be seen; put the case that he habitually knew of their being imprisoned, whipped, transported, neglected, cast out, qualified in all ways for the hangman, and growing up to be hanged. Put the case that pretty nigh all the children he saw in his daily business life, he had reason to look upon as so much spawn, to develop into the fish that were to come to his net —to be prosecuted, defended, forsworn, made orphans, bedevilled somehow. (424–25)

Molly's story replays Mrs. Joe's in several ways. Both women are associated with prodigious strength and untamed nature. Mrs. Joe brings up Pip by hand, while Molly literally possesses murderous hands. Both mothers are indifferent to their children's needs. Mrs. Joe's phallic Tickler and impregnable bib, stuck full of pins and needles, have their counterpart in Molly's disfigured wrists, deeply and widely scarred, and vice-like hands, which Jaggers fetishistically exhibits to Pip.[36] Both women are married to husbands who cannot prevent their adored children from maternal abuse. In short, Molly and Mrs. Joe are sisters under the skin, and they narcissistically injure their children in similar ways.

Pip and Estella share, then, similar types of parents or parent surrogates, and they look to the same adoptive mother for support. Their attraction to each other is thus also incestuous. On another level, in loving Estella, Pip may well by trying to win the love of the mother who stands behind both of them, Miss Havisham. Before he can recreate his parents, however, Pip must first acknowledge his ambivalence toward the fathers who have failed him.

Pip is particularly indignant at Jaggers, his inscrutable guardian.

Standing at the center of mystery and authority in the novel, Jaggers alone knows the secrets of Estella's mother and Pip's real benefactor. His God-like denunciations of misconduct strike terror into criminals, and he remains the one character associated with omniscience and omnipotence. Despite his formidable authority, he symbolizes the principle of benign neglect, as is suggested by the compulsive washing of his hands. He remains detached even when he knows that his intervention would be helpful. "Of course you'll go wrong somehow," he tells Pip, "but that's no fault of mine" (194). Jaggers represents another variation on the theme of the neglectful father. He intimidates Molly into giving up her child yet hands Estella over to an embittered and vengeful woman who succeeds in dehumanizing her. It is particularly ironic that Jaggers permanently separates mother from daughter while employing Molly as his own housekeeper. He does not become Estella's guardian; had he done so, he could have saved at least one child from the atmosphere of evil he knows all too well.[37]

Magwitch has also been a derelict father, though not by choice. Pip's relationship to his second father is fraught with ambiguity. *Great Expectations* opens with the terrified boy in the same position as the young William in *Frankenstein*. In both stories, a frightful creature confronts a child and demands help. Pip watches in horror as the convict devours ravenously a piece of bread, uttering monstrous imprecations. Unlike William, Pip generously befriends the outcast and averts violence. Pip later profits from his compassionate act and rises in the world. Magwitch's unexpected arrival proves shattering to Pip. No longer the innocent boy of the past, Pip, now a snobbish gentleman, recoils in horror from the creature. "The imaginary student pursued by the misshapen creature he had impiously made, was not more wretched than I, pursued by the creature who had made me, and recoiling from him with a stronger repulsion, the more he admired me and the fonder he was of me" (354).

The imaginary student is, of course, Victor Frankenstein, with whom Pip identifies. Pip's counteridentification with the Frankenstein Creature reveals the effort to deny his kinship to the alienated figure. All three characters, the Frankenstein Creature, Magwitch, and Pip, have been rendered into monsters, banished from society. Pip's reading of *Frankenstein* reveals his empathic failure toward both Mary

Shelley's "fictional" Creature and the "real" Magwitch. The parallels between the two novels are inexact but fascinating. *Frankenstein* is a novel about absent mothers and cold, rejecting fathers, the opposite of *Great Expectations*. Pip is pursued by the monster, not out of hostility, but out of love and admiration.[38] Pip and Magwitch are inextricably entwined in each other's life, each creating and being created by the other. Pip befriends Magwitch in the cemetery and inspires the convict to become a new man; Magwitch later befriends Pip and enables him to become a gentleman. Magwitch's unexpected return allows Pip to work through his feelings of guilt and reach a new understanding about the nature of monsters. Pip and Magwitch grow to love each other; to this extent, *Great Expectations* revises the ending of *Frankenstein* and fulfills its title.

Magwitch's devotion to Pip reflects elements of both narcissistic love and object love. Magwitch sees Pip mainly as an extension of himself, a means of self-vindication. "All I've got ain't mine; it's yourn," he triumphantly proclaims to Pip. "I've come to the old country fur to see my gentleman spend his money *like* a gentleman. That'll be *my* pleasure. *My* pleasure 'ull be fur to see him do it" (347). Magwitch's use of first person reveals his self-preoccupation, his inability to see Pip as distinct from himself. Magwitch does not consider whether his own pleasure coincides with Pip's best interests. Nor does Magwitch realize that he has narcissistically overinvested himself in Pip's life. By contrast, Magwitch's counterpart, Miss Havisham, acknowledges her own manipulation of Estella shortly before fire consumes the elderly woman's emotionally charred heart. One wonders whether Pip would have turned into the stony Estella had Magwitch lived with him every day. Few children would not be damaged by a parent's incessant brooding over past injustices, passion for revenge, and overcontrolling behavior.

There is a more generous side to Magwitch, however, which cannot be reduced to selfishness. Surveying Pip with a look of "admiring proprietorship" (348), Magwitch nevertheless genuinely delights in Pip's life. Of all the real and sham benefactors in Pip's life, only Magwitch offers the mirroring and confirming responses that strengthen his self-esteem. If Magwitch's insight into Pip's story is limited, his good will is limitless. Equally important, he understands Pip's initial inability to love him. Magwitch offers Pip unconditional love; and once he sees Pip, he offers to remove himself from his dear boy's life, knowing that Pip can be a gentleman without him.

Albert Hutter has remarked that "Pip seems capable of loving Magwitch only to the degree that Magwitch is helpless and endangered."[39] It's true that there is a role reversal between Pip and Magwitch, with the son now nursing the dying father. It's also true that Magwitch's death relieves Pip from the burden of living with a man whose habits and manners are so alien to his own. But Pip's idealization of Magwitch is affirmative to the extent that it represents an attempt to preserve a benevolent parent. Pip needs to believe in Magwitch's goodness and altruistic devotion. Unlike Victor Frankenstein and the elderly De Lacey, Magwitch does not finally abandon the child. Nor does the child abandon the parent, as the dying Magwitch tells Pip. "You've never deserted me, dear boy" (469).

Pip delays falling ill until Magwitch dies. The mysterious illness seems to be a nervous breakdown, Pip's self-punishment for his ambivalence toward his two fathers. In the faithful Magwitch, Pip sees a much better man than he has himself lately been to Joe. Magwitch and Joe are linked in Pip's imagination; for all their differences, the two men are versions of the idealized father. Fever-ridden, the delirious Pip hears himself say to two sheriff's men who have come to arrest him for his debts: "If you take me from here, I think I shall die by the way" (471). Can we not hear in Pip's words an echo of Dickens' father as he was being carried off to the Marshalsea Debtors' Prison? John Dickens believed, like Pip, that the sun had set upon him forever. So, too, did Charles Dickens believe his own sun had prematurely set. Through Pip's story, Dickens relived the traumatic warehouse experience but changed the ending of the script. In the recast story of *Great Expectations,* the helpless Pip, infantilized by illness, transforms the human figures hovering before him into a single image, that of Joe. By becoming a child again, Pip reenacts his sick childhood, but with a difference, for now he receives Joe's loving ministrations. No longer rendered helpless by his shrewish wife, Joe miraculously pays off the son's debts and averts catastrophe. Surely we can appreciate Dickens' private allusion to Joe's earlier visit to the "Blacking Ware'us." The father now redeems himself, transforming his past neglect into a present act of caring and rescue.

Only a Scrooge will observe that Dickens' fantasy remains the stuff of wish fulfillment, utterly remote from reality. But such fantasies are deeply satisfying, even if they subvert realistic characterization. Dickens had an unusually powerful need for idealizing relationships, and sometimes this misled him into creating sentimentalized characters who are too good to be true. Dickens' suspicion of self-aggrandizement and self-preoccupation compelled him to eliminate these qualities from his noblest characters. To this extent, Dickens shared the Victorian affirmation of self-forgetfulness as an antidote to narcissism.

Pip heals himself, more convincingly, through his commitment to others, most notably, Herbert Pocket. The two characters are, in accordance with the dominant structural principle in the novel, mirror images of each other. Herbert is the "pale young gentleman" who comically provokes Pip into a fight when they encounter each other for the first time at Satis Hall. To his astonishment, Pip has no difficulty in knocking him down. Pip takes gloomy satisfaction in the victory, however, regarding himself as a "species of savage young wolf, or other wild beast" (121). When they meet again in London, they become close friends. Pip admires Herbert's frank and easy nature, his generosity and hopefulness. Pip senses, though, that Herbert will never be very successful or rich, a premonition that proves to be less accurate about Herbert than about himself.

Like Pip, Herbert suffers childhood deprivation. They are raised by harsh mothers and ineffective fathers. "Mr and Mrs Pocket's children," Pip wryly observes, "were not growing up or being brought up, but were tumbling up" (209). Mrs. Pocket does not batter her children, but her absentmindedness is no less harmful than Mrs. Joe's battering of Pip. Mrs. Pocket's obliviousness to her children at first seems comic; the seven of them are in various stages of tumbling as the mother leisurely reads a book and engages in polite discussion with Pip. There is also something comic about her pretensions to royalty. But when Mrs. Pocket remains indifferent to the serious threats to her children's welfare, including the dangerous household instruments with which they are playing, the mood changes from playfulness to anger. " 'Good God!' cried Mr Pocket, in an outbreak of desolate desperation. 'Are infants to be nutcrackered into their tombs, and is nobody to save them?' " (217). The two young men develop a close bond, each mirroring the other's hopes. Each is necessary for the other's self-definition. Pip gloomily tells Herbert about his hopeless love for Estella and his low status in London. "I was a blacksmith's boy but yesterday; I am—what shall I say I am—to-day?" Herbert has the perfect answer: "a good fellow, with impetu-osity and hesitation, boldness and diffidence, action and dreaming, curiously mixed in him"(269).

Pip's decision to assist Herbert represents a healthy commitment to self and other. Pip sees Herbert both as a reflection of himself and as an autonomous other. Pip befriends Herbert, not in order to live vicariously through him or revenge himself upon society, as both Magwitch and Miss Havisham have done, but to aid a deserving young man. By befriending Herbert, Pip befriends himself. "It was the only good thing I had done, and the only completed thing I had done, since I was first apprised of my great expectations" (427). In the penultimate chapter of the story, Pip tells us about his happiness working with Herbert in the firm of Clarriker and Company. By this time, the owner has betrayed Pip's secret to Herbert, who is amazed that his closest friend has made possible his advancement in the busi-ness world. Pip wonders how he could have once conceived the idea of Herbert's inaptitude, until he realizes that the inaptitude was never in his friend at all, but in himself. The insight represents one more act of self-liberation.

Nor is Pip the only character who achieves insight and self-forgive-ness. Magwitch dies contentedly, with no regrets about having re-turned, under penalty of execution, to see his fine young gentleman. Miss Havisham dies, begging forgiveness from Pip for her crimes against him and Estella. In her will, she leaves her considerable for-tune to Herbert's father, as Pip has requested her to do. Pip's two mothers, Mrs. Joe and Miss Havisham, both apologize to Pip; suffer-ing teaches them to understand the pain they have caused others. Pip is implicated in their deaths and must atone for them. Twice he has had premonitions of Miss Havisham's death, the first time after Estella humiliates him at Satis House, the second time after he confronts his sham benefactor to express indignation. Pip tries to forgive Miss Havisham but cannot overcome his anger. As he leaves her for the last time, an early childhood premonition of her death compels him to return to Satis House, where he sees her sitting by the fireplace. Suddenly she is engulfed in flames. In taking off his great-coat and throwing her down, Pip not only smothers the flames, but also enacts a violent sexual assault.[40] Yet rage gives way to reparation, and Pip accepts Miss Havisham's forgiveness, in turn, seeking forgiveness from Joe and Biddy for his neglect of them.

Estella also softens in time, as both endings of *Great Expectations* imply. In the original ending, Pip encounters Estella in London, where she tells him that she has been greatly changed. Pip infers from her appearance that "suffering had been stronger than Miss Havisham's teaching, and had given her a heart to understand what my heart used to be" (496). There is no hope of a permanent union between them. The original ending is powerful in its simplicity and consistent in its theme of loss. In the revised ending, which Dickens was persuaded to write by his friend Edward Bulwer-Lytton to avoid disappointing multitudes of readers, Estella earnestly seeks Pip's forgiveness and expresses the wish to remain friends. Pip sees "no shadow of another parting from her." Some critics are disturbed by the happy ending, which appears to contradict the painful sacrifices Pip has been forced to make. The haunting imagery of the revised ending is too beautiful to dismiss, however, and it is possible to justify Pip's chastened reunion with Estella.

So much has been written about the two endings of *Great Expectations* that it is difficult to contribute anything new to the critical debate. But I may observe that the controversy over the endings reflects, significantly, the dispute between the two leading theorists of narcissism. The original ending, in which Pip and Estella briefly meet each other and go their separate ways, implies the guarded approach to narcissism taken by Otto Kernberg and classical analysts. In this view, the narcissist's coldness, self-preoccupation, and shallow emotional life suggest that Estella will make an unsuitable companion for Pip. They must remain apart because Pip's idealization of Estella would only heighten her grandiosity—and perhaps his own. By contrast, the revised ending, in which Pip sees no shadow of another parting from Estella, implies the hopeful approach taken by Heinz Kohut and self psychologists. In this view, narcissism is not a pathological phenomenon but a developmental arrest. Just as Miss Havisham sees in Pip a mirror of what she once felt herself, so will Estella see in Pip a reflection of grandiosity tamed. Pip's idealization of Estella will enable her to experience healthy self-love for the first time.

Regardless of which ending we prefer, *Great Expectations* remains Dickens' supreme insight into the destructive consequences of the crime against the child. Dickens has been aptly called the "greatest literary psychopathologist since Shakespeare,"[41] and his novels reflect profound insight into narcissistic disorders. All is not resolved at the end of the novel.[42] Orlick, Pip's disowned self, remains beyond rehabilitation. After trying to kill Pip, Orlick breaks into Pumblechook's house, achieving fitting revenge on the man who earlier tormented Pip and posed as his sham benefactor. Few readers will fail to appreciate Orlick's treatment of the imposter, who has his nose pulled and his mouth stuffed full of flowering annuals. Dickens allows Pip to humiliate, vicariously, his old humiliator. Dickens knows Orlick too intimately to believe that narcissistic forces can ever be defeated in all people. There will always be Orlicks as well as imposters like Pumblechook, who hypocritically accuses Pip of "ingratitoode" toward his benefactor. There will also be sons like Wemmick, who remains hopelessly split between his public and private sides. "Every man's business," he reproaches Pip in Little Britain, "is portable property" (421). At his home in Walworth, however, Wemmick is a model son to his Aged Parent. Perhaps such splits are inevitable in a world in which authority figures obsessively wash their hands of all responsibility.

Dickens understood better than anyone the nature of the splits engendered by childhood trauma. Forster notes Dickens' conflicting sides, "a stern and even cold isolation of self-reliance side by side with a susceptivity almost feminine and the most eager craving for sympathy." In an 1862 letter to Forster, Dickens refers to his experiences at Warren's Blacking Warehouse, noting that the "never to be forgotten misery of that old time, bred a certain shrinking sensitiveness in a certain ill-clad ill-fed child, that I have found come back in the never to be forgotten misery of this later time" (Forster, 41). In *Great Expectations*, Dickens succeeds in evoking the never to be forgotten misery of an earlier time; and in doing so, he recasts autobiography into fiction and avenges the crime against the child.[43]

FIVE

The Aesthetics of Narcissism in
The Picture of Dorian Gray

Oscar Wilde's prose poem "The Disciple" offers a startling revision of Ovid's myth of Echo and Narcissus. The poem opens with the weeping Oreads mourning Narcissus' death. Attempting to console the reflecting pool, which has changed from a cup of sweet water into one of salt tears, the Oreads exclaim: "We do not wonder that you should mourn in this manner for Narcissus, so beautiful was he."[1] "But was Narcissus beautiful?" the pool asks unexpectedly. "Who should know that better than you?" the mountain nymphs answer, relating how Narcissus regularly neglected them in favor of the pool, on whose banks he would lie to gaze at his own beauty reflected in the water. The poem ends with the pool's astonishing explanation for its mournful tears. "But I loved Narcissus because, as he lay on my banks and looked down at me, in the mirror of his eyes I saw ever my own beauty mirrored."

In Ovid's account, Narcissus is the only character who may be viewed as narcissistic; in Wilde's revision, nature (the pool) is no less self-preoccupied, oblivious to the human objects surrounding it. Not even the Oreads' sympathy can rouse the pool from self-pity. Ovid treats Narcissus satirically, laughing at his vanity and self-deception; Wilde treats Narcissus reverently, admiring his youth and beauty. For Wilde, Narcissus embodies tragic beauty that approaches spiritual dimensions. The lack of critical distance between the poet and his characters parallels the absence of boundaries between Narcissus and the pool. "The Disciple" reveals Wilde's fascination with Narcissus, the artist of the beautiful, doomed by the aesthetic pleasure that enthralls him. A disciple of Narcissus, Wilde was so fond of the poem that he repeated it one night after dinner to André Gide, who quotes it without commentary in his curious book on Wilde.[2]

Hovering behind Wilde's aesthetics is the haunting figure of Narcissus, mourning elusive beauty. Narcissus figures prominently also in Wilde's short stories[3] and two of his major works: *Intentions*, his critical manifesto on aesthetics, and *The Picture of Dorian Gray*, his only novel, both published in book form in 1891. Beginning with Otto Rank, psychoanalysts recognized the importance of narcissism in Wilde's writings, particularly the theme of the double.[4] As early as 1922, Leo Kaplan commented on Dorian Gray's narcissism (spelled *narcism*).[5] Alexander Grinstein's 1973 essay on Oscar Wilde, part of a book-length study that apparently has not yet been published, reads *The Picture of Dorian Gray* as disguised autobiography.[6] Jerome Kavka's article appeared in 1975, emphasizing the early developmental failures contributing to the lack of object love in Wilde's writings.[7] Bernard Green's 1979 paper analyzes the effects of distortion of the self in Wilde's novel.[8] Two other psychoanalytic studies deserve mention: Karl Beckson's 1983 account of the sibling rivalry between Oscar and Willie Wilde[9] and Ellie Ragland-Sullivan's 1986 Lacanian interpretation of *The Picture of Dorian Gray*.[10]

What has not yet been explored, however, is the extent to which Wilde's theory of aesthetics rests upon an essentially narcissistic foundation. Wilde articulates a theory of art in which the worship of beauty, in the form of self-love, has transcendent significance. "To love oneself is the beginning of a life-long romance," Wilde writes in "Phrases and Philosophies for the Use of the Young" (1894).[11] Notwithstanding his delight in outrageous paradoxes, Wilde was intensely serious about creating a "new Hedonism" in which the aesthete worshiped Narcissus' two divine gifts, youth and beauty. No mere dandy, Wilde's aesthete is a tragic figure, willing to incur public censure and even martyrdom in the pursuit of beauty. Wilde defines aestheticism as nothing less than the "search after the secret of life"[12]—a search that recalls Victor Frankenstein's fervent longing to unlock the mysteries of heaven and earth. Both *Frankenstein* and *The Picture of Dorian Gray* dramatize the narcissistic pursuit of perfection; Victor Frankenstein's journey toward forbidden knowledge anticipates Do-

rian Gray's quest for ageless beauty. Unlike *Frankenstein*, which
repudiates the creator's monstrous egotism, *The Picture of Dorian
Gray* is reluctant to renounce self-love. Despite the protagonist's
suicide, *The Picture of Dorian Gray* remains one of the most narcissistic novels in the language.

In suggesting that Wilde's theory of art is highly narcissistic, I do
not intend to reduce a complicated theory of aesthetics to a personality disorder. Wilde was a leading artist and critic, and one does him
an injustice by searching only for symptoms of personal conflict in his
writings. His influential theory of "art for art's sake" cannot be
properly understood without an appreciation of the literary tradition,
especially his reaction against the Romantic idea of nature.[13] Wilde
deliberately used wit, irony, paradox, and exaggeration to startle and
delight his readers, and he was the most brilliant dramatist (and
conversationalist) of his age. *Intentions* affirms the fertility of Wilde's
imagination and his genius for creating unforgettable aphorisms. Dying
in the same year, 1900, in which Freud published *The Interpretation
of Dreams*, Wilde would hardly have welcomed a psychoanalytic
study of narcissism.

We can indeed infer Wilde's objections to psychoanalyzing art
from his memorable description of Whistler's art lectures to an aghast
Victorian audience. "The scene was in every way delightful; he stood
there, a miniature Mephistopheles mocking the majority! he was like
a brilliant surgeon lecturing to a class composed of subjects destined
ultimately for dissection, and solemnly assuring them how valuable to
science their maladies were, and how absolutely uninteresting the
slightest symptoms of health on their part would be" (*The Artist as
Critic*, 14). Though he identifies with Whistler's irreverent remarks,
Wilde would have opposed any attempt to dissect literature or view it
as "symptomatic" of anything other than art. He would have shared
Nabokov's contempt for psychoanalysis, viewing Freud as a miniature
Mephistopheles or "Viennese witch doctor," perpetrating a cruel hoax
on an unsuspecting public.

Nor is Richard Ellmann, the author of the latest and best biography
of Wilde, sympathetic to psychoanalysis. His monumental *Oscar Wilde*
(1987),[14] published a few months after his death, will surely take its
place next to his celebrated biographies of Yeats and Joyce as a model
of painstaking scholarship and literary taste. Ellmann's biography

demonstrates Wilde's generosity of spirit, playfulness, and creativity. Ellmann does not significantly alter our interpretation of Wilde's life or art, but he succeeds in replacing the attitude of severity that has characterized many of the biographers with one of extraordinary sympathy. Ellmann might not appreciate the comparison, but his biography is Kohutian in its empathic mirroring of Wilde's most generous impulses.

Unfortunately, Ellmann's biography remains averse to psychological interpretations of Wilde's life. The biographer implicitly dismisses any attempt to trace back the tragedies of Wilde's adult life to early childhood conflicts. We learn nothing new, for example, about Wilde's relationship to his parents or the sources of his homosexuality. Nor does Ellmann analyze Wilde's fatal attraction to people who preyed upon him. In portraying a heroic Wilde who is more sinned at than sinning, Ellmann remains silent on the reasons for Wilde's complicity in his own victimization.

Without performing the artistic postmortem that Wilde accused James Whistler of doing, we can explore the signs of illness and health in Wilde's life and art. We can examine, moreover, the underlying adaptive strategies that enabled him to transmute personal conflicts into impersonal art. The creative process was for Wilde, as it was for so many other writers,[15] a counterphobic activity, an attempt to resolve inner tensions. In worshiping beauty, however, Wilde became a disciple of a most unreliable figure, Narcissus, and sought love and admiration from the most self-centered individuals. Wilde's narcissistic conflicts were unusually intense, and they contributed to the formation of an aesthetic in which the artist takes on qualities of both Narcissus and Christ. The creative process ultimately failed to rescue Wilde from his private suffering; working against the salutary implications of creativity was Wilde's self-fulfilling belief that the artist, like Narcissus and Christ, was doomed to suffer.

Wilde elaborates his philosophy of art in the four essays that make up *Intentions:* "The Decay of Lying," "Pen, Pencil and Poison," "The Critic as Artist," and "The Truth of Masks." In "The Decay of Lying," he defines the four doctrines of the new aesthetics: "Art never expresses anything but itself. It has an independent life, just as Thought has, and develops purely on its own lines"; "All bad art comes from returning to Life and Nature, and elevating them into ideals"; "Life imitates Art far more than Art imitates Life"; and "Lying, the telling of beautiful untrue things, is the proper aim of Art" (*The Artist as Critic,* 319–20). Central to Wilde's theory of aesthetics is the absolute separation between art and life. The idealization of art implies, for Wilde, the devaluation of nature. He views nature as highly imperfect, even deformed. "My own experience is that the more we study Art, the less we care for Nature. What Art really reveals to us is Nature's lack of design, her curious crudities, her extraordinary monotony, her absolutely unfinished condition." By contrast, "Art is our spirited protest, our gallant attempt to teach Nature her proper place" (290–91).

Wilde emphasizes throughout *Intentions* the art-nature dichotomy, associating art with health and nature with illness. "One touch of Nature may make the whole world kin, but two touches of Nature will destroy any work of Art" (301). Nature is infectious, he continues, and must be avoided. People are interesting not for their inner natures but for their masks. Anticipating existentialist and poststructuralist assumptions, Wilde goes on to deny the objective existence of nature, arguing that people discover in nature only what they bring to it. "Nature is no great mother who has borne us. She is our creation. It is in our brain that she quickens to life" (312).

Throughout "The Critic as Artist" runs the idea that life is inevitably painful and disappointing. Wilde defines these disappointments, significantly, in purely aesthetic terms, as if he were a drama critic pointing out the defects of a play. "For Life is terribly deficient in form. Its catastrophes happen in the wrong way and to the wrong people. There is a grotesque horror about its comedies, and its tragedies seem to culminate in farce. One is always wounded when one approaches it. Things last either too long, or not long enough" (*The Artist as Critic,* 375). The only escape from the imperfection of life is through the perfection of art. "Art does not hurt us. The tears that we shed at a play are a type of the exquisite sterile emotions that it is the function of Art to awaken. We weep, but we are not wounded. We grieve, but our grief is not bitter." For Wilde, art represents a higher reality in which people experience emotions without being hurt by them. "It is through Art, and through Art only, that we can realize our perfection; through Art, and through Art only, that we can shield ourselves from the sordid perils of actual existence" (380).

What are the psychobiographical implications of Wilde's theory of art in *Intentions*? What does the theory reveal, for example, about the subjective world of the theorist? We know that every judgment has substantive and revelatory dimensions. In *Faces in a Cloud* (1979), Robert Stolorow and George Atwood argue that, insofar as the observer is also the observed, "the subjective world of the [personality] theorist is inevitably translated into his metapsychological conceptions and hypotheses regarding human nature, limiting the generality of his theoretical constructions and lending them a coloration expressive of his personal existence as an individual." [16] Personality theory is neither validated nor invalidated by the subjective elements derived from the personality theorist. "If psychologists were transcendent beings capable of viewing the world from a standpoint of unconditioned objectivity, they could approach the study of the human condition unaffected by factors that are a part of the very phenomena they are seeking to understand. Since this is not the case, however, all theories of personality will remain colored by subjective and personal influences" (18).

Literary theory, no less than personality theory, reflects subjective influences. Accordingly, we may inquire into the personal elements of Wilde's theory of impersonal art. In particular, how do we interpret Wilde's rigid separation of art and life? Why does he strenuously insist upon the autonomy of the artist? Why does he seem so contemptuous of nature, referring to her "curious crudities"? Rather than suggesting that the artist's creativity is analogous to nature's procreativity, why does Wilde refuse to concede any power or beauty to instinctual life? Why does he believe that only through art can we protect ourselves from sordid reality? What is striking about Wilde's criticism, Richard Ellmann observes in his introduction to *The Artist as Critic*, is that "by its creation of beauty art reproaches the world, calling attention to the world's faults through their very omission; so the sterility of art is an affront or a parable" (xxvii). But what is the meaning of this reproach?

Wilde's absolute dualism of art and nature, like that of mind and body, denies the interrelationship of subject and object. Had he emphasized the dialectical tension between art and nature, mind and body, he would have been on much sounder ground, philosophically and pyschologically. Wilde's dichotomy of art (perfection) and life (imperfection) reflects, from the viewpoint of object relations, a fundamental split between the good and bad self. The opposition between idealization (of art) and devaluation (of life) is a familiar pattern of narcissistic thinking. "My own experience is that the more we study Art, the less we care for Nature" (*The Artist as Critic*, 290). The problem with Wilde's aesthetic philosophy is that the artist is forced to expend valuable energy to maintain his existence in a hostile world. The artist—and, by analogy, the grandiose self—can maintain his tenuous existence only through a massive denial of his own nature.

Underlying Wilde's aesthetics is a rescue fantasy, in which the artist's creation of beauty is a refuge against sordid reality. We may recall Freud's classic essay "A Special Type of Choice of Object Made by Men" (1910), in which he theorizes that a man's wish to rescue a prostitute represents the son's efforts to rescue the mother from the father, the boy's rival in love.[17] Freud interprets the rescue fantasy in terms of the Oedipus complex, which he introduces for the first time in this essay. In Wilde's rescue fantasy, the artist must save the fallen woman from her own imperfect nature. The artist alone can transform nature into a higher reality.

Interestingly, one of Freud's most provocative suggestions, that the son wishes to have the mother for himself and present her with a child, may be seen in the magical potency with which Wilde endows his artists. Unlike promiscuous nature, the artist is restrained in his creativity; but this restraint makes the artist more truly creative than nature since, as Wilde explained to André Gide, the work of art is always unique and nonduplicable. Thus, while a narcissus flower may be as beautiful as a work of art, a natural flower is not as unique as an artistic one (*Oscar Wilde: In Memoriam*, 6). Anticipating Nabokov, Wilde insists that only the artist can create reality; only the artist can lie truthfully.

Wilde's characterization of nature reveals the child's deep disappointment with the mother. One senses, here and elsewhere, early childhood loss—not necessarily the death of a parent or sibling, but the absence of a good enough mother to create a sense of basic trust. "Nature is no great mother who has borne us." Mothers, as we shall see in *The Picture of Dorian Gray*, are identified with affectation, possessiveness, and stifling love. There are, it seems, two mothers in Wilde's writings, the devalued "natural" mother, deformed by "curious crudities," and the idealized "artistic" mother, to whom the aesthete remains devoted. The artistic mother is the "goddess whose mystery it is his province to intensify, and whose majesty his privilege to make more marvellous in the eyes of men" (*The Artist as Critic*, 373). Wilde's aesthetic theory contains hostile and reparative elements: hostility is directed at mother nature, the bad object, while reparation is achieved through the healing power of the artistic muse, the good object. Rejecting nature for art, Wilde affirms the wish for ecstatic merger with an idealized object.

Intentions thus reveals Wilde's lifelong preoccupation with the aesthetics of narcissism. It was a preoccupation shaped by aesthetic and psychological needs: aesthetic, in that it reflected Wilde's belief in art for art's sake; psychological, in that it coincided with a highly narcissistic personality structure. Wilde affirms the artist's omnipotent control, unfettered by moral, ethical, or social obligations. Art reproaches nature by creating a compensatory world where the pleasure principle is the primary motive. But beauty remains elusive and ephemeral, and the artist catches only reflections of it. Believing that real beauty inheres in artistic creations, not in natural copies, Wilde insists that the artist must be prepared to show us the masks of characters. Characters are interesting, he insists, only in their masks, not in the reality behind the masks. At times Wilde denies that there is anything behind or underneath the mask, while at other times he implies that the artist must avoid writing about deeper reality. Unmasked, Wilde's worshiper of beauty turns out to be a familiar figure. "It is only the gods who taste of death. Apollo has passed away, but Hyacinth, whom men say he slew, lives on. Nero and Narcissus are always with us" (*The Artist as Critic*, 434).

Narcissus also dwells in *The Picture of Dorian Gray*. The preface to the novel boldly echoes the same aesthetic principles Wilde announces in *Intentions*. The artist's sole purpose is to create beauty, which itself is "quite useless," neither moral nor immoral. The artist is concerned with form not content, art not life. Both *Intentions* and *The Picture of Dorian Gray* reveal the same identity theme. An identity theme, Norman Holland suggests, is the "one theme or style permeating all aspects of an individual's life."[18] An identity theme implies an unchanging self but also shows the self's ability to develop by transmuting new experiences into variations of this unchanging identity theme.

Wilde's identity theme remains remarkably constant: the worship of an elusive beauty that liberates the artist's imagination while dooming him, paradoxically, to eternal mourning. Dorian Gray unhappily discovers the same identity theme.

Wilde's aesthetician in *The Picture of Dorian Gray* is Lord Henry Wotton, the scintillating conversationalist whose witty epigrams and paradoxes constitute the imaginative center of the story. "Prince Paradox," Lord Henry delights in transforming platitudes into outrageous aphorisms. "There is only one thing in the world worse than being talked about, and that is not being talked about";[19] "Being natural is simply a pose, and the most irritating pose I know" (4); "I can believe anything, provided that it is quite incredible" (5); "The only way to get rid of a temptation is to yield to it" (18); "It is only shallow people who do not judge by appearances" (22). Lord Henry voices Wilde's most strongly held views on art, including the belief that "Beauty is a form of Genius—is higher, indeed, than Genius, as it needs no explanation" (21). Like Wilde, Lord Henry idealizes art and devalues nature, and he displays an aversion to quotidian reality. "Don't squander the gold of your days," he tells Dorian, "listening to the tedious, trying to improve the hopeless failure, or giving away your life to the ignorant, the common, and the vulgar. These are the sickly aims, the false ideals, of our age" (22). As in *Intentions, The Picture of Dorian Gray* simultaneously idealizes art and devalues life.

Through Lord Henry, Wilde delivers some of the sharpest satirical commentary found anywhere in his writings. Significantly, one of Lord Henry's favorite targets is the family. "I don't care for brothers," he tells Basil Hallward. "My elder brother won't die, and my younger brothers never seem to do anything else." When Basil expresses indignation over the remark, Lord Henry backs off, saying he was not quite serious. "But I can't help detesting my relations. I suppose it comes from the fact that none of us can stand other people having the same faults as ourselves" (8–9). The remark is unusually self-disclosing, suggesting that Lord Henry's devaluation of others stems from self-devaluation. So too does narcissism, excessive self-preoccupation, stem from low self-esteem. The narrator, whose authorial voice is usually indistinguishable from Lord Henry's, later elaborates on the theme of intergenerational strife: "Children begin

by loving their parents; as they grow older they judge them; sometimes they forgive them" (66).[20]

In addition, women and marriage come under Lord Henry's satirical attack. The "one charm of marriage," he tells Basil, "is that it
makes a life of deception absolutely necessary for both parties" (4).
Although the "both" removes women from special attack, the novel
is filled with misogynistic statements uttered by Lord Henry, the
narrator, and Dorian. Lord Henry comments, for example, on wom-
en's fondness for using the word *always*. "Always! That is a dreadful
word. It makes me shudder when I hear it. Women are so fond of
using it. They spoil every romance by trying to make it last for ever"
(23). Later he tells Dorian that "women, as some witty Frenchman
once put it, inspire us with the desire to do masterpieces, and always
prevent us from carrying them out" (79). Evidently, Lord Henry is
not "always" bothered by the dreadful word he associates with women.

Strangely unmoved by Sibyl Vane's suicide, Lord Henry consoles
Dorian with the following rationalization. "If you had married this
girl you would have been wretched. Of course you would have treated
her kindly. One can always be kind to people about whom one cares
nothing. But she would have soon found out that you were absolutely
indifferent to her" (99). Dorian also rationalizes the suicide, thinking
that "women were better suited to bear sorrow than men. They lived
on their emotions. They only thought of their emotions" (91). Lord
Henry later observes to Dorian, in the most virulently misogynistic
passage in the novel, "I am afraid that women appreciate cruelty,
downright cruelty, more than anything else. They have wonderfully
primitive instincts. We have emancipated them, but they remain slaves
looking for their masters, all the same. They love being dominated"
(102).

Lord Henry's impulse toward domination is one of his most striking features. Intellectually, he exerts nearly total control over Dorian
Gray, reducing the youth into an *objet d'art*. Lord Henry's obsession
with control contradicts his statements that all influence is harmful,
perhaps suggesting his unconscious admission of guilt. "There is no
such thing as a good influence," he lectures Dorian. "All influence is
immoral—immoral from the scientific point of view" (17). At the
novel's close, Lord Henry vigorously denies Dorian's claim that he

has been "poisoned" by a book sent to him by his mentor. "Art has no influence upon action. It annihilates the desire to act. It is superbly sterile. The books that the world calls immoral are books that show the world its own shame. That is all" (218). Lord Henry's haughty punctuation, "That is all," recalls Wilde's similar mannerism in the preface: "There is no such thing as a moral or an immoral book. Books are well written, or badly written. That is all." *That is all*, like *certainly*, is a term that generally camouflages uncertainty. We have already seen how the idea of the sterility or uselessness of art dominates the discussion in *Intentions*, in which Wilde asserts that art is above or beyond the influence of life. How, then, do we explain the contradiction between Lord Henry's overcontrolling personality, on the one hand, and his denunciations of control, on the other?

Sophie Freud has defined the concept of narcissism as a "condition where one simultaneously overloves and underloves oneself, without being able to strike a harmonious balance."[21] Overlove is "one particular form of love that has grown toxic because it has grown out of bounds." Similarly, we can define narcissism as a condition where one simultaneously overcontrols and undercontrols, without being able to strike a harmonious balance. Like overlove, overcontrol is toxic.

Viewed from this perspective, Lord Henry's wish to dominate Dorian Gray, to transmute him into a work of perfect art, reveals the emotional toxicity of an overcontrolling parent. Aesthetician, philosopher, and social critic, Lord Henry is also Dorian Gray's surrogate father and thus resembles Basil Hallward, the artist who paints Dorian's portrait. Both Lord Henry and Basil "create" Dorian, the former through the seductive panegyric on youth, the latter through the painting. Both Lord Henry and Basil become surrogate fathers to the unformed youth, and both find "something fascinating in this son of Love and Death" (36).

For Basil Hallward, Dorian Gray is nothing less than the ruling passion of his life. From the moment he meets Dorian, Basil is dominated by him. The painter worships the youth as the "visible incarnation of that unseen ideal whose memory haunts us artists like an exquisite dream" (114), and he grows jealous of everyone to whom Dorian speaks. Like Lord Henry, Basil transforms Dorian into a work of art. Basil's infatuation with Dorian resembles Aschenbach's worship of Tadzio in *Death in Venice*. In both stories, the artist's infatuation with his subject has fatal consequences. Interestingly, Basil cannot bring himself to use the world *love* to describe his feelings for Dorian. The painter acknowledges only an aesthetic appreciation of his subject. In doing so, Basil falls back upon the same radical dichotomy between art and life, form and content that Wilde displays throughout his writings. Basil describes his feelings toward Dorian, not as passionate love, but as a "curious artistic idolatry." As the painter tells Lord Henry, "Dorian Gray is to me simply a motive in art. You might see nothing in him. I see everything in him" (11).

There is nothing simple, of course, about Basil's motives toward Dorian Gray. Fearing his passionate love for Dorian, he attempts to sublimate his unruly emotions into impersonal art. Art becomes, ideally, a safe container for disruptive passion. Emotions, Lord Henry notes, are dangerous precisely because they lead to heightened vulnerability. "The advantage of the emotions is that they lead us astray, and the advantage of Science is that it is not emotional" (40). Lord Henry and Basil worship Dorian in identical aesthetic terms, but Basil allows himself to become emotionally implicated in Dorian's life. Basil's vulnerability makes him the most appealing character in *The Picture of Dorian Gray,* the only one with whom the reader can identify consistently. He is also the most mysterious character in his secret longings and bitter disappointments. In the beginning he tells Lord Henry that he cannot exhibit the painting of Dorian, since "I have put too much of myself into it." Lord Henry responds: "Too much of yourself in it! Upon my word, Basil, I didn't know you were so vain" (2). Lord Henry then points out the physical differences between the rugged strong face of the painter and the delicate features of the subject. "Why, my dear Basil, he is a Narcissus" (3).

In putting too much of himself into his portrait of human nature, in fathering, so to speak, the parentless youth, Basil Hallward authors Dorian Gray's monstrous egotism. Basil resembles another character who creates a figure in his own reflection and then stands appalled by the creation. Basil's laboratory is not Victor Frankenstein's scientific "workshop of filthy creation" but a painter's studio, where the haunting portrait slowly takes on color and shape. Both creators invest themselves totally in their creations, and both are destroyed by their offspring. Basil's disillusionment is slower than Victor's, but no less definite. We feel more sympathy toward Basil, since he is not guilty of Victor's immediate empathic failure. Nor does Basil abandon Dorian; in this case, the creation abandons the creator. Yet we cannot sympathize entirely with the artist who has put too much of himself into his creation and whose own worst qualities are magnified in the portrait. Unlike Victor, Basil knows that the creator always remains part of his creation. He refuses to exhibit the autobiographically revealing portrait because he fears disclosing the secret of his own soul, and he vows not to expose himself to the world's prying eyes. "My heart shall never be put under their microscope" (11).

Basil affirms an exclusively subjectivistic view of art, in which "every portrait that is painted with feeling is a portrait of the artist, not of the sitter. The sitter is merely the accident, the occasion" (5). Curiously, Basil contradicts himself a few pages later when he argues that artists should create beautiful things but should not put their own personalities into them. "We live in an age when men treat art as if it were meant to be a form of autobiography. We have lost the abstract sense of beauty" (11). Basil's contradictory remarks reflect the confusion seen in the preface to *The Picture of Dorian Gray*, where Wilde asserts the familiar position that "To reveal art and conceal the artist is art's aim," a view he endorses in *Intentions;* yet he quickly adds an ambiguous qualification: "The highest as the lowest form of criticism is a mode of autobiography." (xxiii). Art remains for Wilde a projection screen in which the artist, no matter how carefully he guards his privacy, risks self-exposure.

Basil never entirely lays bare his soul or heart to the spectator's microscope, but he does reveal, significantly, many of the fears we saw earlier in Victor Frankenstein. Basil does not have an inflated opinion of himself, as Victor does, but he suspects that his artistic gift has singled him out for punishment: "we shall suffer for what the gods have given us, suffer terribly" (3). Basil's premonition of suffering reflects the artist's estrangement from society. The main danger for Basil, however, lies not in external but internal forces. As in *Frankenstein, The Picture of Dorian Gray* dramatizes the evil within the self: the creator is murdered by his own creation. But what precisely does Basil mean when he admits to putting too much of himself in the portrait of Dorian Gray? What is the mystery underlying the painter's identity?

One explanation, as Jeffrey Meyers and other critics have noted, is that Basil's secret passion for Dorian contains an erotic element. Meyers argues that Basil's "terrible crisis" involves his homosexual love for Dorian. Meyers notes that Basil compares his love for Dorian to the love of Michelangelo, of Winckelmann, and of Shakespeare, whose devotion to the young man of the Sonnets is described by Wilde in another story.[22] Meyers also quotes Auden's observation in his review of Wilde's *Letters* that "the artist and the homosexual are both characterized by a greater-than-normal amount of narcissism." Few analysts are now willing to claim that all artists and homosexuals are narcissistic, but the generalization does apply to Basil. Basil cannot openly express his adoration of Dorian for fear of disclosure, just as Oscar Wilde could not openly write about homosexuality in his novel. Yet during Wilde's notorious trial, the public prosecutors quoted suggestive passages from *The Picture of Dorian Gray* to "prove" the artist's homosexuality.[23] It is no wonder, then, that Basil fears baring his soul.

Basil's mystery, however, cannot be entirely explained by his homosexuality. He does not only wish to go to bed with Dorian but also to devour, absorb, incorporate him. Basil's passion for Dorian is a metaphor of the longing to fuse with an idealized self in an ecstatic merger. The desire to possess Dorian is so intense that Basil refuses at first to disclose the youth's name to Lord Henry. "When I like people immensely I never tell their names to any one. It is like surrendering a part of them" (4). Basil's real fear is not that others will learn of his secret passion for Dorian, but that the painter's separation from his subject will prove fatal. Unable to view the portrait as a transitional object, a potential space between self and other, the creator cannot live apart from his creation. Only through merger with an idealized selfobject can Basil maintain his tenuous self-esteem.

Basil's desire to possess has its corollary in the fear of being possessed, as he confides to Lord Henry. "I knew that I had come face to face with some one whose mere personality was so fascinating that, if I allowed it to do so, it would absorb my whole nature, my whole soul, my very art itself. I did not want any external influence in my life" (6). Words like *absorb* and *influence* suggest the fear of engulfment, identity loss. Later confessing to Dorian that he has become hopelessly absorbed in the youth, Basil returns to the image of Narcissus Lord Henry used earlier: "You had leant over the still pool of some Greek woodland, and seen in the water's silent silver the marvel of your own face" (114).

Unable to reconcile the powerful wish to merge with Dorian Gray with the no less intense fear of being merged, Basil Hallward finds himself in a perplexing situation. Just as the analyst must maintain proper distance from the patient, neither too close nor too far, so must the artist maintain the right distance. Basil's artistic problem of locating the proper distance from his subject is also the psychological problem of locating the proper distance in interpersonal relationships. The lack of distance between painter and subject suggests the lack of clear boundaries in the artist's personal relationships. Basil suffers, then, from the unresolved boundary issues typical of narcissistic disorders. His failure to solve the problem of distance proves fatal.

Basil's predicament recalls the child's ambivalence toward the mother. "The child's pre-oedipal dilemma," Judith Ruderman writes in her study of D. H. Lawrence, "is that his need for the mother's nurture and protection stimulates a desire to return to the womb, but this regressive dependency means that the child will in effect die, having been annihilated by the devouring, engulfing mother."[24] If the child does not learn to separate from the mother during childhood, then he or she may repeat in later life the early conflicts associated with the failure to achieve separation-individuation: blurred self-object boundaries, splitting between the good and bad mother, lack of object constancy, and problems of empathy.[25] The child must master the developmental tasks associated with separation-individuation to have a healthy sense of self.

In *Frankenstein*, we saw how Victor's urge to become a father is motivated by the belief that a new species would bless him as its creator and source. Victor expects nothing less than complete gratitude and obedience from his child. The same wish may be seen in Miss Havisham's efforts to exert omnipotent control over Estella in *Great Expectations*. Similarly, Basil wishes to create a new and perfect species that will bless him as its creator. Basil's idealization of Dorian has two interrelated aims: to recover and resurrect his own childhood and to become a perfect parent to Dorian. The beautiful youth is the ideal that gives form and meaning to Basil's life. The painter presumably wishes to become a beautiful youth; failing that, he wishes to

father a beautiful youth. By creating a perfect work, the artist participates vicariously in its immortal beauty.

For a time, Basil's idealization sustains his life and art, yet ultimately he becomes victimized by his obsession. "I couldn't be happy
if I didn't see him every day," Basil confesses to Lord Henry. "He is
absolutely necessary to me" (9). Dorian's departure results in the loss
of Basil's creativity. Part of the tragedy of *The Picture of Dorian Gray*
lies in the fact that idealizations cannot be sustained. The closer Basil
looks at Dorian, the more disillusioned the painter becomes with the
portrait. Good objects turn out to be bad objects, idealism fades into
cynicism, outer beauty highlights inner ugliness. Basil's idealization
proves to be a falsification of reality, suggesting that the alluring image
has always concealed a fearful truth.

Like the Frankenstein Creature, Heathcliff, and Pip, Dorian has
never known his parents. His father, a penniless soldier, is killed in a
duel a few months after his marriage, and his mother dies shortly after
his birth. Growing up in a loveless environment, Dorian is raised by
a hateful grandfather who, according to rumor, is responsible for
engineering his son-in-law's death. In *Frankenstein*, the Creature is
rejected by two father surrogates, Victor and De Lacey; in *The Picture
of Dorian Gray*, the beautiful youth is pursued by two father surrogates. Basil and Lord Henry represent the idealistic and cynical sides
of the same self. Both men compete for Dorian's affection, and when
Dorian's choice becomes clear, the painter sadly retires. Lord Henry
does not reject Dorian,' but he does, significantly, vanish at the end of
the story, when Dorian most needs help. In *Frankenstein*, the dead
mother remains idealized, her image kept alive in the miniature portrait Victor's brother William wears round his neck. In *The Picture of
Dorian Gray*, the dead mother is not idealized, and there is apparently
no trace of her existence in Dorian's life. Or is there?

There is only one mother in *The Picture of Dorian Gray*, and she is
not biologically related to the handsome youth. Mrs. Vane is the
mother of another beautiful youth, Sibyl, the actress to whom Dorian
is briefly engaged. Yet Mrs. Vane's true relationship to Dorian is far
closer than that of merely a potential mother-in-law. Mrs. Vane is a
"faded, tired-looking woman" whose obsession in life is to see her
daughter become a famous actress. As her name indicates, she is an
insincere, shallow woman. Every aspect of Mrs. Vane's appearance

represents bad art: her "crooked, false jewelled fingers [which] gave grotesqueness to the words," "those false theatrical gestures that so often become a mode of second nature to a stage-player," and her "tawdry theatrical dress" (59–62). Mrs. Vane's statement to her daughter is revealing. "I am only happy, Sibyl, when I see you act. You must not think of anything but your acting" (59–60). With her overcontrolling personality, her efforts to live vicariously through her daughter, and her conditional love, Mrs. Vane represents the quintessential narcissistic mother.

Mrs. Vane effectively renders Sibyl into a "caged bird." By acting well, both in life and on the stage, Sibyl remains her mother's dutiful daughter; by acting poorly, Sibyl attempts vainly to rebel against her mother's rigid control. Either way, she remains a prisoner. Sibyl's decision to act poorly on the stage results in Dorian's murderous rejection of her. Reduced to an echo by her narcissistic mother and lover, Sibyl commits suicide, her life imitating the tragic role she has played on the stage.

Sybil does not allow herself to rebel against her mother until it is too late, but there is open tension between Mrs. Vane and her son. A clumsy, boorish youth, James Vane voices the narrator's severe disapproval of the mother. After describing Mrs. Vane's "shallow secret nature," the narrator extends his disapproval into a sweeping condemnation of all women. "Women defend themselves by attacking, just as they attack by sudden and strange surrenders" (63). James's hatred of his mother's affectations clearly reflects the authorial point of view. "He was conscious also of the shallowness and vanity of his mother's nature, and in that saw infinite peril for Sibyl and Sibyl's happiness" (66).

The misogynistic statements in *The Picture of Dorian Gray* all point in the direction of Mrs. Vane. We can now see a relationship between the overcontrolling mother and her would-be son-in-law. Vain Dorian Gray is the true son of Mrs. Vane! Each is a reflection of the other's insincerity and shallowness. Sibyl is the innocent victim caught in their crossfire. Mrs. Vane and Dorian are happy only when they can control Sibyl—only when she acts well on the stage. Both use Sibyl for their own selfish purposes. Mrs. Vane consents to her daughter's marriage out of the mistaken belief that the wealthy Dorian Gray will elevate her own social status. Dorian's mad infatuation

arises from the various roles Sibyl enacts. One evening he sees her as
Rosalind, the next evening as Imogen. "I love Sibyl Vane. I want to
place her on a pedestal of gold, and to see the world worship the
woman who is mine" (77). Neither Dorian nor Mrs. Vane values
Sibyl for what she is, but only for what they wish her to be.

Indeed, Dorian and Mrs. Vane are strikingly similar. They are
alternately overloving and underloving, possessive, covertly hostile,
and theatrical. Dorian's pretext for rejecting Sibyl is that she is a bad
actress: "You are shallow and stupid," he says in disgust (87), recalling James Vane's earlier condemnation of his mother's "shallowness
and vanity" (66). In rejecting Sibyl, Dorian seems to be rejecting Mrs.
Vane—a transference no critic has pointed out.[26] Dorian's anger at
Sibyl's poor stage performance coincides with Mrs. Vane's silent disappointment with her. "He had dreamed of her as a great artist, had
given his love to her because he had thought her great. Then she had
disappointed him. She had been shallow and unworthy" (91).

Dorian's feelings toward Sibyl revolve around two poles, idealization and devaluation, "good art" and "bad art." There is no middle
ground, no recognition of the good enough mother or good enough
artist. In rejecting Sibyl, Dorian may be rejecting his own mother as
well as his own shallowness and vanity. It is ironic that Sibyl becomes
infatuated with a man who not only loves conditionally, as her mother
does, but whose insistence upon acting and role playing echoes Mrs.
Vane's statements. Sibyl thus unconsciously chooses a man who embodies her mother's corrupt values. By killing herself, Sibyl may be
symbolically killing her mother and fiancé. She is also conforming
obediently to their expectations of an "artistic" performance. Thus,
Dorian refers admiringly to the suicide as "one of the great romantic
tragedies of the age," "her finest tragedy" (109). For Sibyl, as for the
speaker in Sylvia Plath's "Lady Lazarus," dying is an art, like everything else; she does it exceptionally well.

In casting off Sibyl Vane, Dorian enacts Narcissus' rejection of
Echo. But Dorian himself is an echo of others: an echo of Mrs. Vane,
punishing her daughter for not acting well; an echo of Basil Hallward,
whose portrait of vain beauty has prompted life to imitate art; and an
echo of Lord Henry Wotton, whose philosophy of hedonism has
been acted out with a vengeance. These echoes reverberate throughout
The Picture of Dorian Gray, uttering a death knell for romance. The

violent ending of Dorian's romance repeats earlier breakups of romantic love experienced by his mother and Mrs. Vane. Wilde describes a
world in which romance gives way to empty theater, marriage paro-
dies love, and object love disguises narcissistic love. In a world without real love, where a *"grande passion* is the privilege of people who
have nothing to do" (48), Lord Henry's cynical observation contains
more sadness than sparkle.

After rejecting Sibyl Vane, Dorian tries to make restitution, but it
is too late. Besides, he would rather worship a martyred actress than
respect a living woman. He murders Basil when the artist discovers
the painting's fearful corruption. Dorian's corruption intensifies, and
he poisons everyone with whom he comes into contact, men and
women. Toward the end, he momentarily convinces himself that he
has altruistically spared the life of a young innocent woman named
Hetty Merton, whose reputation he decides not to ruin. A glance at
the hypocritical smile of the portrait shatters his rationalization. Dorian is past redemption. In a moment of rage, he picks up the knife he
has used to murder Basil and slashes the hateful portrait, thereby
stabbing himself in the heart.

All the characters in *The Picture of Dorian Gray* are reduced,
finally, to echoes—all, that is, except for Lord Henry, whose voice
dominates the novel. Lord Henry's epigrammatic brilliance never
loses its confidence, and he remains "Prince Paradox" to the end.
"The way of paradoxes," a minor character observes, "is the way of
truth. To test Reality we must see it on the tight-rope. When the
Verities become acrobats we can judge them" (39). Wilde is so infatuated with Lord Henry's acrobatics that he never topples him from the
tight-rope. It is impossible to accept Christopher Nassaar's conclusion
that Wilde undercuts Lord Henry at the end of the story. "When
Dorian dies, Wotton, the Satan-figure of *The Picture of Dorian Gray,*
suffers the very terrible fate of losing his soul."[27] The point is not that
Lord Henry has lost his soul—he has never had one to lose—but that
Wilde has never distanced himself from the character. "Wotton's
epigrams are so much Wilde's own," Masao Miyoshi correctly points
out, "that they would blend completely in any Wildean essay or
letter. His expression of the new hedonism and aestheticism of the
Fin-de-siècle is clearly Wilde's."[28] Of all the mad infatuations in *The*

Picture of Dorian Gray, the only one that survives is Wilde's adoring treatment of Lord Henry.

Wilde was contradictory about the meaning of *The Picture of Dorian Gray.* In a series of angry and defensive letters published in British newspapers, the novelist sounded at times like Lord Henry in isolating art from life:

I am quite incapable of understanding how any work of art can be criticised from a moral standpoint. The sphere of art and the sphere of ethics are absolutely distinct and separate; and it is to the confusion between the two that we owe the appearance of Mrs Grundy, that amusing old lady who represents the only original form of humour that the middle classes of this country have been able to produce.[29]

One day later, Wilde reversed himself and revealed the "terrible moral" in his novel:

All excess, as well as all renunciation, brings its own punishment. The painter, Basil Hallward, worshipping physical beauty far too much, as most painters do, dies by the hand of one in whose soul he has created a monstrous and absurd vanity. Dorian Gray, having led a life of mere sensation and pleasure, tries to kill conscience, and at that moment kills himself. Lord Henry Wotton seeks to be merely the spectator of life. He finds that those who reject the battle are more deeply wounded than those who take part in it. (*The Letters of Oscar Wilde,* 259)

Notwithstanding these comments, Wilde does not show us Lord Henry's response to Dorian's death, and we can only conclude that the novelist was temperamentally unable to renounce Prince Paradox. And when Wilde writes, in another letter, that "Lord Henry Wotton's views on marriage are quite monstrous, and I highly disapprove of them" (*The Letters of Oscar Wilde,* 264), we are reminded of D. H. Lawrence's shrewd observation: never trust the teller, only the tale.

The tale of Wilde's life is no less contradictory than the tale of his art. Despite his insistence upon the separation of life and art, Wilde confused the two, to the detriment of both. "Life has been your art," Lord Henry tells Dorian (217), anticipating a comment Wilde later expressed to André Gide. "Would you like to know the great drama of my life?—It's that I've put my genius into my life; I've put only my talent into my works" (*Oscar Wilde: In Memoriam*, 16n). Wilde's life and art, like Dorian's, seemed to be governed by the aesthetics of narcissism. In an example of life eerily imitating art, Wilde completed *The Picture of Dorian Gray* and then fell madly in love with a beautiful but vindictive youth, Lord Alfred Douglas, whose influence on him was no less injurious than Lord Henry's on Dorian. One cannot help being struck by the extent to which Wilde, perceiving "Bosie," as he fondly called him, to be a Narcissus, succumbed to the role of Echo. Enraptured by Douglas, who was sixteen years younger, Wilde describes him at the beginning of their relationship in 1892 as "quite like a narcissus—so white and gold. . . . Bosie is so tired: he lies like a hyacinth on the sofa, and I worship him" (*The Letters of Oscar Wilde*, 314). Douglas, in turn, worshiped Wilde, though not with the same constancy. "When you are not on your pedestal you are not interesting. The next time you are ill I will go away at once."[30] While awaiting sentence in prison in 1895, Wilde contemplated the agonizing separation from the beloved youth. "O my love, you whom I cherish above all things, white narcissus in an unmown field, think of the burden which falls to you, a burden which love alone can make light" (*The Letters of Oscar Wilde*, 398).

In prison Wilde was able to analyze with more objectivity his destructive relationship to Douglas. The analysis appears in *De Profundis* (1897), a book-length letter written to his lover. At times painfully self-analytical, at other times merely self-pitying, *De Profundis* is always moving, if only because Wilde drops Lord Henry Wotton's cynical mask to expose the intense suffering in his life. Wilde's attitude toward self-analysis significantly changes here. Lord Henry, echoing Tiresias' remarks in Ovid's myth of Echo and Narcissus, advises against self-awareness. "Knowledge would be fatal" (206). Elsewhere Wilde comments: "Only the shallow know themselves" (*The Artist as Critic*, 434). But in *De Profundis*, Wilde explores for the first time his disastrous involvement with Douglas. Sounding like a disillusioned Basil Hallward, Wilde writes: "I blame myself for allowing an unintellectual friendship, a friendship whose primary aim was not the creation and contemplation of beautiful things, entirely to dominate my life."[31]

Like Basil, Wilde finds himself absorbed by love, to the point where self-object boundaries dissolve; but unlike Basil, who claims to have been inspired by the presence of Dorian Gray, Wilde admits that friendship with Douglas has destroyed his own creativity. "During the whole time we were together I never wrote one single line" (*De Profundis*, 5), a statement later challenged by Douglas.[32] Wilde does not analyze the transference implications of his relationship to Douglas, but he does comment perceptively on the extent to which Douglas' behavior was determined by deep anger toward his father, the Marquess of Queensbury, who originally accused Wilde of sodomizing his son. Writes Wilde: "You thought again that in attacking your own father with dreadful letters, abusive telegrams, and insulting post cards, you were really fighting your mother's battles, coming forward as her champion, and avenging the no doubt terrible wrongs and sufferings of her married life. It was quite an illusion on your part, one of your worst indeed" (32). Observing that Douglas' hatred of his father was of such stature that it "entirely outstripped, overthrew, and overshadowed your love for me," Wilde refers to himself as the "stalking-horse for both of you, and a mode of attack as well as a mode of shelter." Speaking as both a devastated lover and detached analyst, Wilde remarks: "I could have held up a mirror to you, and shown you such an image of yourself that you would not have recognised it as your own till you found it mimicking back your gestures of horror, and then you would have known whose shape it was, and hated it and yourself for ever" (42).

Remembering Basil Hallward's observation that every portrait reveals the artist more than the sitter, we may inquire into the stalking-horses in Wilde's life. Wilde did not look deeply enough into himself to analyze, as he had done with Douglas, the extent to which he found himself unconsciously fighting his mother's battles, avenging the terrible wrongs and sufferings of her married life. Wilde's father, Sir William Wilde, was an eminent eye and ear surgeon in Dublin. He wrote numerous books on a variety of subjects, ranging from aural surgery to Irish history. He was also a notorious womanizer and had at least three illegitimate children by the time he married. His distinguished medical career was cut short by alcoholism, scandal, and a volatile temper. Wilde's mother was an Irish nationalist known as "Speranza," who early in life wrote fiery articles urging Ireland's independence from Great Britain. She later established a literary salon and dabbled in poetry, philosophy, and politics. Their marriage may not have been as stormy as that of Douglas' parents, who eventually divorced, but clearly Wilde witnessed throughout childhood many angry battles between his mother and father and also learned about the public disgrace arising from his father's promiscuity.

Despite numerous biographies of Oscar Wilde and his family, despite the fact, as his bibliographer points out, that there is probably more written about Wilde than about any other modern writer,[33] we cannot easily describe his relationship to his parents. The most compelling psychobiographical detail is that Lady Wilde dressed her son in girls' clothes for the first decade of his life. Lady Wilde's treatment of her son appears in the following recollection by Luther Munday, who knew the family:

Lady Wilde lived opposite our lodgings in Park Street where we lived in those days. Meeting her at Mrs Dallas Glyn's in Mount Street (where I first met Willie and Oscar, her sons), Lady Wilde told the assembled guests, not in a whisper either, that, in her intense desire for a daughter, she thought and willed incessantly. Further that, to compensate for her bitter disappointment when Oscar was born, she treated him for ten whole years as if he had been her daughter, carrying out this treatment in every detail of dress, habit, and companions.[34]

Curiously, this detail has been ignored or dismissed by nearly all of Wilde's biographers. H. Montgomery Hyde's response is typical. "Victorian mothers were accustomed to dress their children of either sex in petticoats and skirts until they were six or seven years old."[35] Ellmann makes the same point in his biography, noting that "however accommodating it is to see a maternal smothering of masculinity as having contributed to his homosexuality, there is reason to be sceptical" (17). But Lady Wilde's treatment of her son went far beyond the bounds of what was culturally acceptable, and in light of the current research on gender identity, it is impossible to believe that Oscar Wilde's "female" childhood did not play a decisive role in his personality development.

Robert Stoller, one of the leading authorities on gender research, argues that a person's core gender identity, the feeling of being either masculine or feminine, is usually established by the second or third year of life. Stoller's pioneering study *Sex and Gender* (1968), discusses the three sources of core gender identity: "the anatomy and physiology of the genitalia; the attitudes of parents, siblings, and peers toward the child's gender role; and a biological force that can more or less modify the attitudinal (environmental) forces."[36] Stoller places greatest emphasis on the second source, the parent-child relationship, which includes the parents' own gender identities, the quality of their marriage, the child's identification with both sexes, and the child's Oedipal and pre-Oedipal development.

One of the rare but potentially malignant sexual disorders Stoller describes is male childhood transsexualism. The boy is anatomically normal but dressed in a girl's clothes and treated as if he were female. The mother typically regards her son as beautiful, encourages his feminine behavior, and daydreams what he might look like as a grown woman. Stoller's research indicates that the mother of such a child tends herself to have a confused gender identity, having been dressed in a boy's clothes when she was younger. She typically experiences emptiness, incompleteness, and low self-esteem. The father tends to be literally absent from the family, or "dynamically" absent: his "absence is a most living, tantalizing one—as compared to the 'static' absence of a dead or divorced father" (*Sex and Gender*, 97). Stoller does not make the connection, but there seems to be a parallel between the transsexual child and Narcissus, both pursuing an elusive shadow. The dynamics of the transsexual child include an extreme symbiotic identification with an intrusive mother and a counteridentification with an absent father.

Stoller's description of the family dynamics of the transsexual child parallels Kernberg's discussion of the factors contributing to pathological narcissism. There is, for instance, the mother-child symbiotic union, resulting in blurred self-object boundaries and identity confusion. There is also the mother's pathological identification with her son, who becomes, in Stoller's words, *"his mother's feminized phallus"* (120). The mother's oversolicitousness usually conceals deep anger toward men. The mother of a transsexual or transvestite unconsciously damages her son's masculinity in order to express rage toward the men who have failed her. The father is a co-conspirator in this process, either remaining absent from the family while the mother is feminizing the son or passively accepting his son's humiliation.

Oscar Wilde was not a "pure culture" of male childhood transsexualism, and there is no concrete evidence that he actually thought of himself in the wrong body, which is the usual definition of the disorder. As a young man, he had love affairs with women; he later married and had two children. He appeared to have a close and loving relationship with his mother. According to Vyvyan Holland (Oscar Wilde's son), his father worshiped Lady Wilde.[37] None of Wilde's biographers has hinted at any serious mother-son conflict. "No one knew better than you how deeply I loved and honoured her," Wilde wrote from prison to Douglas after Lady Wilde's death. "Her death was terrible to me; but I, once a lord of language, have no words in which to express my anguish and my shame" (*De Profundis*, 51).

There was a darker side, however, to the mother-son relationship. Vyvyan Holland reports sadly that just as Lady Wilde decisively favored her older son, Willie, over her younger son, Oscar, so did Oscar favor his older son, Cyril, over the younger one. Vyvyan acknowledges, moreover, that "both my parents had hoped for a girl as their second child, just as my grandmother had hoped for a girl when my father was born" (*Son of Oscar Wilde*, 25). Hence the androgynous name *Vyvyan*. To be dressed as a girl for years, to have one's masculinity mocked, to be raised as a replacement for another, to be taught that appearance has no relation to reality: how can this not affect profoundly a child's imagination? There was thus from the beginning of Oscar Wilde's life a fundamental nonacceptance of his being. Lady Wilde's devaluation of her son's masculinity may well have been a response to her husband's Don Juanism, a form of sexual acting out that usually conceals intense hostility to women as well as anxiety over one's malehood. Given Sir William's temper, reputation, and personal appearance,[38] it must have been particularly difficult for his son to identify with him. A disappointed mother who treats her son as a daughter, a father who is increasingly absent from the family —this is precisely the parental background that gives rise to childhood transsexualism. The son's identification with the mother may have been strengthened by a disease from which they both apparently suffered. George Bernard Shaw reports that Lady Wilde was afflicted with gigantism, which, unchecked, results in acromegaly, producing an enlargement of the hands and feet. Shaw believed that Oscar Wilde also suffered from the same condition.[39] If so, it may have reinforced the son's belief that he was an extension of his mother, the two of them cohabiting the same body.

We can now understand better Oscar Wilde's gender conflicts and identity confusion. The inability of his fictional characters to serve as healthy, joyful mirrors seems to reflect the novelist's own mirroring difficulties. "A person who is systematically and inaccurately mirrored," Bernard Green writes, "must cope with the discrepancy between whom he is experienced to be by another (mirroring) and whom he experiences himself to be. Further, a person subjected to a distorted mirroring relationship will be crippled to a greater or lesser degree in his capacity to accurately mirror another."[40] Basil Hallward's fear of being absorbed by Dorian Gray reflects the fear of maternal devouring that Wilde probably experienced himself. By remaining fused with his mother, Wilde earned her love; by separating himself from his mother, he incurred inevitable ridicule from the masculine world. "Each man kills the thing he loves," Wilde writes in "The Ballad of Reading Gaol" (*The Works of Oscar Wilde*, 823)—an insight that reveals the danger of overlove.

Both of Wilde's parents were accomplished writers, but he identified particularly with his mother's values and perceptions, especially her penchant for theatricality. He certainly identified with her inflated opinion of her own literary stature. Lady Wilde's biographer reports her grandiose belief that she was the "acknowledged voice in poetry among all the poets in Ireland."[41] Wilde imitated his mother's eccentricities and conceits, her posings and histrionics. Mrs. Vane seems to be only a slight exaggeration of Lady Wilde. James Vane's criticisms of his mother's affectations would thus seem to represent Oscar Wilde's criticisms of his own mother.

Not surprisingly, the years of childhood transsexuality produced a violent backlash of misogyny. Wilde's biographers have written about his "reverence for his mother,"[42] but they have not attempted to reconcile this with his offensive statements about women. Ellmann, for example, never raises this subject. How ironic that the son of Speranza, one of the most ardent feminists of her time, turned out to be a secret woman-hater. The matricidal imagery in *The Picture of Dorian Gray* reveals the extent to which Wilde recoiled from women. Since a male transsexual experiences female love as engulfment, any intimate relationship with a woman poses the threat of identity loss. Even as he identified closely with both the erotic and artistic aspects of women, Wilde expressed rage for having been captured by them, deprived of his maleness. His image of beauty was incarnated in the male body. Dorian is most attracted to Sibyl Vane when she plays the role of Rosalind, disguised in a boy's clothes.

Interestingly, Dorian's initial description of Sibyl resembles Wilde's description in 1883 of his future wife. A first-hand account of the young Constance Wilde confirms her slim figure and "almost boyish face."[43] Like Dorian, Wilde was attracted to androgynous women. When Mrs. Wilde's body changed as a result of two pregnancies, her husband became repelled, saying to a male friend in disgust: "How can one desire what is shapeless, deformed, ugly? Desire is killed by maternity; passion buried in conception."[44] Wilde apparently never resumed intercourse with his wife after the birth of their second son.

Seeking to resurrect the defeated father, Wilde dramatizes Dorian Gray's desire to merge with Lord Henry and Basil Hallward. Only a powerful masculine figure could offset the mother's overcloseness. Few novels are more dissimilar than *The Picture of Dorian Gray* and *Sons and Lovers,* yet both portray the horror of possessive maternal love, the son's reparative impulse toward the father, and the power of male bonding. Without the presence of what Peter Blos calls the "dyadic" (or pre–Oedipal) father, the boy's efforts to distance himself from the symbiotic mother become more problematic.[45] In Wilde's case, the search for the idealized male led him to seek out younger men, in most cases, teenage boys. Ellmann characteristically portrays this aspect of Wilde's life in the most positive way. "What seems to characterize all Wilde's affairs is that he got to know the boys as individuals, treated them handsomely, allowed them to refuse his attentions without becoming rancorous, and did not corrupt them. They were already prostitutes" (368). Surely this interpretation sanitizes one of the most tortured aspects of Wilde's life.[46]

It seems likely that Wilde's fascination with perversion arose as a way of coping with a threat to his gender identity. Stoller defines perversion as the "erotic form of hatred": a "perversion is the reliving of actual historical sexual trauma aimed precisely at one's sex (an anatomical state) or gender identity (masculinity or femininity)."[47] Stoller equates perversion, not with sexual orientation, but with the interplay between hostility and sexual desire. The perverse act temporarily erases past sexual trauma by converting the passive victim into the active victimizer. Even as Wilde worshiped male beauty and was prepared to give up everything for forbidden love, he created situations in which he sabotaged his chance for any meaningful love relationship. Wilde's promiscuity, critics have pointed out, is reminiscent of his father's. Indeed, the parallels between father and son are suggestive. Like Sir William, Oscar Wilde became an absent or expelled father to his own children. After her husband was imprisoned, Constance Wilde changed the name of her children to protect them from the public scandal, and they grew up thinking their father was dead.

In light of the years in which Lady Wilde dressed her son in girls' clothes and treated him as a female *objet d'art,* we can now appreciate Oscar Wilde's aesthetics of narcissism. The image of perfect male beauty Wilde pursued in his life and embodied in his novel was the creation of a writer who was treated as his mother's feminized phallus. From the beginning of Wilde's life there was an irresolvable split between appearance and reality, art and life. Wilde elaborated a philosophy of art in which nature was seemingly transformed and improved upon by art. Like Dorian, he elevated the life of the dandy into an ideal, banishing nature from his aesthetic system. Yet nature could not be permanently defied.

Nature's revenge compelled Wilde to seek out elusive narcissistic love. Fertile as his imagination was, he could not convincingly imagine object love. In one of his wittiest epigrams he writes: "To love oneself is the beginning of a life-long romance." But Wilde was aware of the treachery of highly narcissistic love. Realizing this, he identified the artist with Christ in an attempt to unify aesthetics and religion. His "greatest ambition," he said near the end of his life, was to be remembered as the "man who reclothed the sublimest conception which the world has ever known—the Salvation of Humanity, the Sacrifice of Himself upon the Cross by Christ—with new and burning words, with new and illuminating symbols, with new and divine vision, free from the accretions of cant which the centuries have gathered around it."[48] That Wilde succeeded for a time in realizing his greatest ambition is a tribute to his remarkable creative talent. *The Picture of Dorian Gray* remains his flawed masterpiece, a novel that uncannily looks backward to Ovid's ancient myth of Echo and Narcissus and forward to the contemporary personality disorder.

Infanticide and Object Loss in
Jude the Obscure

Little Father Time's suicide in *Jude the Obscure* (1895) is the turning point of a novel demonstrating the cruelty that pervades nature and society. As if the boy's suicide is not terrible enough, Hardy has him hang his younger half-brother and half-sister, the three children suspended from closet hooks. Located near Father Time's body is a note with the victim's last words: *"Done because we are too menny."* [1] The suicide letter reveals the boy's belief that his father, Jude Fawley, and stepmother, Sue Bridehead, would be better off without the children, who only add to the couple's woes in a Malthusian world. Jude sees his son's suicide as symbolic of an impending universal death wish, and he mournfully reassures Sue that she could not have averted the tragedy. "It was in his nature to do it. The doctor says there are such boys springing up amongst us—boys of a sort unknown in the last generation—the outcome of new views of life." These boys, adds Jude, see all the terrors of life before they are strong enough to resist them. "He says it is the beginning of the coming universal wish not to live. He's an advanced man, the doctor: but he can give no consolation to—" (406).

Curiously, although no subject is more important to society than the nurture of its children, the double murder and suicide in *Jude the Obscure* have elicited virtually no literary commentary—a scholarly neglect confirming Father Time's judgment that the world would be better off without the children. The dearth of criticism is more surprising in light of the fact that the violent deaths of the three children represent, in Ian Gregor's words, the "most terrible scene in Hardy's fiction, indeed it might be reasonably argued in English fiction."² Nearly all readers have agreed with Irving Howe's conclusion that the suicide is aesthetically botched: "botched not in conception but in execution: it was a genuine insight to present the little boy as one of those who were losing the will to live, but a failure in tact to burden him with so much philosophical weight."³ Howe consigns this observation to a parenthesis, however, and Hardy's critics have condemned Father Time's suicide without investigating the underlying causes.

There are, admittedly, several objections that may be raised to a psychological interpretation of the double murder and suicide. Father Time is clearly an allegorical, not a realistic, character. Few literary children have appeared so relentlessly morbid and fatalistic, and his melodramatic entrance and exit strain credibility. To take seriously his fears and vulnerability may strike some readers as misplaced critical attention. Does it matter how Hardy disposes of the three shadowy children, two of whom are neither named nor described?

Despite these criticisms, *Jude the Obscure* remains one of the most psychologically rich novels in our language, as the published criticism confirms.⁴ However artistically contrived Father Time's ending may be, the fictional suicide reveals many of the characteristics of real-life suicides. More importantly, Father Time's actions foreshadow the murderous impulses culminating in Sue's grim return to her former husband, Richard Phillotson, and Jude's own self-destruction. Father Time is not biologically related to Sue, but he is the true heir to the gloomy philosophy of his father and adoptive mother. Although Jude and Sue attribute Father Time's death to his "incurably sad nature," the suicide is the logical result of a series of narcissistic injuries involving defective parenting. This is a more disturbing interpretation of Father Time's suicide, since it implicates the parents in the children's deaths.

To be sure, from the beginning of the novel, Hardy seems to be indicting nature, specifically, the brutality of a scheme in which the living are condemned to a woeful existence. Nature itself appears to be a defective parent, allowing one species to survive, temporarily, at the expense of another. An early incident, young Jude's identification with a flock of rooks scavenging for food, evokes Hardy's pessimistic naturalism. "They seemed, like himself, to be living in a world which did not want them" (11). Instead of scaring away the birds to prevent them from devouring the produce destined for human consumption, as Farmer Troutham has paid him to do, Jude allows them to feed off the land. He is swiftly punished for the act. The narrator remarks upon the "flaw in the terrestrial scheme, by which what was good for God's birds was bad for God's gardener" (13). To be alive is to be victimized, the novel suggests, and the Tennysonian belief in nature "red in tooth and claw" pervades Wessex. Jude cannot walk across a pasture without thinking about the coupled earthworms waiting to be crushed on the damp ground. "Nature's logic was too horrid for him to care for. That mercy towards one set of creatures was cruelty towards another sickened his sense of harmony" (15).

Although the narrator ascribes these gloomy thoughts to Jude's "weakness of character," reflective of an unusually sensitive disposition, the other major figures in the story echo the awareness of injustice. Jude's dismay during the pig-killing scene with Arabella foreshadows Sue's horror at the thought of pigeons intended for Sunday dinner. "O why should Nature's law be mutual butchery!" she exclaims (371). Phillotson similarly observes to Arabella that "Cruelty is the law pervading all nature and society; and we can't get out of it if we would!" (384). *Jude the Obscure* "fluctuates between two opposing views of 'nature,' " Robert B. Heilman notes, "between a romantic naturalism . . . and the pessimistic aftermath of scientific naturalism."[5] Nature itself appears to be fundamentally defective, perpetuating suffering and death.

To demonstrate the unfortunate consequences of nature, Hardy introduces Little Father Time into the novel. He is the accidental product of the ill-fated marriage between Jude and Arabella. Born eight months after Arabella left England for Australia, the boy spends his early years with her. Arabella hands over the unwanted child to her parents, who in turn decide they no longer wish to be "encumbered" with him. Arabella then turns him over to Jude. Symptomatic of Father Time's past treatment is the fact that he was never christened, because, he explains, "if I died in damnation, 'twould save the expense of a Christian funeral" (337). His mother and grandparents name him "Little Father Time" because of his aged appearance. He is, the narrator states, "Age masquerading as Juvenility, and doing it so badly that his real self showed through crevices" (332). Sue observes that his face is like the tragic mask of Melpomene, the muse of tragedy. A younger and more extreme portrait of Jude, Father Time is obsessed with death and indignant over the inevitable termination of life. His response to flowers seems almost pathological, especially coming from a child. "I should like the flowers very very much, if I didn't keep on thinking they'd be all withered in a few days!" (358). By the same logic he might have concluded that the flowers' fragility compels us to admire their beauty and vitality. The lively exchange in *Sons and Lovers* on how to pick flowers is missing from *Jude the Obscure*. Unlike Jude, Father Time makes no effort to escape his surroundings or pursue a better life; for this reason he remains pathetic, not tragic, defeated too easily and quickly.

Jude agrees to accept his newly discovered son, telling Sue: "I don't like to leave the unfortunate little fellow to neglect. Just think of his life in a Lambeth pothouse, and all its evil influences, with a parent who doesn't want him, and has, indeed, hardly seen him, and a stepfather who doesn't know him" (330). Jude recognizes that a child's healthy development depends upon loving parents and a friendly environment. Sue intuitively empathizes with Father Time's situation, and she is moved to tears when he calls her "mother." But she is distressed by the physical resemblance between Arabella and Father Time, which causes Jude to exclaim: "Jealous little Sue!" (335). Ironically, Little Father Time shares his adoptive mother's gloomy temperament. A number of years pass, with Father Time bringing unexpected joy into his parents' lives. Even though Jude and Sue live together without marrying, consequently suffering social ostracism, they are portrayed as loving, conscientious parents. Jude's decision to move elsewhere for employment prompts Sue to reaffirm her allegiance to Father Time. "But whatever we do, wherever we go, you won't take him away from me, Jude dear? I could not let him go now! The cloud upon his young mind makes him so pathetic to me; I do hope to lift it some day!" (361). Jude reassures her that the family will remain intact.

The crucial scene preceding the children's deaths takes place in Part Sixth, ii, when Sue and Father Time are together in a cheerless room of a lodging house from which they have just been ordered to leave. Opposite the lodging house stands Sarcophagus College, whose outer walls "threw their four centuries of gloom, bigotry, and decay into the little room she occupied" (401). Despondent over the loss of lodgings and Jude's declining prospects for employment, Sue mirrors this gloom to Father Time. When he asks her if he can do anything to help the family, she replies: "No! All is trouble, adversity and suffering!" (402). As the dialogue continues, it becomes increasingly clear that Sue's despair exacerbates the boy's innately melancholy temperament:

> "Father went away to give us children room, didn't he?"
> "Partly."
> "It would be better to be out o' the world than in it, wouldn't it?"
> "It would almost, dear."
> "'Tis because of us children, too, isn't it, that you can't get a good lodging?"
> "Well—people do object to children sometimes."
> "Then if children make so much trouble, why do people have 'em?"
> "O—because it is a law of nature."
> "But we don't ask to be born?"
> "No indeed." (402)

Instead of heeding the child's cry for help, Sue validates Father Time's worst fears—namely, that he and the other two children are responsible for the family's desperate situation. Sue repeatedly misses the opportunity to allay his suspicion of being unwanted and unloved. In the next line Father Time expresses the fear of becoming a burden to his family, a fear intensified by the fact that Sue is not his biological mother and, therefore, under no obligation to care for him. "I oughtn't to have come to 'ee—that's the real truth! I troubled 'em in Australia, and I trouble folk here. I wish I hadn't been born!"

Here is the perfect moment for Sue to reassure Father Time that he is indeed loved by his parents. If they didn't want him, she could have truthfully said, they never would have consented to adopt him. With luck and determination, she might have added, their lives will improve. However allegorical Father Time's role may be in the novel, during this scene he acts and talks like a scared child. The reader responds to him as if he is fully human, deserving of sympathy. Father Time needs simply to be reassured that the family's circumstances will improve in the future. Indeed, he expects only a reasonable reassurance, not a rosy promise of future happiness. He certainly does not need to hear that unwanted children are responsible for their parents' suffering. How does Sue respond to his wish never to have been born? "You couldn't help it, my dear."

Sue's empathic failure triggers Father Time's inner violence, and his statements become increasingly frantic. "I think that whenever children be born that are not wanted they should be killed directly, before their souls come to 'em, and not allowed to grow big and walk about!" (402). These unwanted children are Father Time and his two siblings. Father Time contemplates infanticide because Sue has already given up on him; she does nothing to diminish his despair because she shares it fully. The narrator similarly regards Father Time's pessimism as philosophically justified and, hence, beyond disagreement. "Sue did not reply" to the boy's accusations, the narrator tell us, since she was "doubtfully pondering how to treat this too reflective child" (402). Father Time *is* too reflective, but that is not the issue. His thinking remains morbid, obsessional, and frighteningly simplistic in its solution to suffering.

Mary Jacobus refers to Sue's "mistaken honesty" in telling Father Time that another child is on the way,[6] but Sue's real mistake lies in her failure to understand her child's needs. She equates Father Time's pessimism with profundity, resolves silently to be "honest and candid" with him, as if he were a mature adult rather than a terrified child, and then informs him that she is pregnant again. The information predictably drives him into a frenzy. The dialogue closes with the distracted boy vowing that "if we children was gone there'd be no trouble at all!" Sue answers, "don't think that, dear" (403). Even when she tries to be reassuring, she succeeds only in confirming his fears. The next time she sees him, the three children are hanging from their necks. Devastated by the sight, Sue prematurely goes into labor and suffers a miscarriage.

Jude and Sue adopt Father Time to avoid exposing him to further parental neglect, yet, as the final dialogue between mother and son indicates, it would be hard to imagine a more chilling family environment for the child. Sue is not an abusive or overcontrolling mother, as Mrs. Joe and Miss Havisham are in *Great Expectations,* and she does not deliberately intend to harm Father Time. She is a depressed mother, not a sadistic one, and since she cannot help herself, readers may reasonably ask how she can be expected to help others, especially someone intent upon killing himself and his two siblings. And yet, unlike Father Time, Sue is an adult, therefore, responsible for the consequences of her actions. However much we empathize with Sue, we cannot suspend our judgment of her.

Jude the Obscure implies that suicide runs in families, like a defective gene passed from one doomed generation to another, but a more plausible explanation for this family curse lies in environmental and interactional causes. Sue remains only partly aware of this. She reads Father Time's suicide letter and breaks down, convinced that their previous conversation has triggered his violence. Sue and Jude plausibly conjecture that upon waking from sleep, Father Time was unable to find his mother and, fearing abandonment, committed the double murder and suicide. Sue accepts responsibility for Father Time's actions, but her explanations mitigate her complicity in the boy's suicide. Perhaps she should have told him all the "facts of life" or none of them, as she says. Nevertheless, the disclosure of the pregnancy is less wounding to Father Time's self-esteem than her failure to convince him that he is wanted and loved.[7]

By projecting her morbidity onto Father Time and confirming his infanticidal fantasies, Sue effectively places a noose around the child's neck. Father Time's inability to enjoy flowers because they will be withered in a few days has its counterpart in Sue's rationalization of the children's deaths. "It is best, perhaps, that they should be gone. —Yes—I see it is! Better that they should be plucked fresh than stay to wither away miserably!" (409). Jude remains supportive, agreeing that what has happened is probably for the best. "Some say that the elders should rejoice when their children die in infancy" (409). Jude does not rejoice at the children's deaths, but he remains unaware of how his statements here and elsewhere mirror the self-destructive philosophy that has victimized the Fawleys. Even the attending physician's interpretation of Father Time's suicide—"the beginning of the coming universal wish not to live"—contains a subtle rationalization. If nothing could have been done to prevent the three deaths, then no one is to blame for the tragedy.

Sue's empathic failure is striking. Her inconsistency of love and self-distraction overwhelm Father Time, as they later do Jude. The defective maternal mirroring represents Father Time's final narcissistic injury.[8] By treating Father Time as an extension of herself, Sue acts out her own unresolved inner conflicts. Moreover, by reinforcing

Father Time's suspicion that all children are monstrous, she repeats Victor Frankenstein's abandonment of the Creature. Sue is the opposite of the healthy mother Alice Miller writes about in *Prisoners of Childhood:* "If a child is lucky enough to grow up with a mirroring mother, who allows herself to be cathected narcissistically, who is at the child's disposal—that is, a mother who allows herself to be 'made use of' as a function of the child's narcissistic development, . . . then a healthy self-feeling can gradually develop in the growing child."[9] The issue is not whether Sue is a perfect mother, but whether she is a good enough mother who can prepare her children for the vicissitudes of life.

In suggesting that Sue is implicated in her children's deaths, I raise several questions. How is her abandonment of Father Time related to other conflicts in her life? Why does she forsake Jude, the man she loves, for Phillotson, whom she does not love? How does she enact the roles of both Narcissus and Echo?

Sue's contradictions are dazzling. Intellectually liberated but emotionally repressed, she claims to reject the church's outmoded teachings but then embraces reactionary dogma. Refined and ethereal—Jude calls her a "phantasmal, bodiless, creature" with hardly any "animal passion" (312)—Sue arouses men mainly to reject them. Torn between the conflicting claims of body and mind, she sacrifices the integrity of both in a futile quest for self-absolution. The pattern of her behavior suggests defiance, guilt, self-punishment, and abject submission. "There was no limit to the strange and unnecessary penances which Sue would meekly undertake when in a contrite mood" (322). Early in the story she buys two plaster statuettes of Venus and Apollo, symbolic of her attraction to classical beauty and wisdom, respectively; but when the landlady asks her to identify the objects, she dissembles, claiming they are casts of St. Peter and Mary Magdalene. She cannot tell the truth to Jude, not even after the landlady has spitefully shattered the pagan objects.

To understand the origins of Sue's conflicts, we must examine her childhood, but unfortunately, Hardy passes over this period, as Albert J. Guerard points out. "The origin of Sue's epicene reticence lies somewhere in her childhood, of which Hardy tells us almost nothing; the origin of her moral masochism lies there also."[10] Hardy gives us an important clue, though, about her history before introducing her into the story—a "friendly intimacy" with a Christminster undergraduate. Sue accepted his invitation to live with him in London, but when she arrived there and realized his intentions, she made a counterproposal—to live with him in a sexless union. Sue's relationship with the Christminster undergraduate remains ambiguous. Was she aware of the sexual implications of his invitation to live with him, and, if so, for what reasons did she decline a passionate romance? Several possibilities come to mind, including fear of pregnancy and threat of social ostracism. The friends shared a sitting room for fifteen months, until he was taken ill and forced to go abroad. Although the shadowy episode represents part of her struggle to emancipate herself from repressive social conventions, Sue blames herself for the undergraduate's death. It remains unclear whether she actually intended to hurt him. In narrating the student's account of their relationship, she seems to accept his version of reality, including his censure. "He said I was breaking his heart by holding out against him so long at such close quarters; he could never have believed it of woman. I might play that game once too often, he said. He came home merely to die. His death caused a terrible remorse in me for my cruelty—though I hope he died of consumption and not of me entirely" (177–78).

We have no way to authenticate what actually happened between Sue and the Christminster undergraduate, but we can analyze the transference implications of Sue's narrating style. Just as patients' stories in psychoanalysis repeat the themes and conflicts of their past, so do fictional characters' narrating styles represent "memorializations of their unresolved pasts."[11] Expressing the hope that the student died of consumption and not from herself, Sue reveals a tendency to hold herself responsible for all the failures in her relationships. In characterizing the young man as a victim of love, she depicts herself as a victimizer. She feels remorse for her cruelty but also satisfaction over her power, even though in hurting others, she hurts herself. Jude is understandably horrified by Sue's story, which provokes her to say, with a "contralto note of tragedy" in her voice: "I wouldn't have told you if I had known!" (178). But Sue knows how Jude will react to the story. Like Estella, who repeatedly warns Pip that she will break his heart if he becomes romantically involved with her, Sue forewarns

Jude about the dangers of intimacy with her—a heeding he fatally disregards.

Sue's relationships with Phillotson and Jude are replays of the unhappy union with the Christminster undergraduate. Phillotson is a hardworking school teacher whose name evokes his conventional social views and stolid character. Eighteen years older than Sue, he is a father figure to her, a fact that troubles his rival, Jude. Despite the temperamental and age differences between teacher and student, they enter into a chilling marriage and wisely agree to a divorce when their incompatibility becomes apparent. Sue moves in with Jude and bears two children. After their deaths, Sue inexplicably returns to Phillotson and remarries him. As Mrs. Edlin observes at the end, "Weddings be funerals a' b'lieve nowadays" (481).

Sue marries Phillotson largely to seek revenge on Jude, who she incorrectly believes has betrayed her. The engagement and marriage to Phillotson follow Jude's disclosure of his imprudent marriage to Arabella. As if to hurt Jude further, Sue asks him to give her away at the wedding. She even teases him by calling him "father," a term for the man who gives away the bride. The rejected suitor represses his response to the word: "Jude could have said 'Phillotson's age entitles him to be called that!' But he would not annoy her by such a cheap retort" (206). During a morning walk, Sue and Jude find themselves in front of the church where the scheduled marriage is to take place. She holds Jude's arm "almost as if she loved him," and they stroll down the nave as if they are married. Sue defends her provocative behavior by saying that she likes "to do things like this." Shortly before the wedding ceremony, Jude reflects on Sue's cruelty toward him, concluding that "possibly she would go on inflicting such pains again and again, and grieving for the sufferer again and again, in all her colossal inconsistency" (210).

Sue's wish to captivate men has Oedipal and pre-Oedipal implications. By marrying Phillotson, she may hope to repair the troubled relationship with her own father. By calling Jude "father," she projects the same complicated symbolism onto him. But if Sue sees Phillotson and Jude as variations of Oedipus, she seems to view herself as a female Narcissus, exerting fatal attraction over men. "I should shock you by letting you know how I give way to my impulses, and how much I feel that I shouldn't have been provided with attractiveness unless it were meant to be exercised! Some women's love of being loved is insatiable; and so, often, is their love of loving" (245). Sue's infatuations end in disillusionment and failure. She later expands upon the reasons for her marriage to Phillotson. "But sometimes a woman's *love of being loved* gets the better of her conscience, and though she is agonized at the thought of treating a man cruelly, she encourages him to love her while she doesn't love him at all. Then, when she sees him suffering, her remorse sets in, and she does what she can to repair the wrong" (290).

Like Narcissus, Sue seems to be in love with the unobtainable, the elusive, the spectral; like other narcissistic lovers, she proceeds from idealization to devaluation. Sue is also an Echo, denying her own independence and free will. Toward the end of the novel, she admits that she began her relationship with Jude in the "selfish and cruel wish" to make his heart ache for her. "I did not exactly flirt with you; but that inborn craving which undermines some women's morals almost more than unbridled passion—the craving to attract and captivate, regardless of the injury it may do the man—was in me; and when I found I had caught you, I was frightened" (426). Although she has grown to love Jude, she abruptly abandons him, causing anguish to them both. "And now you add to your cruelty by leaving me," Jude says, to which she replies: "Ah—yes! The further I flounder, the more harm I do!" (426).

Significantly, Sue's need to be loved by men has little to do with the wish for sexual gratification. She is so horrified at the possibility of intercourse with her husband that she throws herself out of the bedroom window when he accidentally enters her room. Jude calls her return to Phillotson, with whom she has never had sexual relations, a "fanatic prostitution" (436). Sue returns to her former husband presumably to punish herself and Jude for their nonconformist behavior. The "wickedness" of her feelings at the end of the novel is the same self-revulsion she experiences scarcely eight weeks into her first marriage to Phillotson. Denying there is anything wrong with her marriage, Sue delivers to Jude one of the most revealing speeches in the book:

"But it is not as you think!—there is nothing wrong except my own wickedness, I suppose you'd call it—a repugnance on my part, for a reason I cannot disclose, and what would not be admitted as one by the world in general! . . . What tortures me so much is the necessity of being responsive to this man whenever he wishes, good as he is morally!—the dreadful contract to feel in a particular way in a matter whose essence is its voluntariness! . . . I wish he would beat me, or be faithless to me, or do some open thing that I could talk about as a justification for feeling as I do! But he does nothing, except that he has grown a little cold since he has found out how I feel. That's why he didn't come to the funeral. . . . O, I am very miserable—I don't know what to do! . . . Don't come near me, Jude, because you mustn't. Don't—don't!" (255–56)

Sue's speech reveals a multitude of defenses gone awry. The middle sentences confirm the need for outside intervention denied in the beginning and end. Her cry for help anticipates Father Time's appeal for assistance preceding his suicide. Through displacement, Phillotson becomes the hated object, a projection screen for Sue's inner conflicts. Phillotson is not a brutal man; when he releases her from marriage, he shows enlightened judgment. Sue's first marriage to Phillotson may be attributed in part to naïveté and inexperience, but her second marriage suggests an unconscious need to continue her self-punishment. Her sexual surrender takes on the appearance of the "fanatic prostitution" Jude has sadly prophesied.

In remarrying Phillotson, Sue chooses to act out rather than analyze her conflicts. Unable to divorce herself from the institution of marriage she no longer believes in, she falls back upon martyrdom. Even as she punishes herself by returning to a husband she has never loved, she abandons the lover who has remained devoted to her. Sue occupies a dual role in the novel, victim (of Phillotson) and victimizer (of Jude). The roles are interrelated. In terms of ego psychology,[12] she identifies with the aggressor—a process, Anna Freud remarks, in which passive is converted to active. "By impersonating the aggressor, assuming his attributes or imitating his aggression, the child transforms himself from the person threatened into the person who makes the threat."[13] Sue invokes an unsound social code to rationalize an unhealthy psychological situation. The repressive institution of marriage—repressive to Hardy because its rigidity did not allow a relationship to be dissolvable as soon as it became a cruelty to either party —legitimizes her self-punishment.[14] Sue's second marriage thus becomes a more sinister replay of her first marriage, an example of a repetition compulsion principle that dominates *Jude the Obscure*.

In acting out their parents' broken marriages, Sue and Jude demonstrate how the present repeats the past. Sue's family background is almost identical to that of Jude, her first cousin. In endowing them with similar family backgrounds, Hardy intimates their unity of character. "They seem to be one person split in two," Phillotson remarks (276), vexed by his failure to understand either of them. To this extent, Sue and Jude resemble Catherine and Heathcliff in *Wuthering Heights*, who struggle to regain lost unity. The products of broken marriages, Jude and Sue have lost one or both parents at an early age and are raised by indifferent caretakers. According to Arabella, Jude's father ill-used his wife in the same way that Jude's paternal aunt (Sue's mother) mistreated her husband. Both marriages are doomed. After Jude becomes involved with Arabella, his great-aunt, Drusilla Fawley, informs him that his parents never got along with each other, parting company when he was a baby. Jude's mother, continues Arabella, drowned herself shortly afterwards. Drusilla makes no effort to soften the revelation or anticipate its terrible impact upon Jude. Drusilla's empathic failure repeats his mother's earlier rejection of him and foreshadows Sue's rejection of Father Time. After hearing the details of his mother's death, Jude attempts suicide in a similar way by walking on a partly frozen pond. The cracking ice manages to sustain his weight, temporarily thwarting his self-annihilation.

Hardy does not elaborate on the reasons for Jude's half-serious suicide attempt, but the painful repetition of the past cannot be ignored. As with most suicide attempts, including Father Time's, the motivation is overdetermined. Jude's attempt to repeat his mother's suicide is unmistakable, recalling John Bowlby's observation that children who suffer early maternal loss are vulnerable to suicide.[15] Jude's suicide attempt suggests a wish for reunion with the lost mother, a desire for revenge, a need to punish himself for harboring murderous feelings toward the lost love object, and a feeling that life is not worth living. Both Jude and Father Time attempt or commit suicide following maternal loss; they are mirror images of each other, portraits of the same abandoned child. After his mother's death, Jude is raised by a father about whom he never speaks, not even after he has grown up and become a father himself. As with *Frankenstein* and *Wuthering Heights*, *Jude the Obscure* remains preoccupied with the consequences of defective parenting but gives little information about absent parents. After his father's death, Jude is taken in by his great-aunt, who makes it clear that he would have been better off dead, like his parents. "It would ha' been a blessing if Goddy-mighty had took thee too, wi' thy mother and father, poor useless boy!" (8–9).

Against a background of parental loss, Jude develops into a compassionate and idealistic man. Nothing in his family history accounts for his remarkable sensitivity, and for a time it seems as if he has escaped his past. His willingness to adopt Father Time demonstrates his generosity of spirit, and he remains devoted to his wife and children. Jude is a better parent to his newly discovered son than presumably his own parents were to him. Nevertheless, Jude is absent when Father Time most needs him, during the moments preceding the suicide. Although his role in Father Time's suicide is more ambiguous than Sue's, Jude readily accepts the inevitability of his son's death.

Sue's background reveals a similar pattern of parental loss. According to Drusilla, Sue's father offended his wife early in the marriage, and the latter "so disliked living with him afterwards that she went away to London with her little maid" (81). We never discover the length of time she lives with her mother in London or the circumstances of their life. Sue is then brought up by her father to hate her mother's family. Like Eustacia Vye in *The Return of the Native*, another motherless daughter raised by a remote male guardian, Sue grows up to reject conventional society. Her rebellion, no less than Eustacia's, is singularly unsuccessful. Sue's defiance as a twelve-year-old girl, boldly exhibiting her body as she wades into a pond, reveals a spiritedness that contrasts her later inability to be touched by her husband. Her craving for conformity culminates in her sexual surrender to Phillotson. In a novel filled with agonizing self-inflicted deaths, Sue's decision to remarry is one of the most horrifying moments—in effect, another suicide. She returns to her former husband, not to seek a better life, but to punish herself for the past. Sue can survive, paradoxically, only through self-debasement. *Jude the Obscure* reflects a closed system in which loveless marriages, restrictive social conventions, and unmerciful superegos thwart the possibility of a fulfilling life.

Sue's pattern of defiance followed by blind submission suggests, clinically, the child's ambivalence toward the parents: the rejection of the mother, the original love object, followed by the need to recover the lost unity of infancy. Sue and Jude return to the wrong marital partners, and the attempt toward reparation is doomed. From the viewpoint of object relations,[16] Sue and Jude's inner world is precarious and turbulent. Each returns to a despised marital partner, suggesting the child's inability to separate from a defective caretaker. Phillotson and Arabella represent the omnipotent parents who can never be defied successfully. They offer punishment, not love, to the returning child, humbled and broken. Sue's submission to Phillotson parallels Jude's submission to Arabella. Both Sue and Jude regress to infantile modes of behavior (one is creed-drunk, the other is gin-drunk), obliterating themselves in a fatal union with hated love objects.

Object loss is a central theme in *Jude the Obscure,* and Freud's seminal essay "Mourning and Melancholia" (1917) casts light on many of the baffling psychological dynamics of Hardy's characters. Freud's definition of melancholia (depression) describes many of Sue's conflicts: "a profoundly painful dejection, cessation of interest in the outside world, loss of the capacity to love, inhibition of all activity, and a lowering of the self-regarding feelings to a degree that finds utterance in self-reproaches and self-revilings, and culminates in a delusional expectation of punishment."[17] In depression, Freud suggests, "dissatisfaction with the ego on moral grounds is the most outstanding feature" (248). This is especially true of Sue's self-punishing tendencies. Freud argues that the self-recriminations characteristic of depression are "reproaches against a loved object which have been shifted away from it on to the patient's own ego" (248). Depression is related to object loss in that the sadism directed initially against the object is converted to masochism. In both mourning and depression, the loss of an object deprives a person of the love necessary for growth and nurture. Unlike mourning, which is usually a temporary phenomenon, depression may last permanently. Freud viewed depression as arising from hostile feelings, initially directed toward parents, that are internalized, producing guilt and low self-esteem.[18]

Depression is widely regarded as one of the most common of psychiatric illnesses, but there is disagreement over its origin and treatment. Analysts distinguish object-related depression from narcissistic depression.[19] The sense of helplessness and lowered self-esteem are common to both forms of depression, but their origins appear to be different. Object-related depression, which Freud had in mind, awakens virulent aggression toward the disappointing love object. Narcissistic depression, by contrast, originates from disappointments in achieving fantasized or idealized states. For object relations theorists like Otto Kernberg, depression represents the internalization of aggression originally directed toward the rejecting love object. The major conflicts in object-related depression involve aggression: the fear of one's own destructive rage and the fear of retaliation by the object. For theorists like Heinz Kohut, on the other hand, depression represents the inability to merge with the idealized object. The major conflicts in narcissistic depression involve unrealistic or unobtainable goals, such as the pursuit of a perfect relationship.

Elements of both forms of depression appear in *Jude the Obscure*. The family backgrounds of Sue and Jude reflect a long history of parental neglect and abandonment. Both suffer object loss as children and parents. Their sadomasochistic relationship represents a defense against further object loss. That is, the sadist and masochist "play out both sides of the pain-inducing/pain-suffering object relationship."[20] Masochism represents a bond—or, more accurately, a bondage—to the early sadistic object. Contrary to their separation at the end, Sue and Jude remain symbiotically bonded, just as sadism and masochism are inextricably conjoined. The narcissistic element of their depression appears in their failure to merge with healthy, empathic selfobjects. Neither Jude nor Sue can sustain former ambitions, goals, ideals; both fall victim to bitter disillusionment. Sue's movement from social rebellion to repressive conformity parallels Jude's journey from unquestioning acceptance of life to embittered rejection.

Nowhere is Jude's idealizing power more evident than in his desire to pursue a university education at Christminster. The novel opens with Phillotson telling Jude why a university degree is important. "It is the necessary hall-mark of a man who wants to do anything in teaching" (4). Jude invests Christminster with mystical significance, transforming it into a radiant city of light, a "heavenly Jerusalem" (18). The eleven-year-old Jude associates his esteemed schoolteacher with holy Christminster, and he is understandably distressed by Phillotson's departure. Jude's infatuation with Christminster has erotic significance. "He was getting so romantically attached to Christminster that, like a young lover alluding to his mistress, he felt bashful at mentioning its name again" (22). At the same time, Jude speaks of his devotion to Christminster in terms of a son's devotion to his mother. "Yes, Christminster shall be my Alma Mater; and I'll be her beloved son, in whom she shall be well pleased" (41). Before leaving Jude, Phillotson invites him to Christminster, promising never to forget him. The promise is broken years later when Jude visits Phillotson and discovers that the teacher cannot remember him. Jude thus experiences his rejection by Christminster and Phillotson as repetitions of maternal and paternal abandonment.

Jude's lofty idealization of Christminster becomes a deadly mirage, as elusive as Narcissus' reflection. Jude's idealization is really an attempt to compensate for disappointment over parental abandonment. But on discovering the reality of university life, he is dismayed by its hypocrisy, rigidity, and narrowmindedness. Jude suffers other setbacks: he is deceived by the quack Vilbert, who reneges on the promise to supply him with Greek and Latin grammars; he is disillusioned at learning that Phillotson has given up the scheme to receive a university degree; and he is distressed upon receiving a letter from a Christminster professor advising him to renounce intellectual aspirations. We feel Jude's crushing rejection, his outrage at the collapse of his hopes for a university education. And yet, given Jude's impossible idealization of Christminster, we sense that he would have been disillusioned by any university system.

Jude comes to perceive, with Hardy's approval, that "there is something wrong somewhere in our social formulas: what it is can only be discovered by men or women with greater insight than mine, —if, indeed, they ever discover it—at least in our time" (394). Jude does not perceive, however, the narcissistic meaning of his idealizing tendencies. As Kernberg and other analysts point out, defensive idealization conceals fundamentally ambivalent feelings toward the love object, feelings that arise in the early mother-child relationship. The repetitive and compulsive nature of idealization suggests the continual effort to deny the disappointment and aggression associated with early object loss. Jude is eloquent in his social criticism and knowledge of literary and political history, but he is less convincing in his understanding of psychology. Wounded by early narcissistic injuries, Jude is rendered finally into a pining Echo, and his last words echo Job's: *"Let the day perish wherein I was born"* (488).

We can now see more clearly the parallel between Father Time's infanticide and the defective nurturing Jude and Sue received as children. A shadowy bad parent haunts *Jude the Obscure*, linking three generations of Fawleys. Each generation executes a death sentence in the name of the parents. Sue interprets her children's deaths as a sign of divine punishment for her wicked union with Jude. "I see marriage differently now. My babies have been taken from me to show me this! Arabella's child killing mine was a judgment—the right slaying the wrong. What, *What* shall I do! I am such a vile creature—too worthless to mix with ordinary human beings!" (422–23). The reversal is astonishing. She now views Father Time, the murderer of her own children, as an agent of divine retribution, while the two innocent children are evil, like herself. Sue submits herself to a vindictive God, a reflection of her bad father. She seems close to psychotic, lost in a terrible delusion. The violent self-hatred revealed in her speech to Phillotson conceals her infanticidal fantasies, now rationalized in the name of religious purification. "My children—are dead—and it is right that they should be! I am glad—almost. They were sin-begotten. They were sacrificed to teach me how to live!—their death was the first stage of my purification. That's why they have not died in vain! . . . You will take me back?" (439). By splitting the children into good and bad objects, Sue denies her ambivalence toward them, thus preserving her psychic life from massive extinction.

Jude and Sue miss the most terrifying insight of all, the realization that their ambivalence has slain the children. Sue's key admission, that she is "glad—almost" of the children's deaths, betrays an unconscious wish. This explains her complicity in Father Time's decision to annihilate the unwanted children of the world. The boy obediently carries out her wishes. Long before she brings children into the world, Sue has been punishing herself relentlessly for feelings of wickedness. The murders objectify her repressed wishes. By endorsing Father Time's infanticidal actions, Sue reveals herself as the abandoning parent, determined to destroy the hated child within herself. At the same time, she is the abandoned child, intent upon merging with the hated father, Phillotson. Although Jude, Sue, and Father Time refuse to name the bad parent, they create situations in which they punish themselves and the parental surrogates who have failed them. For the tragic protagonists of *Jude the Obscure*, the present repeats the nightmarish past. Hardy's symmetrical plot demonstrates his deterministic view that "What's done can't be undone" (70).

Jude the Obscure portrays Nature as a deficient mother, the law as a repressive father, the two antagonists locked in a deadly, indissolvable marriage. "Radical disorder in the universe is finally matched by radical disorder in human personality," Heilman has remarked about the novel.[21] Hardy's philosophical pessimism cannot be reduced to a single biographical determinant; yet the "General Principles" behind his artistic vision reflect the defective parenting, empathic failure, and object loss implicit in *Jude the Obscure*. In *The Life of Thomas Hardy*, ostensibly written by his second wife, Florence Emily Hardy, but largely ghost-written by the novelist himself, there is an important passage that evokes the spirit of the Fawleys:

General Principles. Law has produced in man a child who cannot but constantly reproach its parent for doing much and yet not all, and constantly say to such parent that it would have been better never to have begun doing than to have *over*done so indecisively; that is, than to have created so far beyond all apparent first intention (on the emotional side), without mending matters by a second intent and execution, to eliminate the evils of the blunder of overdoing. The emotions have no place in a world of defect, and it is a cruel injustice that they should have been developed in it.[22]

Although it is unlikely that Hardy intended this passage either as a criticism of his own parents or as a commentary on *Jude the Obscure*, the novelist's world view reflects the philosophical pessimism in Father Time's farewell speech. It would be misleading, of course, to identify Hardy with a single fictional character, especially with a boy who ends his life before he has a chance to live it. Nevertheless, despite the claim of objectivity in *Jude the Obscure*—"The purpose of a chronicler of moods and deeds does not require him to express his personal views" (348)—the narrator is implicated in the characters' gloomy vision.[23] To give but one example, early in the novel the narrator asks why no one comes along to befriend the young Jude, already disillusioned by his hopeless struggle to master Greek and Latin. "But nobody did come, because nobody does; and under the crushing recognition of his gigantic error Jude continued to wish himself out of the world" (32). In *"I'd Have My Life Unbe"* (1984), Frank Giordano traces the pattern of self-destructive characters in Hardy's world, concluding that, for the novelist, "the desire never to have been born was far more than a traditional poetic trope, while the wish to have his life 'unbe' seems to have recurred often and been very powerful at certain stages."[24]

It is now possible to inquire into the biographical elements of Hardy's novel. Not surprisingly, Hardy insisted that "there is not a scrap of personal detail" in *Jude the Obscure*.[25] There is little in his biography to indicate overt object loss, certainly nothing like the early traumatic loss experienced by Jude and Sue. One fascinating detail emerges, however, about Hardy's entry into the world. When the infant was born, he was presumed dead and cast into a basket by the surgeon in order to attend to the mother, herself in distress. "Dead! Stop a minute: he's alive enough, sure!" the midwife exclaimed (*The Life of Thomas Hardy*, 14). The incident has a tragicomic quality entirely befitting Hardy's later vision of life.[26] As a child, he was extremely delicate and sickly, often cared for by a neighbor. Hardy's biographers acknowledge his inauspicious beginning in life, suggesting a possible link between his early deprivation and life-long bouts of depression. Robert Gittings speaks about an "early thread of perverse morbidity in Hardy, something near abnormality,"[27] while Michael Millgate observes that Hardy's parents took little interest in him because they believed he would die in childhood.[28]

James W. Hamilton, a psychoanalyst, has suggested that the actual circumstances of Hardy's birth burdened him "with profound guilt for having damaged and almost killed his mother," as revealed in his first poem, "Discouragement."[29] An incident in *Tess of the D'Urbervilles* reveals a mother's underloving and overloving tendencies. Hamilton speculates that Tess's ambivalence toward her infant son, aptly named Sorrow (corresponding, perhaps, to the allegorical Father Time in *Jude the Obscure*), may well reflect Jemima Hardy's feelings toward her own child. "When the infant had taken its fill," Hardy writes in *Tess of the D'Urbervilles*, "the young mother sat it upright in her lap, and looking into the far distance dandled it with a gloomy indifference that was almost dislike; then all of a sudden she fell to violently kissing it some dozens of times, as if she could never leave off, the child

crying at the vehemence of an onset which strangely combined pas-
sionateness with contempt."[30] Sorrow's death, like Father Time's,
implicates both nature and nurture: "So passed away Sorrow the
Undesired—that intrusive creature, that bastard gift of shameless
Nature who respects not the social law" (*Tess*, 81).

Hardy's acknowledgement that the fictional portrait of Mrs. Yeobright in *The Return of the Native* was closely based upon his own
mother is also revealing. Closely resembling Mrs. Morel in Lawrence's *Sons and Lovers*, Mrs. Yeobright is an intimidating woman,
alternating between moods of gentleness and anger. Like Paul Morel,
Clym Yeobright is implicated in his mother's death. Michael Millgate
points out in his biography that while Jemima Hardy always com-
manded the unquestioning devotion of her children, she could be
"cold in her manner, intolerant in her views, and tyrannical in her
governance" (21). The same could be said about nearly all parents at
one time or another, but Mrs. Yeobright, like Mrs. Morel, is particularly overbearing.

To what extent did Hardy suffer narcissistic injuries as a consequence of erratic maternal care? Giordano notes that Hardy was
plagued by feelings of low self-esteem, referring to himself on his
forty-seventh birthday as "Thomas the Unworthy" (*The Life of Thomas
Hardy*, 200). Although we do not usually think of Hardy as a mother-
fixated novelist, as we do of D. H. Lawrence, Gittings observes that
he repeatedly fell in love with women (in particular, with several
maternal cousins) who reminded him of his mother. "More than most
mother-fixed youths, Hardy was falling in love with his own mother
over and over again, in a physical and consistent way that was a
typical part of his almost literal-minded nature" (*Young Thomas Hardy*,
64). Hardy's attraction to his cousin, Tryphena Sparks, one of the
chief sources of Sue Bridehead, has generated intense biographical
speculation.[31] Whatever actually happened between Hardy and his
mysterious cousin, Jude and Sue reflect the novelist's fascination with
incestuous love and its elusive, forbidden nature. Hardy's tragic heroes and heroines repeatedly find themselves pursuing the unobtainable. Like Narcissus, they discover the bittersweet quality of infatuation, ending their lives defeated and broken, unable to recover lost
primal unity.

Hardy's little-known novel *The Well-Beloved* (1897) powerfully confirms the narcissistic infatuation to which his characters are particularly vulnerable. Hardy wrote *The Well-Beloved*, subtitled "A Sketch of a Temperament," at about the same time he was working on *Jude the Obscure*. Both novels explore spectral love. Critics generally agree that *The Well-Beloved* is Hardy's most autobiographical novel in its revelations of his unhappy love life. Jocelyn Pierston is a sculptor, not a writer, but like Hardy he is blessed and cursed by a seemingly endless series of blinding infatuations that end in bitter disillusionment. Pierston tires of his lovers as soon as he knows them well, and only one aspect of his life remains constant: the instability of his love. Unusually introspective, Pierston meticulously analyzes his infatuations, lamenting the havoc they wreak upon his life:

To see the creature who has hitherto been perfect, divine, lose under your very gaze the divinity which has informed her, grow commonplace, turn from flame to ashes, from a radiant vitality to a relic, is anything but a pleasure for any man, and has been nothing less than a racking spectacle to my sight. Each mournful emptied shape stands ever after like the nest of some beautiful bird from which the inhabitant has departed and left it to fill with snow.[32]

Pierston's pursuit of the Beloved One, as he calls his elusive love object, suggests defensive idealization, concealing hostility toward women. "Each shape, or embodiment, has been a temporary residence only, which she has entered, lived in awhile, and made her exit from, leaving the substance, so far as I have been concerned, a corpse, worse luck!" (33). Like Narcissus, Pierston realizes that he is doomed to pursue phantoms who vanish upon close approach. Poetic justice catches up with him when he finds himself infatuated hopelessly with a young woman (the daughter of the woman he rejected earlier) who, driven by the same psychology, tantalizes and finally spurns him. Pierston is in love with the idea of love, as Sue Bridehead is. Indeed, Sue's revealing admission, that sometimes her love of being loved gets the better of her conscience, causing her to treat a man cruelly, applies equally well to Pierston. Both Sue and Pierston fail in their reparative efforts to undo the harm they have caused others.

In an illuminating article on *The Well-Beloved* that reveals as much about the creative source of his own fiction as it does about Hardy's, John Fowles has identified the real object of Pierston's hopeless quest. "The vanished young mother of infancy is quite as elusive as the Well-Beloved—indeed, she *is* the Well-Beloved, although the adult writer transmogrifies her according to the pleasures and fancies that have in the older man superseded the nameless ones of the child—most commonly into a young female sexual ideal of some kind, to be attained or pursued (or denied) by himself hiding behind some male character."[33] Intrigued by an interpretation of *The French Lieutenant's Woman* published by the Yale psychoanalyst Gilbert Rose, Fowles posits in Hardy and other novelists an unconscious drive toward the unobtainable. Fowles accepts Rose's thesis that the wish to reestablish unity with the lost mother of infancy is an important motive behind the creative impulse.[34] Behind Tryphena Sparks and the other incarnations of the Well-Beloved, including Sue Bridehead and Tess, both of whom Fowles calls in *The French Lieutenant's Woman* "pure Tryphena in spirit,"[35] lies the pre-Oedipal mother, the muse behind all creativity.

Yet Hardy's maternal muse was profoundly paradoxical, both creative and destructive. *Jude the Obscure* remains his bleakest novel, arguably the bleakest in English literature. Of all Hardy's great tragic novels, *Jude the Obscure* alone lacks convincing affirmation. Despite Hardy's sympathy toward Jude and Sue, he casts them into an indifferent world and then shows, in a novel at once beautiful and terrible, the tragedy of their self-extinction. "How cruel you are," Swinburne wrote to Hardy in an otherwise glowing review the novelist cites in his biography. "Only the great and awful father of 'Pierrette' and 'l'Enfant Maudit' was ever so merciless to his children" (270). Speaking like a disillusioned parent renouncing further children, Hardy observes, in the "Postscript to the Preface" to *Jude the Obscure*, that the experience of writing the book cured him completely of the wish to write additional novels. The novel provoked so much hostility, in fact, that he later referred to a book-burning incident in which the real object of the flames was the novelist himself. It may seem extravagant to compare Father Time's infanticide to Hardy's decision to silence forever his fictional voice. The fact remains, however, that although Hardy published a voluminous amount of poetry in the remaining thirty-three years of his life, he repudiated the art of fiction, perhaps believing, like Father Time, that the world would be better off without him. In that decision lies the greatest loss of all.

SEVEN

Echoes of Rejection in
Sons and Lovers

The first psychoanalytic criticism of *Sons and Lovers* (1912) was written by Lawrence himself. Writing to Edward Garnett one day after sending the manuscript to the publisher, the young novelist reveals the split between Paul Morel's spiritual and sexual love. In Lawrence's Oedipal interpretation, "a woman of character and refinement goes into the lower class, and has no satisfaction in her own life." She rejects her husband and selects her sons as love objects, first the eldest, William, then the second son, Paul. Encouraged by their mother, the sons despise the father and usurp his position in the family. The intense bond between the mother and her sons prevents them from loving women their own age upon reaching manhood. The split kills William and severely injures Paul. Mrs. Morel realizes her destructive effect on the family and dies, leaving Paul also "drifting toward death."[1] Lawrence viewed Paul's problem as symptomatic of the "tragedy of thousands of young men in England," a tragedy the writer felt certain he had transmuted into a "great book."

As Simon O. Lesser and others have shown, there is a striking parallel between *Sons and Lovers* and Freud's "The Most Prevalent Form of Degradation in Erotic Life," also published in 1912.[2] Freud's essay, one of his contributions to the psychology of love, asserts that an incestuous fixation on a mother or sister plays a prominent role in psychological impotence. For certain men who are unusually frustrated by reality and who remain excessively attracted to the mother or sister, a split develops along the two directions personified in art as sacred and profane love. The overvaluation of the mother's sacred love is maintained by the devaluation of the profane love of another woman, such as a prostitute or mistress. For such men, Freud writes in one of his most memorable passages, "where they love they do not desire and where they desire they cannot love."[3] The observation anticipates the same comment made by the oracular Tommy Dukes in *Lady Chatterley's Lover* (1928): "A woman wants you to like her and talk to her, and at the same time love her and desire her; and it seems to me the two things are mutually exclusive."[4]

The spirit of Freudianism was in the air when Lawrence wrote *Sons and Lovers*, but it is unlikely that he read the psychoanalyst's publications at that time. Frieda Lawrence told Frederick J. Hoffman in 1942 that while Lawrence knew about Freud before the final draft of *Sons and Lovers*, he acquired his understanding of psychoanalysis largely through her own interest in the subject. "I was a great Freud admirer; we had long arguments and Lawrence's conclusion was more or less that Freud looked on sex too much from the doctor's point of view, that Freud's 'sex' and 'libido' were too limited and mechanical and that the root was deeper."[5] Lawrence recognized in Freud a formidable opponent and wrote two books, *Psychoanalysis and the Unconscious* and *Fantasia of the Unconscious*, attacking the analyst's bleak vision of the unconscious. Unlike Freud, Lawrence viewed "incest-craving," not as a normal developmental process, but as a pathological result of a parent's sexual demands upon the child.[6]

Lawrence later regretted his Freudian interpretation of *Sons and Lovers*, particularly when critics began to follow his lead in pointing out the novel's incestuous motifs. In 1916 the first important psychoanalytic article appeared on *Sons and Lovers*.[7] Lawrence did not like the interpretation, as he makes clear in an exasperated letter to Barbara Low:

I hated the Psychoanalysis Review of *Sons and Lovers*. You know I think "complexes" are vicious half-statements of the Freudians: sort of can't see wood for trees. When you've said Mutter-complex, you've said nothing—no more than if you called hysteria a nervous disease. Hysteria isn't nerves, a complex is not simply a sex relation: far from it. —My poor book: it was, as art, a fairly complete truth: so they carve a half lie out of it, and say "*Voilà.*" Swine![8]

It has been three quarters of a century since Lawrence offered his Oedipal reading of *Sons and Lovers,* and psychoanalysis has changed profoundly. Readers continue to dissect Paul Morel's mother complex, but few are bold enough to cry *Voilà. Sons and Lovers* remains one of the most psychoanalyzed of all literary texts, and one of the most problematic. The roots of Paul's psychosexual conflicts lie deeper than Lawrence implied in his 1912 summary of the novel. Daniel Weiss's classic study, *Oedipus in Nottingham* (1962),[9] is still illuminating in its detailed account of Lawrence's indebtedness, via Freud, to Sophocles' myth, but in recent years critics have turned to pre-Oedipal issues to account for Lawrence's themes. Just as psychoanalytic theorists have revised their understanding of human development in light of the impressive data suggesting the overwhelming importance of the first year or two of life, when the process of separation and individuation begins, so have psychoanalytic literary critics revised their understanding of Lawrence's life and art. The new interpretation of Lawrence strongly challenges older readings.

Central to the new view of Lawrence is the image of the "devouring mother." The term comes, appropriately enough, from a letter Lawrence wrote to Katherine Mansfield in 1918, warning her of the dangers of the "Mother-incest idea." Enclosing a book by Carl Jung for her and her husband, Middleton Murray, Lawrence launches into an impassioned discussion of mother incest. Yet, even as he warns her that incest can become a dangerous obsession and a falsification of reality, he acknowledges that there is this much truth in it:

at certain periods the man has a desire and a tendency to return unto the woman, make her his goal and end, find his justification in her. In this way he casts himself as it were into her womb, and she, the Magna Mater, receives him with gratification. This is a kind of incest. It seems to me it is what Jack does to you, and what repels and fascinates you. I have done it, and now struggle all my might to get out. In a way, Frieda is the devouring mother.— It is awfully hard, once the sex relation has gone this way, to recover.[10]

Lawrence's candor in writing about his ambivalence toward the "Magna Mater" is startling. He admits, for example, that while Frieda regards his attitude toward women as "antediluvian," he insists that "a woman must yield some sort of precedence [submission] to a man, and he must take his precedence." The belief in male domination would seem to be a compensation for deeply rooted fear of women.

Although Lawrence conceives of the devouring mother in terms of the Oedipus complex, contemporary psychoanalytic critics detect earlier issues of identity and separation-individuation.

Three psychoanalytic studies of Lawrence, all focusing on the mother-son relationship, may be singled out. Marguerite Beede Howe argues in *The Art of the Self in D. H. Lawrence* (1977) that Lawrence's main concern is not blood religion, modern sexuality, nor the vicissitudes of the industrial age, but identity. "This tendency to see existence as relationship, and all relationship as some form of engulfment, is the single most important fact in Lawrence's world view."[11] In *D. H. Lawrence and the Devouring Mother* (1984), Judith Ruderman explores the unresolved pre-Oedipal themes in Lawrence's leadership stories. Citing the research of Erik Erikson, Erich Fromm, and Margaret Mahler, Ruderman discusses how the child's desire to merge with the mother may awaken the fear that dependency leads to death. "The child's pre-oedipal dilemma is that his need for the mother's nurture and protection stimulates a desire to return to the womb, but this regressive dependency means that the child will in effect die, having been annihilated by the devouring, engulfing mother."[12] Daniel Dervin's *A "Strange Sapience"* (1984) links Lawrence's creativity to the conflicts arising toward the end of the first year of life, when the process of object loss, self/separation, and object recovery come to the fore. Relying upon the child development research of Michael Balint and D. W. Winnicott, Dervin emphasizes the mother-child dyad. He suggests that Lawrence "may have countered his fears of maternal envelopment by reproducing and enveloping his own universe of characters."[13] Lawrence's overidealization of the mother, all three critics believe, concealed intense ambivalence.

Until recently, however, most readers accepted Jessie Chambers' statement in *D. H. Lawrence: A Personal Record* that in *Sons and Lovers* Lawrence handed his mother the "laurels of victory."[14] Frieda, who met Lawrence two years after his mother's death, also believed that he glorifies her in *Sons and Lovers*. "He really loved his mother more than any body, even with his other women, real love, sort of Oedipus, his mother must have been adorable."[15] By using *any body* instead of *anybody*, Frieda emphasizes the sexual aspect of Lawrence's love for his mother. Lawrence's statements as a young man support the Oedipal reading of *Sons and Lovers* that he announced to Garnett:

namely, that the son's excessive love for the mother prevented him from loving other women. Jessie Chambers, the source of Miriam Leivers, reports a conversation with Lawrence the day before his mother's funeral in 1910. " 'You know—I've always loved mother,' he said in a strangled voice. 'I know you have,' I replied. 'I don't mean that,' he returned quickly. 'I've *loved* her—like a lover. That's why I could never love you.' "[16]

Many leading scholars continue to affirm the wholesomeness of Lawrence's relationship with his mother and, by extension, Paul's relationship with Mrs. Morel. Critics feel strongly about this issue, for they do not change their minds. Harry T. Moore reports in his revised and enlarged biography, *The Priest of Love* (1974), the view that he first propounded in *The Intelligent Heart* (1954). "The clinical view of Lawrence as a lifelong victim of the Oedipus complex, with all conventional outcroppings of that affliction, including homosexuality, is easily dismissed." Yet the "clinical view" of Lawrence is far more complicated than Moore implies, and no psychoanalytic critic would be inclined to reduce Lawrence (or any other artist, for that matter) to "victim" status. Moore continues to quote approvingly Father William Tiverton's observation in 1951 that some Lawrence critics and biographers have "much exaggerated his Oedipus complex." Moore agrees with Tiverton that after writing *Sons and Lovers,* Lawrence grew "into a separate existence which cannot be interpreted in terms of Mrs Lawrence."[17] Acknowledging the presence of a destructive element in Mrs. Morel's relations with her husband and sons, Keith Sagar nevertheless asserts in *The Art of D. H. Lawrence* (1966) that the "overriding impression is of a normality and strength of character which serves *[sic]* as a standard against which the other women in the novel are judged, and found wanting."[18] In *The Love Ethic of D. H. Lawrence* (1955), Mark Spilka affirms the essential health of Paul's relationship with his mother before William's death. Two decades later, Spilka continues to celebrate the relationship: "Only Paul and his mother, unsentimental and emotionally honest, seem to qualify for maturity—perhaps because of their genuine affection for each other."[19]

And yet there is abundant biographical evidence to suggest Lawrence's awareness of his destructive relationship to his mother. As early as 1910 he refers to their "peculiar fusion of soul." "We have been like one, so sensitive to each other that we never needed words. It has been rather terrible, and has made me, in some respects, abnormal." His conclusion is that "nobody can have the soul of me. My mother has had it, and nobody can have it again. Nobody can come into my very self again, and breathe me like an atmosphere."[20] Today we would call this type of bond a *symbiotic relationship* or, in a different clinical frame, an *enmeshed relationship* and expect to find, as we do throughout Lawrence's writings, strong matricidal imagery. Admitting in 1922 that he had not done justice to Mr. Morel in *Sons and Lovers,* Lawrence came to believe that his mother had turned the children against their father, degraded his manhood, and needlessly provoked scenes of vituperation. "Shaking his head sadly at the memory of that beloved mother, he would add that the righteous woman martyred in her righteousness is a terrible thing and that all self-righteous women ought to be martyred."[21] In *Not I, But the Wind,* Frieda reports Lawrence saying that he would rewrite *Sons and Lovers* if he had the chance. "My mother was wrong, and I thought she was absolutely right." Frieda shrewdly adds: "In his heart of hearts I think he always dreaded women, felt that they were in the end more powerful than men."[22]

Significantly, Lawrence's repressed anger toward his mother was played out in his stormy marriage to Frieda. He was particularly insensitive to Frieda's attachment to her children, whom she was forced to give up when she left her first husband. "You don't care a damn about those brats really, and they don't care about you," Lawrence shouted at her. "My agony over them was my worst crime in his eyes," Frieda believed, sadly concluding that "perhaps he, who had loved his mother so much, felt, somewhere, it was almost impossible for a mother to leave her children."[23]

Though critics have long interpreted Paul Morel as a budding Oedipus, not as a troubled Narcissus, the parallels to Ovid's myth are fascinating. The product of a doting mother and a symbolically absent father, Paul inspires women with thoughts of love. After William dies, Paul becomes the center of his mother's attention. His relationship with Miriam Leivers begins when he is about sixteen, Narcissus' age when he meets Echo. Echo is silenced by the jealous Juno, while Miriam is muted by the jealous Mrs. Morel. The aroused Miriam admires the beautiful youth from a distance until she silently attracts his attention. Paul pursues her ambivalently, desiring her sensuality yet fearing her suffocating love embrace. Fleeing Echo, Narcissus exclaims: "Hands off! embrace me not! May I die before I give you power o'er me!"[24] Fleeing Miriam, Paul exclaims: "You absorb, absorb, as if you must fill yourself up with love, because you've got a shortage somewhere" (274). Like the rejected Echo, Miriam withdraws into herself, hurt and confused. Paul then pursues another woman, Clara Dawes, but inexplicably rejects her. Like Narcissus, he "loves an unsubstantial hope and thinks that substance which is only shadow" (*Metamorphoses*, 153). Worshiped and worshiper, object and subject, Paul is impoverished by his own riches. Empathically bidding his dying mother farewell at the end of the novel, Paul recognizes that a Nemesis awaits him.

Paul is an Echo as well as a Narcissus, and at crucial moments he finds himself involuntarily repeating his mother's actions and thoughts. Mrs. Morel remains the central figure in his life; yet no matter how often he echoes his love for her, he cannot adequately please or fulfill her. Alternately overloving and underloving, she is never able to establish the correct distance from her children. Her love is controlling and possessive, and when Paul grows up, he sees all relationships in the same way, as repetitions of controlling, possessive love. Paul's rejection of Miriam and Clara leads, in turn, to their rejection of him, resulting in his loss of self-esteem and will to live.

Paul's dilemma is to free himself from a mother who lives vicariously through him and who threatens to withdraw her support when he finds other women to love. Frightened by the feelings of fragmentation arising from the loosening of the symbiotic bond, Paul clings to her, though not without growing resentment. He splits his feelings toward Mrs. Morel into the good mother, whom he idealizes, and the bad mother, whom he devalues and then projects onto Miriam and Clara. Repeating the pattern of his mother's relationships, Paul alternates between frenzied pursuit and agonized escape. The major figures in his life function as selfobjects, a projection screen of his guilt and fear. His rejection of Miriam and Clara thus mirrors a larger self-rejection. Paul's defense mechanisms protect his fragile self-esteem, but the cumulative effect of his rejection of women is self-depletion.

The family history of the Morels reveals how psychic injuries are passed on from generation to generation. Gertrude Coppard is the daughter of a solid, middle-class burgher family. Her father is a proud, haughty engineer bitterly galled by poverty; her mother is gentle, humorous, kind. Gertrude favors her mother but resembles her father. The daughter's proud, unyielding temperament and growing bitterness are part of her paternal legacy. She inherits her father's puritanical beliefs, scathing sarcasm, and mistrust of human nature. The novel does not describe the Coppards' marriage, but it is interesting to see how history repeats itself. Gertrude hates her father's overbearing manner but later becomes overbearing to her husband and children. She is capable of expressing gentleness and humor toward her children, but more often we see her resentment and coldness. She is angry over being a woman, and in deprecating her sex, she wishes to be a man: "If *I* were a man, nothing would stop me."[25] Significantly, Miriam and Clara later express the same resentment of men combined with the wish for male power. Mrs. Morel, Miriam, and Clara are portrayed as "superior" women who have no real friends and who remain coolly polite in their dealings with women.

Gertrude Coppard's attraction to Walter Morel is based upon the principle of opposites. She is drawn toward his shining black hair, vigorous beard, and soft, nonintellectual smile. Morel's passion and vitality complement her moral and spiritual temperament: he is Dionysus to her Apollo. The battle begins almost immediately after marriage. Morel soon becomes irresponsible, cruel, violent, and finally indifferent to his family. For her part, Mrs. Morel becomes cynical and embittered. She remains wedded to her husband yet despises him, and their love-hate relationship constitutes the dominant form of bonding in the novel. Only the mother's responsibility to the children prevents the family structure from shattering. From birth, the children grow up with a degraded image of their father. Morel bullies his family, steals from his wife's purse, and drinks himself into a stupor. There are, it is true, a number of early scenes when Walter Morel is portrayed sympathetically. He is in good spirits early in the morning as he prepares for work, and he can be boisterous and playful. He is also a storyteller, exerting a greater impact upon Paul's artistic imagination than Lawrence chooses to admit. Nevertheless, by the time Paul is born, the father has fallen into slow ruin; his body shrinks, his manners deteriorate, and his work declines. "He had denied the God in him" (102). The sympathy expressed toward Morel in the opening pages of the story is soon withdrawn, and his animalistic utterances identify him as a beast: he "sneers," "snarls," "hisses," and speaks "venomously."

Although *Sons and Lovers* vividly dramatizes the children's terror of the drunken father, their terror of the strong-willed mother may be greater. The father is rarely home, while the mother is omnipresent. Even Morel, physically stronger than his wife, remains frightened of her verbal power. "If he sinned, she tortured him. If he drank, and lied, was often a poltroon, sometimes a knave, she wielded the lash unmercifully" (51). A wife who actively despises her husband generally inspires fear in her young children, who recognize that she may also attack them. The threat to withdraw love from a child may be more devastating than actual physical abuse; the threat is less conscious, therefore, not easily defended against. Mrs. Morel is only dimly aware of her ability to inflict injury on her husband and children. When Morel is severely injured in a mining accident, she cannot grieve for him, apart from feeling bitter sorrow. "But still, in her heart of hearts, where the love should have burned, there was a blank" (128). The void in her heart reflects, not an absence of emotion, but an unspeakable rage that approaches murderous intensity. It is as if she has symbolically killed Walter Morel in her heart without formally burying him or mourning his passing. Banished from the family, Morel revenges himself on them by retreating further into alcoholism and by neglecting his health. Only by hurting himself can he hurt others and gain a degree of pity from them. Paul's delicate health may have its sources in the same wish to elicit love and attention.

Few marriages are as chilling as the Morels', but there are curious discrepancies in Paul's portrayal of his parents. He makes no effort to heal the terrible rift between them, and he feels only contempt for the exiled Morel. Why, then, does Paul unexpectedly defend his parents' marriage to outsiders? Contrasting his parents' marriage to that of Baxter and Clara Dawes, Paul tells Miriam that his parents actually received genuine pleasure at first from living together. "My mother, I believe, got *real* joy and satisfaction out of my father at first. I believe she had a passion for him; that's why she stayed with him. After all, they were bound to each other" (381). Apart from the opening pages of the novel, however, we see nothing that is positive about the

Morels' marriage. Mrs. Morel's love for her husband has been in a state of constant decline; "there were many, many stages in the ebbing of her love for him, but it was always ebbing" (84). The periods of temporary truce hardly constitute marital satisfaction. Only from hearsay can Paul have learned about his mother's early passion for his father. Paul praises a marriage here that elsewhere is condemned in the harshest terms. In addition, he extols his mother for qualities that are not dramatized in the story. In claiming that there's "not a tiny bit of feeling of sterility" about his mother (381), Paul contradicts Mrs. Morel's aversion to the instinctual side of life. Moreover, it is impossible to accept the observation that his mother still "feels grateful" for her early experiences with her husband.

There are other inconsistencies in the novel's portrayal of Mrs. Morel. Her reputation in the family as an intellectual with a "curious, receptive mind, which found much pleasure and amusement in listening to other folk" (44) is asserted but not dramatized. We are told that before Mrs. Morel would read a paper to the Women's Guild, the children see her preparing at home, reading, writing, and referring to books. Nevertheless, we don't actually see her writings or hear her literary conversations. Nor do we see her encouraging the children to explore the world of literature. Perhaps Gertrude Morel's curiosity has been destroyed by years of a deadening marriage, but Lawrence does not show her interest in literature, history, or art. She seems more preoccupied with her sons' success in becoming gentlemen than in their intellectual or artistic development. Paul celebrates his mother's virtues mainly to criticize other women, which makes the sincerity of his praise suspect. Shocked by Miriam's intensely possessive love, he contrasts it to his mother's "reserve." "And on such occasions he was thankful in his heart and soul that he had his mother, so sane and wholesome" (203). When we actually see Mrs. Morel interact with her children, however, she does not seem reserved, sane, or wholesome. Is Paul deceiving himself about his mother, and if so, is Lawrence aware of this self-deception?

Paul recognizes that his mother is overloving, overprotective, but fails to see that she is also underloving, underprotective. As I discussed in the chapter on *The Picture of Dorian Gray*, overlove is a form of love that has grown toxic in its intensity. Overlove is close to underlove on the emotional continuum. Sophie Freud's definition of narcissism as a condition in which one simultaneously overloves and underloves oneself captures the paradoxical union of self-love and self-hate. Mrs. Morel's oversolicitousness toward her children thus masks a hostility that Paul cannot bring himself to admit.

Evidence for this interpretation appears in one of Lawrence's best short stories, "The Rocking-Horse Winner," written in 1926. A skeletal *Sons and Lovers*, the story contains the familiar Oedipal triangle: a cold, embittered mother who scorns her husband and demands more money; a weak, ineffectual father who is described as "luckless"; and an adolescent son, coincidentally named Paul, who claims that he will succeed in winning luck and making his mother happy. The story is filled with unmistakable incestuous fantasies, yet what Paul most desires from his mother is not sexual union but simply assurance that he is loved. Like Mrs. Morel, the mother marries for love, but it turns to dust. Most revealing of all, she is incapable of loving her children. They sense this: "They looked at her coldly, as if they were finding fault with her. And hurriedly she felt she must cover up some fault in herself." [26] In the presence of her children, "she always felt the centre of her heart go hard." Dismayed by her coldness, the mother "was all the more gentle and anxious for her children, as if she loved them very much." Yet her oversolicitousness does not fool the family. They know that "at the centre of her heart was a hard little place that could not feel love, no, not for anybody" (790). Paul feverishly rides the rocking horse, wins over seventy thousand pounds, but dies mysteriously from brain fever. His quest to usurp his father's position in the family ends in self-destruction; both father and son are finally defeated, emasculated. At the end of "The Rocking-Horse Winner," the mother remains unable to love her son or recognize her complicity in his death.

Mrs. Morel's ambivalence toward her children is embedded in the novel's subtext. By the time Paul, the third child, is born, the mother no longer feels love for her husband or the desire to have more children. "She had dreaded this baby like a catastrophe, because of her feeling for her husband. And now she felt strangely towards the infant. Her heart was heavy because of the child, almost as if it were unhealthy, or malformed" (73). Mrs. Morel's fear about the baby's health reflects her anger over being pregnant again, as well as an unconscious wish for the baby's death. When the mother does begin to feel a connection with the baby, the love seems strained. "She held it close to her face and breast. With all her force, with all her soul she would make up to it for having brought it into the world unloved. She would love it all the more now it was here; carry it in her love" (74). Despite her determination to love the baby, Mrs. Morel perceives a "reproach" in his look, as if he scolds her for bringing him into the world. Young Paul thus resembles Jude the Obscure and Father Time; all three perceive their unwantedness. Like Sue's feelings toward Jude and Father Time, Mrs. Morel's love for Paul is always tinged with guilt. "She had never expected him to live. And yet he had a great vitality in his young body. Perhaps it would have been a little relief to her if he had died. She always felt a mixture of anguish in her love for him" (105).

There is little doubt about Mrs. Morel's emotional unavailability toward the children or her erratic love. She plays favorites among her family: she is closest to William and then, after his death, to Paul. She has few expectations of her daughter, Annie, and ignores her youngest child, Arthur, because he resembles his father. Mrs. Morel's preoccupation with William leaves little time for the other children. Paul's "fits of depression" (86) as a child seem to be caused by emotional neglect. Shirley Panken has suggested that "Mrs. Morel was sharply fluctuating in her ministrations, focused as she was on William and depressed over the breach with her husband. She thus emerges on the one hand as immensely self-preoccupied, withholding, and abandoning. On the other hand, perhaps concerned by her lack of maternal feeling, she appears guiltily oversolicitous and engulfing."[27] Paul grows up with the feeling that, although he would like to believe "love begets love," experience has taught him the opposite. For most people, he sadly tells Miriam, love is a very terrible thing (217).

William's halfhearted effort to break away from his mother illustrates the Morels' terrible love. He brings home a frivolous and vain woman, Louisa Lily Denys Western ("Gypsy"), whom his mother instantly dislikes. The novel makes it impossible for us to take the young woman seriously. The photograph he sends to Mrs. Morel from London reveals a "handsome brunette, taken in profile, smirking slightly—and, it might be, quite naked, for on the photograph not a scrap of clothing was to be seen, only a naked bust" (142). William feigns surprise that his mother is offended by the racy picture. "I'm sorry you didn't like the photograph," he tells her. "It never occurred to me when I sent it, that you mightn't think it decent" (142–43). Can we believe that the worldly William is truly surprised that his prudish mother will be appalled by the photo? Or is it more likely that William has chosen a woman who will offend his mother's sensibility—and his own?

For all his pretended defiance, William is his mother's son, and he is no less appalled by Gypsy's shamelessness than Mrs. Morel is. He is so verbally brutal to her, in fact, that Mrs. Morel feels compelled to defend her. It is easy to be misled into believing, as John Worthen does, that "far from being possessive, Mrs. Morel is actually sympathetic and understanding. She goes out of her way to be nice to the girl."[28] But the truth is just the contrary: Mrs. Morel can afford to be generous to her defeated rival. William, dutiful son that he is, savages the young woman. "Gyp's shallow," he tells his mother. "Nothing goes deep with her" (178). By attacking Gypsy, William maintains his mother on a pedestal while presenting her with a potential wife whose self-absorption reflects her own. Not that the two women are identical. Gypsy is narcissistic in her self-indulgence and vanity, while Mrs. Morel is narcissistic in her overcontrolling personality, possessiveness, and inability to be a joyful mirror to her children's healthy strivings. The underlying cause of William's premature death is not organic but psychological, as Lawrence intimates to Garnett. "William gives his sex to a fribble, and his mother holds his soul. But the split kills him, because he doesn't know where he is."[29]

William's involvement with Gypsy confirms his mother's dire warnings about defying her authority. Before dying, William predicts Gypsy's faithlessness. "She's very much in love with me *now*," he complains to his mother, "but if I died she'd have forgotten me in three months" (178). Behind William's prediction we can hear Mrs. Morel's bitter forecast of his unhappiness—a prophecy that Mrs. Lawrence actually made about her oldest son, on whom William is based.[30] A few weeks after the death, Mrs. Morel receives a letter from Gypsy, confirming William's prediction. " 'I was at a ball last night. Some delightful people were there, and I enjoyed myself thoroughly,' said the letter. 'I had every dance—did not sit out one' " (187). Would anyone write a letter like this to her deceased fiancé's mother? In portraying Gypsy so negatively, Lawrence sides with the mother's point of view. William's death serves as a stern reminder to Paul about the consequences of growing up, leaving home, and attaching himself to another woman. Paul struggles harder for freedom and independence than William does, yet he too discovers that his mother cannot be defied with impunity.

Paul's pursuit of Miriam Leivers confronts him immediately with his mother's double. With her erotic asceticism, proud humility, and violent spirituality, Miriam mirrors Mrs. Morel's oxymoronic qualities. Attuned to his mother's desperate unhappiness, Paul fails to empathize with Miriam's domestic entrapment. Nor can he understand her wish to have the same opportunities as a man. "Men have everything," Miriam says, to which he naïvely responds: "I should think women ought to be as glad to be women as men are to be men" (204). Paul evades the feminist issue here. He makes little effort to understand the social, political, and economic restrictions women confronted at the turn of the century. The failure becomes more disappointing in that, like so many of Lawrence's heroes, Paul has a "feminine" sensibility: a special sensitivity to feelings, an exquisite appreciation of nature, a talent for art. He prefers speaking to his female coworkers, and, apart from his delight in playing with Miriam's brothers, he shrinks from traditionally defined male activities. At the very least, Mrs. Morel's grief over being born a woman might have sensitized her son to the question of women's rights. Unfortunately, Lawrence never allows Mrs. Morel, Miriam, or Clara Dawes to articulate the case for female equality. Mrs. Morel is so unhappy with her life that she begrudges other women the right to escape the imprisonment of home and hearth. When Paul tells his mother that he intends to teach Miriam algebra, Mrs. Morel sarcastically responds: "I hope she'll get fat on it" (205). Miriam's failure to learn mathematics reinforces Paul's belief that a woman's place is in the home.

Mrs. Morel instinctively recognizes Miriam as a rival. " 'She is one of those who will want to suck a man's soul out till he has none of his own left,' she said to herself; 'and he is just such a gaby as to let himself be absorbed' " (211). Mrs. Morel fears mainly for herself. "She's not like an ordinary woman, who can leave me my share in him. She wants to absorb him. She wants to draw him out and absorb him till there is nothing left of him, even for himself. He will never be a man on his own feet—she will suck him up" (245–46). The oral imagery is striking, recalling Otto Kernberg's observation that the narcissist experiences relationships with others as exploitative, as if he were "squeezing a lemon and then dropping the remains." [31]

Mrs. Morel's fear that Paul will be stolen, seduced, devoured by a hated rival anticipates Clarissa's nightmarish dread that her child will be violated by the spectral Miss Kilman in *Mrs. Dalloway*. Both relationships reflect projective identification: the projection of rage onto another character with whom one then actively identifies. Mrs. Morel acknowledges her own selfishness only once in the novel, when she passionately embraces Paul in "Strife in Love," the chapter containing one of the most transparently Oedipal scenes in literature. Mr. Morel's sudden arrival conveniently allows Mrs. Morel to avoid elaborating on her possessiveness. Paul typically falls back upon blaming others for his failures in love, and Miriam unluckily becomes the battleground on which mother and son act out their larger frustrations.

Paul's confusion toward Miriam shows up sexually. He accuses her of being a nun, hence, of making him into a monk. "In all our relations no body enters. I do not talk to you through the senses— rather through the spirit. That is why we cannot love in the common sense" (309). Chaste Miriam reminds him, first, of a Botticelli Madonna, then, of Miriam's mother. But Paul's important, unconscious association is between Miriam and his own mother. He is sexually attracted to Miriam but uses her "spirituality" as a defense against sexual involvement. "I'm so damned spiritual with *you* always," he cries; "You make me so spiritual . . . and I don't want to be spiritual" (241). Mark Spilka notes that Lawrence's identification of Miriam with maiden-blush implies an unhealthy spirituality, with Paul growing to hate her "worshipful, fawning attitude toward life, an attitude which is consistently revealed by her 'relations' with flowers." [32] The criticism places most of the blame on Miriam. The truth is that Paul hardly gives the understandably frightened young woman a chance to learn how to appreciate the mystery of sensual love.

Consider, for example, Miriam's first symbolic sexual experience, the scene in which Paul vigorously thrusts her forward on the swinging rope. The act predictably elicits her resistance and dread. "He heard the fear in her voice, and desisted. Her heart melted in hot pain when the moment came for him to thrust her forward again" (201).

Critics have interpreted the scene to reveal Miriam's passionless, dis-embodied response to life, her inevitable failure to be awakened by Paul's phallic power.[33] Yet if we look at the scene, not in terms of the "phallic imagination"—the mystical, transcendent thrustings to which Paul aspires—but as a realistic description of an assertive male push-ing too strenuously a shy, introverted teenager on a swing, several problems become evident. First, insofar as swinging on a rope is only remotely analogous to love making, the act remains an imperfect metaphor of sexual experience. Second, Miriam's inability to share Paul's rhapsodic delight in swinging is not necessarily a limitation; elsewhere Paul refuses to participate in traditionally defined male activities without incurring the narrator's disapproval. Finally, Mir-iam may actually be in danger of falling off the swing. She can hardly be reassured by Paul's hypnotic words while swinging: " 'Now I'll die,' he said, in a detached, dreamy voice, as though he were the dying motion of the swing" (200). Consequently, the experience does not accurately test Miriam's ability to enjoy physical intimacy.

When they finally do have sexual intercourse, in the chapter called "The Test on Miriam," Paul is quick to conclude that she will never be able to overcome her sexual repression to enjoy physical intimacy. "Her big brown eyes were watching him, still and resigned and loving; she lay as if she had given herself up to sacrifice: there was her body for him; but the look at the back of her eyes, like a creature awaiting immolation, arrested him, and all his blood fell back" (351). Lawrence's sympathy in the scene is never in question: Paul is the adventurous, articulate male, Miriam the unadventurous, inarticulate female. Paul views the sexual act as a transcendent experience, leading to an apprehension of the creative life force; Miriam, by contrast, sees sexual intercourse merely as part of the procreative process. Paul consistently outargues Miriam, and she acquiesces weakly to his logic. Nearly all of Lawrence's commentators side with Paul's point of view, and few defend Jessie Chambers, on whom Lawrence closely modeled Miriam's character.[34] And yet Paul must accept much of the responsi-bility for their sexual failure. Every test reveals something about the tester, and "The Test on Miriam" highlights the limits of Paul's sensitivity and patience.

It is a truism that when passionate relationships end, lovers often blurt out accusations they later regret. Poets and psychologists long have remarked on how passionate love resembles love sickness. Love and hate are close together, and failed relationships often produce rage, despair, shattered self-esteem—in short, a disabling narcissistic injury. Paul tries to be fair to Miriam when he concludes they ought to end their relationship. He urges upon her a no-fault separation. "I want us to break off—you be free of me, I free of you" (347). Unable to explain his feeling of bondage to her, he thinks: "I don't want another mother." Miriam also feels in bondage to Paul and has her own criticisms of him. Lawrence's attempt to be even-handed about their separation breaks down, however, when he enters Miriam's point of view to reveal that she has always hated Paul because of her inability to control and possess him. Miriam maliciously denies that she has ever loved Paul, a charge that shatters him "like a flash of lightning."

Miriam's dark revelation crushes Paul. "He had wanted to say: 'It has been good, but it is at an end.' And she—she whose love he had believed in when he had despised himself—denied that their love had ever been love" (359). Lawrence portrays Paul as the magnanimous philosophical lover, Miriam as the embittered denier of love. There is also the suggestion that she has cynically exploited Paul throughout the relationship. "She had really played with him, not he with her. She had hidden all her condemnation from him, had flattered him, and despised him. She despised him now" (360). Miriam's devaluation thus nullifies their eight-year friendship, forcing the reader to sympathize with the victimized Paul.

By portraying him as the injured party in love, Lawrence exonerates Paul's treatment of Miriam. Expressed differently, the novelist prefers to see Paul more as a victim than as a victimizer. The narrative structure of *Sons and Lovers* has in a sense engulfed Miriam's identity by merging her voice into Paul's. Much of the difficulty in assessing Lawrence's treatment of Paul and Miriam centers on the question of narrative distance. As many critics have noted, Lawrence is so close to Paul's point of view that he shares the hero's confusion and self-justification. While some critics, like Louis L. Martz, have argued that "Lawrence has invented a successful technique by which he can manage the deep autobiographical problems that underlie the book,"[35] other critics, such as A. H. Gomme, see Lawrence as implicated with Paul in a conspiracy to undermine Miriam's character: "It is as if

Lawrence has established an unholy alliance between Paul and Miriam's unspoken feelings against her conscious and deliberate self," a conspiracy in which "Lawrence has ensured that Miriam's own deepest promptings are already leagued against her."[36] The internal textual falsification occurs (like the earlier one involving Gypsy's unbelievable letter to Mrs. Morel) because Lawrence agrees with Mrs. Morel's devaluation of the women who pursue her sons. The perspective is profoundly colored by Mrs. Morel's bitter experience in love and her tendency to view herself as a martyr. Paul's rejection of Miriam repeats earlier rejections in his life. He finds himself in his mother's situation—rejected, abandoned, betrayed. Like his mother, Paul believes there is no middle ground between love and hate: his feelings toward women fluctuate between idealization and devaluation. Believing earlier that Miriam always worshiped him, he concludes now that she has always despised him.

Paul's need to be martyred in love unites him with his mother's point of view. Both see themselves as long-suffering, self-sacrificial, misunderstood. Although he rejects Miriam's spiritual mysticism, with its "rapture of self-sacrifice," Paul is as self-flagellating as she is. He is capable of being assertive, even combative, but more typically he seems passive in the way in which he pines away from unrequited love. Mrs. Morel rightly fears that her son is becoming self-destructive. "He had that poignant carelessness about himself, his own suffering, his own life, which is a form of slow suicide. It almost broke her heart" (316). Mrs. Morel attributes Paul's dangerous self-withdrawal to Miriam's influence on him, but the truth is that he learned this behavior long before he meets Miriam. Earlier, the narrator suggests why a man may grow indifferent toward his health. "Recklessness is almost a man's revenge on his woman. He feels he is not valued, so he will risk destroying himself to deprive her altogether" (243). The Morel men seem to be intimately acquainted with this recklessness. Walter, William, and now Paul Morel find themselves drifting toward slow suicide, which is their revenge on willful women who threaten their fragile manhood.

Paul cannot bring himself to acknowledge that he seeks revenge on his mother. Miriam remains the scapegoat, and the novel's devaluation of her continues to the end. After Miriam departs from an uninvited visit to the Morels late in the story, Paul overhears Clara say to his mother: "What I hate is the bloodhound quality in Miriam." Mrs. Morel instantly agrees: "Yes; *doesn't* it make you hate her, now!" (390). Paul grows angry at their denunciation of Miriam but agrees with them. In the final chapter, "Derelict," Paul sees Miriam in church and invites her to his rooming house, where she "examined with lingering absorption" his possessions. Miriam looks old, stiff, wooden; her nervous hands clasped on her knee "had still the lack of confidence or repose, the almost hysterical look" (488). The last image of Miriam reflects a repressed, smothering female who will either sacrifice herself to Paul in a loveless marriage or enter the man's world to seek substitute gratification. Her final estimation of Paul—"Suddenly she saw again his lack of religion, his restless instability. He would destroy himself like a perverse child. Well, then, he would!" (490–91)—is so vindictive that we are pushed to reject her point of view in favor of Paul's.

Paul's relationship with Clara Dawes is similarly fraught with ambiguity. A working woman who is separated from her husband, Clara is portrayed as an angry feminist, with a grudge against life and a militant wish to cut herself off from human relationships. Like Miriam, Clara becomes a mother surrogate and, hence, the target of Paul's incestuous fantasies. An early exchange reflects the differences between their points of view. Accusing Paul of being sexist, Clara says: "You would much rather fight for a woman than let her fight for herself." Paul agrees, adding that when a woman fights for herself, "she seems like a dog before a looking-glass, gone into a mad fury with its own shadow." Clara's response—"And *you* are the looking-glass?"—elicits Paul's enigmatic answer: "or the shadow" (290). As Hilary Simpson observes about their use of the mirror image, "Paul suggests that in setting themselves up against men, women gain nothing, since the lots of the two sexes are bound up with each other— man is woman's 'shadow.' Clara takes the reference to the mirror differently, suggesting that what he really means is that man is the mirror in which woman must seek her true self."[37] Paul is enamored of Clara as long as she remains the forbidden (m)other, the wife of another man; but as soon as she gives herself to him, he retreats nervously.

Paul's rejection of Clara is perplexing, since she does not appear to have Miriam's flaws. Clara is not stifled by family life or paralyzed by unhealthy spiritualism. She is outspoken in her beliefs, competent in her work, independent in her personal life. She is better educated than Miriam and more articulate. She also has more options than her unworldly rival. Far from accusing her of being a nun, Paul has a satisfying sexual relationship with Clara, at least in the beginning. Her grudge against men, stemming from her husband's brutal treatment of her, appears to give way to trust and respect. Although she initially objects to Paul picking flowers, she finally allows herself to be "picked" by him, to the pleasure of both. Nevertheless, he rejects her. Why? Even Keith Sagar, who otherwise defends Paul's treatment of women, confesses puzzlement: "I cannot see what prevents a permanent relationship between Paul and Clara."[38]

Mrs. Morel predicts that Paul will soon tire of Clara, and he agrees, complaining that she's "fearfully in love with me, but it's not very deep" (417). Paul thus echoes William's earlier complaint over Gypsy's shallowness. But Clara has not been portrayed as superficial, and she in no way resembles the mindless Gypsy. Paul realizes that there is a problem with his relationships to women, but not what the problem is. Claiming that he loves Miriam and Clara, he mournfully asks: "But *why* don't they hold me?" (418).

Paul's question is misleading, however, since he fears being held by anyone. His impression of Clara's stifling possessiveness remains just that—an impression. Unfortunately, Lawrence feels compelled to validate Paul's fears, at the expense of the novel's objectivity. Had Lawrence maintained essential narrative distance, he would have been able to show that Paul's terror of maternal engulfment prevents an otherwise healthy relationship with Clara from developing. Paul projects this fear onto a woman who has not given any signs of being engulfing. Narrative distance would have allowed Lawrence to separate himself from his hero's anguished confusion. But Lawrence validates Paul's fears by blurring the important differences between Clara and Miriam and by merging both characters into another woman, Mrs. Morel, who is the source of Paul's terror of engulfment. Paul suddenly accuses Clara of sexual insatiability and grows frightened of her unrestrained passion. " 'But what do you always want to be kissing and embracing for?' he said. 'Surely there's a time for everything' " (423). The woman who at first demurely resists Paul's impassioned advances is now transformed into an aggressive sexual creature, pursuing him day and night. Clara's transformation remains improbable, prompting us to question Lawrence's intentions. The novelist alters her character in midstream, making her into an echo of Miriam and, ultimately, Mrs. Morel. In an ironic role reversal, Paul sounds like a reticent Miriam when he accuses Clara of incessantly demanding sex. *"Do* I always want to be kissing you?" Clara asks. "Always," Paul replies (423), and then launches into a dubious intellectual discussion of how the daytime should be reserved for work and the nighttime for love.

Paul extricates himself from Clara by encouraging her unlikely return to her estranged husband. The early description of Baxter Dawes reveals a thoroughly detestable man who has ruined his own life and come close to ruining his wife's as well. "His eyes, dark brown and quick-shifting, were dissolute. They protruded very slightly, and his eyelids hung over them in a way that was half hate" (238). Lawrence is explicitly psychological in his analysis of Dawes's inferiority complex. "His whole manner was of cowed defiance, as if he were ready to knock anybody down who disapproved of him— perhaps because he really disapproved of himself" (238). Apart from a few positive details of the blacksmith's physical appearance, such as his soft brown hair and golden moustache, Dawes's increasingly positive role in Paul's life could not be easily predicted. The early encounters between the two men are distinctly unpromising. Paul has an affair with his wife, provokes him at work, and insults him whenever the opportunity arises.

In addition, Clara is unequivocal about Baxter's brutality. "He— he sort of degraded me. He wanted to bully me because he hadn't got me. And then I felt as if I wanted to run, as if I was fastened and bound up. And he seemed dirty" (334). Paul's response—"I see"—is immediately contradicted by the narrator: "He did not at all see." Paul's empathic failure is distressing, repeating his earlier inability to understand Miriam's domestic entrapment. He defends inexplicably a man whose behavior has been indefensible. Without any evidence, Paul declares that Clara was unfair to Dawes, that it was Clara, in fact, who degraded *him*. Paul tries to convince Clara, moreover, that Dawes still loves her. At the end of the novel, Paul effects a reconciliation between husband and wife, despite the fact that, prior to this scene, Dawes has viciously attacked his rival and come close to killing him—an attack, curiously enough, Paul has gone out of his way to instigate.

Paul's unexpected defense of his adversary arises from the striking similarities between Baxter Dawes and Walter Morel. Both laborers are married to intelligent middle-class women who, failing to accept the men for what they are, strive to make them what they cannot be. The result is predictable. The husbands become abusive, slowly sinking into physical and moral ruin. The men are not without positive qualities: they are initially passionate, instinctual, vital. But these qualities are asserted rather than demonstrated, suggesting an aesthetic problem. Whereas Lawrence sides with Mrs. Morel's point of view against her husband, he now shifts sympathy and supports Baxter Dawes against Clara. Paul remains ambivalent toward Dawes, as Daniel Weiss observes: "In *Sons and Lovers* Paul Morel makes the parricidal gesture against his rival, Baxter Dawes; denies it, allows himself to be beaten; and, in full flight, gives up his rivalry and regresses to his old dependency on his mother, once more a child."[39] Paul merges with Dawes both as a defense against Clara, of whom the two men remain wary, and as an atonement for the ill treatment of his broken-spirited father. Paul's defense of Baxter Dawes thus represents a silent acknowledgment that the Morel family history is more complicated than he has previously admitted. Mark Spilka notes in this context that Paul's troubled relationships with men owe as much to his father's emotional default as to his mother's possessive love.[40]

The problem with this section of the novel is that Baxter Dawes's resurrection remains improbable, artistically and psychologically. Paul's need to make restitution to his father leads him to believe that Baxter is simply another version of Walter Morel. Paul does not see the differences between the two men; neither one is viewed clearly. Paul's sudden sympathy for Dawes would be more meaningful if it did not depend upon the continued hostility toward his father or, more ominously, the withdrawal of sympathy from Clara. He defends the husband by misogynistically attacking the wife. "You imagined him something he wasn't," he charges Clara. "That's just what a woman is. She thinks she knows what's good for a man, and she's going to see he gets it; and no matter if he's starving, he may sit and whistle for what he needs, while she's got him, and is giving him what's good for him" (428). Paul faults Clara for misjudging Dawes's character when, in fact, Paul is the one who casts her into another character, Gertrude Morel, who is responsible for emasculating Walter Morel. Paul even accuses Clara of not knowing the "fearful importance" of marriage and of destroying her husband, whom "a good many women would have given their souls to get" (380). By advising Clara to return to her husband, Paul betrays himself as a false analyst, blinded by countertransference.

In agreeing with Paul's interpretation of her marital failure, Clara becomes another version of the willful but repentant woman who destroys her males, thus justifying Paul's decision to end their relationship. Clara's admission that she has been "vile" to Dawes does not encourage Paul to concede his similar treatment of Miriam. The novel forces Clara to bear the major responsibility for the failure of her relationship with Paul. Her character, moreover, deteriorates. The tongue lashing she gives Paul has the effect of restricting the reader's sympathy for her. "It serves me right," she tells Paul. "I never considered him worth having, and now you don't consider *me*. But it serves me right. He loved me a thousand times better than you ever did" (452). Paul's ineffectual protests only intensify her anger, and she repeats her tormenting words. By portraying Clara as a shrill denier of love, Lawrence exonerates his hero a second time from guilt over the breakup of the relationship. Rejected, Paul can thus fall back upon the role of the injured party in love, which maintains the reader's identification with him.

The Clara who exits *Sons and Lovers* is fundamentally different from the character who enters the novel two hundred pages earlier. One can't help feeling that Lawrence violates Clara's fictional autonomy by burdening her with a symbolism that remains out of character. The once assertive feminist who wisely separated from a bullying husband now wishes to subordinate herself to him. Significantly, her reasons for marital reconciliation do not include love. "She wanted to make restitution. It was not that she loved him. As she looked at him lying there her heart did not warm with love. Only she wanted to humble herself to him, to kneel before him. She wanted now to be self-sacrificial" (453). How can we endorse a reconciliation motivated neither by love nor loyalty but only by self-punishment? Clara's reunion with Baxter Dawes recalls Sue Bridehead's disastrous return to Phillotson in *Jude the Obscure*. Like Sue, Clara humbles herself to her husband in a manner suggestive of a terrified child begging for parental forgiveness. It is impossible to imagine anything other than the continuation of a dreary marriage.

Clara's plea for forgiveness reverberates throughout *Sons and Lovers*. Yet freely given, forgiveness is rare in Lawrence's world. Clara's rejection of Paul is total, with no possibility of future friendship. It echoes other rejections haunting the novel: husbands and wives embittered by marital warfare, parents at odds with their children, men and women turning against their former lovers. No novelist records better than Lawrence the ebb and flow of sympathy, the polarity of hate and love. We rightly celebrate his dynamic vision of emotions that are intense, kinetic, and ever shifting. Yet there is little personal constancy in Lawrence's fictional world. One moment Paul and Baxter Dawes commiserate with each other; the next moment they murderously avoid each other. Their alliance depends as much upon a common resentment of Clara as upon a bond of fellowship. It is as if a mysterious inner contaminant threatens to spoil every relationship.

It is harder for Lawrence's characters to forgive family than friends. No one can fail to be moved by Paul's devoted ministrations to his dying mother; his tenderness surely remains one of the novel's highest achievements. But there is a darker side to his solicitude. The dosage of morphia Paul laces into his mother's night milk is lethal; the drug serves not only to terminate her terrible suffering, but also to free him from her destructive control. Paul's final action, euthanasia and matricide, dramatizes his irresolvable ambivalence.

Significantly, Mrs. Morel still cannot bring herself to make peace with her husband. Even as she lies on her deathbed, she is consumed by the cancerous hate that destroyed her marriage years ago. "Now she hated him. She did not forgive him. She could not bear him to be in the room" (455). True to his mother, Paul shows no forgiveness of his father at the end of the story. After the funeral, Morel sits with his wife's relatives and weeps, saying what a good wife she had been and how he tried to do everything for her. "He had striven all his life to do what he could for her, and he'd nothing to reproach himself with" (472). Morel's denials of self-reproach are intended to convey his shallowness and hypocrisy. Still, it is too easy for Lawrence to dismiss the aging man's right to mourn his wife's passing. By portraying

Morel as an empty sentimentalist, Lawrence denies the opportunity for generous forgiveness. Early in the novel, he describes Paul's hatred of his mother and his silent wish that Morel be killed in the coal pits.[41] At the end of the novel, Paul's attitude toward his father has not appreciably improved.

How do we finally view Paul? Will the loss of his mother foreshadow his drift toward death or return to life? Will he be able to recognize his pathological family structure and exorcise the ghosts of the past? Will he be able to heal narcissistic injuries through work and love? Will he, a painter, develop into the kind of artist Lawrence strove to be, concerned with the resurrection not crucifixion of life? In *Lady Chatterley's Lover*, Lawrence tells us that the novel can "inform and lead into new places the flow of our sympathetic consciousness, and . . . lead our sympathy away in recoil from things gone dead."[42] Will Paul's sympathy find a person or purpose into which to flow? Despite the emotional disengagement at the end, he is, like his mother, a fighter, one individual who will not easily pass out of existence. Insofar as Lawrence describes his hero in the 1912 letter to Garnett as "drifting toward death," he appears to underestimate Paul's tenacious instinct for survival. Lawrence seems too quick to reject his character—a rejection that his fictional characters also tend to make.

Sons and Lovers leaves us, finally, with a number of questions involving not only the Oedipal issues Lawrence consciously saw but the pre-Oedipal issues he unconsciously intuited. He presents us with dualisms of separateness and oneness, alienation and community, distance and closeness.[43] Will Paul realize the narcissistic quality of his imagination and grow into object love? Will he find affirmation in the creative process, believing, as Lawrence did, that "one sheds one[']s sicknesses in books—repeats and presents again one[']s emotions, to be master of them"?[44] The last paragraph of *Sons and Lovers* evokes the image of a world of terrifying darkness surrounding the spectral Paul Morel, but we also glimpse a faintly humming, glowing town in the distance, a gold phosphorescence that points away from the Stygian night.

EIGHT

Heart Problems in
Mrs. Dalloway

Considering how common illness is, how tremendous the spiritual change that it brings, how astonishing, when the lights of health go down, the undiscovered countries that are then disclosed, what wastes and deserts of the soul a slight attack of influenza brings to view, what precipices and lawns sprinkled with bright flowers a little rise of temperature reveals, what ancient and obdurate oaks are uprooted in us by the act of sickness, how we go down into the pit of death and feel the waters of annihilation close above our heads and wake thinking to find ourselves in the presence of the angels and the harpers when we have a tooth out and come to the surface in the dentist's arm-chair and confuse his "Rinse the mouth—rinse the mouth" with the greeting of the Deity stooping from the floor of Heaven to welcome us—when we think of this, as we are so frequently forced to think of it, it becomes strange indeed that illness has not taken its place with love and battle and jealousy among the prime themes of literature.—Virginia Woolf, "On Being Ill"[1]

Considering how common illness was to Virginia Woolf's life, how tremendous the spiritual and psychological changes that it brought, how astonishing, when the lights of health went down, as they frequently did, the undiscovered countries that were then disclosed to her—when we think of this, as we are so frequently forced to think of it—it becomes strange indeed that a study of illness as one of the prime themes of Virginia Woolf's literature has not taken its place with studies of love and jealousy.

"On Being Ill" (1930) eloquently describes the difficulty of writing about an experience everyone has but few dare to transmute into art. A novel devoted to illness is unspectacular, Woolf reminds us, because the drama takes place far from the conventional settings of literature. "Those great wars which the body wages with the mind a slave to it, in the solitude of the bedroom against the assault of fever or the oncome of melancholia, are neglected" (10). Nor are the reasons for the neglect hard to seek. To confront the terrible illnesses that beset body and mind requires the "courage of a lion tamer; a robust philosophy; a reason rooted in the bowels of the earth" (10). Short of these, Woolf continues, "this monster, the body, this miracle, its pain, will soon make us taper into mysticism, or rise, with rapid beats of the wings, into the raptures of transcendentalism." Additionally, readers may complain that illness is devoid of drama or excitement, a novel devoted to influenza lacking in plot. Or the public may complain that there is no love in a novel—wrongly, Woolf notes, since illness often takes on the disguise of love, or self-love. Then there is the problem of language. "English, which can express the thoughts of Hamlet and the tragedy of Lear, has no words for the shiver and the head-ache" (11).

Why, then, would a novelist write about illness? The subject relentlessly reminds us of the blunt truths of existence: human vulnerability, the limitations of reason and will, the inevitability of death. "There is, let us confess it (and illness is the great confessional), a childish outspokenness in illness; things are said, truths blurted out, which the cautious respectability of health conceals" (13). Woolf was intimately familiar with these painful truths, and she wrote about illness with an authenticity that few writers have equaled.

Curiously, "On Being Ill" makes no mention of Virginia Woolf's wrenching struggle with mental illness. She cites examples of physical, not psychological, illness: influenza, typhoid, pneumonia, toothache. With its shimmering prose and incandescent imagery, the essay remains singularly nonautobiographical, nonconfessional. It would be hard to infer from "On Being Ill" that Woolf had already suffered numerous breakdowns, enduring months of enforced solitude and inactivity in various psychiatric hospitals and rest homes. The completion of each book confronted her with paralyzing depression and despair. In light of her suicide in 1941, when she forced a large stone into her pocket and drowned herself in the River Ouse near Brighton, the opening sentence of "On Being Ill" uncannily anticipates her own experience with suffering, "how we go down into the pit of death and feel the waters of annihilation close above our heads."

Numerous biographical and critical studies have illuminated Virginia Woolf's courageous struggle against illness and the extent to which her fictional characters attempt to stave off the waters of annihilation.[2] No one has pointed out, however, the thematic connection between "On Being Ill" and *Mrs. Dalloway* (1925), Woolf's fullest treatment of illness. Much has been written about Septimus Warren Smith's madness and suicide, but Clarissa Dalloway's medical condition has been ignored. We are given few specific details about her heart condition, which apparently originated from an attack of influenza. Clarissa, who is fifty-two, has grown white since her recent illness, is required to take afternoon naps, and ascribes her headaches and sleeplessness to a bad heart. The illness does not incapacitate her, and she remains the imaginative center of the novel. Her vitality and generosity of spirit culminate in her party, a celebration of the interconnectedness of life.

Nevertheless, Clarissa betrays many of the symptoms of psychological illness. She is often on the verge of losing control, succumbing to a panic attack triggered by intense conflicts. The thought of her daughter's tutor, Miss Kilman, sends her into quiet frenzy. Clarissa experiences, from beginning to end, the terror and dread of a self that is always threatening to fragment. She fears, not that she will ultimately die, but that her life will be judged worthless. She fears, in the silent words of her implacable enemy, Miss Kilman, that her life is "not serious," "not good," a "tissue of vanity and deceit."[3] Clarissa's health is further exacerbated by Septimus' suicide, attributed to the delayed effect of shell shock incurred in the Great War. Significantly, Clarissa, Miss Kilman, and Septimus share similar "heart" problems. The three characters demonstrate how truths that are usually concealed by the cautious respectability of health are blurted out in illness.

Many of the symptoms of Clarissa's heart condition would today be associated with a narcissistic disturbance, including low self-esteem, hypersensitivity to criticism, depression, identity diffuseness, and hostility. In addition, her moods alternate between overidealization and (self-)devaluation. In observing this, I do not seek to reduce

Clarissa to a psychiatric case study or define her character in terms of *DSM-III*. Clarissa is not narcissistic in a clinical sense: that is, she is not self-centered, with a grandiose sense of self-importance. She is uninterested in ambition or success; she does not require constant attention and admiration; and she is not exhibitionistic, exploitative, or manipulative. If we view narcissism on a continuum, Clarissa may well remain within the range of "normal," especially in contrast to some of the other characters in *Mrs. Dalloway*. Woolf's portrayal of Clarissa—her extraordinary sensibility and attentiveness to language; her apprehension of beauty; her awareness of the terrors and ecstasies of existence; and her striving for the elusive center of life—transcends the merely clinical.

Clarissa's cardiac condition is a metaphor for an illness that cannot be explained entirely in terms of a physically weakened heart or advancing age. Frequent references to heart imagery underscore her dread and uncertainty. Reflecting upon the bitter argument with Peter Walsh, whose marital offer she rejected years ago, "she had borne about with her for years like an arrow sticking in her heart the grief, the anguish" over his calling her "cold, heartless, a prude" (10). Walking upstairs to take an afternoon nap in her isolated bedroom, she mournfully thinks: "There was an emptiness about the heart of life; an attic room" (45). She broods repeatedly over the elegiac line from *Cymbeline*, "Fear no more the heat o' the sun." She changes the words to fit her thoughts: "Fear no more, says the heart. Fear no more, says the heart" (59). Notwithstanding her magical recitation of the Shakespearean line, Clarissa worries endlessly over her emotional health. Even at the end of the novel, there is "in the depths of her heart an awful fear" (281) that cannot be dispelled. Similar fears beset the other characters. Mrs. Foxcroft is "eating her heart out" (5) over the death of a young man in the war, and Peter still grieves over Clarissa's rejection of him, which, he believes, "almost broke my heart" (62).

Clarissa does not fear a literal heart attack so much as an affective seizure associated with a weak or cold heart. The specter of falling ill, breaking down, becoming dependent upon doctors looms throughout *Mrs. Dalloway*, but the illness is never precisely defined or explained. Characters allude elliptically to illness, as when Hugh Whitbread tersely informs Clarissa that he has brought his wife Evelyn to London "to see doctors" (7). "Was Evelyn ill again?" Clarissa wonders. The question is significant in that "times without number she had visited Evelyn Whitbread in a nursing home" (7). The husband's reply is a masterpiece of evasion: " 'Evelyn was a good deal out of sorts,' said Hugh, intimating . . . that his wife had some internal ailment, nothing serious, which, as an old friend, Clarissa Dalloway would quite understand without requiring him to specify" (7). Clarissa apprehends Hugh's meaning and replies, in a "sisterly" tone: "What a nuisance" (7). She does not question the appropriateness of Hugh's silence, and Evelyn's chronic illness remains mysterious.

Clarissa has no sororal feelings toward another woman whose condition in life seems more desperate than Evelyn Whitbread's. To be sure, Doris Kilman is described in terms, not of medical illness, but of emotional disability. Brooding constantly over her unhappiness, Miss Kilman is filled with rage, bitterness, and jealousy. She is one of the many characters who is guilty of "forcing the soul"—imposing her will onto other people. Most readers have accepted Clarissa's harsh condemnation of Miss Kilman, and, to judge from the published criticism of the novel, about the best one can say on Miss Kilman's behalf is that she cannot understand her violent jealousy of Clarissa or her ferocious urge to possess Clarissa's daughter, Elizabeth. The mere thought of Miss Kilman invariably releases in Clarissa a flood of angry emotion that threatens to wash away her defenses, leaving her vulnerable to total collapse. Yet why should a woman who is socially, economically, and politically powerless succeed in provoking Clarissa's outbursts? Why does the mere thought of Miss Kilman make Clarissa ill, heartless?

Clarissa's first reference to Miss Kilman results in a jarring loss of self-control. She objects to Miss Kilman's religious fanaticism, shabby green mackintosh coat (symbolizing her poverty and disapproval of the wealthy upper class), and proximity to the impressionable Elizabeth. In trying to explain her hatred of Miss Kilman, Clarissa momentarily allows us a glimpse into her nightmarish world. "For it was not her one hated but the idea of her, which undoubtedly had gathered in to itself a great deal that was not Miss Kilman; had become one of those spectres with which one battles in the night; one of those spectres who stand astride us and suck up half our life-blood, dominators and tyrants; for no doubt with another throw of the dice, had the black been uppermost and not the white, she would have loved Miss Kilman! But not in this world. No" (16–17).

Clarissa's outburst only calls attention to her convoluted feelings toward Miss Kilman. It is not clear why she regards Miss Kilman as a specter, parasite, dominator, or tyrant or why she adds that, under different circumstances, she might have loved Miss Kilman. What is clear is that Clarissa sees Miss Kilman, not as a real person, but as a symbol of a monstrous evil or disease able to destroy all that is most dear in life. Clarissa cannot exorcise the nightmare of Miss Kilman, as the following paragraph vividly demonstrates:

> It rasped her, though, to have stirring about in her this brutal monster! to hear twigs cracking and feel hooves planted down in the depths of that leaf-encumbered forest, the soul; never to be content quite, or quite secure, for at any moment the brute would be stirring, this hatred, which, especially since her illness, had power to make her feel scraped, hurt in her spine; gave her physical pain, and made all pleasure in beauty, in friendship, in being well, in being loved and making her home delightful rock, quiver, and bend as if indeed there were a monster grubbing at the roots, as if the whole panoply of content were nothing but self love! this hatred! (17)

Clarissa rejects Miss Kilman, not as one dismisses a nonentity, but as one casts off a diseased part of the self. The idea of Miss Kilman mobilizes all of Clarissa's shadowy fears, insecurities, and persecutory horrors. The last words of the paragraph, the juxtaposition of *self love* and *hatred,* demonstrate the paradoxical nature of narcissism, in which self-love conceals self-hate. Clarissa attributes her malignant feelings toward Miss Kilman to her weakened heart. She is right but in an unexpected way. Clarissa fears that she, too, is emotionally disabled, unworthy of being loved, imprisoned by a brute monster from which there is no escape. There are, in effect, two Miss Kilmans in the novel: the "real" Miss Kilman, who does not elicit strongly negative feelings from any other character; and the symbolic or spectral figure, who is a projection screen for Clarissa's worst fears about herself.

Indeed, the spectral Miss Kilman is not only a figment of Clarissa's imagination, but also a Frankenstein Creature, embodying the split off elements of the self. She identifies Miss Kilman as the "brutal monster" whose "hatred" is constantly "stirring," a "monster grubbing at the roots." Clarissa's hatred is no less intense or irrational than Victor's hatred of the Creature, and the result is the same: self-preoccupation, solipsism, and exhaustion. She and Victor spend so much time justifying the rejection of their doubles that they have little energy left for more worthwhile activities, such as hosting a party or engaging in Promethean research. Few critics, though, have seen the psychic connection between Clarissa and Miss Kilman.

Consider the two women's response to rejection. Both experience feelings of jealousy, abandonment, inadequacy, and rage upon learning that they have not been invited to a party. Clarissa is stung by Lady Bruton's not inviting her to a luncheon with Richard, while Miss Kilman is mortified by being excluded from Clarissa's party. The only difference in their response is that Clarissa denies feeling personally hurt. "Millicent Bruton, whose lunch parties were said to be extraordinarily amusing, had not asked her. No vulgar jealousy could separate her from Richard. But she feared time itself, and read on Lady Bruton's face, as if it had been a dial cut in impassive stone, the dwindling of life" (44). Woolf denies that "vulgar jealousy" could separate Clarissa from Richard, but why else is she devastated by Lady Bruton's engagement with Richard? It is misleading to believe that Clarissa's agonized rejection arises from a fear of the passing of time, a convenient rationalization disguised as a metaphysical profundity. The truth is that most if not all jealousy is "vulgar," embarrassing to acknowledge. Clarissa continues to brood over the rejection, feeling herself "suddenly shrivelled, aged, breastless" (45).

Miss Kilman finds herself in a worse predicament. Deprived of Clarissa's social, economic, and marital advantages, she remains alienated from the Dalloways' comfortable world. She is neither intellectual enough to sustain a life of scholarship nor confident enough to enjoy her independence as a free woman. Because of her Germanic ancestry, she is not accepted into English society. Seething with fury, Miss Kilman embraces the church's teachings, but religion offers her little consolation. She sees Clarissa as the embodiment of an affluent, cultured life that is forever denied to an outsider like herself. Miss Kilman's rage toward Clarissa is almost unendurable. "Fool! Simpleton! You who have known neither sorrow nor pleasure; who have trifled your life away! And there rose in her an overmastering desire to overcome her; to unmask her. If she could have felled her it would have eased her" (189). Miss Kilman's desire to unmask Clarissa recalls the Creature's desire to confront Victor; in both cases, despised outsiders demand recognition and acceptance. While this interpretation may be easier to see in *Frankenstein* than in *Mrs. Dalloway,* Miss Kilman views her exclusion from Clarissa's party as nothing less than an effort to destroy her relationship with Elizabeth, a loss that parallels De Lacey's abandonment of the Creature. "She was about to split asunder, she felt. The agony was so terrific. If she could grasp her, if she could clasp her, if she could make her hers absolutely and forever and then die; that was all she wanted" (199–200).

In siding with Clarissa against Miss Kilman, critics have advanced dubious arguments. Alex Page's conclusion that Clarissa "exercises masterly control over her hate for Miss Kilman and the latter's religious ecstasies and espousal of causes"[4] is as bewildering as Jeremy Hawthorn's assertion that Clarissa is pleased that Miss Kilman detests her, since it confirms the former's identity.[5] On the contrary: Clarissa sees in Miss Kilman qualities that she hates in herself. Alice van Buren Kelley has even suggested that Miss Kilman's physical unattractiveness should be held against her. She "is painfully homely; and beauty . . . is often a path to unity."[6] In accepting Clarissa's harsh judgment of Miss Kilman, these critics repeat her empathic failure.

Indeed, despite the many sensitive feminist interpretations of *Mrs. Dalloway,* few critics have defended a fictional character whose outward situation—a single woman committed to both a career and socially enlightened causes—would appear to make her sympathetic to feminist goals.[7] Female readers are thus forced to counteridentify with Miss Kilman, the one character in *Mrs. Dalloway* who might view herself as a feminist or seek support from the feminist movement. Whereas the novel allows us to sympathize with Clarissa's fears and desires, identify with her defeats and triumphs, no such sympathy or understanding is allowed for Miss Kilman. Why? The explanation is not simply because Miss Kilman is often overcome by bitterness, jealousy, and hate. So is Clarissa. Is it because of Miss Kilman's "religious fanaticism" or her desire to "force the soul"? Perhaps, but in another context, we would admire the strength of her convictions, especially in contrast to Clarissa's questionable attitude of noncommital. If anything, the fact that Miss Kilman has, as Richard acknowledges, "a really historical mind" (16) should make her a more sympathetic character. Nor can we criticize a woman who "out of her meagre income set aside so much for causes she believed in" (190).

Why, then, do we find ourselves denying sympathy to a woman who desperately needs to be accepted and understood, while we side with another woman, Clarissa, whose judgments of people can be so harsh? The prevailing critical attitude toward Miss Kilman is that she is dangerous because she poses a threat to Elizabeth's safety. Upon closer scrutiny, however, this is the most illogical explanation of all. The novel asks us to believe that there is an undeclared war between Clarissa and Miss Kilman over the possession of Elizabeth, as if two warring countries were struggling to annex a neighboring territory. It is true that Miss Kilman wants to make Elizabeth "hers absolutely and forever and then die." Yet Clarissa has no reason to fear that Elizabeth cannot take care of herself. Elizabeth is depicted as an unusually healthy and stable young woman with a firm sense of self. She thus differs from Clarissa and Miss Kilman, whose extreme self-consciousness and instability leave them at the mercy of hidden terrors. Elizabeth seems capable of extricating herself from any potentially dangerous situation. No matter how angry Miss Kilman may feel toward Clarissa, there is no evidence to suggest that she contemplates kidnapping her student or improperly treating her. This seems too obvious to mention were it not for the fact that Clarissa feels that Miss Kilman will literally steal or violate Elizabeth. Clarissa transforms her obscure and powerless rival into her chief enemy, silently accusing Miss Kilman of sexually violating Elizabeth. "Kilman her enemy. That was satisfying; that was real. Ah, how she hated her— hot, hypocritical, corrupt; with all that power; Elizabeth's seducer; the woman who had crept in to steal and defile (Richard would say, What nonsense!). She hated her: she loved her. It was enemies one wanted, not friends" (265–66).

This is not the first time Clarissa ambiguously concedes that she hates and loves Miss Kilman. Earlier, we recall, she acknowledges that, had circumstances been different, she would have loved Miss Kilman. Their intense ambivalence toward each other is centered on Elizabeth, whom each woman tries to rescue from the other. Both vie for her attention. Curiously, neither Clarissa nor Miss Kilman seems particularly interested in spending much time with Elizabeth; they appear less interested in winning her than in making sure that the other loses her. Nor does Elizabeth seem close to her mother or tutor.

Clarissa's sexualization of her anxiety over losing Elizabeth is also puzzling. She refers to Miss Kilman as Elizabeth's "seducer," the woman who had "crept in to steal and defile her." Does she seriously believe that Miss Kilman will seduce or molest Elizabeth? Her fear of Miss Kilman seems to contain an element of homophobia. Since we know that Clarissa has not had sexual relations with her husband for years ("she could not dispel a virginity preserved through childbirth which clung to her like a sheet" [46]) and has had affairs with other women, why does she project homophobic feelings onto Miss Kilman, whose sexual orientation remains ambiguous?[8] She knows that she is being irrational here; "Richard would say," she tells us parenthetically, "What nonsense!" (266). Nevertheless, Clarissa remains haunted by the spectral Miss Kilman.

From a Kohutian point of view, Clarissa experiences Miss Kilman not as an autonomous object, separate and independent from the self, but as a selfobject, an archaic part of the self. More specifically, Miss Kilman represents the claims of the grandiose self, demanding approval. In embodying narcissistic hunger and narcissistic rage, Miss Kilman recalls not only the Frankenstein Creature, but Pip's shadowy Nemesis, Orlick. The chocolate eclairs she greedily devours cannot satisfy her appetite for praise and validation. Clarissa similarly experiences this hunger, but in despising Miss Kilman, she feels only greater self-depletion.

Other psychoanalytic perspectives yield similar conclusions about Clarissa's relationship with Miss Kilman. Viewed from Melanie Klein's object relations theory, Miss Kilman is the target of Clarissa's tendency toward projective identification: the projection of virulent sexual and aggressive impulses onto another person, with whom one then actively identifies. Otto Kernberg would emphasize Clarissa's oral rage, paranoia, and dependency, which become magnified in Miss Kilman. Each sees the other, not as a victim, deserving sympathy and understanding, but as a victimizer. Otto Rank would see Miss Kilman as Clarissa's dark double; Miss Kilman's name symbolizes the lethal danger she poses to Clarissa. These interpretations stress the extent to which Miss Kilman represents Clarissa's disowned self. Clarissa is a gracious hostess to everyone except Miss Kilman; Miss Kilman is a historian but not a psychologist. Both are patients in search of an empathic analyst, and both turn to Elizabeth for support.

I can now suggest why Clarissa and Miss Kilman compete for

Elizabeth's love. They need her primarily as an admired, omnipotent selfobject who will restore their shattered self-esteem. Miss Kilman's need to possess Elizabeth is a symptom of a deeper need to fuse with an idealized love object. Her love for Elizabeth reveals a narcissistic object choice; that is, she cannot realistically see Elizabeth as an autonomous object, distinct from herself. Instead, Miss Kilman sees in Elizabeth the repository of all joy, hope, and power. Her reaction to Elizabeth's departure evokes the image of a child mourning the death of his or her mother.[9] Unable to imagine a life apart from her, Miss Kilman would prefer to die with Elizabeth than live without her.

Indeed, Miss Kilman's relationship to Elizabeth is less that of a teacher than a child, with Elizabeth exerting a calming, maternal influence on the terrified older woman. The loss of Elizabeth constitutes nothing less than the loss of the idealized mother. Fear of the lost love object suggests early traumatic loss, such as the death of a parent, or a pattern of rejections by insufficiently loving parents. "Disappointment in the idealized mother," Kohut writes in *The Analysis of the Self,* "may have been due to the unreliability of her empathy and her depressed moods, or may be related to her physical illnesses, or her absence or death."[10] Narcissistic hunger drives Clarissa and Miss Kilman to Elizabeth, but the young woman cannot fulfill the impossible role that is expected of her, thus intensifying their search for an omnipotent object.

Kohut notes in *The Restoration of the Self* that the "consequence of the parental self-object's inability to be the joyful mirror to a child's healthy assertiveness may be a lifetime of abrasiveness, bitterness, and sadistic control that cannot be discharged."[11] He argues that empathy is as important, psychologically, for human survival as oxygen is, physiologically. An environment devoid of empathy becomes life-threatening. Such is the way in which Clarissa and Miss Kilman darkly mirror each other's fears. This is also true of Clarissa's other psychological double, Septimus Warren Smith. He suffers from a lifetime of abrasiveness, bitterness, and sadistic control—symptoms of a heart problem that Clarissa and Miss Kilman know too well.

"No one kills from hatred," Septimus thinks early in the novel (35). Contrary to the assertion, his suicide demonstrates the outcome of murderous self-hate. Critics have long been fascinated by his psychological complexity, and his life and death take on the appearance of a psychiatric case study.[12] The novel portrays his death as heroic defiance against a repressive medical establishment that would institutionalize a person against his own will, confer patient status on him, and deprive him of all his liberties. Insofar as the suicide is structured as a viable alternative to psychiatric incarceration, we are encouraged to endorse Septimus' final act.[13] But without condoning the horrors of the psychiatric state, we may question whether Septimus' suicide is an act of creative defiance.

Septimus is one of the first to enlist in the Great War. He achieves "manliness" in the French trenches, is promoted, and develops a camaraderie with an older officer named Evans. Woolf's description of the two men evokes the simplicity and innocence of their relationship. "It was a case of two dogs playing on a hearth-rug; one worrying a paper screw, snarling, snapping, giving a pinch, now and then, at the old dog's ear; the other lying somnolent, blinking at the fire, raising a paw, turning and growling good-temperedly" (130). The two men are inseparable. "They had to be together, share with each other, fight with each other, quarrel with each other." When Evans is killed shortly before the Armistice, Septimus congratulates himself on his detachment. The line "He could not feel" (131) becomes a leitmotif in the novel.

Around this time, Septimus develops severe psychotic symptoms, particularly hallucinations: an old woman's head in the middle of a fern, faces laughing at him from a wall, a dog turning into a man, red flowers growing through his flesh. He sees Evans returned from the dead, wearing a gray suit. Along with the hallucinations come headaches, sleeplessness, terrifying dreams. Lucrezia, whom he has married in a fit of panic, explains her husband's mystifying illness as the result of "working too hard." He becomes increasingly suicidal and misanthropic. "He would argue with her about killing themselves; and explain how wicked people were; how he could see them making up lies as they passed in the street. He knew all their thoughts, he said; he knew everything. He knew the meaning of the world, he said" (100). Septimus condemns human nature as a breed of lustful animals, claiming that "love between man and woman was repulsive to Shakespeare. The business of copulation was filth to him before the end" (134). Septimus' most despairing statement is summed up in some of the most savage words in the novel: "For the truth is (let her ignore it) that human beings have neither kindness, nor faith, nor charity beyond what serves to increase the pleasure of the moment. They hunt in packs. Their packs scour the desert and vanish screaming into the wilderness. They desert the fallen" (135).

Why cannot Septimus mourn his friend's death? This is, no doubt, one of the most intriguing psychological questions in *Mrs. Dalloway*. The most obvious interpretation is that the horrors of war prevent Septimus from expressing the commitment to love and friendship that would be appropriate in peacetime. To allow oneself to become emotionally invested in another person may be dangerous on a battlefield. War encourages soldiers to hunt in packs; to renounce kindness, faith, and charity; to desert the fallen. By refusing to grieve his friend's loss, Septimus demonstrates his link to the lustful animals who have no lasting emotions but only whims and vanities.

Septimus' major defense mechanism consists of depersonalization, or what R.D. Laing calls in *The Divided Self* "petrification": "turning, or being turned, from a live person into a dead thing, into a stone, into a robot, an automaton, without personal autonomy of action, an *it* without subjectivity."[14] Laing points out that petrification is the most dangerous defense mechanism:

In the schizophrenic, two main motives form into one force operating in the direction of promoting a state of death-in-life. There is the primary guilt of having no right to life in the first place, and hence of being entitled at most only to a dead life. Secondly, it is probably the most extreme defensive posture that can be adopted. One no longer fears being crushed, engulfed, overwhelmed by realness and aliveness (whether they arise in other people, in "inner" feelings or emotions, etc.), since one is already dead. Being dead, one cannot die, and one cannot kill. *(The Divided Self,* 176)

Such is Septimus' state. Contrary to his earlier denial that "nobody kills from hatred," Septimus fears both killing and being killed. The paranoid belief that others are talking behind his back, conspiring against him, reveals the expectation of punishment. Like other psychotics, he maintains that people can read his thoughts, uncover his secret crimes. What crimes? Crimes of heartlessness, crimes of selfishness. Septimus cannot forgive Evans for dying and leaving him defenseless in a frightening world. Evans' death only magnifies Septimus' guilt, since he cannot logically blame his absent friend for abandoning him. Septimus' grandiosity, a characteristic symptom of a severe narcissistic disturbance, compensates for his feelings of worthlessness. Insofar as no one in the novel, least of all the uncomprehending doctors, is capable of grasping the psychological dynamics of grieving, Septimus cannot work through his anger and guilt.

Woolf's portrait of Septimus Warren Smith uncannily anticipates what has become called *post-traumatic stress disorder* (PTSD)—intense and persistent anxiety following a traumatic event. The term appeared for the first time in *DMS-III*, but its symptoms have been recognized for a long time. During World War I, for example, soldiers who suffered from the anxiety-based disorder were referred to as *shell-shocked*. Septimus' condition illustrates all the major characteristics of PTSD: his symptoms arise from a traumatic event; the symptoms appear continually and in several forms, including intrusive recollections and recurrent dreams; and he experiences a numbing of emotional responsiveness. He suffers from other symptoms associated with the disorder, such as sleep disturbances, short attention span, and panic attacks. Interestingly, of the three major causes of post-traumatic stress disorder—natural disasters, the taking of hostages, and military combat—Septimus falls into the last category, in that his self-reproaches, feelings of failure, paranoia, and hostility are more prominent in survivors of war than in survivors of natural disasters or hostage situations. [15]

Septimus also dramatizes the link between narcissism and post-traumatic stress disorder. Until recently, the relationship between preexisting personality disorders and the development of PTSD has been hinted at but not actually tested. In a 1985 study, a group of 114 Vietnam veterans was given an elaborate questionnaire designed to specify variables associated with the onset of PTSD. The questionnaire assessed the relationship between premorbid personality disorders and PTSD. Respondents were asked whether, at the time they entered the war, they felt that they were persons of "unusual importance and uniqueness and capable of doing truly great things in life." There was a strong correlation between narcissistic factors, particularly grandiosity, and the development of PTSD. The researchers were initially perplexed by the high incidence of narcissism among the Vietnam soldiers, whose average age was nineteen; pathological narcissism generally does not occur until people are in their thirties and forties. Self-esteem and identity formation are crucial developmental issues during early adulthood, however. Thus, war is especially traumatic to those suffering from a fragile sense of self. The researchers concluded that the Vietnam combat experience "may have intensified and, perhaps, negatively affected the normative developmental task of establishing a coherent and positive sense of personal identity."[16]

Septimus' failure to grieve foreshadows a problem that has affected not only Vietnam soldiers but Holocaust survivors. We can use the insights gleaned from World War II victims to illuminate his private nightmare. In the afterword to Claudine Vegh's *I Didn't Say Good-bye*, a series of interviews of children of Holocaust victims, Bruno Bettelheim discusses children who remain silent over the sudden loss of a parent. Bettelheim, himself a concentration camp victim, argues that to share one's catastrophic experience with other people is to receive their assurances of acceptance and understanding. This the survivor does not wish to do. "Others might believe they understood the victim's agonies after they have listened to him talk about them, while he knows that by comprehending the facts they know nothing about the all pervasive nature of his sufferings."[17] Another reason for the survivor's silence involves the denial of death. "If one's parents were possibly still alive, how could one talk about them as dead? Only by not talking about them could one prevent others from insisting that the parents had died and continue to believe in their eventual return" (171). The avoidance of suffering or, paradoxically, the embracing of a mourning that is never completed, enables the survivor to maintain his or her suffering indefinitely, thereby avoiding final separation from lost loved ones.

Septimus' inability to mourn arises from contradictory motives. Being symbolically dead, he feels no pain, no need to acknowledge feelings of rage and abandonment. Being silent about his grief, he retains his unique relationship to Evans. Septimus thus possesses the memory of his departed friend, in whose eventual return he continues to believe.

Septimus' relationship to Evans parallels Miss Kilman's relationship to Elizabeth. Miss Kilman, we recall, cannot endure the thought of separation from Elizabeth, the idealized love object. Nor can Septimus live without his beloved Evans. There is even the suggestion of the *wish* to kill the love object as a way to possess it, completely and exclusively. Also, Septimus and Miss Kilman rely upon splitting as a defense against ambivalence. Miss Kilman perceives Elizabeth and Clarissa as the good and bad objects, respectively; the two objects must be kept apart, indicating the inability to integrate loved and hated elements of the self. Septimus idealizes Evans, but where is the bad object in his life? Although the novel omits any mention of his parents, we do not have to look very far to discover the objects of Septimus' displaced aggression: his two physicians, Holmes and Sir William Bradshaw, symbols of repressive male authority.

Beginning with Evelyn Whitbread's repeated trips to the doctors, all the references to the medical establishment in *Mrs. Dalloway* evoke strenuous protest and resentment. Clarissa is well acquainted with the doctors. Accustomed to being in bed with headaches, she had once gone with someone to ask Sir William's advice about a psychiatric question. "He had been perfectly right; extremely sensible. But Heavens—what a relief to get out to the street again!" (278). Clarissa recalls "some poor wretch" crying in the waiting room. She later confides her disapproval of the eminent psychiatrist to her husband, who agrees with her judgment. These references suggest a pattern of prolonged illness and enforced dependency upon medical treatment. They also prepare us for Septimus' more serious confrontation with the doctors.

Dr. Holmes is Septimus' first physician. A general practitioner with over forty years' experience, he is appallingly obtuse and insensitive. He assures Lucrezia there is nothing seriously wrong with her husband, a judgment she repeats until its falseness becomes undeniable. No Sherlock Holmes, the physician simply advises Septimus to take two tablets of bromide dissolved in a glass of water at bedtime. The epitome of triumphant health, Holmes cannot fathom mental illness, which he equates with moral failure. He speaks condescendingly to Septimus and Lucrezia; his affable tone masks impatience. On the third visit, he gives Lucrezia a "friendly push" to get past her into Septimus' bedroom. Holmes becomes increasingly intrusive, and, not surprisingly, Septimus experiences him as a sinister threat, a persecutory object. "Holmes was on him. Dr. Holmes came quite regularly every day. Once you stumble, Septimus wrote on the back of a postcard, human nature is on you. Holmes is on you. Their only chance was to escape, without letting Holmes know; to Italy—anywhere, anywhere, away from Dr. Holmes" (139).

Ironically, there is an objective basis for Septimus' paranoia: Holmes *does* persecute his patient, driving him to death. Woolf implies that, had the physician not stormed into Septimus' house to imprison him in one of Sir William's notorious rest homes, Septimus might have recovered on his own. Indeed, in the moments preceding Holmes's approach, Septimus' madness lifts, and he regains self-control. But by this time it is too late, for Lucrezia cannot block Holmes's violent entry. Hearing the doctor advance up the stairs, Septimus feels cornered, with nowhere to go except through the window. Woolf endorses Septimus' rage and despair, validates his method of escape from intolerable authority. To eliminate any ambiguity about Holmes's evil character or complicity in Septimus' death, the novelist has the physician utter a monstrous judgment of the young man's death. " 'The coward!' cried Dr. Holmes, bursting the door open" (226). A moment later he magnanimously decides no one is to blame for the suicide.

Nearly all critics agree that Virginia Woolf's treatment of her fictional doctors was influenced by autobiographical factors, namely, bitterness toward her own psychiatrists. Disagreement arises, however, over whether the novelist is fair or balanced in her portrayal of Drs. Holmes and Bradshaw. Beverly Ann Schlack argues that "Septimus' hatred of his doctors is appropriately psychotic. But Holmes and Bradshaw are also the object of Virginia Woolf's hatred, an authorial hatred so stubbornly relentless as to become gratuitous."[18] Woolf was too close to Septimus' problems to be sufficiently objective, Schlack concludes. Moreover, since Holmes has not caused Septimus' illness, it is misleading to place the major blame on him. By validating Septimus' worst fears, the novelist shifts the responsibility for his suicide away from the patient and onto the medical establishment. She concedes this by saying that "Dr. Holmes seemed to stand for something horrible" to Septimus (213), an obscurely evil aspect of human nature.

A more sinister version of Dr. Holmes, Sir William Bradshaw has the "reputation (of the utmost importance in dealing with nerve cases) not merely of lightning skill, and almost infallible accuracy in diagnosis but of sympathy; tact; understanding of the human soul" (144). The language satirizes the religious aura of psychiatrists, twentieth-century secular priests. Sir William doesn't speak about his patients' disabilities, but about their need to maintain a "sense of proportion."[19] He treats "nerve cases" like Septimus with the rest cure, a euphemism for confining patients against their will in an isolated setting, depriving them of companionship and books, force feeding them until they become overweight and compliant, and breaking their spirit until in desperation they are ready to return to the outside world. It is the same psychiatric nightmare that Charlotte Perkins Gilman satirizes so effectively in her 1899 masterpiece, *The Yellow Wallpaper*. To Sir William, the rest cure is benevolent and enlightened; to his patients, it is paternalistic and reactionary. "Naked, defenceless, the exhausted, the friendless received the impress of Sir William's will. He swooped; he devoured. He shut people up" (154). Unlike the speechless Septimus, whose only method to defy Sir William's patriarchal authority is through suicide, Woolf summons all her novelistic fury to express outrage against the medical establishment. She portrays Sir William as a philistine, a worshiper of Mammon, and she completes her revenge by marrying him to a woman who is quietly, discreetly, losing her mind.

Both Clarissa and Septimus view Sir William as the common enemy, and Woolf supports their defiance of his evil power. Hearing about Septimus' suicide, Clarissa responds with immediate sympathy. The boundary between self and other dissolves as she instantly participates in his death. "Always her body went through it first, when she was told, suddenly, of an accident; her dress flamed, her body burnt" (280). Although she has not met the young man nor witnessed his death, Clarissa narrates the details of his gruesome ending. Woolf endows Clarissa with authorial omniscience, transforming her into a novelist whose imagination apprehends the final seconds of Septimus' life. Every detail of the Icarian fall seizes her attention. "He had thrown himself from a window. Up had flashed the ground; through him, blundering, bruising, went the rusty spikes. There he lay with a thud, thud, thud in his brain, and then a suffocation of blackness. So she saw it. But why had he done it?" (280).

Septimus' death represents one of the most mystical descriptions of suicide in literature. "Death was defiance. Death was an attempt to communicate; people feeling the impossibility of reaching the centre which, mystically, evaded them; closeness drew apart; rapture faded, one was alone. There was an embrace in death" (280–281). Woolf emphasizes, not the negation and despair with which suicide is usually associated, but the liberation it brings from suffering. Clarissa is momentarily disgraced by Septimus' suicide, fearing it will destroy her party. But disgrace soon gives way to exhilaration as she rejoices in his defiance. She participates vicariously in the suicide, experiencing release from her own fears of fragmentation and loneliness. "She felt somehow very like him—the young man who had killed himself. She felt glad that he had done it; thrown it away" (283).

In approving the suicide, however, Woolf overidentifies with her two characters. It is surely easier for us to accept the affirmative implications of Clarissa's party than to celebrate a suicide. A party brings people together and strengthens human ties; a suicide destroys human ties. To view suicide as a mystical or heroic act is to require a suspension of disbelief that, notwithstanding Coleridge's injunction, few of us would be willing to make. Ironically, the language surrounding Septimus' suicide "taper[s] into mysticism, or rise[s], with rapid beats of the wings, into the raptures of transcendentalism"— responses that Woolf wisely cautions against in "On Being Ill" (10). This section of *Mrs. Dalloway* thus contradicts the aesthetic principles Woolf announces in the essay, where she tells us that to confront the terrible illnesses that beset mind and body requires the "courage of a lion tamer; a robust philosophy; a reason rooted in the bowels of the earth." Why, then, does Septimus' suicide cause Clarissa's courage, philosophy, and reason to falter?

Without reducing Clarissa to Septimus, we may observe their essential similarities. Both experience feelings of dread, apprehension, and ecstasy. They display rapid alternations of mood, ranging from terror to exaltation. Both are visionary artist figures, apprehending, as does their creator, the miracles, revelations, and agonies of human existence. Their visions "proffer great cornucopias full of fruit to the solitary traveller" (86). Septimus' euphoric vision cannot be dismissed as mania, and his illness is never severe enough to dull his imagination. Nature comes alive to both characters, and it is into nature that they seek to merge. When Septimus' brain goes dark from his plunge, Clarissa continues to see with his eyes, intuit beauty with his imagery.

With their intense love and violent hate, horror of heterosexuality and celebration of innocent homosexuality, they are indeed psychological doubles. Both are married to spouses who do not understand their fears or experience their intensity of feeling. They also resemble each other physically: Septimus is "beak-nosed" (20), while Clarissa's face is "beaked like a bird's" (14). Both wish to soar, like Daedalus, above the labyrinth of experience, freeing themselves from the constraints of reality. They strive for the elusive center of life, a mystical flight that impels Septimus out of this world.

Indeed, Clarissa's identification with Septimus is so strong that, upon learning of his suicidal leap, she moves toward a window, from where she contemplates his death. It is at this moment that Clarissa's hold on life is most precarious. Woolf erased any doubt about Clarissa's self-destructive tendencies by acknowledging in the introduction to the 1928 Modern Library edition of *Mrs. Dalloway* that in the first version of the story, Septimus, "who is later intended to be [Clarissa's] double," did not exist. Rather, "Mrs. Dalloway was originally intended to kill herself, or perhaps merely to die at the end of the party."[20] Unlike Septimus, Clarissa draws back from the window and returns to life.

Whereas Septimus falls to his death, Clarissa falls back upon her strong and sensible husband. Richard Dalloway allows Clarissa the necessary space denied to her by the possessive Peter Walsh. Richard is Clarissa's "foundation" (43), embodying the unwavering structure and stability of a healthy self. An empathic husband, he calms Clarissa's anxieties, allays her paranoid dread of Miss Kilman, and sees to it that his wife receives an hour's complete rest after lunch—a rest cure to which she does not object. Richard respects the gulf that exists between husband and wife. His temperament is the opposite of Clarissa's: he is sure of his identity, confident of his work, secure in his relations with others. Unlike Clarissa, who agonizes over whether she made the right marital decision, Richard rejoices in their union. He is both a protective father and an adoring husband.

Like everyone, Richard has his limitations. He seeks to assuage Clarissa's fears without trying to understand them. As valuable as his support is, he prefers to make the necessary accommodations and adjustments to his wife's heart condition rather than grasp its psychological implications. His solicitous daily reminder to her, "an hour's complete rest after luncheon," originates from a doctor's order. Clarissa realizes that "it was like him to take what doctors said literally; part of his adorable, divine simplicity, which no one had to the same extent" (181–82). Richard is thus implicated, however innocently, in the repressive medical treatment that Woolf attacks throughout *Mrs. Dalloway*. Richard remains a sympathetic, generous character; yet we suspect that the novelist is holding back a fuller description of the Dalloways' marriage, particularly the problems that almost inevitably arise when a spouse suffers from serious, long-term illness.

In fact, there is a character through whom Woolf expresses the feelings of confusion, helplessness, and resentment a healthy individual may experience toward a chronically ill husband or wife. The character is Lucrezia, a less benign version of Richard. Lucrezia becomes increasingly distraught over Septimus' madness, unable to endure her disastrous marriage. "For she could stand it no longer. Dr. Holmes might say there was nothing the matter. Far rather would she that he were dead! She could not sit beside him when he stared so and did not see her and made everything terrible; sky and tree, children playing, dragging carts, blowing whistles, falling down; all were terrible. And he would not kill himself; and she could tell no one" (33). Lucrezia believes that Septimus' illness is caused by his selfish lack of consideration for her; and she is infuriated by his ineffective doctors, who either deny he is ill (Holmes) or proclaim he is too ill to remain at home (Bradshaw). Nor can she understand Sir William's reason for taking Septimus away from her: "the people we care for most are not good for us when we are ill" (146), the psychiatrist says. Realizing that no one can understand her anguish, Lucrezia is condemned to live with the memory of a husband who dutifully carries out her death wish.

Unlike Septimus, who has no living friends, Clarissa has Sally Seton, a dear childhood companion to whose extraordinary beauty Clarissa is magnetized. Passionate, unconventional, daring, Sally is bursting with ideas and vitality. The memory of Sally awakens a purity of emotion within Clarissa that she feels toward no other character:

The strange thing, on looking back, was the purity, the integrity, of her feeling for Sally. It was not like one's feeling for a man. It was completely disinterested, and besides, it had a quality which could only exist between women, between women just grown up. It was protective, on her side; sprang from a sense of being in league together, a presentiment of something that was bound to part them (they spoke of marriage always as a catastrophe), which led to this chivalry, this protective feeling which was much more on her side than Sally's. (50)

Clarissa's admiration of Sally Seton poses the same problem as Septimus' defensive idealization of Evans. Her language—words like *purity, integrity,* and *completely disinterested*—evokes an idealized relationship, free of ambivalence. Clarissa evades love's unruly side, emotions like jealousy. The idealization of Sally is further called into question by the physical and emotional changes accompanying Clarissa's recent heart problem, which erodes all pleasure in beauty, friendship, and love.

Clarissa's relationship to Sally raises additional questions. As youths, they spoke of marriage "always as a catastrophe." Did each woman come to regard the other's marriage as an abandonment of principles —or principals? Upon Sally's instigation, they intended to found a society to abolish private property. Did Clarissa's attitude toward Sally change when the once-defiant socialist married a wealthy factory owner? Clarissa does not trust herself to disapprove of Sally's marriage, though this has not stopped Sally from criticizing Clarissa's marriage. Twice in the above passage, for example, Clarissa implies she was more protective of Sally than Sally was of her. According to Peter Walsh, Sally shared his objections to Richard Dalloway; Clarissa dimly remembers, in fact, one of Sally's unkind remarks about Richard, who "would never be in the Cabinet because he had a second-class brain" (183). Before Sally shows up unexpectedly at the party, Clarissa recalls another disturbing memory of her friend, a scene occurring years ago during a luncheon when she mistakenly calls Richard "Wickham" and Sally mockingly repeats Richard's correction, "My name is Dalloway" (92), until Clarissa flares up. The distressing incident almost ended their friendship.

In short, Clarissa's idealization of Sally Seton is undercut by the reality of their relationship. Her friendship for Sally is almost as illusory as Septimus' hallucination of Evans. During the party, Sally tells Peter that, despite the many invitations she has extended to Clarissa over the years, the Dalloways never visited Sally and her husband. Clarissa would not come, she says, adding that "Clarissa was at heart a snob—one had to admit it, a snob" (289). And despite Clarissa's heartfelt greeting of Sally at the party, the two friends have nothing to say to each other. Clarissa is thus not entirely candid about her feelings for Sally.

What is Clarissa repressing? In a key moment of the narrative, she recalls something that provides a clue, a love scene that ended in horrified disappointment for her three decades ago, in the 1890s, at her ancestral home at Bourton. The memory takes on a dream-like quality, revealing displacement, condensation, and symbolization. The major participants are Clarissa, her father, Sally, and Peter Walsh. Sally, looking radiant in her pink gauze dress, stood by the fireplace talking to Clarissa's father, "who had begun to be attracted rather against his will" (52). Sally's beautiful voice made everything she said sound like a "caress." Clarissa does not elaborate on the disturbing erotic implications of her father's involuntary attraction to her best friend. The next detail is Sally's abrupt suggestion, motivated by embarrassment or awkwardness, for the entire group to proceed on a walk outside the house. Trailing the others in the small group, Clarissa and Sally set out on their walk together. Decades later, Clarissa remembers how important this experience was to her. "Then came the most exquisite moment of her whole life passing a stone urn with flowers in it. Sally stopped; picked a flower; kissed her on the lips. The whole world might have turned upside down!" (52). Clarissa felt as if she had just been given an infinitely precious gift, like a diamond, and told to preserve it forever.

Peter Walsh's untimely arrival shattered Clarissa's precious moment. "It was like running one's face against a granite wall in the darkness! It was shocking; it was horrible." Significantly, Clarissa maintains that it was Sally, not herself, who experienced the horror of the moment. "She felt only how Sally was being mauled already; maltreated; she felt his hostility; his jealousy; his determination to break into their companionship" (53). The memory ends with Clarissa repeating to herself, "Oh this horror!" (53), as if she had known all along that "something would interrupt, would embitter her moment of happiness."

The Oedipal implications are intriguing, beginning with Clarissa's silence over her father's attraction to Sally. Few daughters would be happy about the situation, especially when one's father is aloof and petulant, as Justin Parry is. Rather than desiring her father or viewing Sally primarily as a rival, as a classic Oedipal interpretation would suggest, she feels protective of her companion. She does not accuse her father of wishing to "steal and defile" Sally. (Clarissa uses these words, remember, to accuse Miss Kilman of desiring to violate Elizabeth.) But Clarissa does blame Peter for shattering her intimacy with Sally. Outraged by his belittling remark about star-gazing, she accuses Peter of mauling and mistreating Sally, of trying to break up their companionship.

Clarissa invests Peter with complex symbolism. He is a rejected suitor whose approval she still yearns for after many years, an intimidating authority figure whose "unsentimental" judgments continue to wound her. She repeatedly concedes a dependency upon Peter's judgments, and she tries, with limited success, to emulate his authoritative pronouncements, which carry over into the sphere of language and literature. "It was the state of the world that interested him; Wagner, Pope's poetry, people's characters eternally, and the defects of her own soul. How he scolded her! How they argued!" (9). But Peter's aversion to sentimentality is a mixed blessing; he remains critical of all emotion, whether it is posturing or not. His devaluation of the heart, his demeaning statements about women, and his deprecation of Clarissa's instincts are typical of Virginia Woolf's father figures.

Biographers have identified Peter Walsh with Woolf's own father, Sir Leslie Stephen, the eminent literary critic.[21] A fuller portrait of Woolf's father appears in the character of the selfish and tyrannical Mr. Ramsay in *To the Lighthouse*. Clarissa's fear of failure seems to originate from an emotionally obtuse parent who invokes "unsentimentality" as proscriptively as the other father figure in the novel, Sir William Bradshaw, invokes "proportion" to his benumbed patients. Her anger toward Peter represents, transferentially, the daughter's fear of a menacing father. Clarissa's dread of male sexuality is mirrored in the ever-present knife Peter fondles, to her horror and disgust.[22] Peter's knife symbolizes the cutting remarks of Justin Parry, who is antithetical to the nurturing Richard Dalloway.

The pre-Oedipal meaning of Clarissa's recollection of Bourton highlights a different element of her disappointment in love. Clarissa knows that, however much she would like to, she cannot possess

Sally's exclusive love and attention. Sally symbolizes the power to arouse uncritical love from men and women alike. She is unthreatened by Mr. Parry's inappropriate attraction, unperturbed by Peter's untimely appearance. Her laughter at Peter's star-gazing remark only intensifies Clarissa's grief. Peter's foolish question contains unexpected meaning. Everyone is dazzled by Sally Seton's radiant brilliance; she renders men and women into star-gazers. Clarissa cannot compete with a woman who enjoys being admired by others and who is the center of attention wherever she goes. Clarissa, not Sally, experiences Peter (and Parry) as a rival in love. Peter's presence becomes the pretext for Clarissa's failure to gain exclusive control of Sally's love.

Clarissa's relationship to Sally Seton dramatizes one of the central problems in *Mrs. Dalloway*, reconciling distance and desire. Clarissa, Miss Kilman, and Septimus desire to merge with an omnipotent object, on the one hand, and maintain separation, on the other. Woolf rejects the smothering possessiveness of Peter Walsh and Miss Kilman, yet sympathizes with Septimus' desire for reunion with Evans, the lost love object. Clarissa preserves distance from Richard through a room of her own, yet she exhibits a powerful wish to fuse with Sally. Woolf reveals the consequences of the failure to resolve distance and desire. Excessive distance leads to loneliness and fragmentation, while unmediated desire results in identity loss and engulfment.

Pre-Oedipal issues, or what Margaret Mahler calls in *The Psychological Birth of the Human Infant* (1975) the process of separation-individuation, are at the heart of Clarissa's conflicts. Mahler defines separation-individuation as the "establishment of a sense of separateness from, and relation to, a world of reality, particularly with regard to the experiences of *one's own body* and to the principal representative of the world as the infant experiences it, the *primary love object*."[23] The never-ending intrapsychic process reverberates throughout the life cycle. Mahler conceives of separation and individuation as two complementary developments: separation consists of the "child's emergence from a symbiotic fusion with the mother," while individuation consists of "those achievements marking the child's assumption of his own individual characteristics" (4). Mahler uses the term *symbiosis*, not in the biological sense of a mutually beneficial relationship between two separate individuals, but in the psychological sense of "that state of undifferentiation, of fusion with mother, in which the 'I' is not yet differentiated from the 'not-I' and in which inside and outside are only gradually coming to be sensed as different" (44). Although the concept of symbiosis may not be as complete as originally hypothesized, the lifelong yearning for reunion with the early mother remains a valid clinical observation. In this context, it is interesting to note James Naremore's comment that the method of narration in *Mrs. Dalloway* implies that "there is no clear boundary between the 'inside' and the 'outside,' just as there is no clear boundary between Virginia Woolf's characters or between the author and her materials."[24]

As in *Wuthering Heights*, *Mrs. Dalloway* yields few clues about the absent mother. Clarissa's silence becomes more puzzling in light of the wealth of information she offers about her friends and casual acquaintances. It is as if she has come into the world motherless, living fifty years without maternal roots. It is not that she was born without a mother, like the Frankenstein Creature, or lost her mother at childbirth, like Catherine Linton. Nor does she suffer from the problems of defective mothering that we have seen in the other novels —having a shrewish mother *(Great Expectations)*, a false, theatrical mother *(The Picture of Dorian Gray)*, an indifferent or infanticidal mother *(Jude the Obscure)*, or an alternately overloving and underloving mother *(Sons and Lovers)*. Rather, Clarissa simply does not refer to her mother; nor does Woolf.

Yet, as a mother herself, Clarissa may wonder about the history of mother-daughter relationships in her family. The only detail about her early family life comes from Peter, who refers to the accidental death of her sister Sylvia by a falling tree. Peter's parenthetical comment raises more questions than it answers: "all Justin Parry's fault— all his carelessness" (117–18). Clarissa witnessed the tragic death of her sister, a girl "on the verge of life, the most gifted of them" (118). The experience, she tells Peter, "was enough to turn one bitter." Woolf does not reveal whether Clarissa was able to mourn the death, as Septimus was unable to do, but Peter's offhand remark provokes questions for Woolf's psychobiographers.

Indeed, critics have become increasingly preoccupied with the theme of loss in Woolf's life. Howard Harpur views Sylvia's accidental death as having an autobiographical parallel in the early death of Virginia

Woolf's beloved half-sister, Stella.[25] Phyllis Rose argues that Woolf's hunger for her mother's affection "ended catastrophically with her mother's death, and instead of the real woman who inspired in her growing daughter a mixture of hatred and love, an idealized phantom mother haunted her mind."[26] Mark Spilka devotes an entire book, *Virginia Woolf's Quarrel with Grieving*, to the subject of failed mourning.[27] Ellen Rosenman shows, in *The Invisible Presence*, how "alongside the celebration of the feminine stands an intense anxiety about motherhood and a need to reconstitute femininity to exclude its dangerous emotional and biological contingencies."[28] And Shirley Panken suggests in *Virginia Woolf and the "Lust of Creation"* that Woolf's "sense of unlovability, her vast, unmet need for maternal support," arose from the failure to grieve her mother's death.[29]

These studies emphasize the importance of the mother-daughter relationship in Woolf's life and art, along with the search for pre-Oedipal unity. Woolf's first major breakdown occurred in 1895, immediately after her mother's premature death. Virginia, then thirteen, was unable to grieve the loss. Her failure to mourn becomes more significant in light of a later admission, in a 1924 diary entry, that she inappropriately laughed at her mother's deathbed, an act she kept secret from everyone.

We can now see more clearly how Clarissa's relationship to Elizabeth betrays the symptoms of "heart disease" arising from narcissistic injuries. Walking toward a flower shop, Clarissa reflects upon how she and her daughter have entirely different values and interests. A disquieting thought suddenly comes to her. "Elizabeth really cared for her dog most of all" (15). Clarissa's only consolation is that Elizabeth loves her dog more than she loves Miss Kilman. It is a disturbing consolation, however, and Clarissa fears that she will be judged a bad mother and lose her family. Nor are her doubts allayed by Elizabeth, who rarely thinks about her except in relation to Miss Kilman. Elizabeth is consistently more interested in her father than in her mother and in London, "so dreary compared with being alone in the country with her father and the dogs" (204).

Despite the appearance of a satisfactory relationship, there is very little communication between mother and daughter, no displays of affection, intimacy, or shared experience. Peter Walsh's objection to Clarissa's greeting, "here is my Elizabeth," reveals that there is something not quite right about the mother-daughter relationship, suggesting that "things are what they're not" (84). Sally has always thought that Clarissa is "unmaternal" (290), a feeling that Clarissa shares about herself. Miss Kilman's inordinate fear of seeing Elizabeth turn against her coincides precisely with Clarissa's own heartache about losing her daughter. At the end of the novel, Elizabeth radiantly moves toward her proud father, who is unable to contain his joy at seeing her. Richard, not Clarissa, is the nurturant parent in *Mrs. Dalloway*.

Mrs. Dalloway leaves us, finally, with a variety of heart problems inaccessible to cardiologists. In rejecting psychiatry as forcing the soul,[30] Woolf's characters rule out other ways to unburden their hearts to each other. Neither Lucrezia nor the doctors ask why Septimus wishes to kill himself, why he cannot enter into the mourning process that will release him from the straitjacket of guilt and suffering. Clarissa rejects Septimus' deadly view from the window, but fails to question why his suicide is her own personal "disaster—her disgrace" (282). Septimus dies, believing he has committed an appalling crime. Clarissa lives, believing life is good but always on the brink of being extinguished by an illness with the power to destroy all pleasure in beauty, friendship, and love. She experiences, it is true, temporary relief through her vicarious participation in Septimus' flight. The violent death of her suicidal double allows her to vent her rage toward the doctors who would force their will upon helpless individuals. Her therapeutic relief is short-lived, however, since she never discovers how the repressive doctors symbolize more deeply rooted problems in her life.

By refusing to make peace with her other spectral double, Miss Kilman, Clarissa avoids reconciling the good and bad elements of her own self. There are times when she comes close to effecting a reconciliation, as when rationally confronting her fear of Miss Kilman, who begins to lose "her malignity, her size" (190). The truce never occurs, however, and Clarissa doesn't invite Miss Kilman to the party. "I never go to parties," Miss Kilman confides to Elizabeth, "People don't ask me to parties—and she knew as she said it that it was this egotism that was her undoing" (200). To herself she thinks, "Why should they ask me? . . . I'm plain, I'm unhappy" (200). Notwithstanding the obvious differences between the worlds of *Frankenstein* and *Mrs. Dalloway*, Miss Kilman's feelings of anguished rejection are not very different from the Creature's feelings over his banishment from society or, for that matter, from the feelings of characters as diverse as the young Pip, Heathcliff, or Father Time in their desperate situations. Had Clarissa extended the guest list to Miss Kilman, *Mrs. Dalloway* would have ended more affirmatively, on a note of heartening self-reconciliation. Clarissa would have displayed the generosity of which she is capable, and Miss Kilman might have felt less of an outsider. Miss Kilman also would have discovered her kinship to the other guests. Her favorite subject, we are told, is her own suffering; she likes best "people who were ill" (200). In this respect, she would have much to talk about with Clarissa and her friends.

As *Mrs. Dalloway* draws to a close, Clarissa experiences an intensity of emotion that belies her earlier complaints of fatigue and age. She feels at her party the "intoxication of the moment, that dilatation of the nerves of the heart itself till it seemed to quiver." She also senses, however, that her triumphs "had a hollowness; at arm's length they were, not in the heart" (265). As usual, Clarissa is overly harsh on herself. For despite all her limitations, she remains the magical center of the novel, the character "with that extraordinary gift, the woman's gift, of making a world of her own wherever she happened to be" (114). It is a gift that Virginia Woolf displayed, not in the parties she hosted, but in the novels she wrought. In writing about her characters' heart problems, she makes us aware of how precious life is, how terror and ecstasy are part of a heightened awareness of existence. "What does the brain matter," Sally asks on the last page, "compared with the heart?" *Mrs. Dalloway* demonstrates, with heart-rending power, Virginia Woolf's awareness that illness must take its place with love and battle and jealousy among the prime themes of literature.

Epilogue

Along with love, battle, and jealousy, narcissism must take its place among the prime themes of literature. However we conceptualize it, self-love will always be with us, in its healthy and unhealthy forms. In writing about warm-hearted and cold-hearted characters, we inevitably touch upon narcissistic issues. Viewed closely, every age reveals the culture of narcissism.

And yet there are dangers in writing about narcissism, as my own study demonstrates inadvertently. In judging fictional or real characters as excessively narcissistic, we attach negative labels to them and thus isolate one thread of a rich tapestry. All psychiatric classifications are reductive, and characters are always more complex than their diagnoses. Contrary to what Dr. Spielvogel tells Peter Tarnopol in Roth's *My Life as a Man*, the word *narcissism* is not purely descriptive or value-free.[1] There is no surer way to provoke a narcissistic reaction than to call a person narcissistic; the word is bound to be experienced as an insult. Although narcissism is not exclusively or predominantly pathological, it is unlikely that Kohut and his followers will succeed entirely in overcoming our prejudicial attitude toward self-love. The term *pathological narcissism* will probably always remain redundant.

While writing this book, I have become uncomfortably aware of my ambivalence toward narcissism. Which is to say, I have become ambivalent toward my own narcissism. Readers will note the inconsistency of my empathy, the pattern of my idealizations and devaluations, the limits of my ability to understand other points of view. My theoretical and gender bias must also be evident by now. I believe strongly that psychoanalysis and feminism, long adversaries, are potentially natural allies in their aim of empowerment. My reading of Sue Bridehead, however, reveals traditionally male psychoanalytic assumptions that will prove offensive to some feminists. Sophie Freud's response to my chapter on *Jude the Obscure* is worth quoting:

> You can see that I am still in disagreement with your treatment of Sue, because it is such a reminder of the long years of mother blaming that we indulged in, in our child guidance clinics. Your accusing her, above all, to form "the noose around his neck," seemed truly an empathic failure on your part. I tried to put myself into Sue's shoes, and I found I could understand her words to the child, and even her motivation to return to her dead marriage. She had tried to live a free and independent unconventional life, and it brought about the deaths of three children. It was such a loud heaven-sent condemnation (by which I mean a condemnation of conventions and society) that she simply gave up on life. She returned to being a good little mouse child/wife with no more wishes and plans of her own. It was the very opposite of a narcissistic gesture; she gave up on any narcissistic strivings that she might once have had. [2]

I admire Professor Freud's truly empathic stance and feel chastened by the limits of my understanding. Why am I so judgmental of Sue? I'm not sure. Perhaps my life experience prevents me from fully identifying with the desperation of someone in her situation. (I tend to be overprotective, not underprotective, and therefore make different parenting errors than Sue does.) It may be that, despite my affirmation of the good enough mother, I still desire the perfect mother and reject imperfect mothers such as Sue. For whatever reason, I cannot prevent myself from implicating her in Father Time's double murder and suicide. No matter how many times I reread *Jude the Obscure,* I am still unable to resolve the conflict between remaining accepting and empathic, on the one hand, and critical and detached, on the other. The tension dramatizes the debate between two fundamentally opposed approaches to narcissism: Kohut's affirmation of warm empathy and Kernberg's insistence upon cool detachment.

Analysts speak about countertransference problems awakened by narcissistic patients; literary critics need to recognize countertransference problems awakened by fictional characters. No subject is more treacherous to write about than narcissism, for it inevitably calls attention to the writer's grandiosity and exhibitionism. When I began

Narcissism and the Novel, I desired to contribute to a new understanding of seven classic novels that have delighted millions of readers
and generated countless scholarly books and articles. Like Victor, I
was deeply smitten with the thirst for knowledge, and I wanted to
shine, to become a benefactor of my species. "So much has been
done, exclaimed the soul of Frankenstein,—more, far more, will I
achieve: treading in the steps already marked, I will pioneer a new
way, explore unknown powers, and unfold to the world the deepest
mysteries of creation."[3]

In concluding the book, however, I realize that I have not unfolded
to the world the deepest mysteries of narcissism. I am now struck by
the grandiosity of my efforts to understand an elusive subject. In my
darker moments I fear that I have produced, to quote M. Frankenstein's dismissal of Cornelius Agrippa, "sad trash." Victor's horror
upon the completion of his work only slightly exaggerates the anxieties many authors feel about their own texts. "I had worked hard for
nearly two years, for the sole purpose of infusing life into an inani-
mate body. For this I had deprived myself of rest and health. I had
desired it with an ardour that far exceeded moderation; but now that
I had finished, the beauty of the dream vanished, and breathless
horror and disgust filled my heart" (57). The pale student of unhallowed arts spent only two years working on his hideous creature; I
have now spent four. Nor are my ardor and self-doubt less intense
than Victor's.

I mention these details to suggest how the mechanisms of idealization and devaluation affect fictional and real authors alike. Literary
critics do not generally discuss in print their narcissistic strivings and
defenses, yet our silence only reinforces the belief that self-seeking is
illegitimate. Kohut is surely right to suggest that we must acknowledge the legitimacy of narcissistic forces, so that we can transform
grandiosity and exhibitionism into realistic self-esteem and self-plea-
sure. Only then will we be comfortable with our own narcissism.

It is now time to send this book into the world, where it will
succeed or fail on its own terms and take its place among the prolifer-
ating studies of narcissism. I no longer idealize nor devalue my creation; it will neither "bless me as its creator and source," as Victor
once expected from the Creature, nor, I hope, be judged a "deformed

and abortive creation." Mary Shelley's heart-felt words in the Introduction to *Frankenstein* capture how I feel toward my own work. "I
bid my hideous progeny go forth and prosper. I have an affection for
it, for it was the offspring of happy days, when death and grief were
but words, which found no true echo in my heart" (10).

Notes

I. Introduction: Narcissus Revisited: From Myth to Case Study

1. Ovid, *Metamorphoses*, Frank Justus Miller, trans. (Cambridge: Harvard University Press, repr. 1936), 157. All references are to this edition.

2. E. J. Kenney suggests that Ovid was probably the first to combine the stories of Narcissus and Echo. See his notes in Ovid, *Metamorphoses*, A.D. Melville, trans. (New York: Oxford University Press, 1986), 392. No fan of psychoanalysis, Kenney writes that Ovid "would no doubt have been amused to see the second metamorphosis inflicted on his hero by Sigmund Freud."

3. Douglas Bush, *Mythology and the Renaissance Tradition in English Poetry* (New York: Norton, rev. ed., 1963).

4. Louise Vinge, *The Narcissus Theme in Western European Literature up to the Early Nineteenth Century*, Robert Dewsnap and Nigel Reeves, trans. (Lund: Gleerups, 1967).

5. Linda Hutcheon, *Narcissistic Narrative: The Metafictional Paradox* (Waterloo, Ont.: Wilfred Laurier University Press, 1980). Other studies of narcissism in literature include Robert M. MacLean's *Narcissus and the Voyeur* (The Hague: Mouton, 1979), which argues that the faculty of observation finds no reflection of itself in the world; Barbara A. Schapiro's *The Romantic Mother* (Baltimore: Johns Hopkins University Press, 1983), a psychoanalytic discussion of narcissistic patterns in Romantic English poetry; Lawrence Thornton's *Unbodied Hope* (Lewisburg: Bucknell University Press, 1984), an account of narcissism in selected modern novels; Joyce Warren's *The American Narcissus* (New Brunswick: Rutgers University Press, 1984), a study of women and individualism in nineteenth-century American fiction; Lynne Layton and Barbara A. Schapiro's *Narcissism & the Text* (New York: New York University Press, 1986), an analysis of literature from a Kohutian self psychology

point of view; and Julia Kristeva's *Tales of Love* (New York: Columbia University Press, 1987), an evocative study of the depiction of love in literature.

6. Havelock Ellis, "The Conception of Narcissism," in *Studies in the Psychology of Sex* (New York: Random House, 1937), 2: 362. Ellis' first mention of the psychological implications of the Narcissus myth appears in "Auto-Erotism, a Psychological Study," published in the St. Louis *Alienist and Neurologist*, vol. 19 (April 1898).

7. Herbert Marcuse, *Eros and Civilization* (New York: Vintage, 1961), 154.

8. T.S. Eliot, *The Waste Land*, in *The Complete Poems and Plays: 1909–1950* (New York: Harcourt, Brace and World, 1952). See also *The Waste Land: A Facsimile and Transcript of the Original Drafts*, Valerie Eliot, ed. (New York: Harcourt Brace Jovanovich, 1971).

9. Christopher Lasch, *The Culture of Narcissism* (New York: Norton, 1979), xv. Lasch is dazzling in his pursuit of narcissism but dismissive in his categorical rejection of so much that is valuable in American society. His tone, moreover, is often supercilious, as when he observes that "it is a tribute to the peculiar horror of contemporary life that it makes the worst features of earlier times—the stupefaction of the masses, the obsessed and driven lives of the bourgeoisie—seem attractive by comparison" (99). Indeed, one wonders whether Lasch is himself implicated in the narcissism he is trying to analyze. In a subsequent book, *The Minimal Self* (New York: Norton, 1984), Lasch seems to take a more tolerant view of narcissism, arguing that the reader will find "no indignant outcry against contemporary 'hedonism,' self-seeking, egoism, indifference to the general good—the traits commonly associated with 'narcissism' " (15).

10. Paul Zweig, *The Heresy of Self-Love* (New York: Basic Books, 1968), preface.

11. Pausanias, *Guide to Greece*, Peter Levi, trans. (New York: Penguin, 1979), 1: 376.

12. See Robert Graves, *The Greek Myths* (Baltimore: Penguin, 1955), 1: 287.

13. Tobin Siebers, *The Mirror of Medusa* (Berkeley: University of California Press, 1983), 74.

14. Robert Langbaum, *The Mysteries of Identity* (New York: Oxford University Press, 1977), 6.

15. Hyman Spotnitz and Philip Resnikoff, "The Myths of Narcissus," *The Psychoanalytic Review*, 14 (1954): 174. See also Spotnitz's later article, "Narcissus as Myth, Narcissus as Patient," written in the form of an imaginary exchange between Narcissus and his analyst, in Marie Coleman Nelson, ed., *The Narcissistic Condition* (New York: Human Sciences Press, 1977).

16. Sigmund Freud, *Beyond the Pleasure Principle* (1920), in James Strachey et al., eds. *The Standard Edition of the Complete Psychological Works of Sigmund Freud* (London: Hogarth Press, 1955), 18: 14–16. Henceforth

all references to Freud, unless otherwise noted, come from the twenty-four volume *Standard Edition* (London: Hogarth Press, 1953–1974).

17. Sophie Freud, "Paradoxes of Parenthood: On the Impossibility of Raising Children Perfectly," in Philip J. Davis and David Park, eds., *No Way: The Nature of the Impossible* (New York: Freeman, 1987).

18. Peter Blos, *Son and Father* (New York: Free Press, 1985).

19. Lionel Trilling, "Freud and Literature," *The Liberal Imagination* (Garden City: Anchor Books, 1953), 32.

20. Margaret S. Mahler, Fred Pine, and Anni Bergman, *The Psychological Birth of the Human Infant* (New York: Basic Books, 1975).

21. Martin S. Bergmann, "The Legend of Narcissus," *American Imago*, 41 (1984): 394.

22. Victoria Hamilton, *Narcissus and Oedipus* (London: Routledge and Kegan Paul, 1982), 127. See also Juliet Mitchell, *Psycho-Analysis and Feminism* (New York: Vintage, 1975), 30–41, for a discussion of the role of Echo in the development of narcissism.

23. For a deconstructive reading of Ovid's myth, see John Brenkman, "Narcissus in the Text," *The Georgia Review*, 30 (1976): 293–327.

24. See Jorge Luis Maldonado, "Narcissism and Unconscious Communication," *International Journal of Psycho-Analysis*, 68 (1987): 379–87.

25. For a psychoanalytic view of the meaning of emptiness, see Melvin Singer, "The Experience of Emptiness in Narcissistic and Borderline States," parts 1 and 2, *The International Review of Psycho-Analysis*, 4 (1977): 459–79.

26. Otto Rank, *The Double* (1914), Harry Tucker, Jr., trans. and ed. (Chapel Hill, N.C.: University of North Carolina Press, 1971; repr. New York: New American Library, 1979), 86. All references are to the 1979 edition.

27. Sigmund Freud, "On Narcissism: An Introduction" (1914), *Standard Edition*, 14: 85. All references are to this edition.

28. Sigmund Freud, *Three Essays on the Theory of Sexuality* (1905), *Standard Edition*, 7: 145n.

29. Ernest Jones, *The Life and Work of Sigmund Freud* (New York: Basic Books, 1955), 2: 302. All references are to this edition.

30. Sigmund Freud, *Introductory Lectures on Psycho-Analysis* (1916–1917), *Standard Edition*, 16: 284–85. All references are to this edition.

31. Reuben Fine, *Narcissism, the Self, and Society* (New York: Columbia University Press, 1986), 36. All references are to this edition.

32. Sigmund Freud, *Analysis of a Phobia in a Five-Year-Old Boy* (1909), *Standard Edition*, 10: 145–46. Freud elaborated on this in "On Psycho-Analysis" (1913): "psycho-analysis has demonstrated that there is no fundamental difference, but only one of degree, between the mental life of normal people, of neurotics and of psychotics" (*Standard Edition*, 12: 210).

33. Sigmund Freud, "A Difficulty in the Path of Psycho-Analysis" (1917),

Standard Edition, 17: 139. In *The Ego and the Id* (1923), however, Freud identifies the id, not the ego, as the reservoir of libido.

34. Sigmund Freud, *Group Psychology and the Analysis of the Ego* (1921), *Standard Edition*, 18: 113.

35. Emanuel Peterfreund, "Some Critical Comments on Psychoanalytic Conceptualizations of Infancy," *International Journal of Psycho-Analysis* 59 (1978): 427.

36. Daniel N. Stern, *The Interpersonal World of the Infant* (New York: Basic Books, 1985), 10. All references are to this edition.

37. Sigmund Freud, "Extracts from Freud's Footnotes to His Translation of Charcot's *Tuesday Lectures*" (1892–1894), *Standard Edition*, 1: 139.

38. Sigmund Freud, "Psycho-Analysis" (1923), *Standard Edition*, 18: 253.

39. For a more extended critique of Freud's view of women, see Sarah Kofman, "The Narcissistic Woman: Freud and Girard," *Diacritics*, 10 (1980): 36–45. See also Lucy Freeman and Herbert S. Strean, *Freud and Women* (New York: Frederick Ungar, 1981).

40. Ellis, "The Conception of Narcissism," 355.

41. James Masterson, *The Narcissistic and Borderline Disorders* (New York: Brunner/Mazel, 1981), 14.

42. Sophie Freud, "An Overview of the Concept of Narcissism," *Social Casework* 58 (March 1977): 142. For a discussion of how narcissistic issues affect males and females differently, see Carol Gilligan, *In a Different Voice* (Cambridge: Harvard University Press, 1982). Gilligan maintains that men and women experience differently relationships and issues of dependency:

> For boys and men, separation and individuation are critically tied to gender identity since separation from the mother is essential for the development of masculinity. For girls and women, issues of femininity or feminine identity do not depend on the achievement of separation from the mother or on the process of individuation. Since masculinity is defined through separation while femininity is defined through attachment, male gender identity is threatened by intimacy while female gender identity is threatened by separation. Thus males tend to have difficulty with relationships, while females tend to have problems with individuation. (8)

43. Robert Holt, "Beyond Vitalism & Mechanism: Freud's Concept of Psychic Energy." Quoted by Ben Bursten, "The Narcissistic Course," in Marie Coleman Nelson, ed. *The Narcissistic Condition*, 107.

44. Heinz Kohut, *The Search for the Self*, Paul H. Ornstein, ed. (New York: International Universities Press, 1978), 2: 618–19. All references are to this edition.

45. Sigmund Freud, "Mourning and Melancholia" (1917), *Standard Edition*, 14: 251.

46. Sydney Pulver, "Narcissism: The Term and the Concept," *Journal of the American Psychoanalytic Association*, 18 (1970): 319.

47. American Psychiatric Association, *Diagnostic and Statistical Manual of*

Mental Disorders, 3rd ed. (Washington, D.C.: American Psychiatric Association, 1980), 315. The revised edition of *DSM-III*, published in 1987, has compressed but not significantly altered the definition of narcissistic personality disorder.

48. Richard D. Chessick, *Psychology of the Self and the Treatment of Narcissism* (Northvale, N.J.: Jason Aronson, 1985), 7.

49. Monica Carsky and Steven Ellman, "Otto Kernberg: Psychoanalysis and Object Relations Theory; The Beginnings of an Integrative Approach," in Joseph Reppen, ed., *Beyond Freud* (Hillsdale, N.J.: Analytic Press, 1985), 257.

50. Otto Kernberg, *Borderline Conditions and Pathological Narcissism* (New York: Jason Aronson, 1975). All references are to this edition.

51. Edith Jacobson, *The Self and the Object World* (New York: International Universities Press, 1964).

52. Heinz Hartmann, *Essays on Ego Psychology* (New York: International Universities Press, 1964), 113–41.

53. In Janet Malcolm's lively exposé, *Psychoanalysis: The Impossible Profession* (New York: Vintage, 1982), a forty-one-year-old analyst makes the following remark about Kernberg's formidable self-confidence: "There's the rest of us, crushed under the ton of bricks we call our ambiguity about our patients, which we drag about with us day after day, and there's Kernberg, who gets up on a rostrum and talks about his cases as if they were nose jobs" (111–12).

54. For a lucid discussion of the differences between the two approaches to narcissism, see Gillian A. Russell, "Narcissism and the Narcissistic Personality Disorder: A Comparison of the Theories of Kernberg and Kohut," *British Journal of Medical Psychology*, 58 (1985): 137–48.

55. Erich Fromm, "Selfishness and Self-Love," *Psychiatry*, 2 (1939): 523.

56. Heinz Kohut, *The Analysis of the Self* (New York: International Universities Press, 1971), 220. All references are to this edition.

57. Heinz Kohut, "Reflections," in Arnold Goldberg, ed., *Advances in Self Psychology* (New York: International Universities Press, 1980), 478.

58. Jacques Lacan, *The Language of the Self*, Anthony Wilden, trans. (New York: Delta, 1975).

59. Jacques Lacan, *The Seminar of Jacques Lacan*, John Forrester, trans. (Cambridge: Cambridge University Press, 1988), book 2, 166. All references are to this edition.

60. Ellie Ragland-Sullivan, *Jacques Lacan and the Philosophy of Psychoanalysis* (Urbana: University of Illinois Press, 1986). See also Catherine Clément, *The Lives and Legends of Jacques Lacan*, Arthur Goldhammer, trans. (New York: Columbia University Press, 1983). Art Berman's *From the New Criticism to Deconstruction* (Urbana: University of Illinois Press, 1988) is helpful in showing how Lacanian theory relates to literary criticism.

61. Daniel Dervin, "Lacanian Mirrors and Literary Reflections," *Journal of*

the *Philadelphia Association for Psychoanalysis*, 7 (1980): 139. See also Dervin's "Roland Barthes: The Text as Self, the Self as Text," *The Psychoanalytic Review* 74 (1987): 279–92. Norman Holland offers additional criticisms of Lacanian theory in *The I* (New Haven: Yale University Press, 1985).

62. Sigmund Freud, "Recommendations to Physicians Practising Psycho-Analysis" (1912), *Standard Edition*, 12: 115–16.

63. Ernest S. Wolf, "Empathy and Countertransference," in Arnold Goldberg, ed., *The Future of Psychoanalysis* (New York: International Universities Press, 1983), 310.

64. Heinz Kohut, "Introspection, Empathy and Psychoanalysis," *Journal of the American Psychoanalytic Association*, 7 (1959): 459–83.

65. Joseph D. Lichtenberg, "Is There a Psychoanalytic Weltanschauung?" In Arnold Goldberg, ed., *The Future of Psychoanalysis*, 226.

66. Heinz Kohut, "Reflections," in Goldberg, ed., *Advances in Self Psychology*, 483.

67. Martin Buber, *I and Thou* (1922), Walter Kaufmann, trans. (New York: Scribner's, 1970).

68. Heinz Kohut, *How Does Analysis Cure?*, Arnold Goldberg, ed. (Chicago: University of Chicago Press, 1984), 83.

69. Heinz Kohut, "Selected Problems of Self Psychological Theory," in Joseph D. Lichtenberg and Samuel Kaplan, eds., *Reflections on Self Psychology*, (Hillsdale, N.J.: Analytic Press, 1983), 388.

70. Morris Eagle, *Recent Developments in Psychoanalysis* (New York: McGraw-Hill, 1984), 60.

71. Steven Marcus, "The Psychoanalytic Self," *Southern Review*, 22 (1986): 324.

72. Harold Bloom, *The Anxiety of Influence* (New York: Oxford University Press, 1973).

73. Philip Roth, *My Life as a Man* (1974), (New York: Bantam, 1975), 258.

74. Nancy C. Andreasen, "Suffering and Art: A Defense of Sanity," in Joanne Trautmann, ed., *Healing Arts in Dialogue* (Carbondale: Southern Illinois University Press, 1981), 34.

75. Cited in Michael J. Goldstein, Bruce L. Baker, and Kay R. Jamison, *Abnormal Psychology*, 2nd ed. (Boston: Little, Brown, 1986), 222.

76. See Peter L. Rudnytsky, *Freud and Oedipus* (New York: Columbia University Press, 1987).

77. George Pickering, *Creative Malady* (1974), (New York: Delta, 1976), 19.

78. See Jeffrey Berman, *Joseph Conrad: Writing as Rescue* (New York: Astra Books, 1977).

79. Sigmund Freud, *Leonardo da Vinci and a Memory of His Childhood* (1910), *Standard Edition*, 11: 107.

80. Sigmund Freud, *Civilization and Its Discontents* (1930), *Standard Edition*, 21: 81.

81. Sigmund Freud, *New Introductory Lectures on Psycho-Analysis* (1933), *Standard Edition*, 22: 160.

82. Jack J. Spector, *The Aesthetics of Freud* (New York: McGraw-Hill, 1974), 78.

83. Sigmund Freud, "Dostoevsky and Parricide" (1928), *Standard Edition*, 21: 177.

84. Sigmund Freud, *New Introductory Lectures on Psycho-Analysis* (1933), *Standard Edition*, 22: 161n.

85. Sigmund Freud, "On the Teaching of Psycho-Analysis in Universities" (1919), *Standard Edition*, 17: 173.

86. Sigmund Freud, "A Short Account of Psycho-Analysis" (1924), *Standard Edition*, 19: 208.

87. Harold Bloom, "Sigmund Freud, the Greatest Modern Writer," *New York Times Book Review*, March 23, 1986.

88. Peter Brooks, "The Idea of a Psychoanalytic Literary Criticism," *Critical Inquiry*, 13 (1987): 334.

89. Peter Brooks, *Reading for the Plot* (New York: Knopf, 1984), 322.

90. See Seymour Fisher and Roger P. Greenberg, *The Scientific Credibility of Freud's Theories and Therapy* (New York: Basic Books, 1977).

91. See Frederick Crews, "In the Big House of Theory," *New York Review of Books*, May 29, 1986, 36–42.

92. Jacques Derrida, "Coming Into One's Own," in Geoffrey H. Hartman, ed., *Psychoanalysis and the Question of the Text* (Baltimore: Johns Hopkins University Press, 1978). Derrida's essay is part of a much longer work, *The Post Card: From Socrates to Freud and Beyond* (Chicago: University of Chicago Press, 1987), that has recently been translated into English.

93. Elizabeth Freund, *The Return of the Reader* (London: Methuen, 1987), 47.

94. Murray M. Schwartz, "Critic, Define Thyself," in Hartman, ed., *Psychoanalysis and the Question of the Text*, 12.

95. Sigmund Freud, "Delusions and Dreams in Jensen's *Gradiva*" (1907), *Standard Edition*, 9: 43–44.

96. Meredith Skura, *The Literary Use of the Psychoanalytic Process* (New Haven: Yale University Press, 1981), 30.

97. Baruch Hochman, *Character in Literature* (Ithaca: Cornell University Press, 1985), 7. See also Hochman's discussion of the mimetic novel in *The Test of Character* (Rutherford, N.J.: Fairleigh Dickinson University Press, 1983).

98. Bernard J. Paris, *A Psychological Approach to Fiction* (Bloomington: Indiana University Press, 1974), 4.

99. Barbara Johnson, "Teaching Deconstructively," in G. Douglas Atkins and Michael L. Johnson, eds., *Writing and Reading Differently: Deconstruction and the Teaching of Composition and Literature* (Lawrence: University of Kansas Press, 1985), 140.

100. Daniel R. Schwarz, *The Humanistic Heritage* (Philadelphia: University of Pennsylvania Press, 1986), 4.
101. Heinz Lichtenstein, *The Dilemma of Identity* (New York: Jason Aronson, repr. 1983), 103.
102. Norman N. Holland, *The I* (New Haven: Yale University Press, 1985), 35.
103. Richard Freadman, *Eliot, James and the Fictional Self* (London: Macmillan, 1986), 20–21.
104. Erik H. Erikson, *Childhood and Society* (1950), rev. ed. (New York: Norton, 1963), 279.
105. For a discussion of Philip Roth's relationship to his real and fictional analysts, see Jeffrey Berman, *The Talking Cure: Literary Representations of Psychoanalysis* (New York: New York University Press, 1985).
106. See Ned Lukacher, *Primal Scenes: Literature, Philosophy, Psychoanalysis* (Ithaca: Cornell University Press, 1986). For a review of Lukacher's book, see Jeffrey Berman, *The Psychoanalytic Review,* 75 (1988): 179–84.
107. Steven Marcus, "Freud and Dora," in Charles Bernheimer and Claire Kahane, eds., *In Dora's Case* (New York: Columbia University Press, 1985).
108. See, for example, Masao Miyoshi, *The Divided Self* (New York: New York University Press, 1969).
109. D.H. Lawrence, *Lady Chatterley's Lover* (1928), (New York: Grove Press, 1962), 146.
110. Bruno Bettelheim, *The Uses of Enchantment* (New York: Vintage, 1977), 145.
111. Marshall W. Alcorn, Jr., and Mark Bracher, "Literature, Psychoanalysis, and the Re-Formation of the Self: A New Direction for Reader-Response Theory," *PMLA* 100, 3 (May 1985): 349.
112. Walter Slatoff, *The Look of Distance* (Columbus: Ohio State University Press, 1985). See also his *With Respect to Readers* (Ithaca: Cornell University Press, 1970).
113. See Jane Gallop, "Lacan and Literature: A Case for Transference," *Poetics* 13 (1984): 301–8.
114. D.W. Winnicott, "Transitional Objects and Transitional Phenomena," *International Journal of Psycho-Analysis* 34 (1953): 94.

2. *Frankenstein;* or, The Modern Narcissus

1. Mary Shelley, *Frankenstein; or The Modern Prometheus* (1831), M.K. Joseph, ed. (New York: Oxford University Press, 1969; repr. 1984), 9. All references are to this edition.
2. For a selected chronology of *Frankenstein* films, see Martin Tropp, *Mary Shelley's Monster* (Boston: Houghton Mifflin, 1976), 169–74.

3. Otto Rank, *The Double* (1914), Harry Tucker, Jr., trans. and ed. (Chapel Hill, N.C.: University of North Carolina Press, 1971; repr. New York: New American Library, 1979).

4. Morton Kaplan and Robert Kloss, *The Unspoken Motive* (New York: Free Press, 1973). A complete listing of all the books and essays exploring the theme of the double in *Frankenstein* would have to include virtually everything published on the novel in the last fifteen years. A book not often cited by Shelley critics is Masao Miyoshi's *The Divided Self* (New York: New York University Press, 1969). Miyoshi points out the essential oneness of Victor and the Monster (84).

5. In the original 1818 edition of *Frankenstein*, Elizabeth is described as Victor's cousin, while in the 1831 revision she is described as an Italian foundling adopted by the Frankensteins. For a detailed examination of the differences between the two manuscripts, see Mary Shelley, *Frankenstein; or The Modern Prometheus: The 1818 Text*, James Rieger, ed. (Indianapolis: Bobbs-Merrill, 1974; repr. Chicago: University of Chicago Press, 1982).

6. Ellen Moers, "Female Gothic," repr. in George Levine and U.C. Knoepflmacher, eds., *The Endurance of Frankenstein* (Berkeley: University of California Press, 1979; repr. 1982), 87. All references are to the 1982 edition. For a discussion of the way in which maternity often provokes mental breakdown, see Marilyn Yalom, *Maternity, Mortality, and the Literature of Madness* (University Park: Pennsylvania State University Press, 1985). Although Yalom does not discuss Mary Shelley, *Frankenstein* illustrates the thesis that many women experience childbirth as a form of torture, "a unique encounter with existential aloneness, akin to mental breakdown and dying" (7).

7. J.M. Hill, "*Frankenstein* and the Physiognomy of Desire," *American Imago* 32, 4 (1975): 335.

8. Gerhard Joseph, "Frankenstein's Dream: The Child as Father of the Monster," *Hartford Studies in Literature*, 7, 2 (1975): 97–115.

9. Gordon D. Hirsch, "The Monster Was a Lady: On the Psychology of Mary Shelley's *Frankenstein*," *Hartford Studies in Literature*, 7, 2 (1975): 135.

10. Marc A. Rubenstein, "'My Accursed Origin': The Search for the Mother in *Frankenstein*," *Studies in Romanticism*, 15, 2 (1976): 165.

11. Trop, *Mary Shelley's Monster;* David Ketterer, *Frankenstein's Creation: The Book, The Monster, and Human Reality* (Victoria, B.C.: University of Victoria, 1979).

12. U.C. Knoepflmacher, "Thoughts on the Aggression of Daughters," in Levine and Knoepflmacher, eds., *The Endurance of Frankenstein*.

13. Wayne A. Myers, "Mary Shelley's *Frankenstein*: Creativity and the Psychology of the Exception," in Robert Langs, ed., *International Journal of Psychoanalytic Psychotherapy* (New York: Jason Aronson, 1982–1983), vol. 9.

14. Mary Poovey, *The Proper Lady and the Woman Writer* (Chicago: University of Chicago Press, 1984).
15. William Veeder, *Mary Shelley & Frankenstein* (Chicago: University of Chicago Press, 1986).
16. Trop observes in *Mary Shelley's Monster:* "Frankenstein could almost be labeled a narcissistic schizophrenic, or what Freud called a paraphrenic: 'They suffer from megalomania and have withdrawn their interest from the external world (people and things.)' The paraphrenic is also preoccupied with 'the lost narcissism of his childhood—the time when he was his own ideal!' " (48). Despite the awkwardness in terminology—"narcissistic schizophrenic" conflates two quite different psychiatric classifications—Trop accurately describes crucial elements of Victor Frankenstein's personality. In "Frankenstein and Other Monsters: An Examination of the Concepts of Destructive Narcissism, and Perverse Relationships Between Parts of the Self as Seen in the Gothic Novel," *International Review of Psycho-Analysis* 12 (1985):101–8, Stanley Gold views the Creature as the split-off narcissistic aspect of the self. Despite the lengthy title of the essay, Gold devotes only a few paragraphs to an analysis of *Frankenstein*.
17. Quoted by William A. Walling, *Mary Shelley* (New York: Twayne, 1972), 49. It is interesting to note that despite Percy Bysshe Shelley's insightful comment on *Frankenstein*, several critics have suggested that the fictional Victor mirrors Mary Shelley's ambivalent feelings toward her husband. Christopher Small observes that "Frankenstein himself is clearly and to some extent must intentionally have been a portrayal of Shelley, and Shelley can scarcely have been unaware of it, if only on account of his name. Frankenstein's first name is Victor, the same (presumably in earnest of a life of mental fight and spiritual conquest) that Shelley took for himself on a number of occasions in boyhood and later" (*Ariel Like a Harpy* [London: Victor Gollancz, 1972], 101). George Levine makes a similar point, arguing that *Frankenstein* "dramatizes, whatever its intentions, the deadliness of Shelley, her husband's, idealizing and rebellion" (*The Realistic Imagination* [Chicago: University of Chicago Press, 1981], 26.) In *Shelley & Zastrozzi* (London: Gregg/Archive, 1965), Eustace Chesser suggests that "Shelley was narcissistic, to such a degree that it was a barrier to the formation of other relationships" (25.)
18. George Levine, "The Ambiguous Heritage of *Frankenstein*," in Levine and Knoepflmacher, eds. *The Endurance of Frankenstein*, 8.
19. Otto Kernberg, *Borderline Conditions and Pathological Narcissism* (New York: Jason Aronson, 1975), 264. All references are to this edition.
20. Lillian Feder, *Madness in Literature* (Princeton: Princeton University Press, 1980), 9. For an extended discussion of the similarities and differences between fictional and psychiatric accounts of mental illness, see Jeffrey Berman, *The Talking Cure: Literary Representations of Psychoanalysis* (New York: New York University Press, 1985).

21. Small, *Ariel Like a Harpy*, 65–66.

22. Biographers and critics long have been fascinated by Mary Shelley's decision to name the murdered boy in *Frankenstein* William when, at the same time, her own baby had the same name. "It is almost inconceivable," an early biographer wrote in dismay, "that Mary could allow herself to introduce a baby boy into her book; deliberately call him William, describe him in terms identical with those in which she portrays her own child in one of her letters—and then let Frankenstein's monster waylay this innocent in a woodland dell and murder him by strangling" (Richard Church, *Mary Shelley* [London: Gerald Howe, 1928], 54–55). To make matters worse, the real William died shortly after *Frankenstein* was completed, a chilling example, or so it may have seemed, of life imitating art. David Ketterer calls the decision to name the fictional child William an "act of prescient masochism" *(Frankenstein's Creation*, 42.) Mary Shelley's father, to whom she dedicated *Frankenstein*, and her half-brother were also named William, suggesting the depth of her ambivalence toward the name. As Knoepflmacher notes in "Thoughts on the Aggression of Daughters," "The destruction of little William can obviously be related to Mary Shelley's own muted hostility toward her younger half-brother: unlike herself, the younger William Godwin possessed a mother and, as a male, had received his father's identity and approbation. Simultaneously, however, the Monster's murder of the little boy must also be recognized as a self-mutilation which the novel as a whole tries to resist and conquer" (103).

23. In dying in order to save Elizabeth, Mme. Frankenstein seems to be reenacting the situation of Mary Wollstonecraft, whose death made possible her daughter Mary's life. The "calm death" Mary Shelley ascribes to Mme. Frankenstein may well represent the novelist's efforts to assuage her mother's suffering and mitigate the daughter's complicity in the death.

24. M.K. Joseph, "Introduction" to *Frankenstein; or The Modern Prometheus*, x.

25. Elizabeth Nitchie, *Mary Shelley* (New Brunswick, N.J.: Rutgers University Press, 1953), 96.

26. Heinz Kohut, "Thoughts on Narcissism and Narcissistic Rage," *The Psychoanalytic Study of the Child*, 27 (1972): 380. All references are to this edition.

27. Walling, *Mary Shelley*, 36.

28. Heinz Kohut, "Reflections," in Arnold Goldberg, ed., *Advances in Self Psychology* (New York: International Universities Press, 1980), 516.

29. Ketterer, *Frankenstein's Creation*, 11.

3. Attachment and Loss in *Wuthering Heights*

1. Emily Brontë, *Wuthering Heights* (1847), (Harmondsworth, Middlesex, Eng.: Penguin, 1965; repr. 1985), 70. All references to *Wuthering Heights* are from the 1985 edition.
2. Dorothy Van Ghent, *The English Novel* (New York: Rinehart, 1953; repr. New York: Harper and Row, 1967), 187.
3. Eric Solomon, "The Incest Theme in *Wuthering Heights*," *Nineteenth-Century Fiction* 14 (1959): 80–83. See also Giles Mitchell, "Incest, Demonism, and Death in *Wuthering Heights*," *Literature and Psychology* 23 (1973): 27–36. For a recent discussion of the incest theme in literature, see James B. Twitchell, *Forbidden Partners* (New York: Columbia University Press, 1987).
4. Thomas Moser, "What is the Matter with Emily Jane?: Conflicting Impulses in *Wuthering Heights*," *Nineteenth-Century Fiction* 17 (1962): 1–17.
5. See Ruth M. Adams, "*Wuthering Heights*: The Land East of Eden," *Nineteenth-Century Fiction* 13 (1958): 58–62; Edgar F. Shannon, "Lockwood's Dreams and the Exegesis of *Wuthering Heights*," *Nineteenth-Century Fiction* 14 (1959): 95–109; Robert C. McKibbon, "The Image of the Book in *Wuthering Heights*," *Nineteenth-Century Fiction* 15 (1960): 159–69; Ronald E. Fine, "Lockwood's Dreams and the Key to *Wuthering Heights*, *Nineteenth-Century Fiction*, 24 (1969): 16–30; Michael D. Reed, "The Power of *Wuthering Heights*: A Psychoanalytic Examination," *Psychocultural Review* 1 (1977): 21–42. For a discussion of the novel's preoccupation with childhood, see Irving H. Buchen, "Emily Brontë and the Metaphysics of Childhood and Love," *Nineteenth-Century Fiction* 22 (1967): 63–70.
6. Patricia Meyer Spacks, *The Female Imagination* (New York: Knopf, 1975; repr. New York: Avon, 1976), 176.
7. Helene Moglen, "The Double Vision of *Wuthering Heights*: A Clarifying View of Female Development," *The Centennial Review*, 15 (1971): 391–405. For a more recent study of female identity in *Wuthering Heights*, see Margaret Homans, *Women Writers and Poetic Identity* (Princeton: Princeton University Press, 1980).
8. Leo Bersani, *A Future for Astyanax* (Boston: Little, Brown, 1976), 214.
9. Sandra M. Gilbert and Susan Gubar, *The Madwoman in the Attic* (New Haven: Yale University Press, 1979), 251.
10. Philip K. Wion, "The Absent Mother in Emily Brontë's *Wuthering Heights*," *American Imago* 42 (1985): 143–64.
11. Sigmund Freud, "Female Sexuality" (1931), *Standard Edition*, 21: 226.
12. John Bowlby, *Attachment and Loss*, 3 vols. (New York: Basic Books, 1969–1980). All references are to this edition.

13. Sigmund Freud, "Remembering, Repeating and Working-Through" (1914), *Standard Edition*, 12: 147–56.
14. Stanley L. Olinick and Laura Tracy, "Transference Perspectives of Story Telling," *The Psychoanalytic Review* 74 (1987): 323.
15. Wade Thompson, "Infanticide and Sadism in *Wuthering Heights*," *PMLA* 78 (1963): 71.
16. James Hafley, "The Villain in *Wuthering Heights*," *Nineteenth-Century Fiction* 13 (1958):199–215.
17. See J. Hillis Miller, *The Disappearance of God* (Cambridge: Harvard University Press, 1963; repr. New York: Schocken, 1965) for an illuminating discussion of Joseph's religious significance in *Wuthering Heights*.
18. Gilbert and Gubar, *Madwoman*, 281. For a similar interpretation of Edgar, see James H. Kavanagh, *Emily Brontë* (Oxford: Basil Blackwell, 1985), 41.
19. Richard Benvenuto, *Emily Brontë* (Boston: Twayne, 1982), 114–15.
20. Moser, "What Is the Matter with Emily Jane?" 15.
21. Bersani, *A Future for Astyanax*, 202.
22. Arnold Kettle, "Emily Brontë: *Wuthering Heights*" in Thomas A. Vogler, ed., *Twentieth Century Interpretations of Wuthering Heights* (Englewood Cliffs, N.J.: Prentice Hall, 1968), 40.
23. See William A. Madden, "*Wuthering Heights*: The Binding of Passion," *Nineteenth-Century Fiction* 27 (1972):142.
24. Emily Jane Brontë, "Filial Love," in *Five Essays Written in French*, Lorine White Nagel, trans. (Austin: University of Texas Press, 1948; repr. Folcroft, Penn.: Folcroft Library Editions, 1974), 13–14. All quotations come from the 1974 edition.
25. John Lock and Canon W. T. Dixon, *A Man of Sorrow: The Life, Letters and Times of the Rev. Patrick Brontë* (London: Nelson, 1965), 368.
26. Winifred Gérin, *Emily Brontë* (Oxford: Clarendon Press, 1971), 252.
27. Edward Chitham, *A Life of Emily Brontë* (Oxford: Blackwell, 1987), 233.
28. Emily Jane Brontë, "Portrait," in *Five Essays Written in French*, 12.
29. See Stevie Davies, *Emily Brontë: The Artist as a Free Woman* (Manchester, Eng.: Carcanet Press, 1983), 16.

4. The Autobiography of Fiction:
The Crime Against the Child in *Great Expectations*

1. John Forster, *The Life of Charles Dickens*, 2 vols. (London: Chapman and Hall, 1872; repr. 1899), 1:28. All references are to vol. 1 of the 1899 ed.
2. Edgar Johnson, *Charles Dickens: His Tragedy and Triumph*, 2 vols. (New York: Simon and Schuster, 1952), 1:45.

3. Michael Slater, *Dickens and Women* (London: J. M. Dent and Sons, 1983), 11.

4. Gwen Watkins, *Dickens in Search of Himself* (London: Macmillan, 1987).

5. Linda A. Pollock, *Forgotten Children* (Cambridge: Cambridge University Press, 1983), 62–63.

6. F. M. L. Thompson, *The Rise of Respectable Society* (Cambridge: Harvard University Press, 1988), 137.

7. Dorothy Van Ghent, *The English Novel* (New York: Rinehart, 1953; rpt. New York: Harper & Row, 1967), p. 166.

8. Frank Donovan, *Dickens and Youth* (New York: Dodd, Mead, 1968), 3.

9. Angus Wilson, "Dickens on Children and Childhood," in Michael Slater, ed., *Dickens 1970* (New York: Stein and Day, 1970), 208. See also Vereen M. Bell, "Parents and Children in *Great Expectations*," *The Victorian Newsletter* 27 (1965):21–24.

10. Arthur A. Adrian, *Dickens and the Parent-Child Relationship* (Athens: Ohio University Press, 1984), preface. For a specialized study of the father-daughter relationship, see Catarina Ericsson, *A Child Is a Child, You Know: The Inversion of Father and Daughter in Dickens's Novels* (Stockholm: Acta Universitatis Stockholmiensis, 1986). Ericsson argues in this doctoral dissertation published by the University of Stockholm that a prominent motif in Dickens' novels is the inverted father-daughter relationship, in which "the more severely flawed the father is, the more beautiful shines the devotion of the daughter." (Abstract)

11. Erik H. Erikson, *Childhood and Society*, 2d ed. (New York: Norton, 1963), 247–48.

12. Edmund Wilson, "Dickens: The Two Scrooges," in *The Wound and the Bow* (Cambridge, Mass.: Houghton Mifflin, 1941; repr. New York: Oxford University Press, 1965), 14.

13. Albert D. Hutter, "Reconstructive Autobiography: The Experience at Warren's Blacking," in Robert B. Partlow, Jr., ed., *Dickens Studies Annual* (Carbondale: Southern Illinois University Press, 1977), 6:9.

14. It should be noted that many of Dickens' observations in the Autobiographical Fragment appear word for word in Chapter 11 of *David Copperfield*, published in 1850. To cite but one of many examples, in the Autobiographical Fragment, Dickens writes: "That I suffered in secret, and that I suffered exquisitely, no one ever knew but I. How much I suffered, it is, as I have said already, utterly beyond my power to tell. No man's imagination can overstep the reality. But I kept my own counsel, and I did my work" (Forster, *Dickens*, 30). Compare this to David Copperfield's account: "That I suffered in secret, and that I suffered exquisitely, no one ever knew but I. How much I suffered, it is, as I have said already, utterly beyond my power to tell. But I kept my own counsel, and I did my work" (*David Copperfield* [New York: Bantam, 1981], 150).

15. Heinz Kohut, "Thoughts on Narcissism and Narcissistic Rage," in *The*

Psychoanalytic Study of the Child, 27 (1972):380. All references are to this edition.

16. Sigmund Freud, *Beyond the Pleasure Principle* (1920), *Standard Edition*, vol. 18.

17. Anna Freud, *The Ego and the Mechanisms of Defense*, rev. ed. (New York: International Universities Press, 1966), 113.

18. Robert Stoller, *Observing the Erotic Imagination* (New Haven: Yale University Press, 1985), viii.

19. Leonard F. Manheim, "Dickens and Psychoanalysis: A Memoir," in Michael Timko, Fred Kaplan, and Edward Guiliano, eds. *Dickens Studies Annual* (New York: AMS Press, 1983), 11:343.

20. Charles Dickens, *Great Expectations* (1860), (Harmondsworth, Middlesex, Eng.: Penguin, 1965; repr. 1985), 40. All references to *Great Expectations* are to the 1985 edition.

21. Ian Watt, "Oral Dickens," in Robert B. Partlow, Jr., ed., *Dickens Studies Annual* (Carbondale: Southern Illinois University Press, 1974), 3:170.

22. Curt Hartog, "The Rape of Miss Havisham," *Studies in the Novel*, 14 (1982):250.

23. Lawrence Jay Dessner, "*Great Expectations:* 'The Ghost of a Man's Own Father,' " *PMLA* 91 (1976):444.

24. For psychoanalytic discussions of Dickens' relationship to his father, see Branwen Bailey Pratt, "Dickens and Father: Notes on the Family Romance," *Hartford Studies in Literature* 8 (1976):4–22; and Dianne F. Sadoff, *Monsters of Affection* (Baltimore: Johns Hopkins University Press, 1982).

25. For a useful critique of psychoanalytic approaches to Dickens, see Michael Steig, "Dickens' Characters and Psychoanalytic Criticism," *Hartford Studies in Literature* 8 (1976):38–45. Steig, a prolific psychoanalytic critic, urges others to be humble enough to acknowledge that "it is not so much that Dickens wrote better than he knew, but that on the evidence of the texts he knew an astonishing amount" (44).

26. See Karen Horney, "The Dread of Woman," *International Journal of Psycho-Analysis*, 13 (1932):348–60.

27. Q. D. Leavis, "How We Must Read *Great Expectations*," in F. R. Leavis and Q. D. Leavis, *Dickens, the Novelist* (London: Chatto and Windus, 1970), 321. In *Dickens and the Art of Analogy* (New York: Schocken, 1970), H. M. Daleski also questions Moynahan's thesis that Pip and Orlick are doubles, though Daleski concedes that Orlick's criminality may reflect Dickens' unconscious identification with him (243).

28. Julian Moynahan, "The Hero's Guilt: The Case of *Great Expectations*," *Essays in Criticism* 10 (1960):67.

29. J. Hillis Miller, *Charles Dickens: The World of His Novels* (Cambridge: Harvard University Press, 1958; repr. Bloomington: Indiana University Press, 1969), 257.

30. Nancy Chodorow, *The Reproduction of Mothering* (Berkeley: University of California Press, 1978), 90. All references are to this edition.

31. See Dorothy Dinnerstein, *The Mermaid and the Minotaur* (New York: Harper and Row, 1977), and Carol Gilligan, *In a Different Voice* (Cambridge: Harvard University Press, 1982).

32. See David S. Werman and Theodore J. Jacobs, "Thomas Hardy's '*The Well-Beloved*' and the Nature of Infatuation," *International Review of Psycho-Analysis* 10 (1983):447–57.

33. Heinz Kohut, *The Analysis of the Self* (New York: International Universities Press, 1971).

34. Karl P. Wentersdorf, "Mirror Images in *Great Expectations*," *Nineteenth-Century Fiction* 21 (1966):203–24.

35. Lawrence Frank, *Charles Dickens and the Romantic Self* (Lincoln: University of Nebraska Press, 1984), 164. In a similar context, Taylor Stoehr observes in *Dickens: The Dreamer's Stance* (Ithaca: Cornell University Press, 1965) that "We are at first led to believe that Estella's inability to love is to blame, but in fact the hindrance to his sexual satisfaction is Pip's own inability to love" (120).

36. One of the most curious moments in *Great Expectations* occurs when Jaggers exhibits Molly's scarred and disfigured wrists to Pip. " 'There's power here,' said Mr Jaggers, coolly tracing out the sinews with his forefinger. 'Very few men have the power of wrist that this woman has. It's remarkable what mere force of grip there is in these hands. I have had occasion to notice many hands; but I never saw stronger in that respect, man's or woman's, than these' " (237).

37. For a discussion of Jaggers as a fallen Providence, see Anthony Winner, "Character and Knowledge in Dickens: The Enigma of Jaggers," in Robert B. Partlow, Jr., ed., *Dickens Studies Annual* (Carbondale: Southern Illinois University Press, 1974), 3:100–121.

38. See Joseph Gold, *Charles Dickens: Radical Moralist* (Minneapolis: University of Minnesota Press, 1972), 248.

39. Albert D. Hutter, "Crime and Fantasy in *Great Expectations*," in Frederick Crews, ed. *Psychoanalysis & Literary Process* (Cambridge, Mass.: Winthrop Publishers, 1970), 28.

40. See Hartog, "The Rape of Miss Havisham," 259. See also James Leo Spenko, "The Return of the Repressed in *Great Expectations*," *Literature and Psychology* 30 (1980):133–46.

41. Leonard Manheim, "Dickens' Fools and Madmen," in Robert B. Partlow, Jr., ed., *Dickens Studies Annual* (Carbondale: Southern Illinois University Press, 1972), 2:74.

42. Steven Connor concludes in *Charles Dickens* (Oxford: Basil Blackwell, 1985) that *Great Expectations* offers two equally inadequate models for life in society: a retreat into "narcissistic domesticity, in which the individual forgets or misrecognizes the complexity of the relationships which constitute his being"; or an acceptance of the inevitability of a split self,

leading to a "surrender to alienation" (143–44). Connor's interpretation seems unduly pessimistic, for it overlooks the extent to which the self can be healed through empathy.

43. After I completed *Narcissism and the Novel*, Fred Kaplan's biography of Dickens appeared. His interpretation of Dickens' experience at Warren's Blacking coincides essentially with my own. Kaplan notes that Dickens' "references to his parents in his letters and in his fiction suggest that the infant had both a heightened sense of dependence and a strong fear of their untrustworthiness, particularly his mother's" (*Dickens: A Biography* [New York: Morrow, 1988], 19). Kaplan concludes that as a result of his bitter disappointment with his mother, Dickens divided his pain into "the two women of his fantasy life, the oppressive, witchlike, or carelessly self-indulgent mother he felt he had, and the idealized, loving antimother of wish fulfillment" (44).

5. The Aesthetics of Narcissism in
The Picture of Dorian Gray

1. Oscar Wilde, "The Disciple," in *The Works of Oscar Wilde*, G. F. Maine, ed. (New York: Dutton, 1954), 844. All references are to this edition.

2. André Gide, *Oscar Wilde: In Memoriam*, Bernard Frechtman, trans. (New York: Philosophical Library, 1949), 3–4. All references are to this edition.

3. An extended reference to Narcissus appears in Wilde's short story "The Star-Child": "Indeed, he was as one enamoured of beauty, and would mock at the weakly and ill-favoured, and make jest of them; and himself he loved, and in summer, when the winds were still, he would lie by the well in the priest's orchard and look down at the marvel of his own face, and laugh for the pleasure he had in his fairness" (*The Works of Oscar Wilde*, 276). Interestingly, the Star-Child is turned into a toad because he rejects his mother. Other references to Narcissus may be found in the following poems: "The Garden of Eros," "The Burden of Itys," "Athanasia," "Charmides," "Panthea," and "Désespoir." For a brief discussion of the Narcissus image in Wilde's short stories, see Rodney Shewan, *Oscar Wilde: Art and Egotism* (London: Macmillan, 1977), 52–53.

4. See Otto Rank, *The Double* (1914), Harry Tucker, Jr., trans. and ed. (Chapel Hill, N. C.: University of North Carolina Press, 1971; repr. New York: New American Library, 1979); Masao Miyoshi, *The Divided Self* (New York: New York University Press, 1969); Robert Rogers, *A Psychoanalytic Study of the Double in Literature* (Detroit: Wayne State University Press, 1970); and C. F. Keppler, *The Literature of the Second Self* (Tucson: University of Arizona Press, 1972).

5. Leo Kaplan, "Analysis of *The Picture of Dorian Gray*," A. Green, trans. *Psyche and Eros* 3 (1922):8–21. See also Edmund Bergler, " 'Salome':

The Turning Point in the Life of Oscar Wilde," *The Psychoanalytic Review* 43 (1956):97–103.

6. Alexander Grinstein, "On Oscar Wilde," *Annual of Psychoanalysis* 1 (1973):345–62.

7. Jerome Kavka, "Oscar Wilde's Narcissism," *Annual of Psychoanalysis* 3 (1975):397–408.

8. Bernard A. Green, "The Effects of Distortions of the Self: A Study of *The Picture of Dorian Gray*," *Annual of Psychoanalysis* 7 (1979):391–410.

9. Karl Beckson, "The Importance of Being Angry: The Mutual Antagonism of Oscar and Willie Wilde," in Norman Kiell, ed., *Blood Brothers: Siblings as Writers* (New York: International Universities Press, 1983).

10. Ellie Ragland-Sullivan, "The Phenomenon of Aging in Oscar Wilde's *Picture of Dorian Gray*: A Lacanian View," in Kathleen Woodward and Murray M. Schwartz, eds., *Memory and Desire* (Bloomington: Indiana University Press, 1986).

11. Oscar Wilde, "Phrases and Philosophies for the Use of the Young," in Richard Ellmann, ed. *The Artist as Critic: Critical Writings of Oscar Wilde* (New York: Random House, 1968), 434. All references are to this edition.

12. E. H. Mikhail, ed., *Oscar Wilde: Interviews and Recollections* (London: Macmillan, 1979)1:37.

13. See Hilda Schiff, "Nature and Art in Oscar Wilde's 'The Decay of Lying,' " in Sybil Rosenfeld, ed., *Essays and Studies Collected for the English Association* (New York: Humanities Press, 1965).

14. Richard Ellmann, *Oscar Wilde* (London: Hamish Hamilton, 1987). All references are to this edition.

15. See Jeffrey Berman, *The Talking Cure: Literary Representations of Psychoanalysis* (New York: New York University Press, 1985).

16. Robert D. Stolorow and George E. Atwood, *Faces in a Cloud* (New York: Jason Aronson, 1979), 17.

17. Sigmund Freud, "A Special Type of Choice of Object Made by Men" (1910), *Standard Edition*, vol. 11. For a summary of the concept of rescue fantasies, see Aaron H. Esman, "Rescue Fantasies," *Psychoanalytic Quarterly* 51 (1987):263–70.

18. Norman N. Holland, *5 Readers Reading* (New Haven: Yale University Press, 1975), 61.

19. Oscar Wilde, *The Picture of Dorian Gray* (1891), Isobel Murray, ed. (Oxford: Oxford University Press, 1974; repr. 1982), 2. All references are to the 1982 edition.

20. Wilde makes the same observation in *A Woman of No Importance*, in Maine, ed., *The Works of Oscar Wilde*, 465.

21. Sophie Freud, "Overloving and Underloving," in Robert Langs, ed., *The Yearbook of Psychoanalysis and Psychotherapy* (New York: Gardner Press, 1987), 2:252. See also her comments on overlove in *My Three Mothers and Other Passions* (New York: New York University Press, 1988).

22. Jeffrey Myers, *Homosexuality and Literature: 1890–1930* (Montreal: McGill–Queen's University Press, 1977), 23.

23. See H. Montgomery Hyde, *The Trials of Oscar Wilde* (London: William Hodge, 1948).

24. Judith Ruderman, *D. H. Lawrence and the Devouring Mother* (Durham, N. C.: Duke University Press, 1984), 9.

25. See Margaret S. Mahler, Fred Pine, and Anni Bergman, *The Psychological Birth of the Human Infant* (New York: Basic Books, 1975).

26. Alexander Grinstein suggests that Wilde unconsciously equates Sibyl with his sister Isola, whose death affected him deeply and may have provoked feelings of guilt ("On Oscar Wilde," 357).

27. Christopher S. Nassaar, *Into the Demon Universe* (New Haven: Yale University Press, 1974), 69.

28. Miyoshi, *The Divided Self*, 314.

29. Rupert Hart-Davis, ed., *The Letters of Oscar Wilde* (New York: Harcourt, Brace and World, 1962), 257. All references are to this edition.

30. Vyvyan Holland, ed. *The Complete Works of Oscar Wilde* (London: Collins, 1966), 887.

31. Oscar Wilde, *De Profundis* (New York: Philosophical Library, 1960), 5. All references are to this edition.

32. See Lord Alfred Douglas, *Oscar Wilde: A Summing-Up* (London: Richards Press, 1940), 114.

33. E. H. Mikhail, *Oscar Wilde: An Annotated Bibliography of Criticism* (London: Macmillan, 1978), x.

34. Mikhail, ed., *Oscar Wilde: Interviews and Recollections*, 1:177. Munday's passage is excerpted from *A Chronicle of Friendships*, originally published in 1912.

35. H. Montgomery Hyde, *Oscar Wilde: A Biography* (London: Eyre Methuen, 1976), 181. Other Wilde biographers who dismiss the importance of this detail include Terence de Vere White, *The Parents of Oscar Wilde* (London: Hodder and Stoughton, 1967); Rupert Croft-Cooke, *The Unrecorded Life of Oscar Wilde* (New York: David McKay, 1972); and Anne Clark Amor, *Mrs. Oscar Wilde* (London: Sidgwick and Jackson, 1983). In *Son of Oscar Wilde* (Westport, Conn.: Greenwood Press, 1954), Vyvyan Holland does not mention the fact that Wilde was dressed as a girl during his childhood, but Holland does mention this in passing in *Oscar Wilde: A Pictorial Biography* (New York: Viking, 1960). There is, amazingly, no reference to this fact in Horace Wyndham's *Speranza: A Biography of Lady Wilde* (London: Boardman, 1951).

36. Robert J. Stoller, *Sex and Gender* (New York: Jason Aronson, 1968), 40.

37. Vyvyan Holland, *Son of Oscar Wilde*, 15. All references are to this edition.

38. Robert Keith Miller observes in *Oscar Wilde* (New York: Ungar, 1982):

"a popular riddle in Dublin society ran: 'Why are Sir William Wilde's nails black?' The answer was, 'Because he scratches himself' "(1–2).
39. Mikhail, *Oscar Wilde: Interviews and Recollections*, 2:403.
40. Green, "The Effects of Distortions of the Self," *Picture of Dorian Gray*, 403.
41. Wyndham, *Speranza*, 163.
42. De Vere White, *The Parents of Oscar Wilde*, 17.
43. Amor, *Mrs. Oscar Wilde*, 59.
44. Ibid., 62. Amor notes that, although Wilde's statement was quoted by the notoriously unreliable Frank Harris, who always imputed the worst possible motives to Wilde, the statement has the ring of truth about it.
45. See Peter Blos, *Son and Father* (New York: Free Press, 1985).
46. In reviewing the enormous commentary that has been written on Oscar Wilde's homosexuality, one is struck by how little we know about the subject. Not only have there been a bewildering number of theories to explain the origins of homosexuality in general and Wilde's homosexuality in particular, but the researcher's (often unconscious) value judgments always come into play, especially when investigating this controversial subject. At one extreme is Macdonald Critchley, a physician (it is unclear whether he is a psychiatrist). "To assert that Oscar Wilde was a psychopath is not going far enough," Critchley states, then invokes the hypothesis of a "constitutional hysterical personality—or hysterical psychopathy, in the German psychiatric sense of the term" to explain Wilde's sexual disorder (*The Black Hole and Other Essays* [London: Pitman, 1964] 18–44).

At the other extreme is A. L. Rowse, whose sentimental defense of Wilde is revealed in the following passage: "He was a child himself, with a child's naïveté; or perhaps the perpetual adolescent. He also had a child's sweetness of nature; there was not a grain of malice or ill will in him—something rare in literary life, where he was often attacked" *Homosexuals in History* [New York: Macmillan, 1977], 164). One wonders whether Critchley and Rowse are talking about the same person.

In otherwise perceptive articles on Wilde's homosexuality, we come across dismaying observations. The distinguished analyst Hendrik M. Ruitenbeek writes in *Homosexuality and Creative Genius* (New York: Astor-Honor, 1967): "There was one final factor which, although it could not possibly have been so causal, may have influenced Oscar's behaviour. This is the teaching of Walter Pater. Pater was a timid, little man who never married. This in itself is a suspicious fact for the psychiatrist, since the normal adult instinct is to seek a mate and those who do not do so must be regarded a little obliquely" (74).

The emerging view inside and outside the psychoanalytic community is that homosexuality is not by itself pathological. Genuine love between two people, whether they are of the same or opposite sex, is always valuable and should be respected wherever and whenever it occurs. It is the quality of one's love, not whether it is heterosexual or homosexual, that is most important.

47. Robert J. Stoller, *Perversion* (New York: Dell, 1975), 6.
48. Mikhail, ed., *Oscar Wilde: Interviews and Recollections*, 2: 316.

6. Infanticide and Object Loss in *Jude the Obscure*

1. Thomas Hardy, *Jude the Obscure* (1895) (London: Macmillan, 1971), 405. All references are to this edition.
2. Ian Gregor, *The Great Web: The Form of Hardy's Major Fiction* (Totowa, N.J.: Rowman and Littlefield, 1974), 22. One of the earliest comments on the double murder and suicide appears in Mrs. Oliphant's review of *Jude the Obscure* in 1896, when she sarcastically asks: "Does Mr. Hardy think this is really a good way of disposing of the unfortunate progeny of such connections? does he recommend it for general adoption?" (in Norman Page, ed., *Jude the Obscure: An Authoritative Text, Backgrounds and Sources, Criticism* [New York: Norton, 1978], 385). Quite apart from her outraged Victorian sensibility, Mrs. Oliphant raises an important question ignored by more astute modern readers. "Mr. Hardy knows, no doubt as everybody does, that the children are a most serious part of the question of the abolition of marriage. Is this the way in which he considers it would be resolved best?" (385). J. I. M. Stewart expresses the point more fairly in *Thomas Hardy: A Critical Biography* (London: Longman, 1971): "Little Father Time scarcely murders his siblings in the closet more effectively than his creator murders him with deadly prose" (189).
3. Irving Howe, *Thomas Hardy* (New York: Macmillan, 1967), 145–46.
4. A complete bibliography of the criticism of *Jude the Obscure* is too long to cite here, but the psychologically oriented reader should consult the following books: J. Hillis Miller, *Thomas Hardy: Distance and Desire* (Cambridge: Harvard University Press, 1970); Perry Meisel, *Thomas Hardy: The Return of the Repressed* (New Haven: Yale University Press, 1972); Geoffrey Thurley, *The Psychology of Hardy's Novels: The Nervous and the Statuesque* (Queensland: University of Queensland Press, 1975); and Rosemary Sumner, *Thomas Hardy: Psychological Novelist* (New York: St. Martin's Press, 1981). The following articles are also of interest: Norman N. Holland, "*Jude the Obscure:* Hardy's Symbolic Indictment of Christianity," *Nineteenth-Century Fiction* 9 (1954):50–60; Michael Steig, "Sue Bridehead," *Novel* 1 (1968):260–66; George Y. Trail, "The Consistency of Hardy's Sue: Bridehead Becomes Electra," *Literature and Psychology* 26 (1976):61–68; and Carol and Duane Edwards, "*Jude the Obscure:* A Psychoanalytic Study," *University of Hartford Studies in Literature* 13 (1981):78–90.

5. Robert B. Heilman, "Introduction," in Thomas Hardy, *Jude the Obscure* (New York: Harper and Row, 1966), 9.

6. Mary Jacobus, "Sue the Obscure," *Essays in Criticism* 25 (1975):319. For additional feminist interpretations of *Jude the Obscure*, see Kate Millett, *Sexual Politics* (1970; New York: Ballantine, 1978); and Penny Boumelha, *Thomas Hardy and Women* (Madison: University of Wisconsin Press, 1982).

7. "Would it have been a lie," Robert Langbaum asks, "to tell the boy she loved him and to have withheld the information about the new baby? For all her beauty, intelligence and idealism, Sue emerges as a charming monster because she lacks instincts" ("Hardy and Lawrence," in Norman Page, ed., *Thomas Hardy Annual No. 3* [London: Macmillan, 1985], 30).

8. Kohut defines the mirror transference as the "therapeutic reinstatement of that normal phase of the development of the grandiose self in which the gleam in the mother's eye, which mirrors the child's exhibitionistic display, and other forms of maternal participation in and response to the child's narcissistic-exhibitionistic enjoyment confirm the child's self-esteem and, by a gradually increasing selectivity of these responses, begin to channel it into realistic directions" (*The Analysis of the Self* [New York: International Universities Press, 1971], 116).

9. Alice Miller, *Prisoners of Childhood*, Ruth Ward, trans. (New York: Basic Books, 1981), 32.

10. Albert J. Guerard, *Thomas Hardy: The Novels and Stories* (Cambridge: Harvard University Press, 1949), 109.

11. Stanley L. Olinick and Laura Tracy, "Transference Perspectives of Story Telling," *The Psychoanalytic Review* 74 (1987):320.

12. Freud's shift away from the biological id to the defensive measures employed against forbidden drives gave rise to ego psychology. The two classic books are Freud's *The Ego and the Id* (1923), *Standard Edition*, vol. 19, where he postulates the ego as a mediating agency between id and superego, and Anna Freud's *The Ego and the Mechanisms of Defense* (1936), rev. ed. (New York: International Universities Press, 1966), an analysis of defense mechanisms.

13. Anna Freud, *The Ego and the Mechanisms of Defense*, 113.

14. See William R. Goetz, "The Felicity and Infelicity of Marriage in *Jude the Obscure*," *Nineteenth-Century Fiction*, 38 (1983):189–213.

15. See John Bowlby, *Attachment and Loss*, 3: *Loss* (New York: Basic Books, 1980).

16. According to object relations theory, internalized objects are created from the child's introjection of parental figures. These internalized objects may or may not correspond closely to external reality. They form a complex inner world of fantasy, shaping the individual's responses to the outer world. Good and bad objects in adult life relate to the earliest objects in childhood; a loss in later life reawakens the anxiety of losing the primary object. Hanna Segal's *Introduction to the Work of Melanie Klein* (New

York: Basic Books, 1974) provides a lucid introduction to object relations theory.

17. Sigmund Freud, "Mourning and Melancholia" (1917), *Standard Edition*, 14:244. All references are to this edition.

18. In two other important essays, " 'A Child Is Being Beaten': A Contribution to the Study of the Origin of Sexual Perversions" (1919), *Standard Edition*, vol. 17, and "The Economic Problem of Masochism" (1924), *Standard Edition*, vol. 19, Freud explores the relationship between masochism and Oedipal drives. He argues that the fantasy of being beaten, which may originate from the incestuous attachment to the father, allows the child to fulfill contradictory aims: to gratify the need for love, and to punish oneself for forbidden urges.

19. See Michael Warren Glazer, "Object-Related Vs. Narcissistic Depression: A Theoretical and Clinical Study," *The Psychoanalytic Review* 66 (1979):323–37.

20. Nicholas C. Avery, "Sadomasochism: A Defense Against Object Loss," *The Psychoanalytic Review* 64 (1977):101.

21. Heilman, "Introduction," 10.

22. Florence Emily Hardy, *The Life of Thomas Hardy, 1840–1928* (London: Macmillan, 1962), 149. All references are to this edition, which combines *The Early Life of Thomas Hardy: 1840–1891* and *The Later Years of Thomas Hardy: 1892–1928*. Compare Hardy's "General Principles" to Jude's condemnation of nature: "And then he again uneasily saw, as he had latterly seen with more and more frequency, the scorn of Nature for man's finer emotions, and her lack of interest in his aspirations" (212).

23. For an opposing interpretation, see Dale Kramer, *Thomas Hardy: The Forms of Tragedy* (Detroit: Wayne State University Press, 1975).

24. Frank R. Giordano, Jr., *"I'd Have My Life Unbe"* (Alabama: University of Alabama Press, 1984), 17.

25. Florence Hardy, *The Life of Thomas Hardy*, 274, 392. For a discussion of the autobiographical elements in *Jude*, see F. B. Pinion, *"Jude the Obscure*: Origins in Life and Literature," in Norman Page, ed. *Thomas Hardy Annual No. 4* (London: Macmillan, 1986), 148–164.

26. For an illuminating discussion of tragicomedy in fiction, see Randall Craig, *The Tragicomic Novel* (Newark: University of Delaware Press, 1989).

27. Robert Gittings, *Young Thomas Hardy* (Boston: Little, Brown, 1975), 35.

28. Michael Millgate, *Thomas Hardy* (New York: Random House, 1982), 16.

29. James W. Hamilton, "The Effect of Early Trauma Upon Thomas Hardy's Literary Career," a paper presented before the Wisconsin Psychoanalytic Study Group (Madison, Wisconsin: April 1982). I am grateful to Dr. Hamilton for sending me a copy of his talk.

30. Thomas Hardy, *Tess of the D'Urbervilles* (1891) (New York: Norton Critical Edition, 1965), 76.

31. See Lois Deacon, *Providence & Mr. Hardy* (London: Hutchinson, 1966). For an incisive critique of Deacon's belief that Hardy actually had an affair with Tryphena Sparks, see Gittings, *Young Thomas Hardy*, 223–29.

32. Thomas Hardy, *The Well-Beloved* (1897) (London: Macmillan, 1960), 38. All references come from this edition.

33. John Fowles, "Hardy and the Hag," in Lance St. John Butler, ed., *Thomas Hardy After Fifty Years* (Totowa, N.J.: Rowman and Littlefield, 1977), 33. For a discussion of Hardy's influence on Fowles, see Peter J. Casagrande, *Hardy's Influence on the Modern Novel* (London: Macmillan, 1987).

34. Gilbert J. Rose, "*The French Lieutenant's Woman:* The Unconscious Significance of a Novel to Its Author," *American Imago*, 29 (1972):165–76. For a psychoanalytic interpretation of *The Well-Beloved*, see David S. Werman and Theodore J. Jacobs, "Thomas Hardy's '*The Well-Beloved*' and the Nature of Infatuation," *International Review of Psycho-Analysis* 10 (1983):447–57.

35. John Fowles, *The French Lieutenant's Woman* (1969) (New York: Signet, 1970), 216.

7. Echoes of Rejection in *Sons and Lovers*

1. D. H. Lawrence, *The Letters of D. H. Lawrence*, James T. Boulton, ed. (Cambridge: Cambridge University Press, 1979), 1:476–77.

2. Simon O. Lesser, *Fiction and the Unconscious* (New York: Vintage, 1957), 175–78.

3. Sigmund Freud, "On the Universal Tendency to Debasement in the Sphere of Love" (1912) (formerly translated as "The Most Prevalent Form of Degradation in Erotic Life), *Standard Edition*, 11:183.

4. D. H. Lawrence, *Lady Chatterley's Lover* (1928) (New York: Grove Press, 1962), 95.

5. Quoted by Frederick J. Hoffman, *Freudianism and the Literary Mind* (1957) 2nd rev. ed. (Baton Rouge: Louisiana State University Press, 1967), 154.

6. For a discussion of Lawrence's quarrel with Freud, see ibid., 151–76; Mark Spilka, *The Love Ethic of D. H. Lawrence* (Bloomington: Indiana University Press, 1955), 60–62, 86–87; Eugene Goodheart, *The Utopian Vision of D. H. Lawrence* (Chicago: University of Chicago Press, 1963), 103–15; Murray M. Schwartz, "D. H. Lawrence and Psychoanalysis: An Introduction," *D. H. Lawrence Review* 10 (1977): 215–22; and Daniel J. Schneider, *D. H. Lawrence: The Artist as Psychologist* (Lawrence: University of Kansas Press, 1984), 249–54.

7. Alfred Booth Kuttner, "A Freudian Appreciation," *The Psychoanalytic Review*, 3 (1916): 293–317; repr. in E. W. Tedlock, Jr., ed., *D. H. Lawrence and Sons and Lovers: Sources and Criticism* (New York: New York University Press, 1965).

8. D. H. Lawrence, *The Letters of D. H. Lawrence*, George J. Zytaruk and James T. Boulton, eds. (Cambridge: Cambridge University Press, 1981), 2:655.

9. Daniel Weiss, *Oedipus in Nottingham* (Seattle: University of Washington Press, 1962).

10. D. H. Lawrence, *The Letters of D. H. Lawrence*, James T. Boulton and Andrew Robertson, eds. (Cambridge: Cambridge University Press, 1984), 3:301–2.

11. Marguerite Beede Howe, *The Art of the Self in D. H. Lawrence* (Athens: Ohio University Press, 1977), 18.

12. Judith Ruderman, *D. H. Lawrence and the Devouring Mother* (Durham, N.C.: Duke University Press, 1984), 9.

13. Daniel Dervin, *A "Strange Sapience": The Creative Imagination of D. H. Lawrence* (Amherst: University of Massachusetts Press, 1984), 10–11.

14. Jessie Chambers, *D. H. Lawrence: A Personal Record* (1935) 2nd ed., with an introduction by J. D. Chambers (New York: Barnes and Noble, 1965), 202.

15. Lawrence, *Letters*, 1:449.

16. Chambers, *D. H. Lawrence: A Personal Record*, 184.

17. Harry T. Moore, *The Priest of Love: A Life of D. H. Lawrence*, rev. ed. (New York: Penguin, 1981), 87.

18. Keith Sagar, *The Art of D. H. Lawrence* (Cambridge: Cambridge University Press, 1966), 21–22. Sagar repeats this judgment in *D. H. Lawrence: Life Into Art* (Athens: University of Georgia Press, 1985).

19. Mark Spilka, "For Mark Schorer with Combative Love: The *Sons and Lovers* manuscript," in Peter Balbert and Phillip L. Marcus, eds. *D. H. Lawrence: A Centenary Consideration* (Ithaca: Cornell University Press, 1985), 39.

20. Lawrence, *Letters*, 1:190–191.

21. Edward Nehls, ed., *D. H. Lawrence: A Composite Biography* (Madison: University of Wisconsin Press, 1958), 2:126.

22. Frieda Lawrence, *Not I, But the Wind* (New York: Viking, 1934), 56–57. Lawrence's strongest indictment of his mother appears in an unpublished autobiographical sketch in the collection of Lawrence papers at the University of Cincinnati Library. The following passage, written late in his life, is quoted by George Ford in *Double Measure* (New York: Holt, Rinehart and Winston, 1965), 43:

> My mother fought with deadly hostility against my father, all her life. He was not hostile, till provoked, then he too was a devil. But my mother began it. She seemed to begrudge his very existence. She begrudged him and hated her own love

for him, she fought against his natural charm, vindictively. And by the time she died, at the age of fifty-five, she neither loved nor hated him any more. She had got over her feeling for him, and was 'Free.' So she died of cancer. Her feeling for us, also was divided. We were her own, therefore she loved us. But we were his, so she despised us a little.

23. Frieda Lawrence, *Not I, But the Wind,* 40.

24. Ovid, *Metamorphoses,* Frank Justus Miller, trans. repr. (Cambridge: Harvard University Press, 1936), 151.

25. D. H. Lawrence, *Sons and Lovers* (1912) (Harmondsworth, Middlesex, Eng.: Penguin, 1981), 43. All references are to this edition.

26. D. H. Lawrence, "The Rocking-Horse Winner," in *The Complete Short Stories* (New York: Viking, 1965), 3:790. The following passages come from this page.

27. Shirley Panken, "Some Psychodynamics in *Sons and Lovers:* A New Look at the Oedipal Theme," *The Psychoanalytic Review:* 61 (Winter 1974–1975):574. Other psychoanalytic interpretations of *Sons and Lovers* include Evelyn J. Hinz, "*Sons and Lovers*: The Archetypal Dimensions of Lawrence's Oedipal Tragedy," *D. H. Lawrence Review* 5 (1972):26–53; and David J. Kleinbard, "Laing, Lawrence, and the Maternal Cannibal," *Psychoanalytic Review* 58 (1971):5–13. One of the earliest and shrewdest psychoanalytic observations about *Sons and Lovers* was made by Karl Menninger in a brief paragraph in *Love Against Hate* (New York: Harcourt, Brace, 1942). Observing that fixations of any type are determined more by hating than loving, Menninger remarks that "persons who have a 'mother fixation' fear their mothers more than their fathers; they fear to leave the mother either for a passive, submissive relation to the father which brings them into competition with the mother, or for active masculine interest in available women" (57).

28. John Worthen, *D. H. Lawrence and the Idea of the Novel* (London: Macmillan, 1979), 40.

29. Lawrence, *Letters* 1:477.

30. See Nehls, ed., *D. H. Lawrence: A Composite Biography,* 3:558, for the autobiographical sources of this scene. Particularly revealing is Mrs. Lawrence's response upon receiving a photograph sent home by her son Ernest, D. H. Lawrence's older brother and the source of William Morel in *Sons and Lovers*. The account comes from Mrs. May Chambers Holbrook, Jessie Chambers' older sister.

> We turned to the photograph again.
> "She's nice, isn't she!" said Bert [D. H. Lawrence], quivering with excitement, and I said she was handsome.
> " 'Handsome is as handsome does,' we shall see!" said the mother, grimly.
> The sister pointed to the family group, saying, "That's him."
> "Fool!" ejaculated the mother. "She knows him, don't you, child? Aye, I wonder how he's changed," she said mournfully. "They're never the same men

once they go out into the world. You lose them—you might as well never have had them." Her tone filled me with sadness as if she were crying, "Woe is me."

31. Otto Kernberg, *Borderline Conditions and Pathological Narcissism* (New York: Jason Aronson, 1975), 233.

32. Spilka, *The Love Ethic of D. H. Lawrence*, 45.

33. See Peter Balbert, "Forging and Feminism," *D. H. Lawrence Review* 11 (1978):93–113.

34. Exceptions to this include Faith Pullin, "Lawrence's Treatment of Women in *Sons and Lovers*," in Anne Smith, ed., *Lawrence and Women* (London: Vision, 1978); and Hilary Simpson, *D. H. Lawrence and Feminism* (Croom Helm: London, 1982). See also Emile Delavenay, "D. H. Lawrence and Jessie Chambers: The Traumatic Experiment," *D. H. Lawrence Review* 12 (1979):305–25.

35. Louis L. Martz, "Portrait of Miriam: A Study in the Design of *Sons and Lovers*," in Maynard Mack and Ian Gregor, eds., *Imagined Worlds* (London: Methuen, 1968), 351.

36. A. H. Gomme, "Jessie Chambers and Miriam Leivers: An Essay on *Sons and Lovers*," in A. H. Gomme, ed., *D. H. Lawrence: A Critical Study of the Major Novels and Other Writings* (New York: Barnes and Noble, 1978), 39. Mark Schorer's famous essay on the problem of point of view in *Sons and Lovers*, "Technique as Discovery," *Hudson Review* 1 (1948): 67–87, still remains one of the best discussions on the subject.

37. Simpson, *D. H. Lawrence and Feminism*, 32–33.

38. Keith Sagar, *The Art of D. H. Lawrence*, quoted in Judith Farr, ed., *Twentieth Century Interpretations of Sons and Lovers* (Englewood Cliffs, N.J.: Prentice-Hall, 1970), 49.

39. Weiss, *Oedipus in Nottingham*, 76.

40. Mark Spilka, "For Mark Schorer with Combative Love," 39.

41. The following passage appears in the 1981 Penguin edition: " 'Make him stop drinking,' he prayed every night. 'Lord, let my father die,' he prayed very often. 'Let him be killed at pit' " (99). In the Viking Critical Edition of *Sons and Lovers*, however, edited by Julian Moynahan (New York: 1968), there is a misprint that must have confused thousands of readers. " 'Make him stop drinking,' he prayed every night. 'Lord, let my father die,' he prayed very often. 'Let him not be killed at pit' " (60).

42. Lawrence, *Lady Chatterley's Lover*, 146.

43. For an excellent discussion of how authors and characters deal with these dualisms, see Walter J. Slatoff, *The Look of Distance* (Columbus: Ohio State University Press, 1985).

44. Lawrence, *Letters* 2:90.

8. Heart Problems in *Mrs. Dalloway*

1. Virginia Woolf, "On Being Ill" (1930), *The Moment and Other Essays* (New York: Harcourt, Brace and Company, 1948), 9. All references are to this edition.

2. The reader who wishes to learn more about Virginia Woolf's life should begin with Quentin Bell, *Virginia Woolf: A Biography* (New York: Harcourt Brace Jovanovich, 1972). Two other valuable biographies are Jean O. Love, *Virginia Woolf: Sources of Madness and Art* (Berkeley: University of California Press, 1977); and Phyllis Rose, *Woman of Letters: A Life of Virginia Woolf* (New York: Oxford University Press, 1978). Leonard Woolf discusses his wife's psychiatric problems in *Beginning Again: An Autobiography of the Years 1911 to 1918* (New York: Harcourt, Brace and World, 1964) and *Downhill All the Way: An Autobiography of the Years 1919 to 1939* (New York: Harcourt, Brace and World, 1967).

   Several critics have explored the link between Virginia Woolf's mental illness and creativity. In *Virginia Woolf and the Androgynous Vision* (New Brunswick, N.J.: Rutgers University Press, 1973), Nancy Topping Bazin argues that Woolf's double vision of reality was a reflection of her experience as a manic-depressive. In *"All that Summer She was Mad": Virginia Woolf and Her Doctors* (London: Junction Books, 1981), Stephen Trombley discusses the presuppositions behind the view that she was mad. Trombley's book is marred, however, by his tendency to deny that Woolf's illness was a psychiatric problem and to blame her breakdowns mainly on her incompetent physicians. Thomas C. Caramagno argues, in "Manic-Depressive Psychosis and Critical Approaches to Virginia Woolf's Life and Work," *PMLA* 103 (1988):10–23, that Woolf's illness was mainly due to a biological problem and, therefore, not explainable in psychoanalytic terms.

3. Virginia Woolf, *Mrs. Dalloway* (New York: Harcourt, Brace and World, 1953), p. 194. All references are to this edition.

4. Alex Page, "A Dangerous Day: Mrs. Dalloway Discovers Her Double," *Modern Fiction Studies* 7 (1961):121.

5. Jeremy Hawthorn, *Virginia Woolf's Mrs. Dalloway: A Study in Alienation* (London: Sussex University Press, 1975), 62.

6. Alice van Buren Kelley, *The Novels of Virginia Woolf: Fact and Vision* (Chicago: University of Chicago Press, 1973), 91.

7. Herbert Marder's perceptive observation in *Feminism and Art* (Chicago: University of Chicago Press, 1968) is worth repeating here: "Miss Kilman belongs to a class of women—poor, half-educated, struggling to earn a living by teaching—for whom Virginia Woolf generally had a good deal of sympathy. . . . It is interesting, therefore, that in this case even Miss Kilman's qualifications as a victim of the patriarchy fail to win her Vir-

ginia Woolf's sympathies. Miss Kilman's antagonist, Clarissa Dalloway, belongs to a fashionable clique with which Virginia Woolf never had much in common, but she obviously found it easier to forgive Clarissa's snobbishness than Kilman's lower-class vulgarity" (96n.) Other critics who question Woolf's unsympathetic treatment of Miss Kilman include Harvena Richter, *Virginia Woolf: The Inward Voyage* (Princeton: Princeton University Press, 1970); and Suzette A. Henke, *"Mrs Dalloway:* The Communion of Saints," in Jane Marcus, ed., *New Feminist Essays on Virginia Woolf* (Lincoln: University of Nebraska Press, 1981).

8. Emily Jensen asserts, but without evidence, that Miss Kilman has the power to love women and defy the heterosexual norms that inhibit Clarissa ("Clarissa Dalloway's Respectable Suicide," in Jane Marcus, ed., *Virginia Woolf: A Feminist Slant* [Lincoln: University of Nebraska Press, 1983]).

9. Phyllis Rose argues convincingly, on both biographical and textual grounds, that Woolf's ambivalence toward Clarissa arises from the novelist's contradictory feelings toward her mother. Rose concludes, based upon an analysis of a deleted early draft of the novel, that Miss Kilman exists to give voice to that part of Virginia Woolf who hates her own mother passionately, "hates her for being trivial, purposeless, resents her for being unfairly blessed" (*Woman of Letters,* 150).

10. Heinz Kohut, *The Analysis of the Self* (New York: International Universities Press, 1971), 53.

11. Heinz Kohut, *The Restoration of the Self* (New York: International Universities Press, 1977), 130.

12. To cite but two critics, see Beverly Ann Schlack, "A Freudian Look at *Mrs. Dalloway,*" *Literature and Psychology* 23 (1973):49–58; and Suzette A. Henke, "Virginia Woolf's Septimus Smith: An Analysis of 'Paraphrenia' and the Schizophrenic Use of Language," *Literature and Psychology* 31 (1981):13–23. For a discussion of how Septimus functions as Clarissa's double, see James Naremore, *The World Without a Self: Virginia Woolf and the Novel* (New Haven: Yale University Press, 1973); Lotus Snow, "The Heat of the Sun: The Double in *Mrs. Dalloway,*" *Research Studies* 41 (1973):75–83; Page, "A Dangerous Day"; and Perry Meisel, *The Absent Father: Virginia Woolf and Walter Pater* (New Haven: Yale University Press, 1980). Critics have pointed out the parallels between Septimus' madness and Woolf's. The novelist originally intended to call Clarissa's suicidal double "Stephen Smith." Stephen was, of course, Virginia's maiden name.

13. Most critics have reacted approvingly to Septimus' suicide, viewing it as a necessary effort to maintain his "purity," "wholeness," and "visionary" temperament. E. F. Shields asserts, for example, that Septimus' suicide is not the act of an unbalanced mind. "Clarissa comes to realize that although it was a desperate act, it was a desperate act of affirmation and not of negation. Septimus throws himself from the window not because he

no longer believes in the value of his own life, but because he believes in it very strongly" ("Death and Individual Values in 'Mrs. Dalloway,' " *Queen's Quarterly* 80 [1973]:85). In *Virginia Woolf* (New York: Columbia University Press, 1979), Michael Rosenthal asserts that "However aberrant his behavior," Septimus "retains a kind of inner purity which makes society and its official guardians of mental and moral stability, like Holmes and Bradshaw, seem far more deranged than he" (91).

Elaine Showalter's valuable observation about Woolf's suicide is relevant to Septimus' suicide. "[T]o see Woolf's suicide as a beautiful act of faith, or a philosophical gesture toward androgyny, is to betray the human pain and rage that she felt; to see the suicide as a proof of her feminine neurosis is to condemn her in death to the stereotype that imprisoned her in life" (*A Literature of Their Own* [Princeton: Princeton University Press, 1977], 278–79).

14. R. D. Laing, *The Divided Self* (Harmondsworth, Middlesex, Eng.: Penguin, 1960; repr. 1970), 46. All references are to the 1970 edition.

15. Michael J. Goldstein, Bruce L. Baker, and Kay R. Jamison, *Abnormal Psychology*, 2nd ed. (Boston: Little, Brown, 1986), 350.

16. John P. Wilson and Gustave E. Krauss, "Predicting Post-Traumatic Stress Disorders Among Vietnam Veterans," in William E. Kelly, ed., *Post-Traumatic Stress Disorder and the War Veteran Patient* (New York: Brunner/Mazel, 1985), 145.

17. Bruno Bettelheim, "Afterword" to Claudine Vegh, *I Didn't Say Goodbye*, Ros Schwartz, trans. (New York: Dutton, 1984). All references are to this edition.

18. Schlack, "A Freudian Look at *Mrs. Dalloway*," 55. Marder makes a similar point in *Feminism and Art*, 49–50.

19. In *Downhill All the Way*, Leonard Woolf mentions that one of the distinguished Harley Street specialists who treated Virginia, Dr. Saintsbury, said to her: "Equanimity—equanimity—practise equanimity, Mrs. Woolf" (51). Dr. Saintsbury's "equanimity" is a probable source of Dr. Bradshaw's "proportion."

Woolf wrote bitterly about her involuntary hospitalizations. For her own descriptions of her psychiatric mistreatment, see Nigel Nicolson, ed., *The Letters of Virginia Woolf: Vol. I: 1888–1912* (New York: Harcourt Brace Jovanovich, 1975), 147, 153, 159, 428; and Nigel Nicolson and Joanne Trautmann, eds., *The Letters of Virginia Woolf: Vol IV: 1929–1931* (New York: Harcourt Brace Jovanovich, 1978). Witness this letter she wrote in 1930, the same year in which she wrote "On Being Ill":

As an experience, madness is terrific I can assure you, and not to be sniffed at; and in its lava I still find most of the things I write about. It shoots out of one everything shaped, final, not in mere driblets, as sanity does. And the six months —not three—that I lay in bed taught me a good deal about what is called oneself.

Indeed I was almost crippled when I came back to the world, unable to move a foot in terror, after that discipline. Think—not one moment's freedom from doctor discipline—perfectly strange—conventional men; 'you shant read this' and 'you shant write a word' and 'you shall lie still and drink milk'—for six months. (*Letters*, 4:180)

20. Virginia Woolf, "Introduction" to *Mrs. Dalloway* (New York: Modern Library, 1928), vi.

21. For a discussion of the father image in Woolf's fiction, see Beverly Ann Schlack, "Fathers in General: The Patriarchy in Virginia Woolf's Fiction," in Marcus, ed., *Virginia Woolf: A Feminist Slant.*

22. In *The Novels of Virginia Woolf* (New York: John Jay Press, 1977), 103–4, Mitchell A. Leaska offers an extended discussion of the knife symbolism in *Mrs. Dalloway.*

23. Margaret Mahler, Fred Pine, and Anni Bergman, *The Psychological Birth of the Human Infant* (New York: Basic Books, 1975), 3. All references are to this edition.

24. Naremore, *The World Without a Self,* 103.

25. Howard Harpur, *Between Language and Silence: The Novels of Virginia Woolf* (Baton Rouge: Louisiana State University Press, 1982).

26. Phyllis Rose, *Woman of Letters,* 115.

27. Mark Spilka, *Virginia Woolf's Quarrel with Grieving* (Lincoln: University of Nebraska Press, 1980).

28. Ellen Bayuk Rosenman, *The Invisible Presence: Virginia Woolf and the Mother-Daughter Relationship* (Baton Rouge: Louisiana State University Press, 1986), 76.

29. Shirley Panken, *Virginia Woolf and the "Lust of Creation"* (New York: State University of New York Press, 1987), 36.

30. Given the psychiatric abuses to which Virginia Woolf was subjected, it is certainly not surprising that she rejected the entire medical approach to mental illness, with its prevailing physicalistic approach at the turn of the century. But it is harder to understand her scornful attitude toward psychoanalysis. In spite of her numerous breakdowns and institutionalizations, she never received psychoanalytic treatment, which would have sought to explain her breakdowns in terms of unconscious forces. Despite Leonard Woolf's great interest in Freud (the Woolfs were the publishers of the Hogarth Press, which published Freud's writings in England) and the fact that Virginia's younger brother, Adrian Stephen, became a psychoanalyst (as did Adrian's wife, Karin), the novelist never expressed personal or intellectual interest in psychoanalysis. The few references to Freud in her writings are very negative. In "Freudian Fiction" (1920), a review of J. D. Beresford's *An Imperfect Mother,* Woolf mocks the pernicious effect of psychoanalysis on literary writers. For a discussion of the Woolfs' attitude toward Freud, see Jan Ellen Goldstein, "The Woolfs' Response to Freud: Water Spiders, Singing Canaries, and the

Second Apple," in Edith Kurzweil and William Phillips, eds., *Literature and Psychoanalysis* (New York: Columbia University Press, 1983).

Interestingly, in *Downhill All the Way*, Leonard Woolf describes the moving interview he and Virginia had with the ailing Freud in 1939, a few months before his death. Leonard Woolf was awed by Freud's genius, regarding him as one of the greatest men alive. Freud, who was "extraordinarily courteous in a formal, old-fashioned way" (168–69), ceremoniously presented Virginia Woolf with a flower—a narcissus.

Epilogue

1. Philip Roth, *My Life as a Man* (New York: Bantam, 1975), 258.
2. Letter from Sophie Freud to Jeffrey Berman, October 9, 1988.
3. Mary Shelley, *Frankenstein; or, The Modern Prometheus*, M. K. Joseph, ed. (New York: Oxford University Press, 1969; repr. 1984), 48. All references are to the 1984 edition.

Bibliography

Adams, Ruth. "*Wuthering Heights:* The Land East of Eden." *Nineteenth-Century Fiction* 13 (1958):58–62.

Adrian, Arthur A. *Dickens and the Parent-Child Relationship*. Athens: Ohio University Press, 1984.

Alcorn, Marshall W., Jr., and Mark Bracher, "Literature, Psychoanalysis, and the Re-Formation of the Self: A New Direction for Reader-Response Theory." *PMLA* 100, 3 (May 1985):342–54.

American Psychiatric Association. *Diagnostic and Statistical Manual of Mental Disorders*. 3rd. ed. Washington, D.C.: American Psychiatric Association, 1980.

Amor, Anne Clark. *Mrs Oscar Wilde*. London: Sidgwick and Jackson, 1983.

Andreasen, Nancy C. "Suffering and Art: A Defense of Sanity." In Joanne Trautmann, ed., *Healing Arts in Dialogue*. Carbondale: Southern Illinois University Press, 1981.

Avery, Nicholas C. "Sadomasochism: A Defense Against Object Loss." *The Psychoanalytic Review* 64 (1977):101–8.

Balbert, Peter. "Forging and Feminism." *D. H. Lawrence Review* 11 (1978):93–113.

———, and Phillip L. Marcus, eds. *D. H. Lawrence: A Centenary Consideration*. Ithaca: Cornell University Press, 1985.

Bazin, Nancy Topping. *Virginia Woolf and the Androgynous Vision*. New Brunswick, N.J.: Rutgers University Press, 1973.

Beckson, Karl. "The Importance of Being Angry: The Mutual Antagonism of Oscar and Willie Wilde." In Norman Kiell, ed., *Blood Brothers: Siblings as Writers*. New York: International Universities Press, 1983.

Bell, Quentin. *Virginia Woolf: A Biography*. 2 vols. New York: Harcourt Brace Jovanovich, 1972.

Bell, Vereen M. "Parents and Children in *Great Expectations*." *Victorian Newsletter* 27 (1965): 21–24.

Benvenuto, Richard. *Emily Brontë*. Boston: Twayne, 1982.

Bergler, Edmund. " 'Salome': The Turning Point in the Life of Oscar Wilde."
The Psychoanalytic Review 43 (1956):97–103.
Bergmann, Martin S. "The Legend of Narcissus." *American Imago* 41
(1984):389–411.
Berman, Art. *From the New Criticism to Deconstruction*. Urbana: University
of Illinois Press, 1988.
Berman, Jeffrey. *Joseph Conrad: Writing as Rescue*. New York: Astra Books,
1977.
————. *The Talking Cure: Literary Representations of Psychoanalysis*. New
York: New York University Press, 1985.
Bersani, Leo. *A Future for Astyanax*. Boston: Little, Brown, 1976.
Bettelheim, Bruno. "Afterword." In Claudine Vegh, *I Didn't Say Goodbye*.
Ros Schwartz, trans. New York: Dutton, 1984.
————. *The Uses of Enchantment*. New York: Vintage, 1977.
Bloom, Harold. "Afterword." In Mary Shelley, *Frankenstein; or, The Mod-
ern Prometheus*. New York: Signet, 1965.
————. *The Anxiety of Influence*. New York: Oxford University Press, 1973.
————. "Sigmund Freud, the Greatest Modern Writer." *New York Times
Book Review*, March 23, 1986.
Blos, Peter. *Son and Father*. New York: Free Press, 1985.
Boumelha, Penny. *Thomas Hardy and Women*. Madison: University of Wis-
consin Press, 1982.
Bowlby, John. *Attachment and Loss*. 3 vols. New York: Basic Books, 1969–
1980.
Brenkman, John. "Narcissus in the Text." *Georgia Review*, 30 (1976):293–
327.
Brontë, Emily. *Wuthering Heights*. (1847). Harmondsworth, Middlesex, Eng.:
Penguin, 1965; repr. 1985.
————. *Five Essays Written in French*. Lorine White Nagel, trans. Austin:
University of Texas Press, 1948; repr. Folcroft, Pennsylvania: Folcroft
Library Editions, 1974.
Brooks, Peter. "The Idea of a Psychoanalytic Literary Criticism." *Critical
Inquiry* 13 (1987):334–48.
————. *Reading for the Plot*. New York: Knopf, 1984.
Buchen, Irving H. "Emily Brontë and the Metaphysics of Childhood and
Love." *Nineteenth-Century Fiction* 22 (1967):63–70.
Bursten, Ben. "The Narcissistic Course." In Marie Coleman Nelson, ed.,
The Narcissistic Condition. New York: Human Sciences Press, 1977.
Bush, Douglas. *Mythology and the Renaissance Tradition in English Poetry*
(1932). Rev. ed. New York: Norton, 1963.
Caramagno, Thomas C. "Manic-Depressive Psychosis and Critical Ap-
proaches to Virginia Woolf's Life and Art." *PMLA* 103 (1988):10–23.
Carsky, Monica, and Steven Ellman. "Otto Kernberg: Psychoanalysis and
Object Relations Theory; The Beginnings of an Integrative Approach." In
Joseph Reppen, ed., *Beyond Freud*. Hillsdale, N.J.: Analytic Press, 1985.

Casagrande, Peter J. *Hardy's Influence on the Modern Novel*. London: Macmillan, 1987.

Chambers, Jessie. *D. H. Lawrence: A Personal Record* (1935). 2nd. ed. J. D. Chambers, introd. and ed. New York: Barnes and Noble, 1965.

Chesser, Eustace. *Shelley & Zastrozzi*. London: Gregg/Archive, 1965.

Chessick, Richard D. *Psychology of the Self and the Treatment of Narcissism*. Northvale, N.J.: Jason Aronson, 1985.

Chitham, Edward. *A Life of Emily Brontë*. Oxford: Basil Blackwell, 1987.

Chodorow, Nancy. *The Reproduction of Mothering*. Berkeley: University of California Press, 1978.

Church, Richard. *Mary Shelley*. London: Gerald Howe, 1928.

Clément, Catherine. *The Lives and Legends of Jacques Lacan*. Arthur Goldhammer, trans. New York: Columbia University Press, 1983.

Connor, Steven. *Charles Dickens*. Oxford: Basil Blackwell, 1985.

Craig, Randall. *The Tragicomic Novel*. Newark: University of Delaware Press, 1989.

Crews, Frederick. "In the Big House of Theory." *New York Review of Books*, May 29, 1986, 36–42.

Critchley, Macdonald. *The Black Hole and Other Essays*. London: Pitman, 1964.

Croft-Cooke, Rupert. *The Unrecorded Life of Oscar Wilde*. New York: David McKay, 1972.

Daleski, H. M. *Dickens and the Art of Analogy*. New York: Schocken, 1970.

Davies, Stevie. *Emily Brontë: The Artist as a Free Woman*. Manchester, Eng.: Carcanet Press, 1983.

Deacon, Lois. *Providence & Mr. Hardy*. London: Hutchinson, 1966.

Delavenay, Emile. "D. H. Lawrence and Jessie Chambers: The Traumatic Experiment." *D. H. Lawrence Review* 12 (1979):305–25.

Derrida, Jacques. "Coming into One's Own." In Geoffrey H. Hartman, ed., *Psychoanalysis and the Question of the Text*. Baltimore: Johns Hopkins University Press, 1978.

Dervin, Daniel. "Lacanian Mirrors and Literary Reflections." *Journal of the Philadelphia Association for Psychoanalysis* 7 (1980):129–42.

———. "Roland Barthes: The Text as Self, the Self as Text." *The Psychoanalytic Review* 74 (1987):279–92.

———. *A "Strange Sapience": The Creative Imagination of D. H. Lawrence*. Amherst: University of Massachusetts Press, 1984.

Dessner, Lawrence Jay. "Great Expectations: 'The Ghost of a Man's Own Father.' " *PMLA* 91 (1976):436–49.

Dickens, Charles. *David Copperfield* (1850). New York: Bantam, 1981.

———. *Great Expectations* (1860). Harmondsworth, Middlesex, Eng.: Penguin, 1965; repr. 1985.

Dinnerstein, Dorothy. *The Mermaid and the Minotaur*. New York: Harper and Row, 1977.

Donovan, Frank. *Dickens and Youth*. New York: Dodd, Mead, 1968.

Douglas, Alfred Lord. *Oscar Wilde: A Summing-Up*. London: Richards Press, 1940.

Eagle, Morris. *Recent Developments in Psychoanalysis*. New York: McGraw-Hill, 1984.

Edwards, Carol and Duane. "*Jude the Obscure:* A Psychoanalytic Study." *University of Hartford Studies in Literature* 13 (1981):78–90.

Eliot, T. S. *The Waste Land* (1922). In *The Complete Poems and Plays: 1909–1950*. New York: Harcourt, Brace and World, 1952.

Ellis, Havelock. "Auto-Erotism, a Psychological Study." St. Louis *Alienist and Neurologist*, vol. 19 (April 1898).

———. "The Conception of Narcissism." *Studies in the Psychology of Sex*. 2 vols. New York: Random House, 1937.

Ellmann, Richard. *Oscar Wilde*. London: Hamish Hamilton, 1987.

———, ed. *The Artist as Critic: Critical Writings of Oscar Wilde*. New York: Random House, 1968.

Ericsson, Catarina. *A Child Is a Child, You Know: The Inversion of Father and Daughter in Dicken's Novels*. Stockholm: Acta Universitatis Stockholmiensis, 1986.

Erikson, Erik H. *Childhood and Society* (1950). Rev. ed. New York: Norton, 1963.

Esman, Aaron H. "Rescue Fantasies." *Psychoanalytic Quarterly* 56 (1987):263–70.

Farr, Judith, ed. *Twentieth Century Interpretations of Sons and Lovers*. Englewood Cliffs, N.J.: Prentice Hall, 1970.

Feder, Lillian. *Madness in Literature*. Princeton: Princeton University Press, 1980.

Fine, Reuben. *Narcissism, the Self, and Society*. New York: Columbia University Press, 1986.

Fine, Ronald E. "Lockwood's Dreams and the Key to *Wuthering Heights*." *Nineteenth-Century Fiction* 24 (1969):16–30.

Fisher, Seymour, and Roger P. Greenberg. *The Scientific Credibility of Freud's Theories and Therapy*. New York: Basic Books, 1977.

Ford, George H. *Double Measure*. New York: Holt, Rinehart and Winston, 1965.

Forster, John. *The Life of Charles Dickens*. 2 vols. London: Chapman and Hall, 1872; repr. 1899.

Fowles, John. "Hardy and the Hag." In Lance St. John Butler, ed., *Thomas Hardy After Fifty Years*. Totowa, N.J.: Rowman and Littlefield, 1977.

———. *The French Lieutenant's Woman*. (1969). New York: Signet, 1970.

Frank, Lawrence. *Charles Dickens and the Romantic Self*. Lincoln: University of Nebraska Press, 1984.

Freadman, Richard. *Eliot, James and the Fictional Self*. London: Macmillan, 1986.

Freeman, Lucy, and Herbert S. Strean. *Freud and Women*. New York: Frederick Ungar, 1981.

Freud, Anna. *The Ego and the Mechanism of Defense* (1936). Rev. ed. New York: International Universities Press, 1966.

Freud, Sigmund. *The Standard Edition of the Complete Psychological Works of Sigmund Freud.* 24 vols. James Strachey ed. and trans. London: Hogarth Press, 1953–1974.

——. *Analysis of a Phobia in a Five-Year-Old Boy* (1909). *Standard Edition,* vol. 10.

——. *Beyond the Pleasure Principle* (1920). *Standard Edition,* vol. 18.

——. *Civilization and Its Discontents.* (1930). *Standard Edition,* vol. 21.

——. "Delusions and Dreams in Jensen's *Gradiva*" (1907). *Standard Edition,* vol. 9.

——. "A Difficulty in the Path of Psycho-Analysis" (1917). *Standard Edition,* vol. 17.

——. "Dostoevsky and Parricide" (1928). *Standard Edition,* vol. 21.

——. "Extracts from Freud's Footnotes to His Translation of Charcot's *Tuesday Lectures*" (1892–1894). *Standard Edition,* vol. 1.

——. "Female Sexuality" (1931). *Standard Edition,* vol. 21.

——. *Group Psychology and the Analysis of the Ego* (1921). *Standard Edition,* vol. 18.

——. *Introductory Lectures on Psycho-Analysis* (1916–1917). *Standard Edition,* vol. 16.

——. *Leonardo da Vinci and a Memory of His Childhood* (1910). *Standard Edition,* vol. 11.

——. "Mourning and Melancholia" (1917). *Standard Edition,* vol. 14.

——. *New Introductory Lectures on Psycho-Analysis* (1933). *Standard Edition,* vol. 22.

——. "On Narcissism: An Introduction" (1914). *Standard Edition,* vol. 14.

——. "On Psycho-Analysis" (1913). *Standard Edition,* vol. 12.

——. "On the Teaching of Psycho-Analysis in Universities" (1919). *Standard Edition,* vol. 17.

——. "On the Universal Tendency To Debasement in the Sphere of Love" (1912). *Standard Edition,* vol. 11.

——. "Psycho-Analysis" (1923). *Standard Edition,* vol. 18.

——. "Recommendations to Physicians Practising Psycho-Analysis" (1912). *Standard Edition,* vol. 12.

——. "Remembering, Repeating and Working-Through" (1914). *Standard Edition,* vol. 12.

——. "A Short Account of Psycho-Analysis" (1924). *Standard Edition,* vol. 19.

——. "A Special Type of Choice of Object Made by Men" (1910). *Standard Edition,* vol. 11.

——. *Three Essays on the Theory of Sexuality* (1905). *Standard Edition,* vol. 7.

Freud, Sophie. *My Three Mothers and Other Passions.* New York: New York University Press, 1988.

———. "Overloving and Underloving." Robert Langs, ed., *The Yearbook of Psychoanalysis and Psychotherapy.* New York: Gardner Press, 1987.

———. "An Overview of the Concept of Narcissism." *Social Casework* 58 (March 1977):136–42.

———. "Paradoxes of Parenthood: On the Impossibility of Raising Children Perfectly." In Philip J. Davis and David Park, eds., *No Way: The Nature of the Impossible.* New York: Freeman, 1987.

Freund, Elizabeth. *The Return of the Reader.* London: Methuen, 1987.

Fromm, Erich. "Selfishness and Self-Love." *Psychiatry* 2 (1939):507–23.

Gallop, Jane. "Lacan and Literature: A Case for Transference." *Poetics* 13 (1984): 301–8.

Gérin, Winifred. *Emily Brontë.* Oxford: Clarendon Press, 1971.

Gide, André. *Oscar Wilde: In Memoriam.* Bernard Frechtman, trans. New York: Philosophical Library, 1949.

Gilbert, Sandra M., and Susan Gubar. *The Madwoman in the Attic.* New Haven: Yale University Press, 1979.

Gilligan, Carol. *In a Different Voice.* Cambridge: Harvard University Press, 1982.

Gilman, Charlotte Perkins. *The Yellow Wallpaper.* (1899). New York: Feminist Press, 1973.

Giordano, Frank R. *"I'd Have My Life Unbe".* Alabama: University of Alabama Press, 1984.

Gittings, Robert. *Young Thomas Hardy.* Boston: Little, Brown, 1975.

Glazer, Michael Warren. "Object-Related Vs. Narcissistic Depression: A Theoretical and Clinical Study." *The Psychoanalytic Review* 66 (1979):323–37.

Goetz, William R. "The Felicity and Infelicity of Marriage in *Jude the Obscure.*" *Nineteenth-Century Fiction* 38 (1983):189–213.

Gold, Joseph. *Charles Dickens: Radical Moralist.* Minneapolis: University of Minnesota Press, 1972.

Gold, Stanley. "Frankenstein and Other Monsters: An Examination of the Concepts of Destructive Narcissism, and Perverse Relationships Between Parts of the Self as Seen in the Gothic Novel." *International Review of Psycho-Analysis* 12 (1985): 101–8.

Goldstein, Jan Ellen. "The Woolfs' Response to Freud: Water Spiders, Singing Canaries, and the Second Apple." In Edith Kurzweil and William Phillips, eds., *Literature and Psychoanalysis.* New York: Columbia University Press, 1983.

Goldstein, Michael J., Bruce L. Baker, and Kay R. Jamison. *Abnormal Psychology.* 2nd ed. Boston: Little, Brown, 1986.

Gomme, A. H., ed. *D. H. Lawrence: A Critical Study of the Major Novels and Other Writings.* New York: Barnes and Noble, 1978.

Goodheart, Eugene. *The Utopian Vision of D. H. Lawrence*. Chicago: University of Chicago Press, 1963.

Graves, Robert. *The Greek Myths*. 2 vols. Baltimore: Penguin, 1955.

Green, Bernard A. "The Effects of Distortions of the Self: A Study of *The Picture of Dorian Gray*." *The Annual of Psychoanalysis* 7 (1979):391–410.

Gregor, Ian. *The Great Web: The Form of Hardy's Major Fiction*. Totowa, N.J.: Rowman and Littlefield, 1974.

Grinstein, Alexander. "On Oscar Wilde." *The Annual of Psychoanalysis* 1 (1973):345–62.

Guerard, Albert J. *Thomas Hardy: The Novels and Stories*. Cambridge: Harvard University Press, 1949.

Hafley, James. "The Villain in *Wuthering Heights*." *Nineteenth-Century Fiction* 13 (1958):199–215.

Hamilton, James W. "The Effect of Early Trauma Upon Thomas Hardy's Literary Career." A paper presented before the Wisconsin Psychoanalytic Study Group. Madison, Wisconsin: April 1982.

Hamilton, Victoria. *Narcissus and Oedipus*. London: Routledge and Kegan Paul, 1982.

Hardy, Florence. *The Life of Thomas Hardy: 1840–1928*. London: Macmillan, 1962.

Hardy, Thomas. *The Return of the Native*. (1878). New York: Harper and Brothers, 1929.

———. *The Well-Beloved* (1897). London: Macmillan, 1960.

———. *Jude the Obscure* (1895). London: Macmillan, 1971.

———. *Tess of the D'Urbervilles* (1891). New York: Norton, 1965.

Harpur, Howard. *Between Language and Silence: The Novels of Virginia Woolf*. Baton Rouge: Louisiana State University Press, 1982.

Hartog, Curt. "The Rape of Miss Havisham." *Studies in the Novel* 14 (1982):248–65.

Hawthorn, Jeremy. *Virginia Woolf's Mrs Dalloway: A Study in Alienation*. London: University of Sussex Press, 1975.

Heilman, Robert B. "Introduction." In Thomas Hardy, *Jude the Obscure*. New York: Harper and Row, 1966.

Henke, Suzette A. "*Mrs Dalloway*: the Communion of Saints." In Jane Marcus, ed., *New Feminist Essays on Virginia Woolf*. Lincoln: University of Nebraska Press, 1981.

———. "Virginia Woolf's Septimus Smith: An Analysis of 'Paraphrenia' and the Schizophrenic Use of Language." *Literature and Psychology* 31 (1981):13–23.

Hill, J. M. "*Frankenstein* and the Physiognomy of Desire." *American Imago* 32, 4 (1975):335–58.

Hinz, Evelyn J. "*Sons and Lovers:* The Archetypal Dimensions of Lawrence's Oedipal Tragedy." *D. H. Lawrence Review* 5 (1972):26–53.

Hirsch, Gordon D. "The Monster Was a Lady: On the Psychology of

Mary Shelley's *Frankenstein*." *Hartford Studies in Literature* 7, 2 (1975): 116–53.

Hochman, Baruch. *Character in Literature*. Ithaca: Cornell University Press, 1985.

———. *The Test of Character*. Rutherford, N.J.: Fairleigh Dickinson University Press, 1983.

Hoffman, Frederick J. *Freudianism and the Literary Mind* (1957). 2nd rev. ed. Baton Rouge: Louisiana State University Press, 1967.

Holland, Norman N. *5 Readers Reading*. New Haven: Yale University Press, 1975.

———. *The I*. New Haven: Yale University Press, 1985.

———. "*Jude the Obscure:* Hardy's Symbolic Indictment of Christianity." *Nineteenth-Century Fiction* 9 (1954):50–60.

Holland, Vyvyan. *Son of Oscar Wilde*. Westport, Conn.: Greenwood Press, 1954.

———. *Oscar Wilde: A Pictorial Biography*. New York: Viking, 1960.

Holt, Robert. "Beyond Vitalism & Mechanism: Freud's Concept of Psychic Energy." In J. Masserman, ed., *Science and Psychoanalysis*. Vol. 2. New York: Grune and Stratton, 1967.

Homans, Margaret. *Women Writers and Poetic Identity*. Princeton: Princeton University Press, 1980.

Horney, Karen. "The Dread of Woman." *International Journal of Psycho-Analysis* 13 (1932):348–60.

Howe, Irving. *Thomas Hardy*. New York: Macmillan, 1967.

Howe, Marguerite Beede. *The Art of the Self in D. H. Lawrence*. Athens: Ohio University Press, 1977.

Hutcheon, Linda. *Narcissistic Narrative: The Metafictional Paradox*. Waterloo, Ont.: Wilfred Laurier University Press, 1980.

Hutter, Albert D. "Crime and Fantasy in *Great Expectations*." In Frederick Crews, ed., *Psychoanalysis & Literary Process*. Cambridge, Mass.: Winthrop Publications, 1970.

———. "Reconstructive Autobiography: The Experience at Warren's Blacking." In Robert B. Partlow, Jr., ed., *Dickens Studies Annual*. Vol. 6. Carbondale: Southern Illinois University Press, 1977.

Hyde, H. Montgomery. *The Trials of Oscar Wilde*. London: William Hodge, 1948.

———. *Oscar Wilde: A Biography*. London: Eyre Methuen, 1976.

Jacobus, Mary. "Sue the Obscure." *Essays in Criticism* 25 (1975):304–28.

Jensen, Emily. "Clarissa Dalloway's Respectable Suicide." In Jane Marcus, ed., *Virginia Woolf: A Feminist Slant*. Lincoln: University of Nebraska Press, 1983.

Johnson, Barbara. "Teaching Deconstructively." In G. Douglas Atkins and Michael L. Johnson, eds., *Writing and Reading Differently: Deconstruction and the Teaching of Composition and Literature*. Lawrence: University of Kansas Press, 1985.

Johnson, Edgar. *Charles Dickens: His Tragedy and Triumph*. 2 vols. New York: Simon and Schuster, 1952.

Jones, Ernest. *The Life and Work of Sigmund Freud*. 3 vols. New York: Basic Books, 1953–1957.

Joseph, Gerhard. "Frankenstein's Dream: The Child as Father of the Monster." *Hartford Studies in Literature* 7, 2 (1975):97–115.

Joseph, M. K. "Introduction." In Mary Shelley, *Frankenstein; or, The Modern Prometheus*. M. K. Joseph, ed. New York: Oxford University Press, 1969; repr. 1984.

Kaplan, Fred. *Dickens: A Biography*. New York: Morrow, 1988.

Kaplan, Leo. "Analysis of *The Picture of Dorian Gray*." A. Green, trans. *Psyche and Eros* 3 (1922):8–21.

Kaplan, Morton, and Robert Kloss. *The Unspoken Motive*. New York: Free Press, 1973.

Kavanagh, James H. *Emily Brontë*. Oxford: Basil Blackwell, 1985.

Kavka, Jerome. "Oscar Wilde's Narcissism." *The Annual of Psychoanalysis* 3 (1975):397–408.

Kelley, Alice van Buren. *The Novels of Virginia Woolf: Fact and Vision*. Chicago: University of Chicago Press, 1973.

Keppler, C. F. *The Literature of the Second Self*. Tucson: University of Arizona Press, 1972.

Kernberg, Otto. *Borderline Conditions and Pathological Narcissism*. New York: Jason Aronson, 1975.

Ketterer, David. *Frankenstein's Creation: The Book, The Monster, and Human Reality*. Victoria, B.C.: University of Victoria, 1979.

Kettle, Arnold. "Emily Brontë: *Wuthering Heights*." In Thomas A. Vogler, ed., *Twentieth Century Interpretations of Wuthering Heights*. Englewood Cliffs, N.J.: Prentice-Hall, 1968.

Kleinbard, David J. "Laing, Lawrence, and the Maternal Cannibal." *The Psychoanalytic Review* 58 (1971):5–13.

Knoepflmacher, U. C. "Thoughts on the Aggression of Daughters." In George Levine and U. C. Knoepflmacher, eds., *The Endurance of Frankenstein*. Berkeley: University of California Press, 1979; repr. 1982.

Kofman, Sarah. "The Narcissistic Woman: Freud and Girard." *Diacritics* 10 (1980):36–45.

Kohut, Heinz. *The Analysis of the Self*. New York: International Universities Press, 1971.

———. *How Does Analysis Cure?* Arnold Goldberg, ed. Chicago: University of Chicago Press, 1984.

———. "Introspection, Empathy and Psychoanalysis." *Journal of the American Psychoanalytic Association* 7 (1959):459–83.

———. "Reflections." In Arnold Goldberg, ed., *Advances in Self Psychology*. New York: International Universities Press, 1980.

———. *The Restoration of the Self*. New York: International Universities Press, 1977.

Kohut, Heinz. *The Search for the Self.* Paul H. Ornstein, ed. 2 vols. New York: International Universities Press, 1978.
———. "Selected Problems in Self Psychological Theory." In Joseph D. Lichtenberg and Samuel Kaplan, eds. *Reflections on Self Psychology.* Hillsdale, N.J.: Analytic Press, 1983.
———. "Thoughts on Narcissism and Narcissistic Rage." *The Psychoanalytic Study of the Child* 27 (1972):360–400.
Kramer, Dale, *Thomas Hardy: The Forms of Tragedy.* Detroit: Wayne State University Press, 1975.
Kristeva, Julia. *Tales of Love.* Leon S. Roudiez, trans. New York: Columbia University Press, 1987.
Kuttner, Alfred Booth. "A Freudian Appreciation." *The Psychoanalytic Review* 3 (1916):293–317. Reprinted in E. W. Tedlock, Jr., ed., *D. H. Lawrence and Sons and Lovers: Sources and Criticism.* New York: New York University Press, 1965.
Lacan, Jacques. *The Seminar of Jacques Lacan.* Jacques-Alain Miller, ed., John Forrester, trans. 2 vols. Cambridge: Cambridge University Press, 1988.
———. *The Language of the Self.* Anthony Wilden, trans. New York: Delta, 1975.
Laing, R. D. *The Divided Self.* Harmondsworth, Middlesex, Eng.: Penguin, 1960; repr. 1970.
Langbaum, Robert. "Hardy and Lawrence." In Norman Page, ed., *Thomas Hardy Annual No. 3.* London: Macmillan, 1985.
———. *The Mysteries of Identity.* New York: Oxford University Press, 1977.
Lasch, Christopher. *The Culture of Narcissism.* New York: Norton, 1979.
———. *The Minimal Self.* New York: Norton, 1984.
Lawrence, D. H. *Lady Chatterley's Lover* (1928). New York: Grove Press, 1962.
———. *The Letters of D. H. Lawrence.* Vol. 1: 1901–1913, James T. Boulton, ed; vol. 2: 1913–1916, George J. Zytaruk and James T. Boulton, eds; vol. 3: 1916–1921, James T. Boulton and Andrew Robertson, eds. Cambridge: Cambridge University Press, 1979–1984.
———. "The Rocking-Horse Winner." *The Complete Short Stories.* New York: Viking, 1965. Vol. 3.
———. *Sons and Lovers.* (1912). Harmondsworth, Middlesex, Eng.: Penguin, 1981.
Lawrence, Frieda. *Not I, But the Wind.* New York: Viking, 1934.
Layton, Lynne, and Barbara A. Schapiro. *Narcissism & the Text: Studies in Literature & the Psychology of the Self.* New York: New York University Press, 1986.
Leaska, Mitchell A. *The Novels of Virginia Woolf.* New York: John Jay Press, 1977.
Leavis, Q. D. "How We Must Read *Great Expectations.*" In F. R. Leavis

and Q. D. Leavis, *Dickens, the Novelist.* London: Chatto and Windus, 1970.

Lesser, Simon O. *Fiction and the Unconscious.* New York: Vintage, 1957.

Levine, George. "The Ambiguous Heritage of *Frankenstein.*" In George Levine and U. C. Knoepflmacher, eds., *The Endurance of Frankenstein.* Berkeley: University of California Press, 1979; repr. 1982.

———. *The Realistic Imagination.* Chicago: University of Chicago Press, 1981.

Lichtenberg, Joseph D. "Is There a Psychoanalytic Weltanschauung?" In Arnold Goldberg, ed., *The Future of Psychoanalysis.* New York: International Universities Press, 1983.

Lichtenstein, Heinz. *The Dilemma of Identity.* New York: Jason Aronson, 1977; repr. 1983.

Lock, John, and Canon W. T. Dixon. *A Man of Sorrow: The Life, Letters and Times of the Rev. Patrick Brontë.* London: Nelson, 1965.

Love, Jean O. *Virginia Woolf: Sources of Madness and Art.* Berkeley: University of California Press, 1977.

Lukacher, Ned. *Primal Scenes: Literature, Philosophy, Psychoanalysis.* Ithaca: Cornell University Press, 1986.

MacLean, Robert M. *Narcissus and the Voyeur.* The Hague: Mouton, 1979.

Madden, William A. "*Wuthering Heights:* The Binding of Passion." *Nineteenth-Century Fiction* 27 (1972):127–54.

Mahler, Margaret S., Fred Pine, and Anni Bergman. *The Psychological Birth of the Human Infant.* New York: Basic Books, 1975.

Malcolm, Janet. *Psychoanalysis: The Impossible Profession.* New York: Vintage, 1982.

Maldonado, Jorge Luis. "Narcissism and Unconscious Communication." *International Journal of Psycho-Analysis* 68 (1987):379–87.

Manheim, Leonard F. "Dickens' Fools and Madmen." In Robert B. Partlow, Jr., ed., *Dickens Studies Annual.* Vol. 2. Carbondale: Southern Illinois University Press, 1972.

———. "Dickens and Psychoanalysis: A Memoir." In Michael Timko, Fred Kaplan, and Edward Guiliano, eds., *Dickens Studies Annual.* Vol. 11. New York: AMS Press, 1983.

Marcus, Jane, ed. *New Feminist Essays on Virginia Woolf.* Lincoln: University of Nebraska Press, 1981.

———, ed. *Virginia Woolf: A Feminist Slant.* Lincoln: University of Nebraska Press, 1983.

Marcus, Steven. "Freud and Dora." In Charles Bernheimer and Claire Kahane, eds. *In Dora's Case.* New York: Columbia University Press, 1985.

———. "The Psychoanalytic Self." *The Southern Review* 22 (1986):308–25.

Marcuse, Herbert. *Eros and Civilization* (1955). New York: Vintage, 1961.

Marder, Herbert. *Feminism and Art.* Chicago: University of Chicago Press, 1968.

Martz, Louis L. "Portrait of Miriam: A Study in the Design of *Sons and*

Lovers." In Maynard Mack and Ian Gregor, eds., *Imagined Worlds.* London: Methuen, 1968.

Masterson, James. *The Narcissistic and Borderline Disorders.* New York: Brunner/Mazel, 1981.

Meisel, Perry. *The Absent Father: Virginia Woolf and Walter Pater.* New Haven: Yale University Press, 1980.

———. *Thomas Hardy: The Return of the Repressed.* New Haven: Yale University Press, 1972.

Menninger, Karl. *Love Against Hate.* New York: Harcourt, Brace, 1942.

Meyers, Jeffrey. *Homosexuality and Literature: 1890–1930.* Montreal: McGill–Queen's University Press, 1977.

Mikhail, E. H. *Oscar Wilde: An Annotated Bibliography of Criticism.* London: Macmillan, 1978.

———. ed. *Oscar Wilde: Interviews and Recollections.* 2 vols. London: Macmillan, 1979.

Miller, Alice. *Prisoners of Childhood.* Ruth Ward, trans. New York: Basic Books, 1981.

Miller, J. Hillis. *Charles Dickens: The World of His Novels.* Cambridge: Harvard University Press, 1958; repr. Bloomington: Indiana University Press, 1969.

———. *The Disappearance of God.* Cambridge: Harvard University Press, 1963; rpt. New York: Schocken, 1965.

———. *Fiction and Repetition.* Cambridge: Harvard University Press, 1982.

———. *Thomas Hardy: Distance and Desire.* Cambridge: Harvard University Press, 1970.

Miller, Robert Keith. *Oscar Wilde.* New York: Ungar, 1982.

Millett, Kate. *Sexual Politics* (1970). New York: Ballantine, 1978.

Millgate, Michael. *Thomas Hardy.* New York: Random, 1982.

Mitchell, Giles. "Incest, Demonism and Death in *Wuthering Heights." Literature and Psychology* 23 (1973):27–36.

Mitchell, Juliet. *Psycho-Analysis and Feminism.* New York: Vintage, 1975.

Miyoshi, Masao. *The Divided Self.* New York: New York University Press, 1969.

McKibbon, Robert C. "The Image of the Book in *Wuthering Heights." Nineteenth-Century Fiction* 15 (1960):159–69.

Moers, Ellen. "Female Gothic." In George Levine and U. C. Knoepflmacher, eds., *The Endurance of Frankenstein.* Berkeley: University of California Press, 1979; repr. 1982.

Moglen, Helene. "The Double Vision of *Wuthering Heights:* A Clarifying View of Female Development." *Centennial Review* 15 (1971):391–405.

Moore, Harry T. *The Priest of Love: A Life of D. H. Lawrence.* New York: Penguin, 1974; rev. ed. 1981.

Moser, Thomas. "What is the Matter with Emily Jane?: Conflicting Impulses in *Wuthering Heights." Nineteenth-Century Fiction* 17 (1962):1–17.

Moynahan, Julian. "The Hero's Guilt: The Case of *Great Expectations.*" *Essays in Criticism* 10 (1960):60–79.

Myers, Wayne A. "Mary Shelley's *Frankenstein:* Creativity and the Psychology of the Exception." In Robert Langs, ed., *International Journal of Psychotherapy.* Vol. 9. New York: Jason Aronson, 1982–1983.

Naremore, James. *The World Without a Self: Virginia Woolf and the Novel.* New Haven: Yale University Press, 1973.

Nassaar, Christopher S. *Into the Demon Universe.* New Haven: Yale University Press, 1974.

Nehls, Edward, ed. *D. H. Lawrence: A Composite Biography.* 3 vols. Madison: University of Wisconsin Press, 1957–1959.

Nitchie, Elizabeth. *Mary Shelley.* New Brunswick, N.J.: Rutgers University Press, 1953.

Olinick, Stanley L., and Laura Tracy. "Transference Perspectives of Story Telling." *The Psychoanalytic Review* 74 (1987):319–31.

Ovid. *Metamorphoses.* Frank Justus Miller, trans. Cambridge: Harvard University Press, 1916; repr. 1936.

Page, Alex. "A Dangerous Day: Mrs. Dalloway Discovers Her Double." *Modern Fiction Studies* 7 (1961):115–24.

Panken, Shirley, "Some Psychodynamics in *Sons and Lovers:* A New Look at the Oedipal Theme." *The Psychoanalytic Review* 61 (Winter 1974–1975):571–89.

———. *Virginia Woolf and the "Lust of Creation".* New York: State University of New York Press, 1987.

Paris, Bernard J. *A Psychological Approach to Fiction.* Bloomington: Indiana University Press, 1974.

Pausanias. *Guide to Greece.* Peter Levi, trans. 2 vols. New York: Penguin, 1979.

Peterfreund, Emanuel. "Some Critical Comments on Psychoanalytic Conceptualizations of Infancy." *International Journal of Psycho-Analysis* 59 (1978):427–41.

Pickering, George. *Creative Malady* (1974). New York: Delta, 1976.

Pinion, F. B. *"Jude the Obscure:* Origins in Life and Literature." In Norman Page, ed., *Thomas Hardy Annual No. 4.* London: Macmillan, 1986.

Pollock, Linda A. *Forgotten Children.* Cambridge: Cambridge University Press, 1983.

Poovey, Mary. *The Proper Lady and the Woman Writer.* Chicago: University of Chicago Press, 1984.

Pratt, Branwen Bailey. "Dickens and Father: Notes on the Family Romance." *Hartford Studies in Literature* 8 (1976):4–22.

Pullin, Faith. "Lawrence's Treatment of Women in *Sons and Lovers.*" In Anne Smith, ed., *Lawrence and Women.* London: Vision, 1978.

Pulver, Sydney. "Narcissism: The Term and the Concept." *Journal of the American Psychoanalytic Association* 18 (1970):319–41.

Ragland-Sullivan, Ellie. *Jacques Lacan and the Philosophy of Psychoanalysis.* University of Illinois Press, 1986.

———. "The Phenomenon of Aging in Oscar Wilde's *Picture of Dorian Gray:* A Lacanian View." In Kathleen Woodward and Murray M. Schwartz, eds. *Memory and Desire.* Bloomington: Indiana University Press, 1986.

Rank, Otto. *The Double* (1914). Harry Tucker, Jr., trans. and ed. Chapel Hill, N.C.: University of North Carolina Press, 1971; repr. New York: New American Library, 1979.

———. *The Trauma of Birth.* New York. Harcourt Brace, 1929.

Reed, Michael D. "The Power of Wuthering Heights: A Psychoanalytic Examination." *Psychocultural Review* 1 (1977):21–42.

Richter, Harvena. *Virginia Woolf: The Inward Voyage.* Princeton: Princeton University Press, 1970.

Rogers, Robert. *A Psychoanalytic Study of the Double in Literature.* Detroit: Wayne State University Press, 1970.

Rose, Gilbert J. *"The French Lieutenant's Woman:* The Unconscious Significance of a Novel to Its Author." *American Imago* 29 (1972):165–76.

Rose, Phyllis. *Woman of Letters: A Life of Virginia Woolf.* New York: Oxford University Press, 1978.

Rosenman, Ellen Bayuk. *The Invisible Presence: Virginia Woolf and the Mother-Daughter Relationship.* Baton Rouge: Louisiana State University Press, 1986.

Rosenthal, Michael. *Virginia Woolf.* New York: Columbia University Press, 1979.

Roth, Philip. *My Life as a Man* (1974). New York: Bantam, 1975.

Rowse, A. L. *Homosexuals in History.* New York: Macmillan, 1977.

Rubenstein, Marc A. " 'My Accursed Origin': The Search for the Mother in *Frankenstein.*" *Studies in Romanticism* 15 (1976):165–94.

Ruderman, Judith. *D. H. Lawrence and the Devouring Mother.* Durham, N.C.: Duke University Press, 1984.

Rudnytsky, Peter L. *Freud and Oedipus.* New York: Columbia University Press, 1987.

Ruitenbeek, Hendrik M. *Homosexuality and Creative Genius.* New York: Astor-Honor, 1967.

Russell, Gillian. "Narcissism and the Narcissistic Personality Disorder: A Comparison of the Theories of Kernberg and Kohut." *British Journal of Medical Psychology* 58 (1985):137–48.

Sadoff, Dianne F. *Monsters of Affection.* Baltimore: Johns Hopkins University Press, 1982.

Sagar, Keith. *The Art of D. H. Lawrence.* Cambridge: Cambridge University Press, 1966.

———. *D. H. Lawrence: Life Into Art.* Athens: University of Georgia Press 1985.

Schapiro, Barbara A. *The Romantic Mother: Narcissistic Patterns in Romantic Poetry.* Baltimore: Johns Hopkins University Press, 1983.

Schiff, Hilda, "Nature and Art in Oscar Wilde's 'The Decay of Lying.' " In Sybil Rosenfield, ed., *Essays and Studies Collected for the English Association*. New York: Humanities Press, 1965.

Schlack, Beverly Ann. "Fathers in General: The Patriarchy in Virginia Woolf's Fiction." In Jane Marcus, ed., *Virginia Woolf: A Feminist Slant*. Lincoln: University of Nebraska Press, 1983.

———. "A Freudian Look at *Mrs. Dalloway*." *Literature and Psychology* 23 (1973):49–58.

Schneider, Daniel J. *D. H. Lawrence: The Artist as Psychologist*. Lawrence: University of Kansas Press, 1984.

Schorer, Mark. "Technique as Discovery." *The Hudson Review* 1 (1948):67–87.

Schwartz, Murray M. "Critic, Define Thyself." In Geoffrey H. Hartman, ed., *Psychoanalysis and the Question of the Text*. Baltimore: Johns Hopkins University Press, 1978.

———. "D. H. Lawrence and Psychoanalysis: An Introduction." *D. H. Lawrence Review* 10 (1977):215–22.

Schwarz, Daniel R. *The Humanistic Heritage*. Philadelphia: University of Pennsylvania Press, 1986.

Segal, Hanna. *Introduction to the Work of Melanie Klein*. New York: Basic Books, 1974.

Shannon, Edgar F. "Lockwood's Dreams and the Exegesis of *Wuthering Heights*." *Nineteenth-Century Fiction* 14 (1959):95–109.

Shelley, Mary. *Frankenstein; or, The Modern Prometheus: The 1818 Text*. James Rieger, ed. Indianapolis: Bobbs-Merrill, 1974; repr. Chicago: University of Chicago Press, 1982.

———. *Frankenstein; or, The Modern Prometheus*. M. K. Joseph, ed. New York: Oxford University Press, 1969; repr. 1984.

Shewan, Rodney. *Oscar Wilde: Art and Egotism*. London: Macmillan, 1977.

Shields, E. F. "Death and Individual Values in 'Mrs Dalloway.' " *Queen's Quarterly* 80 (1973):79–89.

Showalter, Elaine. *A Literature of Their Own*. Princeton: Princeton University Press, 1977.

Siebers, Tobin. *The Mirror of Medusa*. Berkeley: University of California Press, 1983.

Simpson, Hilary. *D. H. Lawrence and Feminism*. London: Croom Helm, 1982.

Singer, Melvin. "The Experience of Emptiness in Narcissistic and Borderline States," parts 1 and 2. *The International Review of Psycho-Analysis* 4 (1977):459–79.

Skura, Meredith. *The Literary Use of the Psychoanalytic Process*. New Haven: Yale University Press, 1981.

Slater, Michael. *Dickens and Women*. London: J. M. Dent and Sons, 1983.

Slatoff, Walter. *The Look of Distance*. Columbus: Ohio State University Press, 1985.

Slatoff, Walter. *With Respect to Readers*. Ithaca: Cornell University Press, 1970.

Small, Christopher. *Ariel Like a Harpy*. London: Victor Gollancz, 1972.

Smith, Anne, ed. *Lawrence and Women*. London: Vision, 1978.

Snow, Lotus. "The Heat of the Sun: The Double in *Mrs. Dalloway*." *Research Studies* 41 (1973):75–83.

Solomon, Eric. "The Incest Theme in *Wuthering Heights*." *Nineteenth-Century Fiction* 14 (1959):80–83.

Spacks, Patricia Meyer. *The Female Imagination*. New York: Knopf, 1975; repr. New York: Avon, 1976.

Spector, Jack J. *The Aesthetics of Freud*. New York: McGraw-Hill, 1974.

Spenko, James Leo. "The Return of the Repressed in *Great Expectations*." *Literature and Psychology* 30 (1980):133–46.

Spilka, Mark. *The Love Ethic of D. H. Lawrence*. Bloomington: University of Indiana Press, 1955.

———. "For Mark Schorer with Combative Love: The *Sons and Lovers* Manuscript." In Peter Balbert and Phillip L. Marcus, eds., *D. H. Lawrence: A Centenary Consideration*. Ithaca: Cornell University Press, 1985.

———. *Virginia Woolf's Quarrel with Grieving*. Lincoln: University of Nebraska Press, 1980.

Spotnitz, Hyman, "Narcissus as Myth, Narcissus as Patient." In Marie Coleman Nelson, ed., *The Narcissistic Condition*. New York: Human Sciences Press, 1977.

———, and Philip Resnikoff. "The Myths of Narcissus." *The Psychoanalytic Review* 41 (1954):173–81.

Steig, Michael. "Dickens' Characters and Psychoanalytic Criticism." *Hartford Studies in Literature* 8 (1976):38–45.

———. "Sue Bridehead." *Novel* 1 (1968):260–66.

Stern, Daniel N. *The Interpersonal World of the Infant*. New York: Basic Books, 1985.

Stewart, J. I. M. *Thomas Hardy: A Critical Biography*. London: Longman, 1971.

Stoehr, Taylor. *Dickens: The Dreamer's Stance*. Ithaca: Cornell University Press, 1965.

Stoller, Robert. *Observing the Erotic Imagination*. New Haven: Yale University Press, 1985.

———. *Perversion*. New York: Dell, 1975.

———. *Sex and Gender*. New York: Jason Aronson, 1968.

Stolorow, Robert D., and George E. Atwood. *Faces in a Cloud*. New York: Jason Aronson, 1979.

Sumner, Rosemary. *Thomas Hardy: Psychological Novelist*. New York: St. Martin's Press, 1981.

Tedlock, E. W., ed. *D. H. Lawrence and Sons and Lovers: Sources and Criticism*. New York: New York University Press, 1965.

Thompson, F. M. L. *The Rise of Respectable Society*. Cambridge: Harvard University Press, 1988.

Thompson, Wade. "Infanticide and Sadism in *Wuthering Heights*." *PMLA* 78 (1963):69–74.

Thornton, Lawrence. *Unbodied Hope: Narcissism and the Modern Novel*. Lewisburg: Bucknell University Press, 1984.

Thurley, Geoffrey. *The Psychology of Hardy's Novels: The Nervous and the Statuesque*. Queensland: University of Queensland Press, 1975.

Trail, George Y. "The Consistency of Hardy's Sue: Bridehead Becomes Electra." *Literature and Psychology* 26 (1976):61–68.

Trilling, Lionel. "Freud and Literature." *The Liberal Imagination*. Garden City: Anchor Books, 1953.

Trombley, Stephen. *"All That Summer She was Mad": Virginia Woolf and Her Doctors*. London: Junction Books, 1981.

Trop, Martin. *Mary Shelley's Monster*. Boston: Houghton Mifflin, 1976.

Twitchell, James B. *Forbidden Partners*. New York: Columbia University Press, 1987.

Van Ghent, Dorothy. *The English Novel*. New York: Rinehart, 1953; repr. New York: Harper & Row, 1967.

Veeder, William. *Mary Shelley & Frankenstein*. Chicago: University of Chicago Press, 1986.

Vinge, Louise. *The Narcissus Theme in Western European Literature up to the Early Nineteenth Century*. Robert Dewsnap and Nigel Reeves, trans. Lund: Gleerups, 1967.

Walling, William. *Mary Shelley*. New York: Twayne, 1972.

Warren, Joyce W. *The American Narcissus*. New Brunswick, N.J.: Rutgers University Press, 1984.

Watkins, Gwen. *Dickens in Search of Himself*. London: Macmillan, 1987.

Watt, Ian. "Oral Dickens." In Robert B. Partlow, ed., *Dickens Studies Annual*. Vol. 3. Carbondale: Southern Illinois University Press, 1974.

Weiss, Daniel. *Oedipus in Nottingham*. Seattle: University of Washington Press, 1962.

Wentersdorf, Karl P. "Mirror Images in *Great Expectations*." *Nineteenth-Century Fiction* 21 (1966):203–24.

Werman, David S., and Theodore J. Jacobs. "Thomas Hardy's 'The Well-Beloved' and the Nature of Infatuation." *International Review of Psycho-Analysis* 10 (1983):477–57.

White, Terence de Vere. *The Parents of Oscar Wilde*. London: Hodder and Stoughton, 1967.

Wilde, Oscar. *The Artist as Critic: Critical Writings of Oscar Wilde*. Richard Ellmann, ed. New York: Viking, 1968.

———. *The Complete Works of Oscar Wilde*. Vyvyan Holland, ed. London: Collins, 1966.

Wilde, Oscar. *The Letters of Oscar Wilde*. Rupert Hart-Davis, ed. New York: Harcourt, Brace and World, 1962.
———. *The Picture of Dorian Gray* (1891). Isobel Murray, ed. Oxford: Oxford University Press, 1974; repr. 1982.
———. *De Profundis* (1897). New York: Philosophical Library, 1960.
———. *The Works of Oscar Wilde*. G. F. Maine, ed. New York: Dutton, 1954.
Wilson, Angus, "Dickens on Children and Childhood." In Michael Slater, ed., *Dickens 1970*. New York: Stein and Day, 1970.
Wilson, Edmund. "Dickens: The Two Scrooges." *The Wound and the Bow*. Cambridge, Massachusetts: Houghton Mifflin, 1941; repr. New York: Oxford University Press, 1965.
Winner, Anthony. "Character and Knowledge in Dickens: The Enigma of Jaggers." Robert B. Partlow, Jr., ed., *Dickens Studies Annual*. Vol. 3. Carbondale: Southern Illinois University Press, 1974.
Winnicott, D. W. "Transitional Objects and Transitional Phenomena." *International Journal of Psycho-Analysis* 34 (1953):89–97.
Wion, Philip K. "The Absent Mother in Emily Brontë's *Wuthering Heights*." *American Imago* 42 (1985):143–64.
Wolf, Ernest S. "Empathy and Countertransference." In Arnold Goldberg, ed., *The Future of Psychoanalysis*. New York: International Universities Press, 1983.
Woolf, Leonard. *Beginning Again: An Autobiography of the Years 1911 to 1918*. New York: Harcourt, Brace and World, 1964.
———. *Downhill All the Way: An Autobiography of the Years 1919 to 1939*. New York: Harcourt, Brace and World, 1967.
Woolf, Virginia. "Freudian Fiction" (1920). Review of *An Imperfect Mother*, by J. D. Beresford. *Contemporary Writers*. London: Hogarth Press, 1965.
———. "Introduction." *Mrs. Dalloway*. New York: Modern Library, 1928.
———. *The Letters of Virginia Woolf*. 5 vols. Nigel Nicolson and Joanne Trautmann, eds. New York: Harcourt Brace Jovanovich, 1975–1979.
———. *Mrs. Dalloway* (1925). New York: Harcourt, Brace and World, 1953.
———. "On Being Ill" (1930). *The Moment and Other Essays*. New York: Harcourt, Brace and Jovanovich, 1948.
———. "A Sketch of the Past." (1940) In *Moments of Being*. Jeanne Schulkind, ed. New York: Harcourt Brace Jovanovich, 1976.
———. *To the Lighthouse*. New York: Harbrace, 1927.
Worthen, John. *D. H. Lawrence and the Idea of the Novel*. London: Macmillan, 1979.
Wyndham, Horace. *Speranza: A Biography of Lady Wilde*. London: Boardman, 1951.
Yalom, Marilyn. *Maternity, Mortality, and the Literature of Madness*. University Park: Pennsylvania State University Press, 1985.
Zweig, Paul. *The Heresy of Self-Love*. New York: Basic Books, 1968.

Index